An Introduction to the UK Economy

UK Economy

Performance and Policy
Second Edition

edited by

PAUL HARE

and

LESLIE SIMPSON

PRENTICE HALL
HARVESTER WHEATSHEAF
*London   New York   Toronto   Sydney   Tokyo   Singapore
Madrid   Mexico City   Munich*

First published 1993 as *British Economic Policy: A Modern Introduction*

This second edition published 1996 by
Prentice Hall/Harvester Wheatsheaf
Campus 400, Maylands Avenue
Hemel Hempstead
Hertfordshire, HP2 7EZ
A division of
Simon & Schuster International Group

Typeset in 9½/12 pt Palatino by Photoprint, Torquay, Devon
Printed and bound in Great Britain by
Hartnolls Limited, Bodmin, Cornwall

Library of Congress Cataloging-in-Publication Data

An introduction to the UK economy : performance and policy / edited
by Paul Hare and Leslie Simpson.
    p.   cm.
Includes bibliographical references and index.
ISBN 0–13–235862–X (alk. paper)
    1. Great Britain–Economic policy.   2. Great Britain–Economic
conditions–1945–1993.   3. Great Britain–Economic conditions–1993–
I. Hare, P.G. II. Simpson, Leslie.
HC256.6. I583   1995
338.941–dc20   95–33967
                                          CIP

British Library Cataloguing in Publication Data

A catalogue record for this book is available
from the British Library

ISBN 0–13–235862–X

---

1 2 3 4 5 00 99 98 97 96

Contents

PART 2 Macroeconomic Policy

Part 3 International Economics

Figures and Tables

About the authors

Note: all authors are in the Heriot-Watt Business School unless otherwise indicated.

The editors

Professor Paul Hare, former head of the Economics Department (1985–90), now director of the Centre for Economic Reform and Transformation and mainly occupied with research on Eastern Europe; also part time at the LSE. He has also worked on public finance issues and on UK economic policy, especially to do with privatisation.

Leslie Simpson, deputy head of the Economics Department, senior lecturer in economics, with interests in environmental economics, macroeconomics and some aspects of public sector economics.

The authors (in alphabetical order)

David Begg, lecturer in transport economics, Napier University, with special interests in the economics of urban transport.

Glen Bramley, Professor of Planning and Housing, Edinburgh College of Art (Heriot-Watt University).

Prabir Bhattacharya, lecturer in economics. He has done substantial research in development economics, mainly to do with unemployment and migration problems.

Peter Clarke, lecturer in economics, with research interests in the aerospace industry, telecommunications, transport economics and health economics.

Hugh Fleming, lecturer in economics. His major interests are exchange rate policy and the international financial markets.

Patrick O'Farrell, Professor in the Economics Department. He carries out research on comparative productivity levels of firms in different areas and, more recently, on business services and their impact on industrial performance.

Shu-Mei Gao, lecturer in economics with interests in econometrics and international trade.

Ian Hirst, Professor of Finance in the Department of Accountancy and Finance. He has previously researched on the financial markets, as well as on investment evaluation techniques.

Ian Paterson, lecturer in economics, specialising in industrial relations, trade union studies and labour market issues.

Stuart Sayer, lecturer in economics at Edinburgh University. Author of books and articles on macroeconomic issues.

Andrew Scott, senior lecturer in the Europa Institute, Edinburgh University, with extensive research on the European Community including several contracts for the Commission; editor of *Journal of Common Market Studies*.

Thomas Torrance, senior lecturer in economics with interests in economic methodology, open-economy macroeconomics, and international trade and finance.

Geoffrey Wyatt, reader in economics, with books and articles on technological change, and a study of financial options and futures markets. More recently, he has been investigating techniques of graphical representation of macro-economic models.

Philip Welham, senior lecturer in economics working on inter-temporal aspects of income and wealth distribution, and with a general interest in public finance.

Preface

In teaching economics it is not easy, especially at the introductory level, to find good books on economic policy which cover the most relevant topics in an interesting and illuminating way, using some theory, presenting some data and stimulating further interest in the subject. There is a tendency to regard economic policy as 'too difficult' for an introductory treatment, and most textbooks reflect this by providing excellent coverage of basic economic theory but relatively little applied or policy-related material. However, we disagree with this view of policy. Rather, we believe that a course in economics which includes a strand of economic policy is likely to be greatly appreciated both by students and their teachers. Not only that, but we consider that many policy issues can be usefully studied with the aid of quite simple economic theory, and that the interplay between theory and policy can be beneficial to both.

This book is intended to demonstrate these points. Its level is introductory, so that it should be suitable for the more advanced school students (taking 'A' levels or Scottish Highers and CSYS) as well as for first-year university and college students. While it uses theory, it does not purport to be a theory text. Accordingly, it should normally be used alongside one of the many good textbooks on introductory economic theory.

This book is, in effect, the second edition of the book *British Economic Policy*, produced by the same editors in 1992. However, although some chapters in this book are merely updated versions of what was done before, there are several new chapters (e.g. Chapters 9, 10, 16 and 17) and many other chapters have been substantially re-written to reflect new policy concerns of the mid-1990s. This made it appropriate to restructure the whole book to divide the material into three main sections, dealing with microeconomic issues, macroeconomic policy, and the international economy. To reflect all these changes, the book has also been re-titled.

For Heriot-Watt University's economics department, and colleagues in nearby institutions, writing this book has been an enormously successful, cooperative venture. As can be seen from the information provided about the authors, most do indeed come from the economics department. It is also the case that almost everyone in the economics department has contributed to the book. Early meetings about the book revealed widespread enthusiasm for the project, and a surprising willingness to agree to fairly tight deadlines in the preparation of draft chapters and the implementation of revisions requested by the editors. Even more surprising, to the editors at least, was the outcome: for all authors not only made promises but they actually delivered the goods, more or less on time. In our experience this is extremely unusual for edited books, but it has enabled us to carry out necessary editing at the time we planned to do so, and to submit a complete text to the publisher exactly when we agreed to.

Doing this obviously required considerable cooperation from the authors, as indicated, but also substantial support from the secretarial staff who typed some of the chapters and prepared many of the figures and diagrams. We owe particular thanks, in this regard, to the economics department's two secretaries, Mrs Jean Roberts and Mrs Pat Chrystal for their valiant efforts.

As editors, we took full advantage of modern word-processing technology by ensuring that all chapters were submitted to us both on paper and on disk. This enabled us to carry out a great deal of minor (and some major) editing without referring back to the individual authors, and to print out revised versions of each chapter. We hope that all authors will be content with the changes we have made to their chapters, and that they can still recognise their own work despite our revisions. In any case, we certainly owe many thanks to our enthusiastic and dedicated authors, both for their own chapters and for the helpful comments and suggestions they provided about other chapters.

Finally, especially in the last weeks of preparing this book, the heavy demands of editorial work inevitably placed great strain on the editors' families. We would like to thank our respective wives and children for their support and tolerance during this especially busy period, and hope they agree with us that the results are worthwhile.

Paul Hare and Leslie Simpson
Edinburgh, March 1995

Glossary of Abbreviations

BATNEEC   best available techniques not entailing excessive cost
BIS   Bank for International Settlements
BPEO   best practicable environmental option
BPM   best practicable means
BT   British Telecom

CAP   Common Agricultural Policy
CFSP   Common Foreign and Security Policy
CIT   comprehensive income tax
CPI   consumer price index

DGFT   Director General of Fair Trading
DTI   Department of Trade and Industry

EAS   Enterprise Allowance Scheme
ECU   European Currency Unit
EIB   European Investment Bank
EMS   European Monetary System
ERM   Exchange Rate Mechanism
ESF   European Social Fund
EU   European Union

G7   seven most developed countries
GATT   General Agreement on Tariffs and Trade
GDP   gross domestic product
GSP   Generalised System of Preferences

HMSO   Her Majesty's Stationery Office

IT   Information Technology

JHA   Justice and Home Affairs

LDC	less developed country
LOB	Location of Offices Bureau
MDC	marginal damage curve
MES	minimum efficient scale
MFA	Multi-fibre Agreement
MITI	Ministry of International Trade and Industry
MLR	minimum lending rate
MMC	Monopolies and Mergers Commission
MTFS	Medium Term Financial Strategy
NAIRU	Non-Accelerating-Inflation-Rate-of-Unemployment
NRA	National Rivers Authority
ODP	Office Development Permits
OECD	Organisation for Economic Cooperation and Development
OFT	Office of Fair Trading
OPEC	Organisation of Petroleum Exporting Countries
PRT	petroleum revenue tax
PSBR	Public Sector Borrowing Requirement
QMV	qualified majority voting
R&D	research and development
RDG	regional development grant
RPI	retail price index
RPIX	retail price index (excludes mortgage services component)
RSA	Regional Selective Assistance
RWA	Regional Water Authorities
SEA	Single European Act
SEAQ	Stock Exchange Automatic Quotations
SSA	Standard Spending Assessment
TES	Temporary Employment Subsidy
TSTWCS	Temporary Short-Time Working Compensation Scheme
VAT	value-added tax
YTS	Youth Training Scheme

CHAPTER 1

Economic policy: the major themes

PAUL HARE

1.1 Introduction

The conduct and nature of economic policy in Britain are very different in the early 1990s from what they were in the 1970s and even from the early 1980s. Several factors have contributed to what amounts to an enormous shift in the policy environment in which Britain now operates, and with which it must come to terms. Many of these factors are related to political and institutional developments in Britain and the world, including Britain's evolving relationship with the European Union (EU), but some of the changes are also associated with developments in economic thinking, with the ways in which we conceptualise the working of policy instruments both in the short run, and in terms of an ultimate influence on longer term performance (such as through growth rates).

1.2 Political and institutional factors

Some of these factors are essentially domestic (though even these have often reflected, or paralleled, developments elsewhere). For instance, the government's more restricted conception of the role of macroeconomic policy in actively guiding the economy in the last decade or so contrasts quite strikingly with more interventionist approaches pursued formerly (by both of the main political parties). Within this, conceptions of fiscal policy have assigned greater importance than before to stability and balance in the government's spending and revenue plans, as against the active use of fiscal levers to promote short-term stabilisation. At the same time, monetary policy was largely used to promote price rather than output stability during the 1980s and early 1990s (prices here including both the domestic price level and the exchange rate), with money supply targets and interest rate targets being emphasised more or less strongly at different times.

Another domestic factor is the greatly increased emphasis on using markets and the private sector to deliver goods and services as against the more traditional reliance on public provision for many items. This has influenced wide areas of policy in the last decade and a half. Associated with this theme is the whole question of the privatisation of housing, public services and public enterprises, as well as the liberalisation of the financial markets and the several stages of legislation on trade unions. Despite this marked change in the philosophy of government, however, the 1980s actually witnessed a *rise* in the share of general government spending in gross domestic product (GDP), as we detail later.

The United Kingdom's economic policy environment has also been increasingly influenced by external factors. In the past, some of these might well have been regarded as constraints on domestic policy-making and to some extent this is correct, of course. However, several of the aspects of policy which are either determined externally or subject to external influence are in policy domains where the most appropriate level of determination nowadays is wider than the nation state. Trade policy, exchange rate policy (including the United Kingdom's membership, for a time, of the Exchange Rate Mechanism (ERM) of the European Monetary System (EMS), and the implications of that), the liberalisation associated with the '1992' programme, and the recent development of European Union (EU), G7 or G24[1] policies towards Eastern Europe are just a few of the domains in this category. Hence it is more relevant, now, to think of the United Kingdom's policy environment in a very wide sense, with different types of policy being determined, quite properly, at different levels. Recognition of this situation has not proved easy for the United Kingdom.

One consequence, however, is that it is no longer possible to discuss most important issues in UK policy without making some reference at least to the EU, and in some cases to wider areas. This is why, in the chapters that follow, many of them have an 'EU dimension' reflecting the influence of European institutions on what would previously have been considered domestic policy. Moreover, this influence is evident not only in the familiar areas of macroeconomic policy, referred to above, but increasingly in microeconomic policy too, including such matters as regional policy, environmental policy, science and technology policy and many others.

Through its efforts to promote mobility across the Community – of goods, services and people – the EU is also contributing towards a process of harmonisation which is having increasingly noticeable effects in the individual member states. Whereas in the past, the EU sought to ensure harmonisation by convergence to common standards, a process fraught with political and technical difficulties (and, sometimes, absurdities), it now seeks to make progress through the mutual recognition of standards adopted in different countries combined, where relevant, with definitions of accepted minimum standards. This approach is proving more acceptable to member states, but in many cases it still requires considerable adaptation of their respective domestic policies.

Aside from the increasing impact of the EU, other international agreements and organisations also influence domestic policy in the United Kingdom, such as the General Agreement on Tariffs and Trade (GATT) in relation to trade policy, following the successful conclusion of the Uruguay Round of trade negotiations,[2] and various international conventions on environmental issues. In the international oil market, the Organisation of Petroleum Exporting Countries (OPEC) remains influential, although its role and policies may well be influenced by the longer term effects of the 1991 Gulf War to expel Iraq from Kuwait. The world oil market will also be influenced by the serious economic situation in the former Soviet Union, since oil production there has fallen considerably since the late 1980s. As a major oil producer itself, the oil price is important for the United Kingdom both in terms of public revenues (a higher price yields higher profits to the producers, and hence more tax revenue) and in terms of costs of production throughout the economy (a lower price obviously helps user industries and sectors).

1.3 Conceptual developments and policy aims

Economic policy used to be thought of in very simple terms, with a list of reasonably widely agreed policy objectives to be achieved by the application of a limited range of macroeconomic policy instruments – monetary and fiscal policy, exchange rate policy. At the level of formal policy analysis relatively little attention was paid to microeconomic issues and economists (as well as policy-makers) believed that some variant of the standard Keynesian model provided an adequate basis for discussion. None of this holds today; indeed, much of it was either rejected or found to be seriously deficient by the early 1980s.

Typical policy objectives included the achievement of full employment, low (and preferably stable) rates of inflation and a satisfactory balance of payments and satisfactory growth, although in practice most attention was focused on the so-called internal and external balances. Internal balance essentially means full employment, but the term is also sometimes used to encompass objectives to do with inflation, as well as with the balance between government income and expenditure. External balance simply refers to the balance of payments including, of course, both the current and capital accounts.

Influenced by Keynesian ideas, for much of the post-war period it was taken for granted that in response to short-term fluctuations in output and employment, the government could and should use a judiciously chosen combination of fiscal and monetary policy, supplemented by exchange rate policy, to reduce their amplitude and duration. It is no longer so clear that this is a viable approach (if it ever was) or, in any case, whether it is desirable. For one thing, this approach was predicated on a conviction that certain empirically established relationships, such as the Phillips curve that appeared to relate the rate of change of money wages (or the rate of change of prices) inversely to the level of unemployment, could be relied on to be tolerably stable under a wide range of alternative economic policies. For another, it involved accepting the notion of a private sector which, while it responded to what the government actually did, was assumed to be rather unsophisticated in that it did not attempt to forecast government actions. This passive conception of the private sector is not accepted nowadays.

Instead, the private sector is regarded as forming a model of the economy which includes views about the government's own behaviour (and, as is well known from the work of Sargent *et al.* on rational expectations models, this can imply the complete ineffectiveness of government policy under certain conditions). Given this, it becomes important for the government's policies, and its statements about its likely future actions, to have credibility and consistency. Among other things, this tends to favour relatively stable, slowly changing policy; it also favours policies which involve some pre-commitment by the government, so that private sector agents can see that the government would incur significant political and/or economic costs by making unexpected changes.

In addition to its role in the macro economy, Keynesian thinking predisposed governments of both major parties towards intervention in other areas of economic life, although to a rather greater extent under Labour governments. This is clear in the nationalised industries (which Conservative governments did not extend, but also did not seek to privatise before 1979, with the sole exception of steel), where large monopolies enjoyed statutory protection extending well beyond areas where arguments about economies of scale could have justified them. In some sectors, such as housing and civil engineering (as well as defence, of course), the government was a dominant or major customer and was thereby able to influence the conditions of operation in these sectors. It did so partly by determining the technical conditions of what it purchased, sometimes without regard to what private sector customers might have wanted (e.g. the serious and costly 'mistakes' in public sector housing), and sometimes through fluctuations in the level and composition of public spending. The latter could easily create conditions of boom or bust in the sectors most closely related to government demands, and at times the resulting instability made planning and long-term investment appear extremely risky.

The government, at both national and local levels, also acted as a regulator in regard to many aspects of private sector activity including safety, consumer protection, planning and building controls, and environmental controls. Intervention of this sort is essential in a modern economy, since private sector agents left to themselves cannot be expected to take proper account of the potentially harmful externalities arising from their decisions, and the need for it did not disappear as Keynesian thinking lost its dominance in the United Kingdom. Nevertheless, there have been widespread criticisms about the bureaucratic, and sometimes over-politicised way, in which such controls are implemented in the United Kingdom, especially now that they are increasingly influenced by EU policies emanating from Brussels.

Increasing awareness of these and other shortcomings of the standard Keynesian package influenced conceptions of the most appropriate policy aims, and approach to economic policy, for the government to pursue. At the macro level, rather than seeking to achieve the short-term stabilisation of output by using the traditional, Keynesian instruments of economic policy, the government increasingly took the view that its role was to provide a stable policy environment within which the private sector could (and presumably would) flourish. The key element of this stability was considered to be the rate of inflation which, accordingly, became the principal policy target from the end of the 1970s onwards. This does not, of course, imply that policy was wholly successful in this regard, as we shall see in the next section. Nor does it imply that the government was no longer concerned about the traditional, Keynesian objectives for the economy – full employment, growth and balance of payments equilibrium.

The instruments used to control inflation changed over the decade, influenced by the prevailing exchange rate regime. For most of the 1980s, the exchange rate was, in theory, floating (albeit a managed float), and the domestic money stock (defined in many different ways) was the principal intermediate policy target, with interest rates being used as the main instrument to achieve it (along with the general stance of the public sector, naturally). Later, the exchange rate of the pound sterling (£) was informally linked to the Deutschmark (DM), and eventually the United Kingdom joined the ERM (though not within the narrow bands; see below for fuller discussion). Thus interest rates were used for a time to keep the pound within its agreed limits in the ERM. To the extent that the financial markets had confidence in these exchange rates, the DM/£ exchange rate effectively provided a nominal anchor to the UK price level, to which UK producers (and consumers) were expected to adapt themselves.

A Conservative government was re-elected with a small majority in Parliament in Spring 1992 while the domestic economy remained in deep recession, facing increasing strains associated with the United Kingdom's position in the ERM. In September 1992 speculative pressures forced sterling out of the ERM (see Chapters 15 and 18 for a fuller discussion of this period), and the currency was effectively devalued. This once more freed the interest rate from the external constraints to which it had been subject, enabling the government to embark on a long, gradual process of interest rate reduction from late 1992 onwards. This contributed to a moderately paced economic recovery which still continues, despite a return to somewhat higher interest rates in 1994 and early 1995.

At the time of writing (Spring 1995), many of the main economic indicators are quite favourable, with inflation down to 2–3 per cent p.a. and appearing to be more stable than in the past, unemployment steadily declining and GDP rising at almost 3 per cent p.a. Moreover, the recent growth appears to have been based mostly on a recovery and expansion of exports, unlike past recoveries that have given greater weight to an expansion of personal consumption. Many firms and industries in the United Kingdom are far more competitive than they were a decade ago, and this has created a situation in which the trade balance is improving as the economy expands, not at all the usual UK position in recent decades. Given these recent developments the government's job, as stated earlier, is to maintain a monetary environment compatible with continuing low inflation. In particular, as the Prime Minister John Major has asserted, there is no need to 'kick-start' the economy by means of expansionary fiscal measures (but see Chapter 11 for some discussion of this point).

An alternative interpretation is somewhat different, however. This is that the recession was caused, and/or the recovery is being delayed, by policy errors. Thus one can easily cite the over-rapid reduction in income taxation which stimulated excessive consumer spending in the late 1980s and helped to foster a new round of inflationary pressure in the United Kingdom, accompanied by massive increases in property prices. The recession left many people with abnormally high debts which they are still striving to reduce, while property prices in many parts of the country, having fallen substantially at the beginning of the 1990s, have so far only recovered a little. In addition, the United Kingdom's late entry into the ERM, at a point when UK inflation was much faster than Germany's, and at a DM/£ rate that was widely considered too high even at the time of entry into the mechanism, created serious difficulties. For although the ERM provided the UK economy with a nominal anchor to restrain inflation (in the absence of effective domestic policies to achieve this outcome), its effectiveness depended on its credibility. As noted above, the position did indeed turn out to be unsustainable.

On balance, we (i.e. the editors) believe that under the conditions of the early 1990s, the government was right to leave the ERM and thereby give itself an additional degree of freedom in its economy policy. Moreover, it is clear that the departure from the ERM, and subsequent economic developments, have been managed in a way that has not given rise to the renewed inflationary pressure that many people feared.

This last observation raises questions about the most suitable wages and incomes policy for the United Kingdom. The government has tended to assert that there is no wages policy, and that 'markets must decide'. This is clearly absurd: for the government is, directly and indirectly, the largest employer in the country, and hence its own approach to wage settlements unavoidably influences the behaviour of the private sector. Conversely, major private sector wage settlements are bound to influence or constrain what the government must pay. Given existing policies towards inflation, the real question is how much unemployment must be tolerated in order to make the desired inflation rate 'stick'. Unfortunately, this is an area where the government has been relatively ineffective in developing new policy in the last decade, with the result that the level of unemployment may have to remain higher than would be necessary with more satisfactory wage-setting arrangements.

Although the 1960s and 1970s did witness an active micro policy, as for instance in areas such as regional policy and industrial policy, this was not really in keeping with the typically neoclassical approach to microeconomic issues that could be found in most economics textbooks of the time. Interestingly, while the neoclassical approach gained greater acceptance among policy-makers in the 1980s, in association with the ascendance of monetarist ideas in macroeconomics, it was accompanied by a new emphasis on what came to be called supply-side economics. This is not easy to define precisely, but the basic idea is simple enough.

Supply-side economics recognises that, even in an essentially competitive economy, certain markets may not work perfectly. This can be due to high taxation (distortions), formal or informal restrictions on competition, or externalities of various sorts, including those due to imperfect information. Politically, supply-side economics was strongly associated with Mrs Thatcher and her advisers in the United Kingdom, and with President Reagan in the United States, but many of its tenets were adopted by other industrialised countries of all political persuasions during the 1980s.

An important aspect of supply-side economics was a strong push to lower tax rates, both on corporations and on personal incomes, in order to stimulate more effective and efficient use of economic resources. Such a trend was evident in many western countries during the 1980s, including the United Kingdom, although ironically, the United Kingdom's reductions in income taxation were almost wholly offset by rises in value added tax (VAT) (see Chapter 7). Given that, it is questionable whether the supposed incentive effects of lower income taxes can have been very significant.

In addition, training and education policy have both received attention as means of improving the general level of skills and improving labour market mobility and flexibility. In practice, however, much of the new training provided by government agencies was of a rather low level and educational reforms, including in higher education, were limited by increasingly stringent budgetary constraints.

Trade union legislation was introduced to limit restrictive practices and make the effective use of strikes more difficult. In the capital market, one of the first steps taken by the Conservative government in 1979 was to abolish all remaining UK controls over capital movements. Other countries also gradually relaxed their controls during the 1980s and early 1990s, and the period witnessed an enormous expansion in the international flow of capital, both for portfolio investment and for investment in new plant and equipment. Within the United Kingdom itself, particular attention was paid to the needs of small firms (which were 'fashionable' for a time, and considered to be 'neglected' by the capital market), as well as to deregulation in the financial markets. Finally, public support for Research and Development (R&D), while much criticised in the United Kingdom for its over-emphasis on military R&D, was focused on information technology and other so-called generic technologies where externality arguments could be deployed to justify it. The United Kingdom lost its technological advantage in some areas, such as electronics and nuclear power, while gaining in such areas as chemicals, drugs and food. As in many other policy domains, R&D was a field that came to be increasingly dominated by EU-level policies from the mid-1980s onwards.

Particularly in the United Kingdom, the housing market has been seen as restricting mobility, partly through problems of local authority tenants finding new accommodation in an area to which they might wish to move, and partly because of highly differentiated house prices across the United Kingdom in the privately owned sector. Both sectors of the market have been distorted by subsidies of various kinds, which governments have been slow to recognise or remove. This is an aspect of supply-side policy that has seen some significant change recently, including the vigorous pursuit of privatisation: much of the local authority-owned housing stock was privatised during the 1980s, mainly by sale to existing residents on favourable terms. Another aspect of housing policy worth noting here has been the gradual reduction of subsidies to private home owners through the provision of tax relief on mortgage interest. In real terms, the amount of a mortgage on which tax relief can be given has declined substantially, as has the maximum rate at which relief is paid.

Another important issue affecting labour supply, wages and unemployment is social security (including housing benefit) and social welfare policy. This has changed during the 1980s and early 1990s, with typical social security payments falling in relation to average money wages, and several elements of policy being more sharply focused on those deemed to be in greatest need. The result of this, and the tax cuts already referred to, has been to increase the inequality of incomes in the United Kingdom during the 1980s; most probably inequality has not increased further in the early 1990s (see Chapter 8).

Partly as a supply-side policy and partly as a means of promoting greater efficiency (and sometimes competition), we must refer to the government's privatisation programme. After a slow start, this gathered pace and resulted in the transfer to private hands of about 10 per cent of the nation's capital stock during the 1980s, with further public asset sales in the early 1990s, leaving very little productive capital outside the private sector. The programme is expected to continue at least through the mid-1990s, and is gradually being extended to new areas (see Chapter 3).

1.4   Economic performance in the 1980s and early 1990s

The 1980s started badly with a very deep recession, and ended badly with another recession from which recovery was initially very slow, although it had gathered pace by early 1995. In between the two recessions, the United

Kingdom enjoyed a period of rapid growth of output and, for many of those in full-time employment, rapidly improving incomes and real living standards. Tighter monetary control was supposed to 'squeeze inflation out of the system', changes in taxation were expected to improve incentives and those firms which survived the tough conditions of the early 1980s should have been 'leaner and fitter'. No doubt many of them were, and still are, although the cost in terms of bankruptcies and unemployment was very high. The question is whether, in the mid- to late 1990s, the policies of the last decade and a half will turn out to have brought about a fundamental change in the United Kingdom's economic behaviour and, therefore, whether their costs will be considered justified in the light of superior UK performance in the coming years.

At present (May 1995) this is still not clear, since although the economy is certainly in the midst of a recovery the growth rate is not very rapid. Moreover, the government has been so concerned to win 'the battle against inflation' that it was prepared to maintain a very tight monetary policy even in the depths of the recession. These and other issues are referred to in later chapters (but see also Smith, 1992; Michie, 1992; Buxton, Chapman and Temple, 1994), so here I confine myself to a brief review of the main macroeconomic indicators for the 1980s and early 1990s, including some comparisons with other industrialised countries. Many indicators not covered here are discussed fully in the chapters that follow (e.g. unemployment, balance of payments, money supply, etc.).

For the period from 1978–93, Table 1.1 shows GDP and its main expenditure components for the United Kingdom and five other developed countries: the chosen comparator countries are the United States (US), Japan, France Germany and Italy. For the same period, and the same six countries, Table 1.2 shows how the consumer price index (consumption price deflator in the table) has moved in each country.

From the data shown in the tables, the evidence for a British economic miracle in the 1980s is quite mixed. Indeed, over the whole period shown the United Kingdom experienced slower overall economic growth (i.e. growth of GDP) than any other country in the tables, and consumer prices rose faster on average than anywhere except Italy. Taking a somewhat shorter period, from 1981–90, however, during which time the UK economy enjoyed unbroken growth, GDP growth was faster than any country in the table except Japan, averaging 2.9 per cent p.a.

Like all the other OECD countries exhibited except the United States, growth of public consumption (government expenditure on goods and services) was slower than that of GDP as a whole. This reflects a tendency throughout the developed world to restrict government spending in recent years, in line with monetarist philosophy which, as we saw above, favoured reducing the role of the government in the economy. On the other hand, the United Kingdom and Italy were the only countries in the tables in which private consumption grew noticeably faster than GDP as a whole. In the case of the United Kingdom, this reflects a tendency for booms to be led by private consumption spending. Thus

Table 1.1 GDP and its components in the United Kingdom and other OECD countries

	United Kingdom						United States						Japan					
Year	GDP	C	G	I	X	M	GDP	C	G	I	X	M	GDP	C	G	I	X	M
1981	75.9	71.2	89.7	60.3	70.7	56.7	78.5	75.7	76.5	81.8	63.9	53.8	68.6	70.9	81.8	60.0	55.5	52.9
1982	77.2	71.9	90.4	63.6	71.3	59.4	76.8	76.5	77.6	75.3	58.1	53.8	70.9	74.0	83.5	60.0	57.7	52.5
1983	80.0	75.2	92.4	66.8	72.6	63.4	79.8	80.0	79.8	80.3	56.0	60.5	72.9	76.6	85.9	59.4	58.7	49.5
1984	81.9	76.7	93.1	72.8	77.4	69.7	84.7	83.9	82.2	93.0	59.9	75.7	76.1	78.7	88.3	62.1	67.4	54.7
1985	84.9	79.6	93.1	75.8	82.0	71.5	87.4	87.6	87.2	97.7	60.6	80.4	80.0	81.4	89.8	65.4	71.7	54.2
1986	88.6	85.1	94.6	77.8	85.6	76.4	89.9	90.7	91.7	98.0	64.6	85.8	82.1	84.1	93.8	68.6	67.9	54.5
1987	92.8	89.6	95.5	85.8	90.6	82.3	92.7	93.3	94.5	97.6	71.3	89.7	85.7	87.7	94.2	75.1	71.0	60.3
1988	97.5	96.3	96.2	97.8	91.0	92.7	96.4	96.6	95.1	101.7	82.6	93.0	91.0	92.3	96.2	84.1	78.6	73.2
1989	99.6	99.4	97.5	103.6	95.2	99.5	98.8	98.5	97.0	101.8	92.4	96.5	95.4	96.2	98.1	91.9	90.4	89.3
1990	100.0	100.0	100.0	100.0	100.0	100.0	100.0	100.0	100.0	100.0	100.0	100.0	100.0	100.0	100.0	100.0	100.0	100.0
1991	98.0	97.8	102.6	90.5	99.3	94.7	99.4	99.6	101.2	92.4	106.3	99.5	104.3	102.2	101.6	103.7	105.1	97.6
1992	97.5	87.8	102.6	89.5	102.4	100.6	101.7	102.3	100.5	97.5	113.4	108.1	105.6	103.9	104.4	102.5	107.9	94.8
1993	99.6	100.4	103.5	89.8	105.5	103.4	104.8	105.7	99.7	108.6	118.0	119.7	105.5	105.0	106.1	100.7	106.8	94.5

	France						Germany						Italy					
Year	GDP	C	G	I	X	M	GDP	C	G	I	X	M	GDP	C	G	I	X	M
1981	80.1	79.2	82.3	78.5	70.6	64.9	80.1	81.1	90.0	81.1	64.3	67.1	80.8	78.3	80.1	81.5	67.9	62.5
1982	82.2	81.9	85.4	77.4	69.4	66.6	79.2	79.8	89.2	76.5	66.6	66.3	80.9	79.2	82.1	77.7	66.3	62.4
1983	82.8	82.7	87.1	74.7	72.0	64.8	80.6	81.0	89.4	78.9	66.1	67.2	81.7	79.8	85.0	77.2	67.8	61.5
1984	83.8	83.6	88.1	72.7	77.0	66.5	82.9	82.5	91.6	79.0	71.9	70.9	83.9	81.3	86.9	80.0	73.6	69.1
1985	85.4	85.6	90.1	75.1	78.5	69.6	84.8	84.0	93.5	79.0	77.7	74.3	86.1	83.7	89.8	80.5	76.0	71.8
1986	87.6	89.0	91.6	78.5	77.3	74.5	86.7	86.9	95.9	81.6	77.1	76.2	88.6	86.9	92.1	82.3	77.9	73.8
1987	89.5	91.5	84.2	82.2	79.7	80.3	87.9	89.9	97.3	83.0	77.0	79.1	91.4	90.5	95.3	86.4	81.5	80.6
1988	93.6	94.5	97.5	90.1	86.1	87.2	91.1	92.1	99.4	86.4	81.0	82.9	94.2	94.2	98.0	92.4	85.9	86.0
1989	97.6	97.4	97.9	97.2	94.9	94.2	94.4	95.0	97.8	91.7	89.6	90.2	97.9	97.6	98.8	96.4	93.5	92.6
1990	100.0	100.0	100.0	100.0	100.0	100.0	100.0	100.0	100.0	100.0	100.0	100.0	100.0	100.0	100.0	100.0	100.0	100.0
1991	100.8	101.4	102.6	99.3	103.8	102.8	105.1	105.7	100.3	105.9	110.9	111.5	101.2	102.7	101.6	100.6	100.5	103.4
1992	102.0	102.7	105.6	96.8	109.0	103.9	106.6	107.9	104.4	105.3	115.6	115.1	102.0	104.1	102.5	98.6	105.6	108.2
1993	101.1	103.4	106.1	91.9	108.5	100.0	104.8	108.1	103.2	96.7	111.8	108.9	101.3	101.9	103.3	87.7	116.2	100.3

Notes: 1. All data are presented in index form in constant prices of 1990, with 1990 values = 100.
2. Notation is standard, so C = private consumption, G = public consumption, I = investment, X = exports, M = imports.
Source: Quarterly National Accounts 1994(4), Paris: OECD.

Table 1.2 Consumption price deflator in the United Kingdom and other OECD countries

Year	United Kingdom	United States	Japan	France	Germany	Italy
1981	62.4	67.7	86.8	62.1	82.6	45.6
1982	67.8	71.6	89.2	69.2	86.8	53.3
1983	71.1	75.0	90.9	75.9	89.6	61.3
1984	74.6	78.0	93.2	81.8	91.9	68.6
1985	78.6	81.0	95.2	86.5	93.5	74.8
1986	81.7	83.5	95.6	88.8	93.0	79.5
1987	85.2	87.0	95.8	91.6	93.4	83.7
1988	89.5	90.7	95.7	94.0	94.7	88.5
1989	94.8	95.1	97.5	97.2	97.4	94.1
1990	100.0	100.0	110.0	100.0	100.0	100.0
1991	107.4	104.2	102.5	103.1	103.7	106.8
1992	112.4	107.5	104.6	105.6	107.7	112.5
1993	116.4	110.1	105.9	107.9	111.1	117.8

Note: 1. All figures are expressed as percentages of the 1990 consumer price level for each country.
Source: Quarterly National Accounts 1994(4), Paris: OECD.

living standards rise for a time, but investment and exports are too weak to sustain the expansion without encountering capacity constraints (in the case of investment) and inflationary pressures, as well as a worsening trade balance. All of this was apparent in the United Kingdom in the second half of the 1980s.

Table 1.1 shows that the United Kingdom's export performance has been the weakest of the countries shown over the 1980s. Thus even when world trade grows rapidly, as it did for much of the 1980s, the United Kingdom enjoys export growth while losing market share to more dynamic competitors, both within the OECD (as in the table) and outside (e.g. Hong Kong, China, etc.). For UK industry this trend is very worrying, since it implies that in an increasing range of branches and product groups, UK firms have been unable to compete effectively in world markets. The most recent, and still continuing recovery, provides the first indication that this pattern may be changing.

One reason for the traditional pattern has undoubtedly been the low rates of investment which characterise the United Kingdom. It is interesting that, with the exception of the United States whose underlying economic situation is even more difficult than that of the United Kingdom, investment by OECD countries grew much faster than GDP as a whole during the 1980s. In the United Kingdom, investment enjoyed a short-lived boom in the late 1980s but has fallen back substantially since 1989, with recovery from the recession only resulting in a significant increase in investment quite recently. Meanwhile, our principal competitors continue to invest at a higher rate, partly because their investment has grown faster than GDP in the last decade, partly because even at the start of this process they were already investing a higher proportion of their GDP. On both counts, the United Kingdom is being left behind.

Turning, finally, to inflation, we have already noted the United Kingdom's poor inflation record in the last decade (see Table 1.2). However, this record is better than that achieved in the United Kingdom during the 1970s, and in the early 1990s inflation has declined to the lowest levels for several decades. Inflation in 1992 was around 4 per cent, and the rate of inflation has fallen further since then. However, as we discuss later, the costs of this achievement may turn out to have been very high.

1.5   Brief introductions to individual chapters

In order to guide the reader through what follows, this section provides some brief introductory remarks on each chapter. Like the book as a whole, the comments are grouped into three subsections: on microeconomic issues, macroeconomic policy and the international economy, respectively.

1.5.1   *Microeconomic issues*

In Part 1 we begin with Peter Clarke's Chapter 2 on industrial policy, covering a diverse field of policy in which any government intervention extending beyond the minimal requirement to set the parameters within which the private sector would operate was generally considered undesirable during the 1980s. After reviewing alternative approaches to industrial policy, notably the neoclassical and 'Austrian' approaches, Chapter 2 sets out the framework of industrial policy in the United Kingdom. In doing so, it reviews the areas of competition policy, regional policy, public support for research and development (R&D) and policy on international trade. Starting from the premise that the function of industrial policy should be to promote international competitiveness, the chapter finds that UK policy has probably had very little net impact in the last decade and a half, even though the existence of the relevant legislation and institutions might help to discourage certain forms of anti-competitive behaviour. Some aspects of industrial policy, such as merger and takeover issues, and some aspects of R&D policy, now fall within the ambit of EU policy. While this can enable a wider, EU view to be taken of industrial concentration, for instance, it can also give rise to conflicts of interest between the EU and member states.

Aside from policy towards private industry and the services sector, the 1980s witnessed a massive programme of privatisation of state-owned firms and industries in the United Kingdom. This transformation is described in Paul Hare's Chapter 3. Even as late as the 1970s, the nationalised sector in the United Kingdom was expanding as new firms were brought into public ownership. At the same time, the government sought to establish a general framework of control over the sector, with policies concerning pricing, investment criteria and financial limits. Increasingly, both public perceptions and comparative analysis agreed that the nationalised sector was not performing well and, as monetarist thinking came to the fore in macro-economics, so privatisation became an increasingly central plank in the government's microeconomic policy. In the course of implementing the programme, many UK citizens became shareholders for the first time. Especially in the public utilities, which remained as virtual monopolies after privatisation, the government established new regulatory bodies to control their pricing and other aspects of their economic behaviour. Towards the end of the 1980s, the government was starting to extend the idea of privatisation to new areas: schooling, the universities, the health service, local authority services, and so on. In the early 1990s it was apparent that the re-elected Conservative government would continue in the same direction, although there was increasing opposition to some of the more extreme proposals, and increasing unease about possible threats to traditionally publicly provided services such as education and health that might result from privatisation.

Since services have received so little attention from policy-makers, and are so rarely covered in economics textbooks, it is appropriate for Chapter 4 to provide some definitions. Some of the key features of services are highlighted, including the increasing interchangeability between goods and services, and the nature of the interaction between supplier and customer: some types of specialised manufacturing become increasingly like services, while some services (e.g. fast food outlets) become more like a production line. Although hard to measure, there is evidence that UK service sector productivity has risen far faster than that of manufacturing in recent decades, while the sector generated over 2 m new jobs in the 1980s. Only a small part of UK regional policy spending has supported services, and at EU level the main emphasis has been on deregulation and the promotion of competition.

In contrast to services, the trade unions did attract substantial amounts of attention from the government in the 1980s, as documented in Chapter 5 by Ian Paterson. He outlines the basic labour market theory which makes it possible to assess the impact of trade unions, and reviews the empirical evidence for the United Kingdom which suggests that the impact has been quite small in practice (despite government assertions to the contrary). In stages during the 1980s and early 1990s, industrial relations legislation was passed to limit trade union powers and immunities, requiring pre-strike ballots, and ending the protection previously given to union closed shops. Although union membership has declined, as has the extent of national pay bargaining in the United Kingdom, the government keeps this area of its policy under continuous review.

Increasingly important at both United Kingdom and EU levels of policy is the control over environmental pollution. As Leslie Simpson emphasises in Chapter 6, the 'common sense' view that all such pollution is a bad thing is simply mistaken. Instead it is essential to consider both the costs and benefits of pollution, which together enable us to determine the 'optimal' level of pollution. Because of the high costs of eliminating some forms of pollution, this optimal level is unlikely to be zero. Nevertheless, since pollution is not normally traded (no price is attached to it), markets left to themselves are most likely to generate more than the optimal level of it (firms treat it as costless, even though it generates social costs). This is why governments seek to regulate pollution. They can do so either through the price mechanism (using taxes and subsidies) or by direct controls and standards. Although the former is usually preferable in theory, the latter is most often employed in practice. The chapter reviews air and water pollution control policy in the United Kingdom, as well as recent legislation to establish an integrated pollution control system. EU environmental policies, as well as measures resulting from the recent Earth Summit, are likely to have a substantial impact on the United Kingdom's pollution controls in the later 1990s.

The next three chapters in Part 1 deal with issues related to government expenditure and taxation, government being broadly interpreted to include the local authorities. Thus Chapter 7, by Philip Welham, deals with public expenditure and taxation; Chapter 8, also by Philip Welham, reviews the distribution of income and wealth, with particular reference to the impact of tax and expenditure policies upon these distributions. Finally Chapter 9, by Glen Bramley, analyses local government services and finance. Between them these chapters cover two of the three traditional areas of public finance, to do with efficient resource allocation and questions of equity. The remaining area, stabilisation policy, is covered in Chapter 11 in Part 2.

Chapter 7 studies the appropriate size of the public sector, the components of government expenditure and the way the tax base and tax rates affect firms' and households' decisions. It concludes that there has almost certainly been too little public spending on education, health and housing, and that despite substantial reductions in income taxation, the overall burden of taxation increased during the 1980s. In the 1990s policy options will be constrained by concern over the government's total borrowing: thus even if income tax rates continue to fall, it will be at the cost of widening the tax base (by removing some existing tax concessions) or by cutting public expenditure.

As Chapter 8 shows, the United Kingdom experienced a reduction in income inequality in the period from 1945 to 1979 but in the 1980s inequality increased again, with further increases likely in the 1990s. Taken as a whole, the tax system has little effect on income distribution, but transfer payments redistribute annual income towards the poor. Nevertheless, the extent of poverty in the United Kingdom increased during the 1980s. The distribution of wealth in the United Kingdom was also becoming more equal in the post-war period, but this trend came to an end around 1976. Since then, it is most likely that the distribution has remained roughly stable.

Chapter 8, by Glen Bramley, discusses the current situation of local government in the United Kingdom. He points out that while local government is responsible for spending the large sum of approximately £75 bn a year, there is no general political consensus concerning the roles and powers of this important group of institutions. In the 1990s local government has been in a state of almost continuous structural, financial and organisational turmoil. The chapter examines the impact on the provision of local services brought about by the following upheavals in local government: the switch to single tier (or unitary) local authorities; the abandonment of the now discredited Community Charge in favour of the Council Tax; and the widespread introduction of such things as compulsory competitive tendering, educational opting out and the increasing reliance on markets (or 'quasi-markets') to provide allocative signals for the use of resources.

The final chapter of Part 1 is David Begg's, on transport policy. This notes that transport is economically special in that it is associated both with increasing returns to scale in the supply of transport infrastructure, and with substantial externalities in the form of congestion costs imposed on other users, especially on the roads. This latter feature has given rise to a great deal of debate about the desirability of road pricing, and consideration of various ways of doing that. Although some countries have undertaken experiments in this area, however, the United Kingdom has not yet done so. Indeed, as far as UK transport policy is concerned, the main elements of the decade and a half have been deregulation (e.g. the buses), commercialisation and privatisation.

1.5.2 *Macroeconomic policy*

Part 2 opens with Stuart Sayer's chapter on fiscal policy and the public sector deficit. This argues that in order to understand the stance of fiscal policy it is necessary to consider what has been happening to the public sector deficit. Whether a particular deficit is sustainable depends on how it is financed – by asset sales, bond issues or by monetary emission – and on its relation to GDP both now and in the future. The latter, of course, depends both on cyclical factors and on longer run growth trends. After discussing a variety of possible cases, including the effects of political pressures and expectations, the chapter ends with a useful check-list of factors to look for in assessing the likely impact of fiscal policy in general, and the Chancellor's budget statements and public expenditure statements in particular.

For much of the period since 1979 controlling inflation has been the government's top priority, but large reductions in inflation were only achieved at very high cost in terms of output and employment, as Geoffrey Wyatt emphasises in Chapter 12. While the government attempted to use monetary targeting to control inflation in the early 1980s, it was doing so at a time when financial markets were undergoing both rapid innovation as well as deregulation. This made it very hard to operate monetary policy effectively, and to interpret monetary indicators. On 8 October 1990 the United Kingdom decided to discard its independent monetary policy, and opted instead for membership of the ERM. For a variety of reasons, discussed in Chapter 12, this change in policy proved unsustainable and on so-called 'Black Wednesday' (16 September 1992) the United Kingdom abandoned the ERM and re-established its own independent monetary control. It remains to be seen whether the current approach, with its stress on setting base rate transparently with reference to monetary conditions as given by a range of indicators to achieve an explicit target for underlying inflation, will be more successful than previous monetary policies.

Partly as a result of the monetary policy pursued in the 1980s, the United Kingdom experienced its highest unemployment rates since the 1930s. This gave rise to much debate about the nature of the resulting unemployment, and in particular about how high unemployment needed to rise in order to restrain and bring down inflation. The policy issues involved here are both important and complex. They are examined in Chapter 13, by Prabir Bhattacharya. He argues that reducing unemployment entails the use of supply-side policies to reduce wage pressure, while aggregate demand is also increased. The inflationary effects of the latter are minimised if new job opportunities can be made available to the long-term unemployed.

As Ian Hirst emphasises in Chapter 14, the UK financial markets changed rapidly during the 1980s. He concentrates on the corporate sector, reviewing the banks, the equity market and the bond markets, as well as important issues to do with takeovers, mergers and corporate governance. There is now less distinction between different types of financial institution than there used to be (which is a mixed blessing, since it gives up some of the benefits of specialisation), greater competition and tougher regulation to protect investors. Whether the reformed system of financial markets functions more effectively as a supplier of risk capital to the corporate sector is not yet clear, since the reforms have not been in place for long, and a recession does not provide the best occasion to assess market performance.

1.5.3   *The international economy*

In Chapter 15, Hugh Fleming analyses the recent behaviour of the sterling exchange rate. In examining the United Kingdom's experience as a member of the ERM from 1990 to 1992, this chapter discusses the enormous difficulties faced by the government in the second half of this period in attempting to keep the pound within 6 per cent of the relatively high target rate of DM 2.95. Eventually the problems proved too great, and on 16 September 1992 sterling was withdrawn from the ERM and returned to a position in which its exchange rate was again determined by market forces in a free float. The chapter also looks at the strict financial criteria laid down by the Treaty of Maastricht (of 7

February 1992) for a single currency in the EU, and concludes that the Treaty timetable is likely to prove overly optimistic.

The current account of the balance of payments is reviewed in detail in Chapter 16 by Thomas Torrance. After presenting some key definitions, the chapter shows that the United Kingdom has moved into increasing deficit in its trade in goods (visible trade), but that this has been offset to varying degrees by surpluses in services trade (the invisibles account). Several conceptual approaches have been developed to explain the current account balance and changes in it over time, including the absorption approach and the elasticities approach. Both of these are explained in the chapter. Given policy-makers' usual concerns about the balance of payments, especially when the current account is in deficit, the chapter raises an interesting question at the end. This asks whether we should always be concerned about a deficit: perhaps there should even be a Queen's Award for imports! The conclusion is that a current account deficit is nothing to worry about if it stems from profitable investment within the economy that local savings are inadequate to finance, and if investors have sufficient confidence in the economy to continue providing the capital flows needed to balance the overall external accounts.

Chapter 17, by Shu-Mei Gao, is concerned with the trends in UK trade and the United Kingdom's trade policy in practice. The chapter starts by examining several explanations for the cause and direction of international trade, essentially various approaches to explaining a country's comparative advantage. Then changes in the structure of the United Kingdom's trade during the last 30 years or so are reviewed, together with the factors which brought about these changes. The instruments of trade policy, such as tariffs and non-tariff barriers, have changed considerably over the period examined, to a large extent as a result of the increasing impact on the United Kingdom of the General Agreement on Tariffs and Trade (GATT; now replaced by the World Trade Organisation (WTO) from January 1995) and the EU on the United Kingdom's trade policy. The result has been a gradual but substantial liberalisation in the United Kingdom's trading environment, to which United Kingdom companies have had to adapt themselves.

The final chapter of the book, Andrew Scott's Chapter 18 on the EU, could have been placed almost anywhere, since it deals with microeconomic, macroeconomic and international issues. Its inclusion in the book reflects the enormous importance of EU policy for the United Kingdom nowadays, not only in connection with the EMS which was already referred to above, but also in connection with agriculture (the Common Agricultural Policy (CAP)), regional policy, technology policy and the whole package of policies to do with the Single European Market (sometimes called the 1992 Initiative, though it only came into force from January 1993). The last of these entailed removing many of the remaining barriers to the movement of goods, capital and people within the EU.

Questions for discussion

1. How did the UK government's approach to economic policy change in the 1980s?
2. Discuss the United Kingdom's economic performance in the 1980s in comparison with other industrialised countries.
3. 'Low income taxes strengthen work incentives, which in turn yield faster growth.' How far does the United Kingdom's experience support this view?
4. Is investment in the United Kingdom too low?
5. Discuss the main ways in which the world economic environment changed in the last decade. Were these changes favourable or unfavourable for the United Kingdom?
6. Has the United Kingdom managed to achieve low inflation and steady growth in the 1990s?

Notes

1. G7 refers to the group of seven most developed countries: the United States, Canada, Japan, Germany, France, Italy and the United Kingdom. G24 refers to the 24 most developed countries (which therefore includes the G7), belonging to the Organisation for Economic Cooperation and Development (OECD), based in Paris. Both groups meet regularly to discuss a wide range of world economic and political issues. Note that strictly speaking, G24 should now be referred to as G25, since Mexico joined the OECD in 1994.
2. Note that from 1 January 1995, GATT has been replaced by a new international organisation, the World Trade Organisation (WTO). Like its predecessor, this organisation is also located in Geneva.

References and further reading

Buxton, T., Chapman, P. and Temple, P. (eds) (1994) *Britain's Economic Performance*, London: Routledge.
Michie, J. (ed.) (1992) *The Economic Legacy 1979–1992*, London: Academic Press.
OECD (1994) *Quarterly National Accounts*, Paris: OECD.
Sargent, T. and Wallace, N. (1975) 'Rational expectations, the optimal money instrument and the optional money supply' *Journal of Political Economy* 83 pp. 241–54.
Smith, D. (1992) *From Boom to Bust: Trial and error in British economic policy*, London: Penguin Books.

PART 1

Microeconomic issues

CHAPTER 2

Industrial economic policy

PETER CLARKE

2.1 Introduction

In this chapter, I maintain that those who argue for the exclusion of government from intervention in industry have not taken into account the policies employed by international competitors in the global market. I conclude that there is a substantial role for government, not only in contributing to the creation of a competitive domestic environment, but also in matching competitors' government support in international markets. In coming to this conclusion I emphasise the process of decision-making as well as the implementation of the policies themselves.

The next section identifies the potential content of industrial policy. This is followed by consideration of the problem or problems which industrial policy must tackle. Next is an investigation of how these problems arose. The identification of the problems and their causes are essential steps in understanding the process of policy determination. The chapter proceeds with a discussion of the constraints within which policy is determined, followed by an examination of the rationale for the different theoretical approaches to industrial policy. There is then a description of the current policy framework and a presentation of the policies adopted by the UK government since 1979, with an evaluation of their effectiveness. This is followed by a section on what are perceived as the successful elements of industrial policy in those countries regarded as 'winners' in the global market. European Union policy and its effects on UK policy-makers provide the final stage of the discussion before the concluding section.

2.2 What is industrial policy?

Industrial policy can involve a wide range of policy instruments. Generally, it includes any policy implemented by government which is directed towards a particular industry, with the objective of improving that industry's competitive position. Policy can be directed, for example, at an infant industry in order to protect its development, or at a mature industry in order to facilitate rationalisation or regeneration. Industrial policy may be conveniently divided into four main policy areas: competition, regional, research and development (R&D) and international trade. Each area can involve a number of individual elements of policy, some of which can have effects in more than one policy area, not always in the desired direction. The list below presents a sample of the policies that are in common use:

1. Protectionism;
2. Export subsidies;
3. Financial assistance to displaced workers;
4. Subsidies for R&D;
5. Education and training;
6. Antitrust policies;
7. Infrastructure support;
8. Direct loans to reduce risk;
9. Tax policy to encourage investment; and
10. Procurement policy of the government.

This list gives an indication of the scope that governments have in aiding industry, and almost all governments use some combination these policies and others, either explicitly or covertly (OECD, 1990).

2.3 What is the problem to be solved?

Industrial policy is not formulated for its own sake, but to solve a particular problem or problems. The initial stage is to identify the problem, and the second is to set a policy objective with the aim of solving it. There has been a great debate as to the extent and significance of Britain's industrial decline. There are those who argue that the structural changes that have taken place in the United Kingdom should be expected in a mature economy and that there is no problem. On the other hand, opponents argue precisely the opposite and look for ways of reversing or slowing down the country's relative industrial decline. One incontestable observation is the decline in the United Kingdom's international competitive position. There has been, over the last four decades, a decline in the United Kingdom's relative importance in world trade (Foreman-Peck, 1991). Data to support this development can be found in the decline in the UK share of world trade, the change from surplus to deficit in the UK balance of trade, the degree of import penetration (see also Chapters 16 and 17).

These two trends in international trade statistics are mutually supportive in providing evidence of the United Kingdom's decline. In a dynamic world economy with many newly industrialised countries, it could be expected that the United Kingdom's share of world trade would fall (see Tables 2.1 and 2.2). However this is no reason why, if it is maintaining its relative competitive position, a long-term manufacturing trade surplus should turn into a deficit.

Table 2.1 Percentage share of world merchandise trade for the United Kingdom (calculated from IMF International Financial Statistics)

1950	1960	1970	1980	1990	1993
10.8	9.1	6.9	5.9	5.5	5.5

Table 2.2 UK visible trade and import penetration

	1979	1981	1983	1985	1987	1989	1991	1993
Value (£ million)								
Exports	40 471	50 668	60 700	77 991	79 446	92 792	103 413	121 414
Imports (fob)	43 814	47 416	62 237	81 336	90 669	116 632	113 697	134 623
Visible balance	−3343	+3252	−1537	−3345	−11223	−23840	−10287	−13209
Import penetration Ratio imports/ home demand	26.9	27.8	31.1	34.3	35.2	35.6	31.2	33.2

Since 1980 there has been an erosion of the United Kingdom's net trade balance in manufacturing, with an overall deficit on trade in manufactured goods appearing for the first time in recent decades in 1983. This situation has persisted even in the recent long recession and into the export-led modest recovery, when it could have been expected that there would have been a significant reduction in imports.

Further supporting evidence of the decline in the United Kingdom's relative competitiveness is the difference in total and labour productivity between the United Kingdom and its major competitors. Statistics show that over the last 20 years the United Kingdom has lagged significantly behind many of its major competitors in productivity growth; this is despite the improvement in both the United Kingdom's total and labour productivity since 1979, primarily due to restructuring during the 1980–2 recession. An illustration of these productivity differences is that in 1991 industrial workers in United Kingdom produced only 65 per cent of German industrial workers.

In addition the United Kingdom has lagged seriously behind its major competitors in manufacturing growth. Further OECD data shows that UK manufacturing growth in output since 1979 has been lower than any other of the 24 OECD countries apart from Greece. The decline in the international competitiveness of the United Kingdom has had repercussions for the economy. The unemployment rate has increased for all the industrialised countries over the last three decades, the EU average increasing from 4.4 per cent to 9.8 per cent between the 1970s and 1980s. The United Kingdom's figure has increased by a larger percentage from 3.9 per cent to 9.8 per cent. Lastly, the United Kingdom has experienced rapid decline in its manufacturing base, has had relatively slow growth over the whole period, and has experienced declining investment in research and development. These changes in the circumstances of the UK economy are all part and parcel of the main problem, the decline in international competitiveness. To some degree they are both contributors to the problem and the consequences of it.

2.4   The reasons for the loss of international competitiveness

If the main industrial problem of the United Kingdom has been correctly identified, the next stage is to diagnose the cause or causes of the problem. Only when this next stage has been completed is it possible to look for policy options. There is no simple, all-embracing explanation of the United Kingdom's decline in international competitiveness. Parts of the problem may be found in non-economic explanations which lie beyond the scope of this chapter. The economic explanations refer to several levels. At the highest level are those which contribute to the creation of the overall economic environment, while those at the lower levels work within that environment. The following contribute to a greater or lesser extent to the United Kingdom's decline in international competitiveness.

First, the United Kingdom has failed to accept that to take part in the world market firms and governments must adopt a global perspective. Most of the growth markets are global markets with fierce international corporate competition often supported domestically by an active government industrial policy.

Secondly, firms in the United Kingdom have a tendency to concentrate on short-term objectives and policies, while the main competitors, Germany and Japan, adopt much longer time horizons. The pressures on corporate management from the financial sector to adopt short-term objectives constrain their ability to take the long-term view required, for example, in investment in research and development (see also the related discussion in Chapter 14).

Thirdly, structural economic relations do not appear to be appropriate for improving international competitiveness. The relationship between the financial and product markets is an example of one of the many structural differences within the British economy compared to those existing in the competitors' economies.

The UK financial sector, although regarded by many as one of the most efficient and competitive in the world, contributes little to funding real investment in the manufacturing sector. The relationship of German banks to the firms they serve, enabling them to provide the main source of corporate finance, and the corresponding position in Japan, contrast significantly with the United Kingdom (Hutton, 1995).

The above explanations of the United Kingdom's problem manifest themselves in lower-level, operational explanations. These include: de-industrialisation, low growth rates, low investment in new plant and machinery and infrastructure, low expenditure on R&D and a poor record in industrial training and education.

Although the above explanations of Britain's relative decline are not exhaustive, they provide much of the background in which past and current, corporate and government policy has been enacted. They represent fundamental characteristics and trends of the UK economy. This does not mean they cannot be altered, as they have been in the past, but it does imply that current policies can either be directed to altering the overall economic environment or they can accept its existence and attempt to work within it. The former requires a long-term perspective while the latter may generate little success working in an inappropriate environment.

De-industrialisation, i.e. the decline in the relative importance of manufacturing output in the economy, is commonly given as a reason for the United Kingdom's demise. It has been argued that the decline of the United Kingdom's share of world trade is synonymous with de-industrialisation. The discussion about the importance of the move away from manufacturing to services has been long and heated. Whatever the merits of the arguments, one consequence of the shift has been the inability of the United Kingdom to generate a balance of trade surplus. There are a number of reasons for this.

First, it has been proposed that the country's relatively poor record in R&D expenditure has resulted in poorer performance in the introduction of new products and processes in UK manufacturing. The allocation of a substantial percentage of R&D expenditure to the defence sector makes very little contribution to improving international competitiveness in the fast-growing global consumer markets. Even the benefits of this R&D, of large defence sector exports, are likely to be eroded in a declining defence market with an increasing number of suppliers, including several from Eastern Europe.

Secondly, the lack of training and industrial education has meant that the United Kingdom has a relatively large proportion of unskilled workers who are unable to be employed in modern management and production methods. Many of our major competitors have superior track records. Thus, the German workforce has twice as many vocationally qualified workers as the United Kingdom. This difference has had a detrimental effect on United Kingdom productivity and has created a vicious circle. Low wages provide, in turn, an incentive for labour intensive production methods which generate low labour productivity, which then justifies the low wages.

2.5 Significant industrial policy interdependencies

It is important to understand the overall economic policy environment in which industrial policy is expected to work. Industrial policy is not determined in a vacuum, and there are important interdependencies between policy domains, including those between:

(a) macroeconomic and microeconomic policy;
(b) governments' and corporations' objectives for industry;
(c) the governments' and corporations' industrial strategies;
(d) the governments' policies in different areas of industrial policy; and
(e) the United Kingdom's and its rival countries' industrial policy.

(*a*) The fiscal and monetary policies employed by government have a significant and continued influence on industrial success. The difficulty arises because macroeconomic policies, implemented to meet macro objectives such as inflation control, can and do have serious implications for firms' success, especially in a recession. Industrial policy cannot be insulated from the effects of the relatively short-term, political cycle. For example, the effect of any industrial policy to stimulate investment in plant and machinery or in research and development expenditure, may be more than offset by restraining macroeconomic policies.

(*b*) Because firms and governments do not always represent the same interest groups in society they are likely to have different objectives. Firms in a recession may have as their sole objective the wish to survive. Therefore they will concentrate on preserving their cash flow by resisting long-term commitments. Governments, on the other hand, may be more interested in stimulating investment in productive capacity to contribute to the climb out of the recession.

(*c*) Even if firms and governments agree on a particular objective, such as maximisation of long-term profits or value added, they may perceive the achievement of that objective by different and sometimes conflicting means. Corporate managers may state that they believe in market competition but many of their actions are an attempt to develop their own market niche or dominant firm position.

(*d*) Because of the range of both industrial policy areas and the policies which can be used in them, there is the possibility that a specific policy which contributes to one objective will be counter-productive in respect to another. The possible conflicts between the use of the patent system and dominant firm policy is a ready example.

(*e*) Lastly, a country involved in international competition cannot determine its industrial policy in ignorance of the actions of its competitors' governments. Policies which exclude government intervention at a domestic level, will fail to improve international competitiveness if other countries' governments are successfully intervening (Audretsch, 1989). The US anti-trust legislation is primarily directed at the limitation of economic power in any market. It takes a dogmatic stance in this respect. It does not provide for a case-by-case investigation as to whether a monopoly could be the best way to achieve economic efficiency. Competition is not only king, irrespective of the costs, it is also all-pervasive. Japan, in contrast, adopts a different attitude. The Japanese have a more receptive policy towards cartels. This incorporates a view of fair trade which assigns priority to international competitiveness over their domestic dominant firm policy. They will also encourage consortia of corporations to undertake R&D jointly.

Many of the criticisms directed at government industrial policy arise because of a failure to understand these relationships. Often policies exacerbate rather than contribute to the solution of problems. It is only when the relationships are fully understood, especially the last, that appropriate policies can be correctly determined and efficiently implemented. Any failure in this respect may not only mean the lack of a level playing field for UK companies, it would imply that their international competitors are playing at a much higher altitude.

2.6 Philosophical rationale of policies

In any debate it is always easiest to make a case for the extremes on either side of the argument. It is the nature of theoretical development in the social sciences that 'progress' is achieved by a new approach attempting to usurp the existing conventional wisdom. Although this may make for interesting reading in the academic journals and lead to the promotion of those involved, it does not always contribute usefully to the determination of policy. This is the case for industrial policy, and particularly in the area of competition policy. The main protagonists in this area represent two views which are diametrically opposed to each other. One argues for a strongly interventionist policy, based on neoclassical economics, the other for a non-interventionist, *laissez-faire* policy based on the Austrian School (Hay and Morris, 1991).

The neoclassical school focuses on the characteristics of markets and particularly on market failure. Market failure exists because not all markets are the same and some forms of market fail to generate optimally efficient results. Although there are a number of market failures, much criticism has been directed at dominant firms and their capacity, by increasing price and reducing output, to reduce economic welfare. This has led to the structure–conduct–performance approach, which emphasises the causal relationships between these three elements. The argument is that once the market structure has been determined then the conduct and performance levels of a market can be predicted. In a competitive market, market pressures lead to long-term normal profits and any long-term dominant firm profits which exist are seen as the result of the abuse of market power.

Competition policy, underpinned by this approach, concentrates on the creation of the appropriate competitive market structure. It takes the position that monopolies, or markets with high concentration, will not lead to the efficient allocation of resources and therefore a policy which will reduce the level of concentration should be implemented. High concentration exists when a large proportion of any product or service market is concentrated in a relatively small number of firms. Therefore, unless there are strong economic efficiency reasons, such concentrated market structures are to be avoided.

The Austrian School attempts to embody a much more complex and dynamic conception of the market environment. It takes the position that as long as market entry is not artificially restricted, long-run allocative and cost efficiency are generated. Entry or even potential entry ensure that firms are always vulnerable to competitive pressures. Large profits, as may be generated by a dominant firm, are viewed as a reward for entrepreneurship and greater efficiency, and a vital element in an active and dynamic economy. Investment in both product and process innovation are seen as responses to the existence of large profits which attract resources to compete for them and may ultimately lead to lower long-run costs.

Policy recommendations based on this school of thought consequently take a much more relaxed attitude to dominant firms and industries with high concentration ratios. It has provided the basis for a *laissez-faire*, non-interventionist posture by government in respect to industrial policy. It has also led to the deregulation of a number of industries, for example, the bus industry in the United Kingdom and the airline industry in the United States.

Adherents to the structure–conduct–performance rationale can adopt a dogmatic approach to competition policy, as in the United States, and automatically restructure markets characterised by a dominant firm. An alternative application involves comparison of the costs and benefits of a dominant firm. Each case is individually investigated to assess whether it does generate net benefits. The Austrian School in its extreme form recommends no government intervention at all, as unconstrained markets in any current guise are deemed to represent the most efficient means of resource allocation. In its qualified form it acknowledges that government can contribute to the creation of the appropriate competitive economic environment. For example, it can legislate against price fixing and horizontal mergers (Hartley and Cooper, 1990).

Although both theoretical approaches have some degree of credibility, there is a difficulty associated with the uncritical acceptance of either as the basis for industrial policy. Neither is appropriate, given the complexity of the economic environment in which industrial policy must work. Both approaches provide some insights to the problem and possible solutions, but they cannot cope with the whole picture. In particular, they are unable to accommodate fully the interrelationships described above, especially those between different countries' industrial policies. This failing of the two philosophical extremes has led to two developments.

An extension of the neoclassical model acknowledges that firms work in an internationally imperfect market and that a significant part of this trade is between industrialised countries and on an intra-industry basis. These features have become so important in the last two decades that they have led to the introduction of a 'new trade theory'. The policy implications of this theoretical development have been to reinforce the case for a role for government intervention, especially in the case of subsidies and taxes.

In the current world market it is Japan that is the current 'winner' in the international market. It would, then, seem sensible to understand the basis on which it sets its industrial policy. Japanese policy reflects elements of both the theoretical extremes portrayed above. It has neither adopted nor rejected either of them exclusively. This has led to the introduction of the concept of the development state or managed economy. In this approach, the government actively participates in forming the appropriate domestic market structure. In Japan overall policy determination is managed by MITI (the Ministry of International Trade and Industry), and includes representation from all sections of the interest groups involved in the industrial sector.

2.7   The current industrial policy framework in the United Kingdom

Some elements of current industrial policy originated over four decades ago. Development was initially slow, but it gathered pace in the 1960s and 1970s (Office of Fair Trading, 1990). The present framework for the four areas is presented below.

2.7.1.   *Competition policy*

This is the area of industrial policy which has in the past attracted most attention. It is the responsibility of the Secretary of State for Trade and Industry (President of the Board of Trade) and involves dominant firms (monopolies), mergers and takeovers, restrictive practices and anticompetitive practices. One of the more controversial elements of policy over the last decade has been the privatisation of public sector organisations. As this topic is dealt with fully in Chapter 3, the only reference to it here concerns its implications for market behaviour where there is a dominant firm. Competition policy is governed by four Acts of Parliament, namely:

1. The Fair Trading Act 1973;
2. The Restrictive Practices Act 1976;
3. The Resale Prices Act 1976; and
4. The Competition Act 1980.

Each Act is directed primarily at a particular aspect of competition policy, the first dealing with mergers, takeovers and monopolies, the second with agreements in restraint of trade, the third with minimum price setting and the last with anticompetitive practices. The above legislation is implemented through two bodies: the Monopolies and Mergers Commission (MMC) and the Office of Fair Trading (OFT), headed by the Director General (DGFT). The Restrictive Practices Court provides the legal decisions in the area of restrictive agreements or minimum resale prices. The OFT oversees the overall state of competition and initiates action when necessary, reports its findings to the Secretary of State, and implements policy. Final decisions rest with the Secretary of State or, within its jurisdiction, with the Restrictive Practices Court.

Dominant firm (monopoly) policy

This area of policy is more commonly known as monopoly policy, but the main focus is not on monopolies, as there are only a few of them in the United Kingdom, but on firms or a group of firms which have a significantly large market share of a good or service. The large market share generates market power and therefore provides firms with the potential to act as if they were monopolies. The need for policy arises because of the conflict between the benefits of large firms, economies of scale, and their potential to exploit their market position and not pass on the benefits of their size to their customers.

For at least four decades, until the mid-1980s, the increase in the size of firms had led to increased market concentration in industry in the United Kingdom (usually measured as the market share of the four largest firms in the sector). In the 1980s there was a halt to this trend, but because of a surge of mergers in the last part of the decade, it is likely to have proved only temporary. This increase in concentration in UK manufacturing, rising from as low as 20 per cent at the end of the Second World War to just under 40 per cent at the present time, has stimulated concern over the potential for firms to exploit their growing market power.

The legislation envisages two stages of investigation. The first is the identification of a dominant firm, and the second the determination as to whether a firm is exploiting its market power. In the United Kingdom under current legislation a monopoly position is considered to exist when a company supplies or purchases at least 25 per cent of UK total market supply. In addition, for the purposes of the Act, monopolies are also said to exist when a group of companies with 25 per cent or more of the market act so as to affect competition. The Secretary of State for Trade and Industry or the DGFT have the right to refer any such company or companies to the MMC. It investigates the company and reports back intimating whether a monopoly exists, and if it is working against the public interest. Initially the relevant legislation was directed at private sector companies only, but since the Competition Act of 1980 public utilities are also liable to scrutiny by the DGFT and investigation by the MMC.

Note that it is not the existence of the monopoly that causes concern but the question whether it may be working against the 'public interest'. What is meant by public interest has given rise to a range of interpretations. The Fair Trading Act 1976 sets out the criteria providing the ground rules for determining what is in public interest:

1. Maintaining and promoting effective competition between persons supplying goods and services in the United Kingdom.
2. Promoting the interests of consumers, purchasers and other users of goods and services in the United Kingdom in respect of their quality and the variety of goods and services supplied.
3. Promoting, through competition, the reduction of costs and the development and use of new techniques and new products; and facilitating the entry of new competitors into existing markets.
4. Maintaining and promoting the balanced distribution of industry and employment in the United Kingdom.
5. Maintaining and promoting the balanced distribution of industry and employment in the United Kingdom.

If the MMC decides that a monopoly exists and that it is acting against the public interest as described above, the Secretary of State has the following alternatives: (a) ask the firm to cease the activities which have given the cause for concern; (b) order the firm to cease its unacceptable activity; or (c) reject the advice of the MMC and leave the firm to continue as it has in the past.

The main difficulties in the application of this policy are twofold. The first surrounds the difficulty of defining what is meant by public interest. The question is not as straightforward as is suggested by the list above. Other factors, not listed above, may be taken into consideration and the relative weighting given to any element in decision-making process is at the MMC's discretion in each case before it. Consequently, the relative merits of each case involve a degree of subjective evaluation. This has led to a lack of consistency between decisions over time, but it has had the advantage that the MMC has the discretion to reflect changes in priorities that have occurred over time. Dominant firm legislation in the United Kingdom therefore provides for a large degree of discretionary power. Discretion exists as to whether the Secretary of State refers a firm to the MMC, and as noted above the MMC has a good deal of discretion to determine whether a firm is acting against the public interest.

The second problem is the relationship between the minimum efficient scale (MES) in an industry; that is, the lowest scale of production at which costs are at a minimum, and the identification of the market a firm is working in. In many industries the MES is greater than the size of the domestic market so government policy which generates domestic competition will lead to higher unit costs. This leads to pressure on governments to accept a wider view of a firm's market than the domestic one.

Mergers and takeovers

The problems faced in this area of competition policy are similar to those of dominant firm or monopoly policy. Mergers and takeovers have repercussions for the degree of market concentration in the economy. The legislation requires investigation of mergers or takeovers which lead to a merged firm having over 25 per cent of a market, or where the companies involved have gross assets above some minimum level. This minimum level has increased over the years and since 1984 has been £30 m. Meeting one or both of the above criteria can lead to reference to the MMC.

Not all types of mergers affect concentration, although all types can affect the level of competitive activity. There are three categories of merger or takeover: horizontal, vertical and conglomerate. Each represents a different strategic response to the conditions in which a corporation works. The first has a direct effect on industry concentration but both of the others can lead to restrictions on competition in the market place. Over the years the relative importance of different types of merger has changed, partly as a response to government legislation. It has been directed primarily at the concentration problem and has led to fewer horizontal and more conglomerate mergers and takeovers.

Once a merger has been brought to the notice of the DGFT he or she initially carries out a preliminary inquiry. If the inquiry finds that there are grounds to believe that the public interest will be detrimentally affected, the DGFT then advises that the Secretary of State should refer the merger to the MMC. It is not an automatic referral, as the Secretary has discretion over the decision. If, after its investigation, the MMC concludes that the merger is against the public interest, it will recommend how the position can be resolved. This may involve rejecting the merger outright or a restructuring of the merger. The final decision as to whether a merger should be referred to the MMC and whether a merger should be allowed to go ahead is left to the Secretary of State.

The legislation makes no presumption about whether mergers are good or bad. Each referral is judged on its own merits to see how it will affect the public interest. One important aspect of the process is that the onus of proof is on the MMC to show that any merger or takeover is against the public interest, rather than on the firms to show that it is in favour of the public interest. There are opportunities for firms to take advice from the OFT as to whether a proposed merger would be referred, and if so, what are the possibilities of reconstructing the merger agreement to avoid a referral.

Once again there is little consistency in the decisions of what is in the public interest. In addition, due to the need for speed there is little time to undertake a thorough investigation as to the relative merits of each proposed merger. Yet one of the major criticisms of this policy concerns the time taken to investigate mergers and takeovers. Although the speed of the average investigation has been reduced from 6 to 3 months this is still a long time in financial sector terms, particularly if the delay puts one firm at a disadvantage. This is the case if there is competitive bidding and one firm's bid is not referred to the MMC while the other or others are. Lastly, the role of the Secretary of State, with the power of veto on referral to the MMC and the right to reject the MMC's recommendation, means that politics are always a factor in decisions (Peacock and Bannock, 1991). At times, this has led to a conflict between President of the Board of Trade and the DGFT and may have contributed to the recent premature resignation of the DGFT.

Restrictive trade practices

The Restrictive Trade Practices Act 1976 covers any agreements between firms in respect to prices, market share, terms and conditions of contracts of supply and distribution, etc. These agreements between firms are viewed as possibly reducing the level of competition. The Act has jurisdiction over all forms of contracts whether explicit or informal, written or verbal.

The agreements, under the Act, must be presented for registration with the DGFT. The DGFT decides whether the agreement has to be registered and, if that is the case, then refers it to the Restrictive Practices Court. It is the Court which decides whether the practice is in the public interest. Such agreements are assumed to be against the public interest until the firms involved can prove otherwise. In order to do so they must show that the advantages of the agreement's existence outweigh the costs, and it must pass through one of the following 'gateways':

1. The agreement is necessary to protect the public from injury in connection with the use of goods;
2. The restriction enables the public to receive specific and substantial benefits;
3. The restriction is reasonably necessary to counteract measures taken by any one person not party to the agreement with an interest to prevent or restrict competition in relation to the trade in which persons party to the agreement are engaged;
4. The restriction is reasonably necessary to enable the persons party to the agreement to negotiate fair terms for the supply of goods to, or the acquisition of goods from, any one person not party thereto who controls a preponderant part of the trade or business of acquiring or supply such goods;
5. The agreement is necessary to prevent a serious and persistent adverse effect on the general level of unemployment;
6. Removal of the restriction would be likely to cause a reduction in the volume or earnings of the export business which is substantial in relation either to the whole export business of the United Kingdom or to the whole business of the trade.

The Restrictive Practices Court decides whether or not an application of a firm to pass through the gateways is upheld. If an agreement is found not to be in the public interest an order is passed for it to be struck down. There are very few agreements which have been held to work in the public interest.

Resale price maintenance

The imposition by any supplier of a minimum resale price is known as resale price maintenance, and is prohibited by the Resale Prices Act of 1976. This Act has banned this activity from all markets except those for books and pharmaceutical products. These two exceptions have been granted on public interest grounds. It is the responsibility of the DGFT to respond to any complaints of price fixing. Normally the DGFT will obtain an agreement from the firm to desist from the action. If they will not the DGFT can apply for a court injunction to prohibit any minimum price agreement. The OFT deals with an average of 30 claims a year, and in recent years these have resulted in four or five firms being requested to stop resale price maintenance. The activity is more prevalent than the above numbers suggest, as it is common practice for firms to recommend prices which by 'convention' are accepted by the trade. Failure to do so by a firm can lead to supply 'difficulties' and consternation throughout the industry.

Anticompetitive practices

The passing of the Competition Act 1980 reflected the, at least publicly proclaimed, procompetitive attitude of the Conservative government. The Act identified the existence of 'anticompetitive practices' as policies which provide firms with advantages over their competitors which are not based on efficiency. The Act empowers the DGFT to investigate a firm which is believed to employ such anticompetitive practices. If evidence is found to support the belief, the DGFT can secure an agreement with the firm to cease the activity. If no such agreement can be obtained, then the case is referred to the MMC to determine whether the anticompetitive practice is against the public interest. A report is forwarded to the Secretary of State who is empowered, if there is a case, to direct the company to stop the practice. As above, in dominant firm policy, there is a problem of definition as to what constitutes an anticompetitive practice. It has been defined by the Act to be: 'a course of trade or business that . . . has or is intended to have or is likely to have the effect of restricting, distorting or preventing competition in connection with the production supply or acquisition of goods'. Interpretations of this definition have so far included predatory pricing, refusal to supply, and particular types of discount. Although it would appear at first sight that there would be numerous cases to be investigated, the Act has had little effect to date on firm practices. This is mainly due to the few cases that have been proposed for examination.

2.7.2 *Regional policy*

The alleviation of disparities in the distribution of prosperity throughout the United Kingdom has provided a rationale for regional policy. Such policy has primarily taken the form of financial support, specifically investment grants, subsidies and tax concessions, as well as constraints on the expansion of firms in prosperous areas of the United Kingdom. There are two stages in policy implementation: first, the identification of the areas of need, and secondly, the determination of the appropriate form of aid.

The main thrust of current policy is to provide support in the regions to small- and medium-sized firms. In the early 1980s duty-free 'freeports' were introduced along with the creation of 'enterprise zones' which were both liable to less planning bureaucracy and exempt from local rates. In 1988 Regional Selective Assistance totally replaced Regional Development Grants. This aid programme is aimed at projects which generate jobs or maintain employment. It is in the form of cash grants with a ceiling of 15 per cent of total expenditure. The objective is to promote firm viability and to encourage firms to remain in their regional location.

2.7.3 *Research and development*

Government participation in R&D has been both direct and indirect. As in all industrial countries the UK government has provided a legal framework to protect the intellectual property rights of inventors, i.e. the patent system. The patent system enables inventors to generate a return on their investment in R&D and therefore encourages firms to enter new markets or introduce new products or processes. On the other hand patents often lead to a market dominated by one firm because of the existence of barriers to entry as the result of the patent. The UK government also intervenes directly in R&D by spending large amounts to fund research projects, both in the defence and civilian sectors.

2.7.4 *International trade*

The protection of domestic industries from foreign competition has often played a critical role in industrial policy. The main instruments of trade policy have been quotas, tariffs, selective assistance to industries and non-tariff barriers. Examples of the latter are the setting of standards, such as lawn-mower noise levels, and market sharing agreements. The development of the EU with its restrictions on the use of quotas and tariffs, and other trade agreements which have a similar effect, have led to a decline in the importance of quotas and tariffs and an increase in the use of non-tariff barriers and market sharing agreements.

2.8 Policies of the Conservative government

The incoming government of 1979 was convinced that the UK's poor international competitive position was due primarily to the intervention of government in the industrial sector. As a consequence the decade that followed saw, in contrast to the 1960s and 1970s, a significant reduction in the role of the Department of Trade and Industry (DTI) in the determination of industrial policy (Johnson, 1991). The DTI decline in importance was reflected in the number of ministers appointed to the post, 13 in 15 years, resulting in a lack of consistency in approach and policy. The first of these DTI ministers, Sir Keith Joseph, set the tone for others to follow in arguing for deregulation and the removal of many of the restrictions on industry. However, during the period that followed there have been periods when the government has adopted an active role, for example in the information technology industry.

One significant measure of the degree of the reduction of government influence in this sector has been the decline in the percentage of government expenditure going to industry, energy, trade and employment. This figure was 5 per cent in 1979–80 and, despite attempts to reduce it by Keith Joseph, it was still the same figure in 1982–3. However, by 1986–7 it had been reduced to 4.2 per cent and to the lower percentage of 4.0 per cent in 1990–1.

2.8.1   Competition policy

The main aim of UK competition policy has been to encourage and enhance the competitive process. The generation of efficient markets in the United Kingdom, it was argued, would produce a leaner and more active industrial sector which would compete more effectively in international markets. Despite these strong views about competition and non-interventionist policy, policy has not reflected a total commitment to competition. It has continued with the pragmatic approach which is accommodated in the legislation. The process of a case-by-case examination meant that any action by firms which reduced competition was not automatically banned; only when a form of market behaviour was found to be, or was likely to be, against the 'public interest' was it prohibited.

Dominant firm policy

The main legislative change in the 1980 Competition Act has been to bring nationalised industries under the monopolies legislation. Sixteen investigations have followed from this change, with over 600 recommendations to increase efficiency. Policy in this area has continued to investigate each suspected dominant firm position individually. The onus is still on the MMC to assess whether the monopoly is acting against the 'public interest'. The case had been made that the MMC's activities have reduced some of the more serious abuses arising from the possession of market power. However, with regard to its stated main objective the MMC has been found to have little effect on maintaining or improving the competitive process. Within its own terms, and allowing for the small number of investigations, it would seem to have continued with its limited success.

The reduction of government involvement in industry led to a radical review of direct government ownership in industry. The transfer of industries from public to private ownership, (privatisation) occurred in the traditional industries, the car industry, steel and shipbuilding, as well as in the high-technology industries such as telecommunications (as we discuss in greater detail in Chapter 3). A number of these corporations transferred were, and because they were not substantially restructured, are still monopolies. This is clearly a lapse from the government's commitment to competitive markets, since the transfer of ownership to the private sector did not change the market structure or the competitive environment and reveals the consequences of a conflict of policy objectives. Recently there have been attempts to introduce competition into these monopoly utilities. In the case of telecommunications the rapid change in technology has led to many potential competitors for British Telecom (BT) thus resolving a difficult regulatory market restructuring problem.

It is difficult to assess the contribution to the improvement of the United Kingdom's international competitiveness made by current dominant firm policy. If this policy does not enhance the competitive process, it is not meeting its current policy objective. Whatever its effects it is unlikely to have made anything other than a very small contribution to improving UK competitiveness. It is also questionable whether the privatisation programme has to date made any significant contribution to competitiveness. It is competitive markets rather than the change of ownership to the private sector that, if anything, would contribute to this objective.

Merger policy

Under the Competition Act of 1980 the guidance for decisions on mergers and takeovers placed the emphasis on whether the merger or any other action was anticompetitive. An investigation into a merger to determine whether there would be anticompetitive consequences was broadened to take into account domestic and foreign suppliers in both the domestic and overseas markets.

In a period during which there was a great deal of merger activity, very few mergers were referred to the MMC. Thus in the years 1965 to 1978 about 2.5 per cent of proposed mergers were referred to the MMC for investigation, the rest being unopposed. In the years 1979–87, of 2070 mergers only 64 were referred to the MMC, amounting to a little over 3 per cent of the total. Of these 64 referrals, 19 were declared against the public interest, 29 were declared as not against the public interest and 16 were abandoned by the firms involved before the MMC reported and the referral was withdrawn.

A criticism of current merger policy is the role played by competition issues to the near exclusion of other aims of industrial policy. It is argued that because merger policy can have enormous effects in other policy areas, such as regional policy, these effects should also be taken into account in the decision. This is an area of potential conflict between the Secretary of State and the MMC. The former is obliged to take the wider view while the latter may have the narrower focus of competition. The decisions that have been taken, because of the subjective evaluation process, have continued to fail to provide a clear set of criteria for the interested parties. There has been a continued lack of consistency in both the referrals to the MMC and in the decisions taken by the MMC and the Secretary of State.

The effectiveness of merger policy should not only be assessed in terms of the numbers of cases investigated. Firms, for example, have moved away from horizontal mergers as a strategic option because of the policy towards them. However, the time and resources required to carry out an investigation will always provide a constraint on the number that can be considered regardless of the cases that in principle should be referred to the MMC. The large number of mergers which took place through the 1980s, and their effect on industrial concentration, does not in itself mean that they affected the degree of competition and were against the public interest. However, it is difficult to obtain systematic information on what consequences they did have on the level of competition.

The broadening of policy to include foreign suppliers and markets in the assessment of the public interest, should be treated with caution. It is an argument sometimes put forward by companies to justify a merger or takeover when in fact there are barriers of entry to the domestic market for foreign firms.

If the effect of merger policy on competition is difficult to identify it is even more difficult to assess its contribution to the improvement in the United Kingdom's international competitiveness. The small numbers investigated suggest that, at best, it can only be small. There are reasons, however, to suggest that it may even exacerbate the United Kingdom's international position. The first is that the more sympathetic approach to mergers and takeovers has led to managers spending much of their time involved in this activity. They are either searching for victim companies to contribute to their own rapid growth, or are defending their company from predators. The opportunity cost is that management has been diverted away from building long-term viable companies capable of competing in global markets. The second is that if UK companies are not to be put in a disadvantaged position, compared to their international competitors, they should be dealt with in the same way by UK policy as their competitors are treated by their own merger legislation.

Restrictive practices policy

By the end of 1991 over 5000 agreements had been registered. Over 50 per cent had been abandoned and approximately 1000 had all restrictions removed. The processing of this large number of cases was facilitated by a number of key cases which set the criteria for rejection for many others. Whether the abandoned agreements were really abandoned or merely replaced by informal arrangements remains a point of conjecture.

In 1976 the Restrictive Practices Act was modified to include services in addition to goods. This change was to generate one of the most important industrial developments of the 1980s, that of the deregulation of the financial sector, with the reorganisation of the Stock Exchange through the 'Big Bang' in 1986 (see Chapter 14 for details). Government action in this area was prompted by a referral of the Stock Exchange restrictive practices to the Court. A deal was made between the Government and the Stock Exchange whereby legislation exempted the Stock Exchange from the restrictive practices Acts in return for a number of changes in practice; for example, the discarding of restricted labour practices and the minimum concession rates.

The effectiveness of this policy is both difficult to assess and all too easy to overstate. The public abandonment of many agreements may have resulted in their materialising as covert agreements out of the public gaze. In addition, there have been doubts placed on the appropriateness of the role of the Court in making judgements on economic issues. What criteria do they use to ensure consistency towards the policy objectives and between cases?

Here again this policy, within its own terms, could be considered to have been relatively successful and to have made a contribution to increases in allocative and cost efficiency. Even if this position can be supported it is a big step to state that it has made a substantial contribution to the competitiveness of the United Kingdom. It is possible that, through its indirect effect on the deregulation of the financial sector, it has had negative effect on competitiveness.

Anticompetitive practices

The 1980 Act reflected a strong commitment to erase anticompetitive forces, but the fact that there have been so few investigations, only an average of less than four a year, suggests window dressing rather than an active concerted policy. It is difficult to see that to date this policy has contributed significantly to any industrial policy objective.

An overall assessment of the role played by the United Kingdom's competition policy in improving its international competitiveness must conclude that it makes, at best, a marginal contribution. Despite the resources directed towards it, its effect on the lower-level, operational objective of increasing competitiveness is also not significant.

2.8.2 *Regional policy*

There have been significant changes in this area of industrial policy during the 1980s. In the early 1980s duty-free 'freeports' were introduced along with the creation of 'enterprise zones' which were exempt from local rates. In the mid-

1980s, the Regional Development Grants system which subsidised investment in particular areas of the country was curtailed and, although its scope was widened to include services, in 1988 it was replaced by Regional Selective Assistance. The main thrust of policy has been to give more support to firms in the regions, particularly to aid small and large firms. In addition there has been a move from automatic to discretionary aid. Regional Selective Assistance helps projects which maintain employment or create additional jobs by providing the minimum resources to encourage supported firms to continue operations in the local area. The areas which qualify for aid have been reduced significantly and as a consequence there has been a large reduction in expenditure as revealed in Table 2.3.

Some regional policy spending has received EU support, athough this has given rise to controversy over the issue of 'additionality' (see Chapter 18 for details).

It is difficult to judge the effect of the changes in regional policy. Previous policies were not considered to be a success as they often only attracted marginal firms or projects which were only viable with assistance and were highly vulnerable in times of recession. The foreign investments that have been attracted into areas of deprivation were more likely to be persuaded by a large, cheap and relatively skilled labour force than some marginal financing. Also, even though such incomers as the Japanese car firms must be of benefit to our balance of trade, they will eventually lead to a decline in the invisibles balance as profits are returned to Japan (see Chapter 16 for relevant definitions).

Table 2.3 Government expenditure on regional preferential assistance to industry

	£ million				
	1983–4	1985–6	1987–8	1989–90	1992–3
Great Britain	648.9	584.1	556.2	539.3	364.0
North	130.2	96.6	109.3	117.0	48.3
Yorkshire and Humberside	36.3	36.4	38.8	32.4	13.7
East Midlands	17.5	8.8	9.4	9.5	1.2
East Anglia	0.0	0.0	0.0	0.0	0.0
South East	0.0	0.0	0.0	0.0	0.0
South West	12.1	12.3	14.8	10.7	8.2
West Midlands[1]	0.0	7.1	19.3	19.9	10.8
North West	104.2	87.5	79.0	74.3	36.8
England	300.3	248.7	270.6	263.8	119.0
Wales	120.0	138.4	132.4	131.7	104.4
Scotland	228.6	197.0	153.2	143.8	140.6

Note: [1] Certain Travel to Work Areas in the West Midlands attained assisted area status on 29 November 1984.

Source: Central Statistical Office, *Regional Trends* 1994.

The reduction in the level of funding and record of failure of regional policy in the past leads to the conclusion that current policy is not any more effective than previous policies. It is difficult to isolate the effect of this policy in an economy where macroeconomic policy has led to radical shifts in regional prosperity. The overheated economy in the mid- to late 1980s, followed by the recession, have had a far greater effect on regional disparities.

2.8.3 *Research and development*

There has been a continuation of the long-term decline in the United Kingdom's private and public expenditure on R&D, and the overall expenditure has continued to be low by international comparison. The low figure is a product of the short time horizons adopted in the private sector and the attribution process in the public sector. This is the situation where programmes funded by the EU are attributed to specific government departments and are included as part of their public expenditure calculations. Despite this latter policy, government has continued to make a substantial contribution but half of its expenditure has been on defence-related projects. These projects are generally large and are concentrated on a few defence contractors. Although these projects are currently important in the world defence market, evidence now confirms that there is little technological transfer between defence and civil sectors. Government support in the civil sector includes the funding of projects in a particular industry or firm, and the support of collaborative projects. The former has been used to fund projects which have widespread potential, such as software development and fibre optics. The objective of the most important collaborative project, the ALVEY project, was to promote research in the information technology industry over an extensive range of key technologies by promoting collaborative projects involving firms and the universities.

There has been a change in the balance of funds from single firm projects to joint research between companies and research units like the universities. There has also been a move to rely on the private sector to finance near-market research, the percentage of business enterprise R&D supported by the government falling from 30 per cent in 1981 to 19.4 per cent in 1987, while the government funds the more basic research. Many of the government's programmes in the mid-1980s were introduced when Kenneth Baker was Secretary of State. It involved targeting a number of what were thought to be critical technological projects. Because it is often difficult to determine all the direct and indirect effects of R&D, even those projects targeted which failed, such as cable networks and the provision of financial services in the home, may eventually be seen to have made a contribution to technological progress.

R&D is one of the most important elements of a successful modern economy. In many world markets corporations compete not with price but through product and process innovation. The fall in the proportion of world patents taken out by UK companies and the large increase recorded by Japanese and other rivals' companies is likely to anticipate a further reduction in the competitive capabilities of the United Kingdom (HMSO, 1992). Unlike the other areas of industrial policy, this area can have a more clearly specified objective, the increase in the number of world patents which, allowing for the time lag, is strongly related to international competitiveness.

The failure of UK policy on R&D to reverse the declining patent record of UK companies does not necessarily mean that the projects were not successful. If they had not been undertaken the United Kingdom's current position might be even worse.

2.8.4 *International trade policy*

The development of the EU and the completion of the Uruguay Round of GATT negotiations (see Chapter 17) have limited the scope for the United Kingdom in this area of industrial policy. Policy can be divided into three areas, namely policy within the EU, policy governed by the World Trade Organisation (WTO, the successor to GATT), and lastly that area which is not constrained by any international trade agreement. However, with the growth of intra-industry trade it is the first policy area which is most important.

Membership of the EU and the development of an integrated market has led to policies to remove any constraints to trade within the EU, while at the same time imposing barriers to any suppliers outside the EU. The reduction of trade barriers between the member countries of the EU stimulated UK imports and exports within the Union, reinforcing a pre-existing trend, while the existence of the Common External Tariff discriminated against goods from countries outside the EU, especially in Britain's case against countries in the Commonwealth.

The exclusion of tariffs as a form of protectionism stimulated the use of alternative policies to form barriers. This occurred in the United Kingdom, although to a lesser extent than in many other countries. A simply applied policy, but one declining in importance, is that of import quotas. This policy was adopted by the United Kingdom in the 1980s to restrict Japanese car imports. More subtle barriers have also been raised, many of which reflect the technical characteristics of the products concerned. Safety requirements, noise levels, exhaust emissions, etc., are all forms of non-tariff barrier that have been used to protect domestic industry against foreign competition.

Given the import penetration experienced in nearly all UK markets it is difficult to argue that where trade policy has been employed it has been successful. It may be the case, however, that if some form of trade policies had not been in place, the current situation would be worse than it is.

2.9 The European Union

The United Kingdom's membership of the EU and the industrial policy adopted by the EU introduce a number of interesting points of discussion, not least because it creates an environment for potential conflict between the governments of the member states themselves and between the individual states and the European Commission. EU industrial policy has slowly evolved since the Treaty of Rome, but with the creation of the Single Market (see Chapter 18) there is a more urgent requirement for a Community industrial policy to ensure consistent policies for all member states. A number of EU policies mirror those of the member countries, but since the objectives of EU policy are set at a different level to those of the member nations, this can generate differences in the appropriate policies (Bayliss and El-Agraa, 1990).

The Treaty of Rome (Articles 85, 86 and 92) provides the basis for the Community policy in this area. It prohibits and declares void agreements and concerted practices that have the object or the effect of preventing, restricting, or distorting competition within the EU, and which affect trade between member states. Member states are also restrained from resourcing or helping in any way their own domestically located producers. These Articles of the Treaty provide the guidelines for policy but leave some leeway for interpretation. The rationale of EU competition policy, for example, is to generate competitive markets, but it is recognised that unconstrained market activity does not necessarily generate efficient and equitable solutions. Therefore the role of competition policy is to ensure that competitive markets will arise and be sustained.

The overall objective of the Commission's policy is to enable EU producers to compete successfully in global markets. This objective is to be achieved by maintaining a favourable business environment, by implementing a positive approach to adjustment, and lastly by keeping an open approach to markets. The first of these is to be achieved by public authorities adopting the appropriate policies, especially infrastructure provision, to facilitate and support the decisions about structural change that producers must take. The second requires the avoidance of defensive, protectionist industrial policies that directly inhibit industrial adjustment. The third takes the view that optimal market allocation will only occur if markets are open, both outside and inside the EC. These points reflect a broadly pro-market approach, with the minimisation of government intervention except for expenditure on industrial infrastructure (Curzon Price, 1990).

Although it is relatively early to assess the effectiveness of European Union industrial policy, there have been a number of clashes between member states and the Commission. One area where a difference of view arises is that of merger decisions. A 1990 EU directive empowered the Commission to monitor all proposed mergers resulting in a combined worldwide turnover of over 5 bn ECU, with at least two of the firms having a turnover of 250 m ECU in the EU, unless two-thirds of either was in a single member state. The problem arises because of differences of opinion over the definition of a market. Does the existence of the Single Market imply that what would have been treated as a monopolistic merger within a member state would be treated differently in the larger EU market? There is nothing new about this problem, since it is a feature of all dominant firm, public policy decisions. However, the problem is exacerbated by the emergence of conflicts of interest between the Commission and the member states involved. These arise, for instance, with the targeting of industries to create Euro-champions, where the Commission generally adopts a sympathetic position while the United Kingdom takes a strongly adverse stance.

One obvious area of difficulty for the United Kingdom is that the EU industrial policy should apply uniformly to all member states. Implicitly, it is assumed that all members are faced by the same set of industrial problems, but there are strong arguments to suggest that the United Kingdom and Germany face quite different problems.

EU policy is still developing, and it is clear that it will continue to have important implications for each member state's industrial policy. However, the complexities of industrial economic problems for both the member states and the Commission are unlikely to lead to a clear, unambiguous policy framework. The commitment to market forces will often be set aside and government intervention will take place at both a member state and at the Union level.

2.10   The competition

It is not always straightforward to transfer the successful elements of other countries' industrial policy to our own without adaptation, so there are no clear policy guidelines to be devised by looking at our international competitors, as each can be said to have adopted policies which are appropriate to its own sociopolitical environment. However, there are a few common threads which reveal that there are a number of different ways to create a successful industrial policy.

The continuing large Japanese trade surplus with the world, and with the United Kingdom in particular, provides us with at least one reason to explore further some of the industrial policy elements that Japan employs. Japan has managed to regulate market forces by forming collusive groups, Keiretsu, with the Ministry of International Trade and Industry (MITI) playing a substantial role, but at the same time promoting vigorous competition between groups in many domestic product markets. This competition ends with a limited number of domestic winners who then go on to dominate global markets.

Japan is now highly innovative, its R&D spending has averaged 3 per cent of gross national product (GNP) and by investing resources in basic research it is providing a substantial base, for example in pharmaceuticals and genetics, to dominate the major industries of the twenty-first century. The industrial sector relies to only a small extent on the equity market for its long-term financing. A significant proportion of corporate funding is provided by the banking system which permits the long-term perspective necessary to enjoy the benefits of the basic research. Further, Japan has been protective towards its domestic markets by creating barriers – real and imaginary – to foreign imports. Lastly, it has encouraged a large number of small- and medium-sized companies which provide the variety and capacity to supply the large, globally well known Japanese corporations.

Germany, despite facing the problem of integration with what was the former German Democratic Republic, with its serious lack of modern infrastructure, minimal modern manufacturing capacity, poor communications and less skilled and productive population, has already managed to out-perform its EU partners. This could not have been achieved without the coordination of the financial and industrial sectors. German companies rely much less on the stock market for their finance than do their counterparts in Britain. Britain has four times the number of companies quoted on the stock market despite being two-thirds the size of the German economy. This means that German companies are less threatened by a possible change of corporate control via takeovers and managers can focus on running the company. Companies generally have a close relationship with a particular bank which provides long-term finance and also has representatives on the main board of the company, providing a good communication link between the two. Daimler–Benz and the Deutscher Bank is an example of this relationship, where the Deutscher Bank patiently financed Daimler–Benz through a dip in its fortunes in the early 1990s.

Another strong component of the German economy is the size and strength of the small and medium enterprise (SME) sector, which is proportionately approximately nearly twice the size of the British sector. In addition, finance to small- and medium-sized companies is supplied via an Industrial Lending Bank which focuses on the specific needs of this important sector of industrial growth. Lastly, Germany has always allocated significant amounts of public money to industrial support, most going to the regions and small firms, with around 20 per cent allocated to R&D support.

Both Japan and Germany have managed in their own way to provide an institutional framework within which market forces can work successfully. Government has not simply provided the appropriate environment for the market but actively participates within it. Their less 'sophisticated' financial sectors have retained their service characteristics and fulfil the needs of their respective industrial sectors.

In contrast in the United Kingdom, the reliance on the equity market encourages companies to adopt short-term planning horizons. Another weakness of the financial sector in the United Kingdom concerns the financing of small- and medium-sized companies. This is primarily provided by the banking sector but often via overdrafts or relatively short-term loan arrangements which are relatively expensive and put pressure on firms for early repayment. Also the banks' decisions to advance money to small companies have relied more on the security that could be offered rather than the economic viability of the project proposed. Consequently there were a record number of SME bankruptcies as a result of the last recession, a significant number of which were considered to be well managed companies. The effect of the extent of these bankruptcies may negatively influence the future level of SME entrepreneurial activity.

2.11 Conclusion

It is only necessary to undertake a brief investigation in order to conclude that all governments of industrialised countries employ some form of industrial policy. The recognition of this fact is an essential element in the determination of any national industrial policy. The Conservative government during the 1980s argued that the United Kingdom's past, poor industrial record was partly due to the intervention of government. They therefore argued, for example, in favour of a reduction in the role of the DTI. At the same time they criticised other governments for adopting a more active role in their industrial sectors. If government industrial policy only works to the detriment of a given country's industrial sector, why should their competitors be concerned about its existence? Clearly this is not the case, and the relevant question then concerns the form that policy should take.

There are no quick and easy answers. The decline of the United Kingdom's international competitive position has taken place over many years and the road to recovery will be long. The duration of the decline suggests that fundamental changes are required in the economic environment within which traditional industrial policy is determined. For example, the relationship between the financial and the industrial sectors might be restructured along similar lines to those in Japan and Germany. Re-industrialisation, which is what is needed, demands a more managed economy, requires an active government role, and should involve more cooperation and coordination between those operating in a given sector. This implies that neither the neoclassical nor the Austrian schools should exclusively provide the basis for policy and that it should be a product of pragmatism, not dogmatism. Pragmatism combined with a clear set of objectives should ensure a consistency of policy with the necessary flexibility required in a rapidly changing world economy.

If the necessary structural changes to the overall economic environment are made, the specific policies adopted in the traditional areas of industrial policy are less critical. First, it is not clear in the cases of competition and regional policy that they have ever made significant contributions to the United Kingdom's international competitiveness. Secondly, membership of the EU and the WTO will increasingly restrict the power of any UK government to employ nurturing or protective policies in support of its domestic industries. Lastly, the one policy area which can contribute to the long-run improvement in international competitiveness, if the regulatory framework allows, is the promotion of research and development. This may require the adoption of a supportive policy towards all research and development, in the form of tax concessions, grants, loans or the purchase of equity capital, or a change in patent law, or it could involve the targeting of specific industries which are judged by all participants in the industrial sector to be important for the future global growth markets.

In conclusion, industrial policy should take cognisance of the relationships set out in Section 2.4, and should therefore comprise a set of non-conflicting policies which are a response to a clear and consistent set of objectives, of which the most important should be the improvement of the United Kingdom's international competitive position.

Questions for discussion

1. What is industrial policy? Describe the main areas of policy and a number of specific policies used within each of those areas.
2. Does the United Kingdom have an international competitiveness problem? If so, what are its causes?
3. What are the problems to be encountered in the determination and the implementation of an effective industrial policy?
4. Present the principal elements of the United Kingdom's competition policy.
5. Describe the two main theoretical approaches to industrial policy.
6. How effective has industrial policy been over the last decade?

References and further reading

Audretsch, D.B. (1989), *The Market and the State*, Hemel Hempstead: Harvester Wheatsheaf.

Bayliss, B.T. and El-Agraa, A.M. (1990) 'Competition and industrial policies with emphasis on competition policy' in *Economics of the European Community* El-Agraa, A. (ed.), Hemel Hempstead: Philip Allan.

Central Statistical Office (1994) *Regional Trends*, London: HMSO.

Curzon Price, V. (1990) 'Competition and industrial policies with emphasis on industrial policy' in *Economics of the European Community* El-Agraa, A. (ed.), Hemel Hempstead: Philip Allan.

Foreman-Peck, J. (1991) 'Trade and the Balance of Payments' in *British Economy since 1945* Crafts, N. F. R. and Woodward, N. (eds) Oxford: Oxford University Press.

Hartley, K. and Hooper, N. (1990) 'Industry and policy' in *Understanding the UK Economy* Curwen, P. (ed.), Basingstoke: Macmillan.

Hay, D.A. and Morris, D.J. (1991) *Industrial Economics and Organization: Theory and Evidence*, Oxford: Oxford University Press.

HMSO (1992) *Science and Technology Issues, A review by Acost*, London: HMSO.

Hutton, W. (1995) *The State We're In*, London: Jonathan Cape.

Johnson, C. (1991) *The Economy under Mrs. Thatcher 1979–1990*, London: Penguin Books.

Office of Fair Trading (1990) *An Outline of United Kingdom Competition Policy*, London: HMSO.

OECD (1990) *Industrial Policy in OECD Countries*, Paris: OECD.

Peacock, A. and Bannock, G. (1991) *Corporate Takeovers and the Public Interest*, Aberdeen: Aberdeen University Press.

Walshe, J. G. (1991) 'Industrial organization and competition policy' in *The British Economy Since 1945* Crafts, N.F.R. and Woodward, N. (eds), Oxford: Clarendon Press.

CHAPTER 3

Privatisation

PAUL HARE

3.1 Introduction

Industries and enterprises in the United Kingdom were mainly nationalised in two waves. The first wave occurred in the late 1940s under the post-war Labour government, and most of the businesses nationalised then belonged to the public utilities: coal, electricity, public transport, gas. These were added to activities already in the public sector, such as the Post Office. The second wave of nationalisation also occurred under a Labour government, this time in the 1970s, and included a number of industrial firms which were considered important for the country's economy, but which for various reasons were failing to compete effectively in the domestic and external markets: among these were British Aerospace, British Shipbuilders, British Leyland (now, in its privatised form, the Rover Group), and the computer firm ICL. The industry with the most chequered history in this period was steel: for it was nationalised in the late 1940s, denationalised (we would now say 'privatised') in the 1950s, and renationalised in the 1960s, only to be privatised once again in the 1980s.

In practically all these cases nationalisation was seen as a solution to a problem. In the first wave of nationalisations, the problem usually had to do with the consequences of years of under-investment and neglect, sometimes exacerbated by the controls which had been in force during the Second World War (1939–45). Later on, it appeared that the issue had more to do with the failure to compete successfully, associated with low innovation, cautious management and more aggressive marketing by firms in other countries. In any case, government ministers undoubtedly hoped that once they had brought certain firms into public ownership, and established new management structures for them, they would not be troubled further. As it turned out, this was a vain hope. There were several reasons for this which need to be understood in order to appreciate the pressures which had built up by 1980 to put the whole process into reverse, and embark on an increasingly ambitious programme of privatisation. Thus the reasons included:

1. The newly nationalised businesses required large amounts of investment

for their modernisation, and had to compete for resources with other parts of the public sector.

2. The managers of the nationalised firms were not presented with clear commercial objectives.

3. The pressures to improve efficiency were sometimes very weak, due to the lack of effective competition, and to the knowledge that bankruptcy would not be permitted even if financial performance was very poor.

These factors led to a number of attempts in the 1960s and 1970s to improve the management framework and financial accountability of the nationalised industries; and when these efforts were perceived to have failed, they contributed to the shift of opinion towards privatisation.

In the next section, I review briefly the attempts to establish a satisfactory management framework for the nationalised industries and look at some evidence on nationalised industry economic performance. Then Section 3.3 surveys the United Kingdom's privatisation programme of the 1980s and early 1990s, both in terms of what actually happened and in terms of the new forms of competition and/or regulation which emerged. This provides the background to Section 3.4 which considers what remains to be privatised and reviews privatisation issues for the mid-1990s, and Section 3.5 which concludes by commenting on the lessons learned from UK privatisation.

3.2   Management of nationalised industries and firms

Most state sector businesses in the United Kingdom were set up as public corporations.[1] Organisationally, these were joint stock companies with the state (in the form of the Treasury) being the sole (or in a few instances such as British Petroleum (BP), the majority) shareholder. Each business had a responsible minister through whom reports to Parliament would be made, and from whom came various directives and advice about the running of the firm or industry. In theory, the boards of the individual nationalised firms could decide on all operational matters for themselves, while they had to seek ministerial permission for strategic decisions concerning major investments. This 'division of labour' looks quite neat on paper, but worked badly in practice: the result was that ministers found themselves 'interfering' in many aspects of their firms' affairs, resulting in blurred responsibility for their ultimate performance.

A further complication was the lack of clear objectives for nationalised firms in the relevant statutes. Often they were enjoined to cover costs 'taking one year with another', or to pay attention to certain social objectives, while general commercial criteria (such as seeking higher profits) or efficiency goals (like raising productivity in a given period) received less emphasis. Moreover, in the public mind many of the nationalised industries were perceived as providing an essential service, in which profit-making was popularly regarded as undesirable. One consequence of this attitude, apparent in much of the popular reporting about present and former nationalised industries and firms, is that they could expect to be criticised more or less whatever their financial performance. If they made losses this represented an unacceptable drain on the public purse, while if they made significant profits they were considered to be profiteering (even when the net return on capital employed was rather low compared to the prevailing private sector norms).

To establish some sort of order in the relationships between nationalised industries and firms and their supervising ministries, the government published White Papers on the topic in 1961, 1967 and finally in 1978 (HM Treasury, 1961, 1967 and 1978). These had to deal with three tasks: establishing a proper financial framework for the sector, and making recommendations both about pricing rules and investment criteria. In the theoretical literature on public sector production the latter two concerns have attracted most of the attention, with well-known arguments for marginal cost pricing, and for investment based on the net present value approach using a discount rate suitable for public sector projects (see Webb, 1973).

Given their importance, these arguments are worth reviewing briefly, which we do with the help of Figure 3.1. The horizontal axis shows the output level of a typical nationalised firm, the vertical axis showing price or cost as appropriate. The short run marginal cost curve, corresponding to a given capital stock, is labelled SRMC. The long run marginal cost curve, which takes account of the incremental capital costs (amortisation plus a normal rate of return on capital) associated with raising output is LRMC; this is drawn

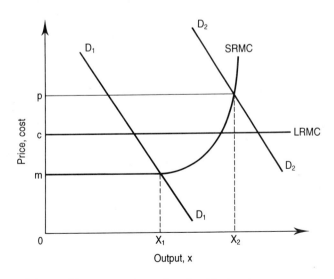

Figure 3.1 Pricing and investment in nationalised industries.

horizontal for simplicity, implying constant returns to scale, but other assumptions are easily incorporated.

In any given period, the best policy is to use the existing capital stock as efficiently as possible. If demand is low, corresponding to the demand curve D_1, this implies that the optimal price, $p_1 = m$ (= SRMC, for output below full capacity), and the level of output will be x_1. Under these conditions, since $p_1 < c$ (LRMC), it is not profitable to undertake further investment. If demand is high, corresponding to the demand curve D_2, the optimal price, $p_2 = p$ (= SRMC, for full capacity output), and the level of output will be x_2. In this case, since $p_2 > c$, new investment will yield more than enough additional revenue to cover the normal return on capital; consequently, new investment is justified.

These basic ideas about pricing can easily be modified to allow for situations where the demand fluctuates considerably (such as electricity over a day, and over the year; or telephone services), or where the pricing structure incorporates a fixed element as well as a price per unit of product consumed; but the formal analysis required to deal with these cases is beyond the scope of this chapter.

Aside from these important allocative issues, the government became increasingly concerned to strengthen financial controls and the 1978 White Paper therefore introduced a system of short-term financial targets (external financing limits (EFL), associated with attempts to determine suitable medium-term financial goals for each firm/industry. The aims were to reduce the burden on the exchequer of loss-making state firms, and to bring the whole sector closer to self-financing.

Under the various policy 'regimes', how did public sector firms perform? Fortunately, several studies have been carried out, covering the 1960s, the 1970s and the first half of the 1980s (see Pryke, 1971, 1981 and 1982; also Molyneux and Thompson, 1987). The third of these studies made comparisons between similar public sector and private sector activities, while the most recent one was able to compare firms still in public ownership with those recently privatised. The results make interesting reading. In the 1960s, it seems that the nationalised industries performed quite well compared to the rest of the economy, in terms of productivity, pricing and profitability; but in the 1970s the situation was far less rosy, with the further enlarged public sector lagging well behind the private sector in terms of productivity improvements, profitability and employment. This is the background against which public opinion gradually shifted to favour privatisation, supported by further critical studies of the nationalised industries, such as Redwood (1980) and Redwood and Hatch (1982). Nevertheless, the most recent study of efficiency shows that performance was better in the 1980s *both* in the recently privatised firms *and* in those remaining in state hands. This suggests that ownership is not the only issue relevant to performance, a point we return to below.

3.3   Privatisation in the 1980s and early 1990s

When the Conservative government came to power in 1979 privatisation was not a central part of its initial programme, although it did speak in general terms about the need to reduce the state's role in the economy. However, it soon started to prepare plans for the privatisation of certain state-owned firms, and for the deregulation of others. The programme which gradually evolved began quite slowly and accelerated through the 1980s, the share of nationalised industries (strictly, public corporations) in the GDP had fallen from around 10 per cent in 1979 to well under 5 per cent in the early 1990s. Moreover, the programme was not confined to the nationalised industries, since it also included publicly owned housing and, increasingly, a wide range of services provided by local authorities and other public bodies (see LeGrand and Robinson, 1984).

In the UK context, therefore, privatisation has to be understood in very broad terms. It includes:

1. The sale of all or part of an existing public company, by public offering or by negotiation with a single buyer.
2. The conversion of part of a public company into a distinct business unit, and its separate sale.
3. The deregulation of a given public company (possibly combined with partial or complete sale).
4. The subsidised sale of council houses to their tenants.
5. The compulsory competitive tendering of local authority services.
6. The introduction of market-type mechanisms into the health service, education and other spheres of public provision (e.g. contracting out, formation of hospital trusts, etc.).

From this list it is apparent that privatisation includes measures to strengthen the scope for competition in areas where it was formerly restricted by statutory monopoly or other constraints. As was implied at the end of the last section, ownership change is only part of the story, albeit an important part.

Such a wide-ranging programme of privatisation inevitably had many goals, the balance between which varied somewhat over time. The most important goal, although not always the most prominent, was that of improving the efficiency of the firms and services concerned. However, others included raising revenue for the Treasury, creating a 'share-owning democracy', facilitating competition between alternative suppliers and encouraging wider home ownership (see Kay *et al.*, 1986).

Not surprisingly, these goals were not always compatible. For instance, raising revenue for the Treasury requires the share price of a given state-owned firm to be as high as possible, while making such shares attractive to the general public sometimes favoured a rather lower price. Also, selling off a statutory monopoly usually contributed little to fostering competition, and even required the establishment of new regulatory bodies to restrain the exploitation of monopoly power. The reason for this is that, at least for the main network utilities, the presence of increasing returns to scale implies that the companies concerned are likely to be natural monopolies. This means that it is efficient for only one firm to supply the market, provided that the firm in question is prevented from taking undue advantage of its position: hence the need for some form of regulation. In any case, even where it would have been feasible, breaking up the firms into smaller units in order to enhance competition would only have been possible at the cost of a lower selling price and hence less revenue for the Treasury.

Despite these and other complications, privatisation in the United Kingdom made remarkable progress in the 1980s and early 1990s. Concerning procedures, for each firm (or group of related firms) being privatised in the United Kingdom, a separate Act of Parliament has to be passed. This Act covers the structure of the new firm or industry, specifies the private sector firms that will result from the privatisation, and includes as necessary the regulatory provisions of the sort just discussed above. Thus to implement a programme on the scale of that seen in the United Kingdom in the last decade and a half, very large amounts of parliamentary time have been required, sometimes to the detriment of legislation in other areas. One wonders, in line with what has been done since 1990 in several of the Eastern European economies in transition (see Estrin, 1994; Ash, Hare and Canning, 1994), whether it might not have been possible to arrange for a general enabling law to be passed, which ministers could then use to make specific arrangements to privatise firms in their respective domains. This would, however, have considerably diluted the extent of parliamentary supervision over the privatisation process.

Two broad sectors were largely state-owned at the start of the UK's privatisation programme, namely energy and transport. In the former, gas, coal and electricity were all in public ownership, being joined in the 1970s by a state-owned oil company, British National Oil Corporation (BNOC, later Britoil); the government also held a substantial shareholding in BP. One of the original arguments for bringing most of the energy sector into public ownership was the view that its different components could benefit from some coordination of investment across the sector, on the basis of agreed projections for the growth of the economy. Typically, energy investments are very costly, take many years to plan and implement, and have long lives. Hence the social costs of mistakes in the sector are likely to be very high. Nevertheless, early post-war attempts to plan the sector largely failed. It became apparent that the government was unable to plan the development of the sector any better than the private sector could do; moreover, the private sector proved increasingly willing to supply the large amounts of capital required to develop energy supplies, as was evident during the 1970s and 1980s as investment in the North Sea (oil and gas) enjoyed an extended boom.

In the case of transport the principal airlines, the railways, much passenger shipping and the freight sector of road transport, as well as the buses were mainly in state hands. The growth of private car ownership, and competition from private firms in other parts of the transport sector, adversely affected the economic conditions of the state-owned firms. It is possible that with better management, and more sustained attempts to plan the relative rates of development of different types of transport, superior outcomes might have been achieved. In practice, coordination was no more effective than in the energy sector, except sometimes at the very local level. Again, therefore, the failure of the state to manage its assets effectively helped to undermine much of the resistance to privatisation that remained.

As the Conservative government's privatisation programme took shape, and it became clear that virtually everything that could be privatised would be, state firms in the 'queue' to be sold off started to prepare themselves for life in the private sector. They did so partly by lobbying government to maintain their existing organisational forms (or to make as little change as possible), hence preserving much of their monopoly power. In this, most firms were remarkably successful. They also took steps to cut costs and rationalise production with much more determination than nationalised industry managers had usually exhibited in the past. This is probably one reason why the most recent study of privatised and state industry performance, reported in the last section, was unable to find significant differences between the two groups of firms.

Another reason has to do with the types of firm likely to 'benefit' from privatisation. Those firms with the greatest potential for cost reduction and/or quality improvement are not the large public utilities whose extensive networks inevitably confer monopoly power, but those in which there is greater scope for competition through new entry or through breaking up the original state-owned firm. Also, firms which have recently reduced costs sharply may have exhausted most of the available opportunities for a time, and may not therefore be able to cut costs much further after privatisation. Now in the United Kingdom, those firms privatised first were not, on the whole, those whose privatisation would have been expected *a priori* to yield the greatest benefits according to these criteria.

In terms of the volumes of assets transferred into private hands, housing privatisation clearly made the largest single contribution, with over 1.5 m local authority and new town tenants buying their houses during the 1980s. These tenants received discounts which were initially set at 50 per cent (of a notional market price), later increased to 60 per cent and then 70 per cent for those with at least three years of a tenancy (see *Social Trends 22*, HMSO, 1992). Sales of the nationalised industries taken together contributed about £42 bn to the Treasury during the period 1979/80 – 1991/2 (source: *Autumn Statement*, HM Treasury, various years). In terms of shareholding, there were several million new shareholders in the United Kingdom as a result of privatisation offerings to the market, although most of the new shareholders only held one or two privatisation stocks and tended not to be active traders. Many of them sold their privatisation stock quite quickly, in order to benefit from an immediate capital gain.

Focusing on the privatisation of the nationalised industries, the public corporations, Table 3.1 indicates that several methods of privatisation were employed. Thus some companies, such as the Rover Group (formerly British Leyland), were sold to single buyers; these were typically cases where the government believed, probably correctly, that there would be limited interest among the general population in buying the shares. In other cases, non-core parts of the business were formed into separate companies and then privatised: an example here is the hotels formerly owned (and badly managed) by British Rail. Then with firms such as BP (in which the government initially held a 51 per cent stake) and British Telecom (BT) (initially wholly state-owned, but privatised in stages), shares were sold by public offering while still leaving the government with a significant shareholding. Finally, some firms were privatised completely by means of a single public offering.

For some of the most complex cases, a good deal of restructuring preceded the actual privatisation, at times accompanied by considerable controversy. This was most evident for the electricity supply industry, where two large producers were established in England and Wales[2] (PowerGen and National Power), together with a separate company managing the national grid, jointly owned by the 12 regionally based distribution companies. In addition, after much debate it was finally accepted by the government that the country's nuclear power stations could not be included in the privatisation as originally envisaged. Accordingly, a separate state-owned company, Nuclear Electric, was formed to manage these assets.[3]

Although in relatively limited spheres it was possible to foster competition in the public utilities, in practice it was expected that they would retain substantial monopoly power in their principal markets. For this reason, new regulatory bodies were established to supervise the industries concerned; the bodies formed up to the end of 1994 are listed in Table 3.2, together with their main roles.

It can be seen that the new regulators usually have a very broad remit. In the case of the Office of Telecommunications (OFTEL), for instance, it not only includes the regulation of BT itself, but also extends to the promotion of competition in the telecommunications market as a whole by creating conditions in which new entrants such as Mercury can survive and prosper, and in which other entrants can get established (this includes conditions for access by other providers to the BT network). There are also powers to monitor customer satisfaction with telecommunications services, and to demand that

Table 3.1 UK privatisation – progress in the 1980s and early 1990s

Name of firm (current)*	Date of privatisation	Method of privatisation
British Aerospace	1981	Share issues, 1981, 1985
British Airways	1986	Public sale of shares
British Coal	None	Privatisation of most remaining pits in late 1994
British Gas	1986	Share issues, 1986, 1988; new regulatory body
British Rail	None	White Paper on rail privatisation published summer 1992, and British Rail reorganised in 1994 into Railtrack and a number of operating companies. Non-rail assets (hotels, other property, etc.) sold in 1980s
British Steel	1984	Share issues 1984–5 and 1988
British Telecom	1984	Public sale of shares; regulatory body (OFTEL)
Electricity Industry	1990	In England and Wales, 12 distribution companies and two generating companies (PowerGen and National Power) privatised by public share offer. Distribution companies jointly own National Grid company. Government retains Nuclear Electric. In Scotland, Scottish Power and Scottish Hydro-Electric privatised by public share offer. New regulatory body (OFFER). Remaining government holdings in PowerGen and National Power sold in 1995
Jaguar Cars	1984	Public sale of shares; company subsequently purchased by the Ford Motor Company
National Bus Company	1980–8	Deregulation, 1980; split into separate, mainly regional companies, majority sold to management by 1988
Regional Water Authorities	1989–90	Public offering of shares; regulatory body (OFWAT)
Rover Group	1987	Formerly part of British Leyland. 'Sold' to British Aerospace under favourable conditions which attracted some EC criticism. Finally sold by British Aerospace to BMW

Notes: The table shows a selection of the major privatisation 'events' during the last decade; it is not a complete listing.

* In many instances firms changed their name upon privatisation, sometimes also at other times; the table shows the most recent name.

Source: Hare and Dunkerley (1991). White Papers and press reports – various.

Table 3.2 New regulatory bodies established in the United Kingdom

Acronym	Full name	Activities
OFTEL	Office of Telecommunications	Established 1984. Regulates BT – inland calls, line rentals, international calls; provides conditions for new entrants such as Mercury; regulates the equipment market; licenses new forms of telecommunications service
OFGAS	Office of Gas Supply	Established 1986. Regulates gas supplies to domestic users – average price per therm. Industrial gas supplies, connections charges, etc. not regulated. Changes in cost of gas to British Gas can be passed forward into prices.
OFWAT	Office of Water Services	Established 1989. Regulates standard domestic and non-domestic supply by 34 water and sewerage companies. Limits price of unmeasured water per customer, and measured water per unit of water
OFFER	Office of Electricity Regulation	Established 1990. Regulates prices for transmission, distribution and supply by the 12 regional electricity companies, overall electricity costs for smaller customers. Generation business is not regulated

Source: Veljanovski (1991).

specified standards be attained by the providers. Finally, OFTEL has powers to regulate new telecommunications services.

As far as BT itself is concerned, OFTEL can impose restraints on pricing policy (including network access charges to other suppliers), and it can impose service quality standards. Clearly, since these controls affect the future profitability of BT, it is important to maintain a reasonably stable, predictable regulatory environment. At the time of privatisation itself, it was also important for investors to know what the initial regulatory regime would be like, so that the share price could be set properly.[4] On the pricing of telecommunications services, OFTEL determines guidelines for BT periodically (initially for 5 years, subsequently for 3-year periods), based on the so-called (RPI-X) formula. In this formula, RPI stands for the annual rate of increase in the retail price index (in per cent), while X denotes a required annual rate of improvement in productivity (also in per cent). Then in setting its prices for a specified basket of services, BT would be allowed to raise its average price by (RPI-X) per cent, with much less (if any) restriction on changes in the relative prices within the basket. For its first 5 years X was set at 3 per cent, so that BT could raise prices by at most 3 per cent below the prevailing rate of inflation; then in 1988 X was raised to 4.5 per cent, and in the most recent reviews it rose further to 6.25 per cent and then to 7.5 per cent, which means that BT is expected to improve its productivity even more rapidly than before. However, the evidence of its profitability, together with cost and price information about telephone companies in other countries suggest that this should be manageable. On the other hand, the frequency of reviews and the gradual tightening of targets, is partly a response to public perceptions that BT had been excessively profitable, and reflects continuing ambivalence over the role of regulation in promoting improved economic performance. As argued in Armstrong, Cowan and Vickers (1994), more attention to the creation of a more competitive environment at the time of privatisation might have been more beneficial.

Related to this last point, a final theme to emphasise here is the relative importance of ownership and competition in the different forms of privatisation. For the standard nationalised industries/firms, the balance is most influenced by the underlying technology of the firms concerned. Thus in the bus industry, deregulation and the promotion of competition came first, followed by the completion of privatisation through ownership change (often by means of management buyouts). The former is generally considered to have exerted the greater impact upon quality of service, consumer choice, and prices. In that situation, privatisation merely allows the formerly state-owned parts of the industry to compete more effectively against new private sector rivals. In telecommunications, even though the promotion of competition fell short of what was needed, the combination of OFTEL regulating BT's core business and promoting competition in the sector, wherever it was feasible, probably did more to improve the performance of the sector than the relatively straightforward ownership change. Hence in most instances, it is not easy to see why an ownership change alone would exert a dramatic effect on an industry's performance, within the context of a predominantly market-type economy like the United Kingdom's.[5]

3.4   Privatisation: issues for the late 1990s

As we have seen, very little remains in the traditional state-owned sector in the United Kingdom following a decade of privatisation. Those businesses which were still state-owned at the start of the 1990s, such as British Coal (sold off in late 1994, as indicated above) and British Rail, did not appear to be promising prospects for privatisation in the 1980s, although possible schemes were considered from time to time and this decade is already witnessing major changes in these industries. The re-elected Conservative government quickly made clear that it envisaged rapid progress here, and a White Paper on rail privatisation was published in 1992 (Department of Transport, 1992). The first steps towards privatisation have already been taken, with the network's track and signals being managed by a new company, Railtrack, the trains themselves being run by a series of mostly regionally based operating companies. It is already clear that the contractual arrangements among these new (albeit still state-owned) companies must be extremely complex, and it remains to be seen whether the flexibility of the formerly integrated rail system can be preserved under the new arrangements. Initial indications are far from encouraging.

At the same time, from the late 1980s onwards, attention turned towards other areas of the public sector, such as the provision of local authority services, the health service and parts of the education system. In addition, existing policies to privatise much of the housing stock held by local authorities and various public sector housing agencies (such as Scottish Homes) are expected to continue.

In local authorities, not only are there increasingly tough requirements to put services which they would previously have supplied themselves, such as street cleaning, repair and maintenance of buildings, etc., out to competitive tender, but some of their major areas of responsibility are being transformed. The most notable instance so far concerns the provision of primary and secondary education, where schools are now able to opt out of local authority control and become self-governing bodies. Their budget then comes directly from the Department of Education, and the only controls over an opted out school are the requirement to follow the National Curriculum and the liability to regular inspections by the Schools Inspectorate (which has itself been privatised).

In the health service, NHS hospitals can now become self-governing trusts, financing their activities by selling their services to other parts of the health service, including directly to private patients. General practitioners (GPs) can also operate more independently of their local health board by becoming budget holders: using their assigned budget, and knowing the costs of different forms of treatment, they can then provide what they judge to be the most appropriate services to different patients. Since these reforms, as well as those affecting schools mentioned above, are both new and only partly implemented, it is too early to assess their impact on the efficiency of resource allocation in these areas. It is important to emphasise, however, that their aim is to make fuller use of market-like mechanisms in health and education, although in doing so the most striking initial change has been an enormous expansion in the administrative costs of providing the relevant services. This reflects the fact that to employ a market-based approach, inputs and outputs must be measured far more carefully, and be associated with particular components of service provision, than formerly. To date, there has been no formal change of ownership over the assets employed to provide health and education services.

An interesting indication of the changing climate of opinion regarding privatisation was provided in late 1994 when the government failed to privatise the Post Office. Although it is widely recognised that the UK Post Office is a well run and efficient operation as compared to many of its state-owned counterparts in other countries, it faces increasingly stiff competition from many private sector suppliers of postal services in the more expensive, business-orientated segments of the market requiring courier services, speedy parcel delivery, etc. The Post Office might well be able to meet such competition very effectively, but it requires substantial investment to enable it to do so, and within the public sector this is subject to Treasury rules and constraints. Hence the main argument for privatisation was that it would enable the Post Office to undertake the necessary investment to cope with competition in the business sector of its market. However, the main argument against was that a more profit-orientated business might wish to shut down many small, village post offices and concentrate on the more profitable, larger centres; there were also fears that a privatised Post Office would eventually be allowed to charge different rates for postage in different parts of the country, reflecting the different costs of service provision. These social, rather than solely economic concerns, convinced enough MPs about the dangers of Post Office privatisation (including its possible effects on their re-election chances!), that the government was unable to pass the necessary legislation.

3.5 Conclusions

What has been learnt from a decade and a half of privatisation in the United Kingdom, and how far will it affect the development of policy in the later 1990s? First, it turned out that privatisation was feasible in much of the state-owned sector, that in most cases it was popular (no doubt partly because of the inducements of low-priced share issues), and that the programme could be designed to satisfy several aims: improving efficiency, widening share ownership, yielding revenue for the Treasury. Secondly, many of the firms/industries privatised were able to resist attempts to restructure them to foster greater competition, and in some cases this required new regulatory bodies to be established to restrict the exploitation of monopoly power post-privatisation. These regulatory bodies have not been completely successful in resolving the resulting problems.

Thirdly, it was nevertheless clear that improvements in overall perform-ance were most likely to occur in those areas where individual incentives would be strongly influenced by privatisation and/or where competition was strengthened. The former was most noticeable in the area of housing privatisation, where in most cases the new private owners were more inclined to spend money on maintaining and improving their property than the former local authority landlords had been. On the other hand, housing privatisation selectively removed from the public sector housing stock many of the better properties, little of the revenues from privatisation could be used to build new public sector houses (because of restrictions imposed by central government), and the ability of local authorities to meet housing needs in their areas was severely undermined. At the same time, some of the new owners experienced financial difficulties due to the combination of high interest rates and deepening recession at the start of the 1990s, and were sometimes unable to retain their new properties. Hence the substantial benefits (both private and social) of much of the housing privatisation must be offset by these negative factors.

Increases in competition were most striking in the aftermath of bus deregulation in the early 1980s, and although many of the companies were eventually fully privatised (often by management buyout, as noted above) it was the competitive environment which did most to stimulate change. Moreover, the change was not confined to the buses, since British Rail was obliged to respond with revised prices and conditions for young travellers and other groups whose cross price elasticity of demand was relatively high.

Fourthly, it now seems very likely that the remaining public sector firms will be privatised before the end of this decade, whether or not they meet any or all of the conditions for privatisation to improve performance. The idea seems to be, quite simply, that the government is unwilling to continue present subsidies, and that it is increasingly prepared to contemplate virtually any degree of contraction or reorganisation as the 'price' for getting these firms out of state hands. In the context of areas of policy such as transport, or energy, where there are important actual and potential interactions between different subsectors of the industry (as noted above), as well as with the users/ customers, such an ideologically based approach to further privatisation has little to recommend it. Nevertheless, the apparent (or perceived) success of privatisation elsewhere is likely to maintain substantial momentum in favour of privatisation under the present government.

Finally, in areas other than housing and the conventional nationalised industry sector, the 'competition' rather than 'ownership' aspect of privatisation will predominate, with an increasing separation between the public financing of various activities and the actual delivery of services. Sometimes, as in competitive tendering of local authority services, bids can come both from the original local authority providers or from private firms. Presumably, when the latter are successful the local authority would have to declare some of its existing staff redundant (some of whom might then be taken on by the new supplier). On the other hand, experience indicates that with outside sourcing of services the monitoring and supervision costs can rise quite sharply, so that the net financial benefits from such provision can be considerably less than anticipated.

Overall, one must judge the results of the United Kingdom's privatisation policy as mixed. Many former public sector businesses and organisations have been transformed, with new management structures, a tougher competitive environment and regulation where appropriate (see Bishop, Kay and Mayer, 1994). However, economic units still in the public sector have undergone roughly parallel changes, so that it is not always evident that privatisation *per se* is what made the difference. Similarly, outside the conventional nationalised industries there has been considerable development of competitive structures and new arrangements to stimulate individual incentives. Much of this is beneficial in that it forces organisations which were otherwise not compelled to think in terms of cutting costs or improving performance to do so, though sometimes (as we noted above) at a heavy cost in terms of their ability to fulfil broader social objectives.

Questions for discussion

1. Why were many firms and industries in the United Kingdom nationalised?
2. Did nationalised industries fail? If so, why? If not, in what respects did they succeed?
3. Discuss the advantages and disadvantages of different methods of privatisation (a) for the government; (b) for shareholders; and (c) for the customers of the given firm.
4. Are there any industries or firms which should not be privatised?
5. Discuss the relative importance of 'ownership' and 'competition' as factors influencing the results of a privatisation. Give examples to illustrate your answer.
6. What were the main aims of privatisation in the United Kingdom during the 1980s, and how far were they achieved?
7. To what extent can regulation impose a competitive-type environment upon a privatised firm?
8. Should privatised firms be required to meet social objectives? If so, how?
9. How far would you expect UK privatisation in the later 1990s to diverge from the 1980s experience?
10. Discuss the likely costs and benefits of privatising *either* the health service, *or* the education service in the United Kingdom.

Notes

1. The most prominent exception being the Post Office, which was run as part of the civil service until 1961. In that year, however, it became a public corporation, which was later split into two public corporations in 1981, when British Telecom was formed.
2. In Scotland, the situation was different. Two firms emerged from the privatisation there, Scottish Power and Scottish Hydro-Electric, both of which are engaged in the production and distribution of electricity.
3. This problem arose because of doubts about the economic viability of these power stations, and uncertainty about the costs of decommissioning them at the

end of their useful lives. PowerGen and National Power were required to purchase specified amounts of their electricity supplies from Nuclear Electric.
4. There is obviously a trade-off between the tightness of regulation and the share price, tougher regulation depressing the share price since it lowers potential profits.
5. The situation would, of course, be rather different in the case of the formerly planned economies of Eastern Europe.

References and further reading

Armstrong, M., Cowan, S. and Vickers, J. (1994) *Regulatory reform: Economic analysis and British experience*, Cambridge, Mass.: MIT Press.

Ash, T., Hare, P. and Canning, A. (1994) 'Privatisation in the former centrally planned economies', ch. 9 in *Privatisation and regulation: A review of the issues* Jackson, P. and Price, C. (eds), London: Longman.

Bishop, M., Kay, J. and Mayer, C. (eds) (1994) *Privatization and Economic Performance*, Oxford: Oxford University Press.

Crafts, N.F.R. and Woodward, N. (1991) *The British Economy Since 1945*, Oxford: Oxford University Press.

Department of Transport (1992) *New Opportunities for the Railways: The privatisation of British Rail* Cm. 2012, Department of Transport, London: HMSO.

Estrin, S. (ed.) (1994) *Privatization in Central and Eastern Europe*, London: Longman.

Hare, P. and Dunkerley, J. (1991) 'Nationalized industries' ch. 12 in Crafts, N.F.R. and Woodward, N. (eds) *The British Economy Since 1945*, Oxford: Oxford University Press.

HM Treasury (1961) *Financial and Economic Obligations of the Nationalised Industries* Cmnd. 1337, London: HMSO.

HM Treasury (1967) *Nationalised Industries: A review of economic and financial objectives* Cmnd. 3437, London: HMSO.

HM Treasury (1978) *The Nationalised Industries*, Cmnd. 7131, London: HMSO.

HMSO (1992) *Social Trends 22*, London: HMSO.

Kay, J. (ed.) (1986) *Privatisation and Regulation: The UK experience*, Oxford: Clarendon Press.

LeGrand, J. and Robinson, R. (eds) (1984) *Privatisation and the Welfare State*, London: Allen & Unwin.

Molyneux, R. and Thompson, D. (1987) 'Nationalised industry performance: still third rate?' *Fiscal Studies* 8(1) pp. 48–82.

Pryke, R. (1971) *Public Enterprise in Practice*, London: McGibbon and Kee.

Pryke, R. (1981) *The Nationalised Industries: Policies and performance since 1968*, Oxford: Martin Robertson.

Pryke, R. (1982) 'The comparative performance of public and private enterprise' *Fiscal Studies* 3(2) pp. 68–81.

Redwood, J. (1980) *Public Enterprise in Crisis: The future of the nationalised industries*, Oxford: Basil Blackwell.

Redwood, J. and Hatch, J. (1982) *Controlling Public Industries*, Oxford: Basil Blackwell.

Stevens, B. (1992) 'Prospects for privatisation in OECᴸ
  Westminster Bank Quarterly Review August pp. 2–22.
Veljanovski, C. (ed.) (1991) *Regulators and the Market*, London: Institu
  Affairs.
Webb, M.G. (1973), *The Economics of Nationalized Industries*, London: Nelsᴜ

CHAPTER 4

The role of services in the economy

PATRICK O'FARRELL AND LESLIE SIMPSON

4.1 Introduction

Services are embodied in all products of an economy, whether these supply the needs of producers or, as they ultimately must, of consumers. Service activities are implicated in every process of economic change whether of restructuring, growth or decline, at local, national and international level, yet they have been seriously neglected by economists. This is partly because many economists treat services as a residual, analogous to the 'non-production' functions of extractive and manufacturing firms. Such a view of services is misleading since many are involved with material processing and the quality of such services directly influences the competitiveness of production (Marshall, 1988; O'Farrell and Hitchens, 1990). Any satisfactory definition must illuminate the economic role of all services, whether they are producer or consumer orientated, in the private or public sector, or concerned with handling information or materials (Wood, 1990, p. 4).

This chapter will review alternative classification schemes for service activities, including the economics approach and the market-based approach. The basic characteristics of services – intangibility, durability, interchange-ability and interaction between customer and supplier – which are alleged to differentiate them from manufactured goods, are then outlined. The chapter then considers the fundamental issue of whether services are a prime mover in economic growth, whether they can exist without prior goods production, or if services must always be dependent upon goods production. Subsequently we examine the problem of measuring service productivity; technology and restructuring in services; the empirical evidence on growth and decline of services in the United Kingdom and the location of business service growth. Finally, the policy response to the growth of service activities is considered.

4.2 Alternative taxonomies of services

While there is not a complete consensus on the definition of services, most authorities consider the services sector to include all economic activities whose output (i) is not a product or construction, (ii) is generally consumed at the time it is produced; and (iii) provides added value in forms (such as convenience, assurance, comfort, knowledge or health) that are essentially intangible concerns of the purchaser. A key characteristic of services is that they offer the expertise necessary to support other economic activities. This expertise may take a wide variety of forms: knowledge of financial markets, research and development in manufacturing, maintenance and repair services, marketing skills, provision for leisure or support for educational and health needs. This view of services is demand-orientated, stressing the worth of materials handling or information services to other production or consumption activities (Marshall, Damesick and Wood, 1987).

However, in order to analyse services in a meaningful way it is useful to distinguish between different categories of services. One important category is those service activities which primarily handle information or data, e.g. research and development (R&D), management consultancy or marketing. Another important distinction is between the two main types of function that services perform. These are: producer (or intermediate) services which provide output which is consumed or used by other industries, e.g. accountancy or market research; and consumer services which produce output direct to consumers or households, e.g. retailing, hotels, cinemas, etc. A further distinction is between basic and non-basic (induced) services. Basic services are orientated to national and international markets and may provide a substantial net balance of payments contribution to a region or country. They are also able to generate self-sustaining growth independent of a particular locality and to yield significant multiplier effects. Other bipolar classifications which may be made between services are privately and publicly provided services and, related to this, marketed and non-marketed services.

4.2.1 *The economics approach*

The notion that the service sector is primarily dependent upon the demands of the 'wealth' creating manufacturing goods sector for its prosperity, and that it is the non-basic component of the national or regional economy incapable of autonomous growth, dates from the thinking of Adam Smith. He distinguished between 'productive' and 'unproductive' labour: 'the labour of a manufacturer adds generally to the value of the materials which he works upon . . . The labour of a menial servant, on the other hand, adds to the value of nothing' (Smith, 1937, p. 314). In Smith's classification, not only menial servants were unproductive but also the sovereign, the army and navy, churchmen, lawyers, physicians and men of letters of all kinds: 'Like the declamation of the actor, the harangue of the orator, or the tune of the musicians, the work of all of them perishes in the instant of its production' (ibid, p. 315). Hence, Smith made tangibility, with its associated quality of durability of the economic activity, the criterion of productiveness (O'Farrell and Hitchens, 1990, p. 164). It was Smith's disciple, J.B. Say, who realised Smith's error and who accepted that 'the professor, the doctor and the actor had claims to be regarded as producers' (Gide and Rist, 1948, p. 35). Despite Alfred Marshall's (1961, p. ix) dictum to the effect that 'there is not in real life a clear line of division between labour that is or is not productive', much of the conventional thinking on the subject of goods and services is based on the assumption of a clear-cut distinction between the two.

The taxonomy most widely used by economists and statisticians is reflected in the Standard Industrial Classification (SIC) (revised 1980) which classifies services by exclusion; they are not agriculture, production or construction (see Table 4.1). Such an approach to taxonomy has severe limitations and inevitably throws up anomolies: for example, there is no logical rationale for the inclusion of printing within manufacturing and computer software within services. Part of the confusion arises from the practice of defining services by listing industries rather than by trying to articulate the essence of service activity that all such industries still share.

The SIC classifies employment by industrial sector – i.e. the eventual product – irrespective of the nature of the particular job. The industrial classification of mechanical engineering, therefore, includes lawyers, typists and accountants. Indeed, more than one-third of those employed in manufacturing industries are in service occupations while almost one-fifth of those employed in service industries hold manual jobs. Conventional economic explanations of the rise of service employment (Clark, 1940) draw to a large degree on the 'sector theories' of economic development which explain the growing prominence of service sector employment in terms of changes in business demand and labour productivity. In this view, as consumer incomes rise, more discretionary spending occurs on higher value goods and quasi-luxury consumer services. Production becomes more technically and organisationally complex to service these needs, and depends critically on high quality research and development and more advanced educational and training programmes (Gershuny and Miles, 1983; Greenfield, 1966). The proportion of workers employed in the actual process of material transformation declines, however, as more capital intensive methods are introduced, while the share of employment in services increases, not only because of increased demand, but also because their 'personal' character limits the application of capital equipment. These trends and a world expansion of markets are accompanied by an increasing domination of business by large, frequently multinational firms.

4.2.2 *Market-based approaches*

The sectoral definitions widely employed by economists do not take account of the different markets served by service industries (Marshall *et al.* 1987, p. 577).

Table 4.1 Employees in employment in Great Britain, 1981 and 1993

Industry	Division class or group	Employees (1000s)		Percentage change 1981–93
		1981	1993	
All industries and services	0–9	21 148	21 024.1	−0.6
Agriculture, forestry and fishing	0	370	238.8	−35.5
Production and construction industries	1–5	7 688	5 263.2	−30.2
Energy and water supplies	1	682	326.7	−52.1
Manufacturing industries	2–4	5 932	4 256.1	−28.2
Construction	5	1 074	780.4	−27.3
Service industries	6–9	13 090	15 422.0	17.8
Distribution, hotels, catering, repairs	6	4 113	4 587.3	11.5
Wholesale distribution	61	840	845.3	0.6
Retail distribution	64–5	2 060	2 340.1	13.6
Hotels and catering	66	938	1 166.2	24.3
Repair of consumer goods and vehicles	67	238	181.4	−23.8
Transport and communication	7	1 406	1 222.5	−13.1
Banking, finance, insurance, etc.	8	1 724	2 695.9	56.4
Banking and finance	81	478	562.6	17.6
Insurance, except social security	82	225	266.1	18.3
Business services	83	831	1 591.9	91.7
Renting of movables	84	91	113.5	24.8
Owning and dealing in real estate	85	98	161.8	65.1
Other services	9	5 846	6 916.4	18.3
Public administration and defence	91	1 505	1 340.4	−10.9
Sanitary services	92	280	439.0	56.8
Education	93	1 492	1 852.9	24.2
Research and development	94	121	84.9	−29.8
Medical and other health services	95	1 285	1 563.1	21.6
Other services (welfare and community)	96	552	938.2	70.0
Recreation and cultural services	97	430	500.8	16.5
Personal services	98	180	197.0	9.4

Source: Employment Gazette, December 1983, October 1994.

Services may be distinguished not only on the basis of their ownership (public or private), markets (final consumers or producers) and product characteristics (material or ephemeral), but also in terms of their commodification (market or non-market provision), the function performed (services for people, goods or money) and the quality of the exchange. However, focusing solely upon service industries plays down the extent to which services and other sectors are interdependent and the fact that many occupations within production perform service functions. The distinction between goods and services is not primarily a matter of the nature of the product, nor even the type of expertise offered; the main economic distinctions that separate different services are concerned with the types of markets served (Marshall *et al.*, 1987, p. 578).

4.2.3   *The nature of services*

An alternative approach to the definitional problems of services is to categorise services according to several characteristics which are alleged to differentiate them from manufactured goods: intangibility, durability, interchangeability and interaction between customer and supplier.

Tangibility

Many authors argue that intangibility is both the only characteristic common to all services and the factor that best distinguishes them from immaterial goods. What is immaterial in services is the performance of the service itself as opposed to the person doing it, any materials used or the good to which a service is attached. There is limited usefulness in distinguishing between companies according to whether they produce goods or services; it may be more useful to distinguish between tangibles and intangibles (Levitt, 1981). All products, whether they are manufactured goods or services, possess some degree of intangibility. Hence, it is useful to define a continuum of intangibility ranging from highly intangible products such as films, insurance or travel at one end to highly tangible ones such as cars, milling machines or face cream at the other end (O'Farrell and Hitchens, 1990, p. 166). However, even the apparently most tangible products, such as a lathe or a washing machine, possess intangible features such as delivering it on time, installation, training in correct operation, servicing, repair and maintenance work which are crucial to the product's successful operation. This emphasises the inability to measure properly the service content of the final output of manufactured goods.

Durability

Durability is a characteristic which has been used to distinguish goods from services, but, as in the case of tangibility, it does not clearly discriminate between them. Much depends on the time span used as the demarcation between perishable, semi-durable and durable. Routine office cleaning, for example, may be classified as a perishable producer service since the premises must be re-cleaned within a short space of time. In the semi-durable category, Greenfield (1966, p. 9) placed advertising services concerned with sales promotion; and among durable producer services he classified services concerned with the strategic direction of the firm, such as those provided by management consultancy firms and R&D projects. A strategic business plan, market research report, computer software, the contract of a solicitor, or the music written by a composer may all have much longer lives than many so-called durable manufactured goods. Hence the concept of durability is not confined to services and is not a valid discriminator between services and manufactured goods.

Interchangeability of goods and services

Services are directly interchangeable with manufacturers in a variety of situations. Few customers care whether a refrigerator manufacturer implements a particular feature through a hardware circuit or by internal software. New computer-aided design can substitute for design equipment, while improved transportation or distribution services can lower a manufacturer's costs as effectively as cutting direct labour or material inputs. Even more fundamentally, products themselves are only physical embodiments of the services they deliver (Quinn, 1988, p. 20). A disk delivers a software program or dataset, a car delivers a service, transport, electrical appliances deliver entertainment, dishwashing, clothes washing and drying, cooking and food storage – all services. Most products, therefore, provide a convenient or less costly form in which to purchase services.

Interaction

A fundamental weakness of many studies in the past is that they have assumed that services perform separate functions from production and consumption. Yet the distinguishing characteristic of service output is that it is primarily a process or activity that produces changes in persons or the goods they possess (Riddle, 1986, p. 11). A primary feature of service production is the complexity of the relationship that exists between the producer and the customer of which there are three general types: (1) the producer may provide services in isolation from the customer, as is the case in many professional services; (2) the customer may self-serve, using equipment and/or procedures arranged and maintained by the producer (e.g. leasing a photocopying machine); (3) the producer and the customer may produce the service in interaction with one another so that the latter affects its performance and quality. Frequently the buyer and seller have to come together to create the service, as in the cases of a haircut, medical consultation, dental treatment or installation of a quality control (QC) system in a manufacturing company. In such instances the quality of the QC system will be greatly facilitated by a clear definition of needs by the firm's management. Therefore, the quality of many services depends not only upon the performance of the supplier, but also on how well the customer performs in interaction with the supplier (O'Farrell and Moffat, 1991). This highlights another important difference between services and manufacturing, namely that the service product is not considered to be output unless it is sold; in other words there must be consumer participation and, inevitably, simultaneity of supply and demand.

4.3 The primacy of goods production or a key role for producer services?

4.3.1 *The role of services in development*

Does the apparent increased domination by services of employment in the late twentieth century-developed economies imply that services are less capable of triggering productivity gains, technological advances, tradeable exports and inter-industry multipliers than are manufacturing industries? Can services be considered 'basic', to be a prime mover and exist without prior goods production, or must services always follow and be dependent upon goods production? Do services play a peripheral, or supportive, role *vis-à-vis* goods production, or do they lie at the heart of any economy and provide the facilitative milieu in which other, especially market-orientated production activities, become possible? We shall consider this question by considering the role of services in production and then the issue of productivity in services.

First, many services, such as medical, legal, entertainment, banking, consultancy and education do not necessitate prior goods production. Such service activities require that there be income for individuals to buy the services. The source of that income can be either a goods or a services producing industry, or other income such as rent, interest, savings or dividends. Secondly, the status of many services as intermediate inputs into industrial production has long been recognised. A substantial proportion of what is characterised as the service sector – distribution, transport, utilities, business or producer and many government services – is linked to an evolving division of labour within primary and secondary industries. Data for the United Kingdom, Australia, Canada and the United States in the 1970s showed that one-third (22–38%) of tertiary sector output (share of GDP), took the form of intermediate services to the 'productive' sectors (Gershuny and Miles, 1983, p. 30). More recently, the OECD analysed GDP data for eight member countries by classifying services (i.e. excluding 'goods' and 'government') into those 'directly linked to goods production', those which 'are a necessary adjunct to the process of producing goods', and 'free-standing services' which are 'bought by households in their capacity as final consumers' (Blade, 1987, pp. 164–5). It was found that on average production-related services contributed 25 per cent of GDP and 'free-standing services' 20 per cent. Another analysis of input–output data from seven OECD countries showed that over 50 per cent of output, on average, of transport, communications, banking and insurance and 'services to firms' industries goes to intermediate consumption, that is to enterprises, as does 25 per cent of distribution and 'various' other services output.

Other studies have also demonstrated the vital function of services within manufacturing: approximately 75 per cent of the total value added in the US goods sector is created by service activities within that sector (Quinn and Gagnon, 1986, p. 101). About 25 per cent of US GNP was accounted for (in 1980) by services used as inputs by goods-producing industries – more than the total value added to GNP by the manufacturing sector (Riddle, 1986, p. 21). Indeed, service occupations have been expanding within manufacturing industry as part of ever-lengthening production sequences necessary to conceive, plan, enable, supervise, produce and maintain the production and distribution of goods. The ability to compete for many firms – both manufacturing and service – is increasingly dependent on the quality of knowledge (information services) at the disposal of management. There has been a rapid increase in demand for advice and information on merger and takeover options, portfolio investments, product design, computer aided manufacturing systems, quality control, commercial and international law, market research, corporate strategy and advertising. To an increasing degree, therefore, it is the services end of the production chain – design, research, quality, style, marketing, delivery, packaging and advertising – which determines the competitiveness of agricultural and manufacturing investment. Services are responsible for a growing share of value added to products. Such service provision may be organised and supplied hierarchically from within the firm, as inputs purchased externally on the market or as downstream external services once the product leaves the factory. Furthermore, government funding of transport, communications and utilities infrastructure, advisory and trade promotion organisations, regional development agencies and training are evidence of the critical role of the state in supplying support services to production. All the evidence therefore points to manufacturing, other service firms and the public sector being important sources of demand for service inputs.

There are two patterns which appear at odds with the notion of services being intermediate inputs to goods production. First, all service groups serve both intermediate and final demand markets. Secondly, a substantial volume of transactions is generated within and between service industries themselves such as links between financial institutions and legal and accountancy services, or between advertising agencies, market consultants and other service firms. In the United Kingdom more of the output from producer service industries goes to other services (22%) than to manufacturing (18%) (Marshall *et al.*, 1987, p. 588). This reinforces the point that some components of producer services have market outlets that are either independent of manufacturing, or embrace both the producer and consumer service sectors (e.g. hotel, travel, banking, legal, consultancy and insurance service companies). Hence, the diversity of services has led to an awareness that the role and contribution of services to production is both more extensive and complex than previously supposed.

The traditional relationship of manufacturing 'demand' determining service 'supply' is no longer applicable for important parts of the two sectors because of various interdependencies between them. Furthermore, there are circumstances where the demand from services had led manufacturing investment. Many goods-producing industries manufacture items such as printing, computer systems and information technology (IT) that are inputs to service industries, i.e. services are the prime movers. Also technological breakthroughs in certain services have stimulated the expansion of important manufacturing industries, as for example with research and development (scientific instruments), health care (medical equipment) and information processing (typewriters, photocopiers, computers). Similarly, the transformation of the form of provision and consumption of some services has led to major surges in demand for a variety of goods such as household appliances, leisure equipment and home improvement supplies. This reflects a move towards the self-service economy where rising costs of labour services have encouraged households to substitute goods for paid services. There is no basis for the belief that goods production is more necessary to an economy, more income-generating, or more wealth-enhancing than services. Therefore, it is argued that the conventional economist's sectoral view of the economy needs to be rethought because it encourages an artificial distinction between goods and services.

Producer services are at the leading edge of the growth in service employment and are central to the economic base of a nation. The key to the dynamics of service growth and uneven spatial development lies in growing intermediate demands for services, frequently operating at an international scale. Indeed, services can be an important element of international trade. First, manufactured exports contain a high proportion of value added due to service inputs, although the service is classified to the manufacturing sector. Secondly, analysis of input–output data for OECD countries by Petit (1986, p. 123) revealed that direct foreign trade accounts on average for 8 per cent of service output. Although trade in services is very difficult to measure accurately, most experts agree that the total volume of services trade is underestimated. One feature of services trade is that most of the facilities and jobs created by services exports are in the user country, for example banks, hotels, retail stores, consultancy firms and advertising agencies. Unlike manufacturers, fewer services are produced in the parent country and exported across borders. In contrast to manufacturing exports, services trade data frequently recognise only the fees or profit margins that services companies can repatriate – a small fraction of their total transactions value.

4.3.2 *Productivity*

Productivity in services is notoriously difficult to measure because of the problems of defining output units and quality differences in services. For example, how does one evaluate the productivity of a medical surgeon who increases the number of operations performed per day from six to 12 but with substantially increased risk to the health of patients? Is the number of letters delivered per postal worker a meaningful productivity measure if more letters are late or lost? Can a university professor be assumed to have enhanced productivity if he has increased the number of research papers published per annum but at a cost in terms of quality? What use are standard economic productivity measures which assume that output value is only equal to its cost?

Investment in new technology by many services has grown markedly with financial services, retailers, distribution and the health sector among the leaders. As workers master new technologies they frequently discover new applications not envisioned in the original investment. Barras (1986) showed services sector productivity in the British economy growing at 2.9 per cent annually (based on the real value of output per employee) from 1960 to 1981, whereas manufacturing productivity grew at less than 1 per cent on the same basis. The primary causes of this phenomenon were (i) the continued demand growth in services, which led to (ii) both capital deepening in services and improved capital quality (output gain per unit of invested capital) within services. The analysis of Barras (1986) suggests that the shift to services has not been an important factor in the slowdown of British national productivity growth.

When services are delivered to manufacturing or other service clients by a business service firm, such as a management consultant, how should productivity be evaluated? First, it could be measured according to the number and quality of reports produced per annum; or, secondly, by the number of clients served. Thirdly, we argue that their economic contribution, at any stage of production, can be measured only in relation to the benefits they bestow, directly or indirectly, on these other activities. The value of service inputs to customers depends on how these are combined with other inputs. This requires a 'total factor productivity' approach to assessing the economic contribution of services to other sectors. This might be assessed by the impact of the service delivered upon the productivity and competitiveness of the client organisations (O'Farrell and Hitchens, 1990, p. 168). This latter is the more meaningful criterion, that is in terms of the effectiveness of the service as viewed from the perspective of the client. In this light the notion of a distinct 'service sector' is misleading, as is that of a manufacturing sector (Wood, 1990 p. 5). Any understanding of services must be based on the reality of economic interdependence.

4.4 Technology and restructuring in services

New technologies have substantially improved performance in many service industries. Jet aircraft made long-haul passage and freight movement efficient. New diagnostics, life support systems and surgical procedures have revolutionised medical practice. New loading, refrigeration and handling techniques have facilitated an expansion of international trade. Electronics information and communication technologies have been widely adopted in the retailing and wholesale trade, engineering design, financial services, communications and entertainment. Such new technologies permit firms to realise new economies of scale and scope. Thus banks, airlines and retailers use their networks to extend into a range of new activities.

The advent of new technology, the internationalisation of markets, increasing cost pressures and trends towards growing concentration via mergers and acquisitions mean that many service sectors are experiencing the type of major restructuring that manufacturing has undergone since the late 1960s. The conventional view of services is that, in contrast to most sectors of modern manufacturing, many parts have until recently been characterised by low concentration ratios due to the ease of entry which leads to the domination of the industry by large numbers of very small enterprises. This is particularly the case in retailing and other consumer and personal services; but this situation is changing. Such evidence as exists appears to show that in most service sectors the concentration ratios are steadily rising (Howells and Green, 1986). In fact, many of the world's largest companies are service enterprises – in hotels, leisure, retailing and financial services, for example. Service multinationals with interests in different service sectors have emerged, as well as companies involved in both manufacturing and services. In fact, the growth of multi-site and multinational service enterprises is helping – along with the similar trends that occur in other sectors of the economy – to integrate regional and subregional economies increasingly into the world economic system.

Accountancy provides an example of a business service sector which has undergone substantial organisational change. Twenty years of rapid structural change following the Second World War, largely involving mergers and acquisition, has resulted in a polarisation of the industry between a very small number of large companies and a vast number of very small practices, with medium-sized operations being squeezed out. Internationalisation of the profession over this period has resulted in both the UK and world markets being dominated by 'the big six' firms which in 1981 audited 493 of the world's top 500 companies.

Retailing is another sector in which concentration is rising and technical changes, combined with cost and competitive pressures, are leading to locational changes. Many of the most famous high street names are now international operators subject to the great competitive pressures that entails. Large multiple retailers now account for over 50 per cent of retail sales in the United Kingdom, while single outlet retailers have around 30 per cent of the market (Howells and Green, 1988). The market share of the multiples continues to rise both in the United Kingdom and other EU countries. Among the multiple chains, there is a move towards non-central stores with greater floorspace, with adverse effects on the 'corner shop'. New technology is providing major opportunities for increased productivity, both in terms of the automation of the check-out operation and the way in which this is linked to improved stock control. The move towards greater sensitivity to consumer demand which this allows is accompanied by a centralisation of distribution facilities which would be impossible without computerisation.

4.5 Growth of the service sector

Growing labour market imbalances, which became apparent in the mid-1970s and which persisted during the 1980s, have resulted in considerable interest in recent years by politicians, policy-makers and academic researchers, in the nature of the job generation process. Attention has turned to the service sector as the major source of new jobs and the only one which appears to offer large-scale employment growth potential. The data in Table 4.1 show that overall employment in Great Britain fell by 0.6 per cent between 1981 and 1993 but that there were considerable between-sector differences in employment change. Manufacturing employment fell by 28 per cent (1 676 000 jobs) while agricultural employment declined by 35 per cent, construction by 27 per cent and energy and water supply by 52 per cent. In contrast, service industries employment increased by 18 per cent overall (2 332 000) and the proportion of people employed in services rose from 62 per cent to 73 per cent. Within the service industry divisions, transport and communications employment fell by 13 per cent, but all other divisions expanded. Distribution, hotels, catering and repairs increased by 12 per cent, banking and insurance by 56 per cent and other services by 18 per cent. The largest growth in employment was recorded by business services with a net increase of 92 per cent (760 000 jobs) followed by other services (welfare and community) where the increase was 70 per cent (386 000 jobs).

4.5.1. *Supply and demand for business services*

Business services perform a crucial function as inputs to other industries in order to improve their competitiveness. The activities usually regarded as business services are listed in Table 4.2 with their standard industrial classification (SIC). The increasing *demand* for the specialist skills of business services in the 1980s emanated from the public and private sector of the economy in response to rapidly changing market, technological and competitive circumstances. Peter Wood (1993) cites a number of sources of 'commercial uncertainty' demanding specialist business service expertise. These include:

- the globalisation of markets – requiring marketing, legal and logistical skills;
- technological change – requiring specialist technical knowledge;
- changes in financial markets – requiring new types of financial control;

Table 4.2 Business service activities

Standard Industrial Classification (SIC)	Activity
8310	Activities auxiliary to banking and finance
8320	Activities auxiliary to insurance
8340	House and estate agents
8350	Legal services
8360	Accountants, auditors, tax experts
8370	Professional and technical services nes
8380	Advertising
8394	Computer services
8395	Business services nes
8396	Central offices not allocated elsewhere
8500	Owning and dealing in real estate

Note: nes = not elsewhere specified.

- adjustments to the regulatory environment – requiring a variety of information and technical skills to respond to changes ranging from privatisation to environmental protection; and
- corporate adaptation to change including mergers and takeovers – requiring management consultancy expertise, not least in the area of human resource management.

The demand for business services in the 1980s was met by a combination of *externalisation*, where clients sought the required expertise outside their own organisation, and *internalisation* which has involved the development of in-house capabilities. Externalisation has resulted in a rapid expansion in the number of business service companies, large and small. While the large organisations developed mainly from the diversification of existing specialist companies, the small firms, many consisting of self-employed individuals, often emerged as the result of a 'spin-off' from the restructuring of larger business services and client organisations (Wood, 1993, section 2, para. 9). Both internalisation and externalisation have contributed to the rapid expansion of business service activities.

4.5.2 *Business services nes (SIC 8395)*

The largest business service group is business services nes (not elsewhere specified), which includes management consultants, market researchers, public relations consultant, document copying, duplicating and tabulating services and other services 'primarily engaged in providing services to other enterprises'. This, collectively, is an extremely dynamic sector of the economy in which employment has expanded dramatically by 162 per cent between 1981 and 1991, a net increase of 248 700 jobs (Table 4.3).

Table 4.3 The regional distribution of business services nes (8395) employment in Great Britain, 1981–91

Region	Employment in business services nes (8395) (1000s) 1981		1991		Change 1981–91	
	No.	(%)	No.	(%)	No.	(%)
Greater London	61.4	40.1	132.3	32.9	70.9	115.4
Rest of South East	28.4	18.5	88.1	21.9	59.7	210.2
East Anglia	2.5	1.6	9.5	2.4	7	280
South West	6.9	4.5	23.0	5.7	16.1	233.3
East Midlands	5.1	3.3	17.6	4.4	12.5	245.1
West Midlands	13.1	8.6	31.1	7.7	18	137.4
North West	12.7	8.3	32.0	8.0	19.3	152
York and Humberside	6.6	4.3	22.0	5.5	15.4	233.3
North	4	2.6	10.7	2.6	6.7	167.5
Wales	3.1	2.0	8.9	2.2	5.8	187.1
Scotland	9.5	6.2	26.8	6.7	17.3	182.1
Great Britain	153.3	100	402	100	248.7	162.2

Source: Wood (1993).

Business service employees include part of the increasing band of Know-ledge Workers (Rajan, 1992), whose three defining characteristics are – higher level education and training – intellectual skills linked to problem solving and decision-making – an ability to take on board a variety of responsibilities. 'Key business service personnel are those who are able to adapt and develop their knowledge to new situations in a flexible manner as they interact with client requirements' (Wood, 1993, section 4, para. 2).

The most striking feature of Table 4.3 is the dominance of Greater London as the centre of business services nes activity in the United Kingdom. By 1991, business services nes firms operating in London employed 132 300 workers, or 33 per cent of the national total. No other city or county approached this concentration of activity. Regionally, the South East England outside London contains the second largest cluster of business service nes employment, with over 88 000 jobs in 1991. The South East as a whole thus accounts for over 54 per cent of total UK employment in this sector. The very clear focus of information-based business services in Britain upon southern England is further highlighted by the fact that by 1991, South West England accounted for nearly as many jobs as Scotland, and more than Wales and Northern England combined.

Trends in the growth of this sector during the 1980s have further reinforced the north–south divide. Thus Table 4.3 shows that between 1981 and 1991, four of the five fastest-growing regions were in southern England (South West, East Anglia, Rest of South East and the East Midlands). In volume terms, the South

East also dominated the growth map, with an extra 130 600 jobs, or 52.5 per cent of the total growth. Hence, the north–south divide in business services widened appreciably between 1981 and 1991. However, the rate of employment growth in London was actually below the average for the whole of Great Britain. This is partly due to a relative decentralisation of business service firms from London into the South East, with relative (but not absolute) losses in London and relative (and absolute) gains in the South East outside London (O'Farrell and Hitchens, 1990, p. 146).

The concentration of business services in major metropolitan regions is related both to the international operation of many service activities, their customers and the positive impact of associated corporate head offices on a network of related specialist suppliers of expertise. Other parts of the country, however, rely heavily upon the contracting-out of service activities by a manufacturing sector facing stiff international competition. Not surprisingly the restructuring of service companies in response to such shifts in demand, including diversification into new growing markets and strategies of specialisation on core businesses, seem to favour metropolitan regions, with the resulting growth of high income professional occupations supporting a range of leisure, recreation and retail services.

4.5.3   *Towards a service economy?*

Since 73 per cent of British employment in 1993 was in services this raises the question as to whether government should intervene to dampen any further trend towards a services economy. Frequently concern is expressed about the decline of the manufacturing sector in the United Kingdom, that the economy cannot endure as simply a services-producing economy, and that only manufacturing represents the creation of 'real' wealth. Those who advocate policies to counter the process of 'de-industrialisation' have in mind a scenario of high-productivity factory workers being replaced by low-productivity fast food restaurant employees, based on the simplistic notion that manufacturing creates more wealth than services. More generally the reasoning for this seems to be that: (i) the production of goods generates more income than the production of services; (ii) the production of services can take place only after the demands for goods have been satisfied; and (iii) the country cannot survive – especially in international trade – by producing only services. Is the economy better off because a consumer spends £100 on golf clubs rather than £100 on green fees – the former being goods, the latter services? This seems doubtful, since the goods purchased are less likely to be 100 per cent domestic value added than the service.

The notion that goods production is more income-generating than services may be linked to the presumption that investment may be more wealth enhancing than current consumption. This would be true of buildings, machine tools or construction machinery – investment goods that can be more wealth-enhancing to the economy than can the production of many specific services. However, many other goods (e.g. processed foods, newspapers, soft drinks, ice cream) are current consumption items. By contrast, education – a major service industry – enjoys the greatest long-term, wealth-producing potential of any industry. An economy could survive and prosper, in theory, producing only services – if that economy's competitive advantages were in the production of services. Hence, the arguments typically advanced for considering service industries as inferior to goods-producing industries seem to have little validity. Yet the concern over the declining manufacturing base in the United Kingdom cannot be dissociated from the apprehension about the rise of services. There is no case for advocating a stronger shift to services or for retarding that shift in some arbitrary way. Government policy should aim at raising productivity throughout the economy, no less in services than in manufacturing. However, as we shall see in the next section, UK industrial policy is predicated on the assumption that goods production is more important than services.

4.6 Services policy

4.6.1 *Office dispersal*

The response of industrial policy to the growth of service activities has been limited. Policy-makers have largely ignored the potential contribution of the sector to economic development due to a perception of services being dependent upon manufacturing. Regional policy has been in operation since 1934 yet only in the last 20 years has the government introduced measures for services. Regional policy was based on influencing the inter-regional move-ment of mobile manufacturing industry through provision of factories, industrial estates, and later loans and grants in the Development Areas, and through floorspace controls in the congested areas, particularly the South East and Midlands.

In the early 1960s the first policy measures towards service activities were introduced – Office Development Permits (ODP) and the formation of the Location of Offices Bureau (LOB) in 1964, initiatives prompted as much by increasing congestion in central London as the needs of the regions for office employment (McCrone, 1968). The Office Industry Development Act applied initially to London and the West Midlands conurbation and required all office developments over 3000 sq.ft to apply for an ODP. Permits were only granted where it could be demonstrated that there was a need for a central area location, that no other suitable accommodation was available, and that the development was 'in the public interest'. In 1966 the controls were extended to the whole of the South East, the West Midlands, East Midlands and East Anglia, but after 1969 the exemption limit was raised to 10 000 sq.ft (Marshall, 1988, p. 206). The Conservative government in 1979 abolished both the ODP system and the LOB.

The implementation of the office dispersal policy was not very successful since it was based on a considerable overestimate of the growth of office employment in central London. From 1965 to 1976, almost 28 million square feet of office floorspace was prohibited in central London under the ODP system, approximately 30 per cent of the floorspace applied for (Alexander, 1979). Nevertheless, between 1966 and 1977 some 145 000 private sector jobs were diverted out of central London (Alexander, 1979). Much of this movement took place over short distances, usually to other parts of the South East. Of the 70 000 jobs decentralised between 1963 and 1970, only about 1 per cent actually moved to the Development Areas.

4.6.2. Government office relocation

In parallel with the government's policy to redistribute private sector office employment, attempts were made to relocate public administration from London. Between 1963 and 1972 some 23 500 civil service jobs were dispersed from central London (Marshall, 1988, p. 208). This policy was more beneficial to Assisted Areas than the decentralisation of private sector office jobs since over 50 per cent were moved to problem regions, notably Scotland, Wales, the North and the North West. Much of the relocation undertaken involved clerical back-office jobs; the high quality headquarter posts remained in London.

In a new phase of relocation policy, the government decided in 1974 to relocate 31 000 civil service jobs outside London over a decade. Some 90 per cent of these jobs were to go to the Assisted Areas: Glasgow, Cardiff, Newport, Mersey and Teeside were the major beneficiaries. Although this programme still continues, a reduction in the projected number of relocated jobs, cutbacks in public expenditure since 1979 and opposition from civil service unions have all reduced the scale of the programme (Marshall, 1988, p. 205). Consequently, while almost 31 000 civil service jobs were dispersed from London between 1963 and 1983, more than one-third of civil service employment is still concentrated in the South East.

4.6.3 Policy instruments

In 1973 the government introduced special incentives – the Service Industry Removal Grants – which provided employee transfer grants of £800 in addition to grants providing rent relief for up to 5 years or to facilitate the purchase of premises (HMSO, 1974). Aid, however, was restricted to mobile projects (those with a choice of location) and those which created a minimum of 10 jobs for transferred firms and 25 jobs for new start-ups in the Assisted Areas. Assistance for local services was excluded. Later a job creation grant was introduced providing £1500 per job in Special Development Areas and £1000 per job in Development Areas (HMSO, 1977). A final increase in the maximum levels for the job creation and employee removal grants to £8000 and £2000, respectively, took place in 1981. The policy was discontinued in 1984 and the job creation element of the scheme incorporated into the more general Regional Selective Assistance programmes, but the employee transfer grants were abolished. The number of awards made was relatively low and the assistance constituted only 1 per cent of regional aid in 1977 (Daniels, 1982). Since 1984 the pressures for decentralisation have diminished and the concentration of business services, financial services, and IT in London and the South East has increased.

4.6.4 *Current policy*

The election of a Conservative government in 1979 brought an immediate commitment to review the system of regional incentives. Following a series of spatial cutbacks in the extent of the Assisted Areas, a White Paper in 1983 proposed, *inter alia*, 'less discrimination against service industries' (HMSO, 1983). A new regional policy was introduced in November 1984 involving a two-tier structure, a redrawn map of Assisted Areas, a new regional development grant (RDG) scheme placing more emphasis upon job creation, a cutback in expenditure and an extension of the eligibility of the service sector. For the first time services qualified for automatic regional assistance and the eligibility criteria were broadened considerably to include a wide range of service activities (Table 4.4). In selecting the services for assistance the DTI targeted 'industries with a choice of location', those which were of 'regional importance', and those which would have little displacement effect (i.e. which would not replace existing jobs). In the first year following the 1984 review, aid to services accounted for one-third of new RDG approved expenditure; but since then the scale of assistance to services has declined (Marshall, 1988, p. 213). Services were also eligible for aid under the Regional Selective Assistance (RSA) scheme assuming they satisfied the criteria of viability, proof of need, efficiency, employment benefit, own contribution to costs and exporting beyond the local area.

The most recent revision to regional policy occurred in March 1988 when the automatic RDG scheme was discontinued. The discretionary RSA scheme continues to be available in development areas and intermediate areas for both manufacturing and qualifying service projects. The changes also included an expansion of government assisted business advisory services available to both manufacturing and service companies which have fewer than 500 employees and wish to use private services in design, quality, marketing, manufacturing systems, business planning and financial and information systems. This Enterprise Initiative scheme involves subsidising the costs of consultancy services of between 5 and 15 days with two-thirds of the cost paid for firms in assisted areas and half in non-assisted locations.

Regional aid is but one component of government assistance to industry which also incorporates nationalised industry support, competition policy,

Table 4.4 The eligibility for regional policy assistance of producer services: 1984 scheme

Scheme	Service eligibility
Regional development grant	Data processing and software development
	Technical design, testing analysis, etc.
	Business services
	Management consultants
	Market research and public relations
	Exhibition contracting and organising
	Industrial research and development services
	Administration, headquarters
	Advertising agencies
	Industrial photographic services
	Venture capital providers
	Credit card companies
	Export houses
	Repair (except for consumer goods & vehicle repair)
	Value added network services
	Cable television
	Mail order houses and similar services provided direct to the public, e.g. football pools
	Freight forwarders
Regional selective assistance RSA grant Training in support of RSA Exchange risk cover	All producer services, unless more specific forms of assistance are available, e.g. for R&D
Government factories	All producer services, although eligibility is subject to job density minima per 1000 sq. ft (apart from Northern Ireland)

Source: Marshall (1988).

employment measures, innovation policy and sector-specific measures (on these, see also Chapter 2). Few schemes are specifically designed for services, the major exception being the computer services field. There is also a variety of schemes which are not restricted to specific sectors; most of these are in the employment and training, export promotion and general business investment field.

4.6.5 *The European Union (EU) and services policy*

Thirty years after the enactment of the Treaty of Rome, barriers to intra-EU trade in services have finally begun to fall. The fragmentation of markets for services has been the result of a combination of two factors: the intrinsic nature of services and government regulations. Regulation plays a dominant role in most service industries. In the presence of market failures, regulation may be justified on grounds of efficiency. Three types of failures are relevant to service industries.

1. Imperfect competition prevails in many services: some industries are natural and/or public monopolies (e.g. the railways) and regulation may be required to prevent monopolistic abuse. Others tend to be oligopolistic (e.g. the banks).
2. The problem of imperfect information pervades many services, inviting government intervention in the form of occupational licensing and certification (e.g. accountancy, law and medicine).
3. Negative externalities arise in certain service industries because of asymmetric information such as in financial services where failure of one institution may cause problems to others. This situation calls for regulation through licensing and certification.

In recent years government regulations have come under severe attack. It was argued that regulation, rather than acting in the public interest, tends to be captured by special groups seeking monopoly rents and doubts were raised about the effectiveness of regulation as an instrument for correcting market failure. These criticisms contributed to the deregulation movement which spread to Britain and throughout Europe in the 1980s. The attempts to open up service markets in Europe go back to the origin of the community. The Treaty of Rome calls for 'restrictions on freedom to provide services within the Community [to] be progressively abolished during the transitional period' (Article 59) and for 'restrictions on the freedom of establishment . . . [to] be abolished by progressive stages in the course of the transitional period' [Article 52]. Liberalisation of trade in services made no significant progress until the mid-1980s because of the high degree of government regulation and the disparity in regulatory régimes between Member States. The 1985 Commission White Paper on *Completing the Internal Market* called for the principle of mutual recognition to be used as a lever for liberalising services trade. The decision to liberalise intra-EU services trade by 1992 was motivated by technological changes, regulatory changes in the United States and the worldwide efforts to liberalise services trade launched as part of the Uruguay Round of GATT negotiations.

Intensifying competition has been the key component of policy pursued by the Commission for completing the internal market in services. So far the emphasis has been upon deregulation, that is, introducing competition in markets hitherto subject to government regulation. As integration in service markets proceeds, another aspect of competition policy will become important, namely tackling barriers to competition erected by companies themselves. Any regulation requires a careful prior assessment of the nature and degree of market failure. As a corollary, there is no single optimal degree of regulation that applies to all sectors. Furthermore, is the appropriate level of regulation local, national, or community wide? The Commission tends only to assume regulatory responsibility at the EU level when it cannot be handled nationally, which raises questions about the appropriate division of regulatory power between the EU and its member states. Also, the issue of the balance between deregulation to make EU markets more competitive and industrial policy to promote the competitiveness of EU firms did not arise in services until recently. The major emphasis has been upon a strict application of the rules of competition in order to eliminate barriers to intra-EU trade in services. Regulatory barriers to world trade have insulated EU firms from foreign corporations and thereby marginalised the question of competitiveness. There is a possible trade-off between competition and competitiveness. The creation of larger service firms through mergers or growth may be important in order to compete against US multinationals in some industries (e.g. air travel) but this would simultaneously stifle competition within the Community. The direction of future EU services policy remains uncertain.

4.7 Conclusions

There is growing evidence that some convergence between manufactured goods and services is taking place, products are ultimately the physical embodiments of the services they supply. The trends towards smaller batch sizes in manufacturing and increased customisation of products are features which make manufacturing more like services. Simultaneously some services (such as fast food outlets and shuttle air services) are taking on production line characteristics and are, therefore, becoming more like manufacturing.

Economists have traditionally classified services by industry and occupation. The standard industrial classification, however, is flawed because it is not founded upon a satisfactory conceptualisation of the nature of service activities but is based upon the eventual product. It is important to note that the distinction between goods and services is not primarily a matter of the nature of the product, nor even the type of expertise offered, the main economic distinctions that separate different services are concerned with the types of markets served.

Alternative approaches to the taxonomic problem of services is to categorise them according to several characteristics which are alleged to differentiate them from manufactured goods: tangibility, durability and interaction between supplier and customer. We have argued that intangibility is inadequate as a definition of services; it is preferable to classify goods and services according to a continuum of relative intangibility. Similarly, durability does not clearly discriminate between goods and services, different degrees of perishability exist among both manufactured goods and services. The nature of the customer–seller interaction represents a more meaningful discriminator: the quality of many services depends not only on the performance of the supplier but also upon how well the consumer performs in interaction with the supplier. The definitional problems of services differ only in degree from those of manufacturing as a whole or for economic market states such as monopoly or market competition.

Productivity in services is notoriously difficult to measure because of the difficulty of defining output and quality differences. Barras (1986) demonstrated that services sector productivity in Britain grew at 2.9 per cent per annum from 1960 to 1981 whereas manufacturing productivity grew at less than 1 per cent. In the case of producer services which satisfy intermediate demand, we argue that productivity should be assessed by the impact of the service delivered upon the competitiveness of the client organisations.

The service sector (SIC divisions 6–9) created 2.333 m net new jobs between 1981 and 1993 (Table 4.1), and the proportion of the UK population employed in services rose from 62 per cent to 73 per cent. Over the same period manufacturing employment declined by 1.676 m jobs (28.2%). Within services the greatest increase was recorded by business services with a net increase of 91.7 per cent or 761 000 jobs between 1981 and 1993.

The long history of British government intervention in industry indicates a consistent bias towards the manufacturing sector. Financial incentives for services were not introduced until the 1960s, involved little job creation and a small share of regional aid. Moreover, expenditure on regional policy has been substantially reduced. The major thrust of EU policy on services has been upon deregulation, by introducing competition in markets hitherto subject to government regulation in order to eliminate barriers to intra-EU trade.

What about the longer-term prospects for growth based upon services? Because the utility of all products and services is created in the mind (i.e. a diamond, a Mozart opera, a Mercedes Benz, a Shakespeare play, a holiday in Italy or a stylish hat may have little functional value relative to its high price) the growth of the services economy is limited only by the capacity of the mind to conceive of activities as having high utility (Quinn, 1988, p. 25). A safer, healthier, better-educated society may be considered to have higher welfare than one with more physical goods. Services such as education, art, music, literature, public health levels, and scientific know-how represent critical investments, yielding higher productivity and living standards both in the present and future.

Questions for discussion

1. Review the weaknesses of the standard industrial classification as a system for classifying services.
2. Examine the characteristics which are alleged to differentiate services from manufactured goods.
3. How do services contribute to the activities of goods producing industries?
4. Examine the contribution of services to productivity growth.

5. What has been the contribution of new technology to the performance of service industries?
6. Outline the major factors responsible for the rapid growth in service employment during the past 20 years.
7. To what extent has the location of business service employment changed between 1981 and 1991?
8. Discuss the extent to which services may be conceptualised as a fundamental part of the 'wealth' creating sector of the economy.
9. Should policy makers be concerned about the increasing proportion of jobs in service industries and the simultaneous decline of manufacturing employment?
10. What has been the response of industrial policy to the growth of service activities?

References and further reading

Alexander, I. (1979) *Office Location and Public Policy*, London: Longman.

Barras, R. (1986) 'A comparison of embodied technical change in services and manufacturing industry' *Applied Economics* 18 pp. 941–58.

Blade, D. (1987) *Goods and Services in OECD Economies*, Paris: OECD.

Bryson, J., Keeble, D.E. and Wood, P.E. (1991) 'The rise of small business service firms and regional development in the United Kingdom: some empirical findings and theoretical issues' Paper presented to RESER Conference, Lyon, September.

Clark, C.A. (1940) *The Conditions of Economic Progress*, London: Macmillan.

Commissioin of the European Communities (1985) *Completing the Internal Market*, White Paper, Brussels: Commission of the European Communities.

Daniels, P.W. (1982) *Service Industries*, Cambridge: Cambridge University Press.

Daniels, P.W. (1989) 'Some perspectives on the geography of services' *Progress in Human Geography* 13(3) pp. 427–33.

Department of Employment (1983) *Employment Gazette*, December, London: Employment Department.

Department of Employment (1994) *Employment Gazette*, October, London: Employment Department.

Gershuny, J. and Miles, I.D. (1983) *The Service Economy: The transformation of employment in industrial societies*, New York: Praeger.

Gide, G. and Rist, C. (1948) *A History of Economic Doctrines*, London: Harrap.

Greenfield, H.I. (1966) *Manpower and the Growth of Producer Services*, New York: Columbia University Press.

Guile, B.R. and Quinn, J.B. (eds) (1988) *Technology in Services: Policies for growth, trade and employment*, Washington: National Academy Press.

HMSO (1977) *Industry Act 1972 Annual Report 1976–77*, London: HMSO.

HMSO (1983) *Regional Industrial Development* Cmnd. 9111, London: HMSO.

HMSO (1994) *Industry Act 1972, Annual Report 1973–74*, London: HMSO.

Howells, J. and Green, A.E. (1986) 'Location technology and industrial organization in UK services' *Progress in Planning* 26 pp. 83–184.

Levitt, T. (1981) 'Marketing intangible products and product intangibles' *Harvard Business Review* 59 pp. 54–102.

Marshall, A. (1961) *Principles of Economics*, 9th edn, London: Macmillan.

Marshall, J.N. (ed.) (1988) *Services and Uneven Development*, Oxford: Oxford University Press.

Marshall, J.N., Damesick, P. and Wood, P. (1987) 'Understanding the location and role of producer services in the United Kingdom' *Environment and Planning A* 19 pp. 575–93.

McCrone, G. (1968) *Regional Policy in Britain*, London: George Allen & Unwin.

O'Farrell, P.N. and Hitchens, D.M. (1990) 'Producer services and regional development: key conceptual issues of taxonomy and quality measurement' *Regional Studies* 24 pp. 163–71.

O'Farrell, P.N. & Moffat, L.A.R. (1991) 'An interaction model of business service production and consumption' *British Journal of Management* 2 pp. 205–21.

Petit, P. (1986) *Slow Growth and the Service Economy*, New York: St Martins Press.

Quinn, J.B. (1988) 'Technology in services: past myths and future challenges' in *Technology in Services: Past myths and future challenges*, Guile, B.R. and Quinn, J.B. (eds), Washington: National Academy Press.

Quinn, J.B. and Gagnon, C.E. (1986) 'Will services follow manufacturing into decline?' *Harvard Business Review* 86(6) pp. 95–106.

Rajan, A. (1992) *Capital People – Skills Strategies for Survival in the Nineties*, London: Industrial Society.

Riddle, D.I. (1986) *Service Led Growth: The role of the service sector in world development*, New York: Praeger.

Smith, A. (1937) *The Wealth of Nations*, New York: Modern Library.

Wood, P. (1990) 'An integrated view of the role of services' in *Managing and Marketing Services in the 1990s* Teare, R., Moutino, L. and Morgan, N., (eds) London: Cassell Education, pp. 3–17.

Wood, P. (1993) 'Implications for employment policy of the growth of business services in the UK during the 1980s and 1990s' *Working Paper No. 1, Business Services Research Project*, Department of Geography, University College London.

CHAPTER 5

Trade unions and industrial relations

IAN PATERSON

5.1 Introduction

Industrial relations legislation has undergone significant change in the period since 1979. Measures taken to limit the powers of trade unions formed part of supply-side economic policy. The government argued that trade unions had become too powerful and had used their powers in ways which pushed up labour costs, restricted productivity improvements and increased the level of unemployment. As Table 5.1 shows, trade union membership had grown rapidly from 10.2 m in 1968 to 13.3 m in 1979, an increase of over 30 per cent. Coupled with this, trade unions had acquired increasing political and economic influence. In part, this was the result of legislation introduced during the 1970s which increased trade union powers at the expense of employers. It

Table 5.1 Trade union membership and density in the United Kingdom: selected years 1968–92

Year	Union membership (1000s)	Potential union membership (1000s)	Union density (%)
1968	10 200	23 203	44.0
1970	11 187	23 050	48.5
1975	12 026	23 548	51.1
1979	13 289	24 393	54.5
1980	12 947	24 485	52.9
1981	12 106	24 265	49.9
1983	11 236	24 134	46.6
1986	10 539	24 807	42.5
1989	10 158	24 404	41.6
1991	9 585	24 503	39.1
1992	9 048	24 584	36.9

Sources: Various issues of the *Employment Gazette* and its occasional *Historical Supplements*. The potential union membership data represent employees in employment with the addition of the unemployed, at June of each year.

was also a consequence of the growth of formal closed shop arrangements. Dunn and Gennard (1984) have shown that by 1978 closed shop arrangements affected at least 5.2 m people, 23 per cent of the labour force.

The government also put considerable emphasis on the conviction that inflexible pay arrangements were a barrier to creating new jobs. It argued that national pay agreements restricted labour flexibility and discouraged the growth of employment opportunities. Employers were therefore urged to decentralise their pay bargaining arrangements. Attention was also given to the role of wages councils, bodies which fixed legal minimum wages in certain industries where collective bargaining arrangements were inadequate. The government argued that wages councils contributed to unemployment and that the national rates they set were inconsistent with the need for flexible pay determination. It introduced legislation to curtail their powers and subsequently abolished them altogether.

5.2   The effects of trade unions

The impact of trade unions on the level of wages and employment can be analysed by making use of microeconomic models of the labour market, although it should be borne in mind that the macroeconomic effects involve wider considerations. Two possibilities are considered, the first where there is a perfectly competitive labour market and the second where a monopsonist has the power to influence wage rates.

In the perfectly competitive model, it is assumed that all workers have the same skill level and perfect information, and will seek employment where wage rates are highest. This case is illustrated in Figure 5.1, where SL is the labour market supply curve. Individual employees will balance the opportunity cost of work – foregone leisure opportunities – against the wage rate to be paid. Assuming that prices are constant, the higher is the wage rate the greater will be the supply of labour. The labour market demand curve, DL, is the horizontal summation of the labour demand curves of individual firms. All firms are profit maximisers and will increase their demand for labour up to the point where the marginal cost of labour – the wage rate under perfect competition – equals the marginal revenue product of labour. Diminishing marginal returns will cause the marginal revenue product of labour to fall in the short run as firms employ more labour. Consequently, the demand for labour will be higher the lower is the wage rate. In this model the labour market is in equilibrium when the wage rate is equal to WE and the level of employment is NE.

Powerful trade unions may be able to secure wages which are above the equilibrium level. The consequence will be a reduction in the demand for labour and an increase in the supply of labour, causing involuntary unemployment. The amount of unemployment which results depends on how far the wage rate is pushed above the equilibrium level, and also on the wage elasticity of the labour market demand and supply schedules. If a trade union negotiated a wage rate of WU in Figure 5.1, the demand for labour would fall from NE to NU and the supply of labour would rise from NE to NA. This would give an excess supply of labour of NA–NU. A national minimum wage fixed at WU would have the same consequences. If the trade union was further able to insist that firms maintain the equilibrium level of employment, NE, this would result in overstaffing, reduced competitiveness and profitability, and might force some firms out of business.

Alternatively, trade unions may be able to raise the equilibrium wage rate by restricting the supply of labour. This could be achieved by controlling employee training or restricting access to jobs by imposing a closed shop. At each wage rate the supply of labour will be reduced so that the labour market supply curve moves to the left. This is indicated in Figure 5.1, with a move to SL1. The result is that the wage rate rises to WU and the equilibrium level of employment falls to NU. Two types of closed shop arrangement may exist. A pre-entry closed shop requires membership of the union prior to employment and is associated with restricting entry. A post-entry closed shop exists where employees must join the union within a short period of being employed.

The case of the monopsonist arises where one employer, or a group of employers acting together, can dominate a labour market. In either case, employment decisions directly affect wage rates. Figure 5.2 demonstrates the extreme case of a single profit-maximising monopsonist. The labour market supply schedule SL, shows how much labour will be supplied at each wage rate. In order to employ more labour the firm must raise the wage rate. Unlike the perfectly competitive model, the marginal cost of labour is greater than the

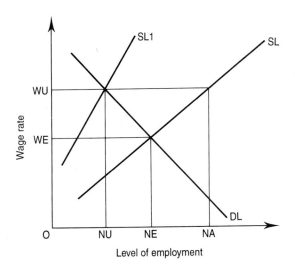

Figure 5.1   Perfect competition model.

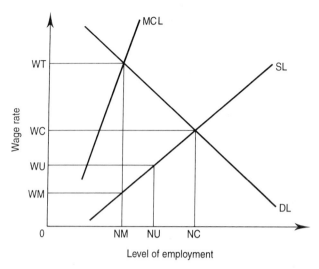

Figure 5.2 Monopsonist model.

wage rate. (If a monopsonist employing 50 workers at a wage rate of £300 per week increases the wage rate to £301 per week to attract an additional employee, the marginal cost of labour will be £301 + (50 × £1) = £351.) This is illustrated by schedule MCL. The monopsonist's demand for labour schedule, DL, shows the marginal revenue product of labour at each level of employment. At the level of employment NM, the marginal cost and marginal revenue product of labour will be equated. In order to employ NM workers the firm will only need to offer a wage rate equal to WM. Compared with the competitive model the equilibrium wage rate and level of employment are lower. If as a result of trade union pressure (or the introduction of a national minimum wage) the wage rate is increased to WU, the level of employment will rise to NU. This is because the marginal cost of labour will now be equal to the negotiated (or minimum) wage rate WU. As the marginal revenue product of labour is greater than the marginal cost of employing additional units of labour for all employees willing to work at the wage rate WU, the level of employment will increase to NU. In Figure 5.2 the level of employment would continue to rise as the trade union negotiates higher wages (or minimum wages are increased) up to the competitive wage rate, WC. Although employment would start to fall if wages were pushed beyond WC, it would remain above NM until the wage rate reached WT.

In both models it has been assumed implicitly that changes in the wage rate do not affect the marginal revenue product of labour. However, it is possible that an increase in wage rates could have the effect of increasing worker productivity. This response to wage increases, known as the efficiency wage effect, is the result of higher wages providing an incentive for employees to work up to their full capabilities and, in addition, reducing labour turnover. A wage increase might also result in an improvement in management efficiency. Where management has relied on low wages in order to remain competitive, the shock of having to pay higher wages may encourage the use of more modern technology and efficient production processes. In both cases there would be an increase in the marginal revenue product of labour at each level of employment, resulting in a shift of the labour demand schedule to the right. It is possible, therefore, that an increase in wage rates might reduce, leave unchanged or even increase the level of employment depending on the structure of the labour market and the impact of the higher wage rate on labour productivity.

The overall effect of trade unions on productivity is not immediately obvious. Different attitudes towards flexibility and technological change will result in different consequences for productivity, even when levels of unionisation are similar. In some cases the existence of trade unions may increase labour productivity. This is likely to be the case where good industrial relations exist and cooperation between employees and employers is encouraged. Unions may support management efforts to reduce inefficiency with resulting increases in output and productivity. Similarly, higher productivity may be expected when union activity keeps managers aware of, and alive to, what is happening around them. Freeman and Medoff (1984) have argued that by giving employees a 'collective voice' in the firm, trade unions improve communications between workers and management. This 'collective voice' contributes to increased productivity, in particular by reducing labour turnover and waste. However, when industrial relations are poor, with employees and employers in frequent conflict, productivity may suffer. Furthermore, by restricting technological change or maintaining restrictive practices, unions may be responsible for low productivity levels. Restrictive practices may be the result of work rules or agreements on staffing levels negotiated between management and trade union representatives. Such agreements have been quite common in the manufacturing sector of British industry. While a decline in agreements of this type was experienced during the 1980s, Millward *et al.* (1992) found that in 1990 bargaining over staffing levels for manual workers still existed in 28 per cent of private manufacturing establishments which recognised trade unions. Overall, the effect of trade unions on productivity may be seen as the net effect of forces pulling in opposite directions. Establishing the outcome is an empirical issue.

5.3 Empirical studies

Studies of the impact of trade unions on wages in Britain clearly indicate a mark-up of union over non-union wages. The mark-up is largest where a closed shop operates, with pre-entry closed shops having the greatest impact on wages. Reviewing several studies that had recently been undertaken, Blanchflower and Oswald (1988) suggested that the average mark-up for union members was 10 per cent or just under, with the bulk of the premium associated with closed shops. Research by Stewart (1991) distinguished between skilled and semi-skilled manual workers. In the case of skilled workers, Stewart found that the average union mark-up in 1984 was insignificant in the absence of a closed shop. However, where a post-entry closed shop existed it was 6 per cent and in pre-entry closed shop situations it rose to 15 per cent. For semi-skilled workers the union mark-up averaged 6 per cent where no closed shop existed, 9 per cent in the case of a post-entry closed shop and 19 per cent in pre-entry closed shop situations.

Conflicting arguments exist regarding the effect of the trade union legislation outlined in Section 5.4 on the ability of unions to bid up wages. Stewart (1991) concluded that there was no evidence that the union mark-up fell between 1980 and 1984. If anything, he found that the mark-up for semi-skilled workers might have risen. However, Gregg and Machin (1992) found that unionised firms experienced slower wage growth than non-union firms between 1984 and 1988, and concluded that this was consistent with a fall in the average union/non-union wage differential in these companies.

Empirical evidence on the consequences of trade union activity for the level and growth of employment is rather limited. Until recently, there was very little research carried out to examine the effects of trade unionism upon jobs at the workplace level, but some has now been published. A study undertaken by Blanchflower, Millward and Oswald (1991), which used data from the Workplace Industrial Relations Surveys of 1980 and 1984, found that trade unions had a negative impact on the growth of employment of the order of three percentage points. In other words, unionised workplaces lost about 3 per cent more jobs, or gained about 3 per cent fewer jobs, each year than non-union establishments. The researchers found that over the period 1980–4, 33 per cent of non-union establishments in the private sector experienced more than 20 per cent employment growth. Only 9 per cent of workplaces in which more than 75 per cent of employees belonged to a union experienced a comparable rise. Furthermore, while 36 per cent of private sector establishments in which unionisation exceeded 75 per cent experienced a greater than 20 per cent reduction in employment, only 15 per cent of non-union workplaces had a comparable fall.

However, Machin and Wadhwani (1991) suggested that the slower employment growth in unionised plants during this period may have been the result of an increase in productivity growth arising from changes in working practices. If trade union legislation, or the higher level of unemployment in the 1980s, had resulted in unions giving up some of their restrictive practices, this could have explained the faster productivity growth and lower levels of employment. Machin and Wadhwani also suggested that during the late 1970s trade unionism and employment growth had been positively correlated.

Empirical studies of the impact of trade unions on productivity levels, while plentiful, do not give a clear answer to the question of whether trade unions generally have a negative or a positive effect on productivity. Wilson (1987) studied 52 firms in the UK metal-working industry taking data over the period 1978–82. He found that in firms where the level of unionisation was less than 50 per cent, unions had negligible effects on productivity. Where the level of unionisation was between 50 per cent and 80 per cent, the effect was positive. For firms in which over 80 per cent of employees were union members, however, the impact on productivity was negative. Machin (1991) used the same dataset as Wilson and found that unions had no damaging effects on productivity, except in large plants with more than 1000 employees.

Another study by Edwards (1987) examined manufacturing plants with more than 250 employees and came to the conclusion that unionisation had little or no effect on productivity levels. A more recent study undertaken by Nickell, Wadhwani and Wall (1992) investigated the impact of trade unions on total factor productivity growth. They used company accounts data in a survey of over 100 manufacturing firms and found that, on average, unionised firms experienced faster productivity growth than non-unionised ones over the period 1979–84. Virtually no difference was found between the average rate of productivity growth of unionised and non-unionised firms for the succeeding two years. Ingram and Lindop (1990) used CBI databank information to examine productivity growth over the period 1987–9. They found that in a period of very rapid productivity growth in the manufacturing sector, non-unionised firms out-performed those that were unionised.

5.4   Industrial relations legislation

Since 1979 the government has instituted a number of statutes affecting British industrial relations. The main issues tackled have been strikes, the closed shop, democracy in trade unions, trade union recognition and minimum wage fixing.

It was the government's view that disruption to production should be minimised by reducing the capacity of unions to call strikes and make them effective. In Britain, unlike most other European countries, the right to strike is not laid down by statute. Instead, statute law has provided immunities from common law judgements concerning conspiracy and liability for damaging an employer's business through strike action, or some other kind of industrial action such as an overtime ban, a go-slow or a work-to-rule. The legislation introduced after 1979 limited the extent of these immunities in various ways.

The Employment Act of 1980 restricted picketing to a person's own workplace, thus outlawing secondary picketing. Consequently, anyone picketing at locations other than their own place of employment became liable to action in the civil courts for interfering with commercial or employment contracts. This statute also restricted the legality of other types of secondary industrial action, such as the 'blacking' of goods. Such action had to be confined to a direct supplier or customer of the employer with whom the trade union was in dispute. The Employment Act of 1990 has since made all secondary industrial action unlawful by removing entirely a trade union's immunity from claims for damages when action is taken against a supplier or customer of the employer with whom the union is in dispute.

The Employment Act of 1982 had earlier abolished the special immunities that had prevented trade unions being sued in their own names. It stipulated that a union would be liable for unlawful industrial action if that action was authorised or endorsed by any committee or official with authority under the union's rules to call industrial action. Limits, however, were placed on the damages courts could award. Formerly, only union officers could be sued for organising unlawful industrial action on behalf of their union – the union's funds were safeguarded. The 1982 Act also attempted to prevent political strikes by requiring that a trade dispute, with its accompanying immunity from civil damages, must 'wholly or mainly' relate to employment matters rather than simply being 'connected with' such matters as was previously the case. The new definition of a trade dispute in the 1982 Act also excluded disputes between employees in an effort to prevent inter-union disputes.

Trade union immunity was further restricted by the Trade Union Act of 1984. This provided that if a union authorised or endorsed strike action without first securing majority support for it in a secret ballot, immunity would be lost. This provision also applied to any other form of industrial action which interfered with or broke employment contracts. The Employment Act of 1988 followed this up by giving union members the right to seek a court order restraining their union from organising industrial action if the ballot requirement had not been met. Moreover, it gave union members the right not to be disciplined by their union for refusing to take part in any form of industrial action. The Trade Union Reform and Employment Rights Act of 1993 required pre-strike ballots to be postal (workplace ballots had earlier been possible) and, unless fewer than 50 union members are involved, to be independently scrutinised. It also required unions to give employers at least seven days' written notice of official industrial action and created a new 'citizen's right' enabling any individual deprived of goods and services because of unlawfully organised industrial action to seek a court order restraining the unlawful action.

The Employment Act of 1990 had earlier made trade unions legally responsible for unofficial strikes called by shop stewards or any lay officer. If industrial action is organised by any union official, the union concerned becomes legally liable unless either a secret ballot has been conducted approving the action or the action is repudiated in writing by the union's executive committee or chief officer. This Act also opened the way for employers to selectively dismiss employees taking unofficial industrial action.

The government's view of the closed shop was that it not only infringed individual liberty, but also caused economic damage by raising labour costs and encouraging inefficient working practices. Statutory support for the closed shop was thus gradually removed in an attempt to stifle it.

The government had inherited a situation in which employers could dismiss anyone for non-membership of a union where a closed shop agreement was in force, unless an employee had a genuine religious objection to union membership. The 1980 Employment Act widened this conscience clause and also sought to protect those already employed when a closed shop was established. Individuals with conscientious or deeply held personal reasons for not wishing to join a union, or who had been engaged before a closed shop agreement was concluded, were given the right not to be dismissed by their employer for non-membership of a union. In addition, the Act also tried to ensure that new closed shops could only be introduced if the great majority of the employees concerned were in favour. It laid down that, unless a new closed shop agreement had been approved by 80 per cent or more of those affected by it, the employer concerned could not legitimately dismiss anyone for not being a union member. A periodic review of existing closed shops was introduced by the 1982 Employment Act. This made dismissal for non-membership of a union unfair unless a closed shop agreement had been approved by 80 per cent of the workforce concerned within the previous five years.

Protection given to employers and employees against the operation of closed shops was widened by the 1988 Employment Act. The Act made dismissal for non-membership of a trade union automatically unfair by repealing the earlier legislative provisions that had allowed employers to dismiss individuals for not being union members where a closed shop had been approved by the required majority. It also removed all legal immunity for industrial action organised by a union to compel an employer to establish or maintain any kind of closed shop arrangement.

The 1990 Employment Act aimed to put an end to the pre-entry closed shop by making it unlawful to deny anyone a job because that person is not a union member. The Act also made it unlawful to refuse to employ someone because he or she is a member of a trade union. Complaints alleging either of these infringements can be made to an industrial tribunal, which has the power to award compensation if any such complaint is upheld.

The government also decided that statutory intervention was appropriate in the internal affairs of trade unions in order to ensure that union leaders were properly accountable to their members and that unrepresentative minorities would be unable to gain control of any union. The implication was that this would make union behaviour more responsive to the national economic interest. The Trade Union Act of 1984 required the members of the principal executive committee of a trade union to be elected by a secret ballot of all the union's members at least once every five years. Enforcement was left in the hands of ordinary union members, who were given the right to apply for a court order requiring their union to comply. The Employment Act of 1988 insisted on postal ballots in elections for union executives, thereby ruling out workplace ballots, and also required independent scrutiny of ballots.

Furthermore, the 1984 Act laid down that a secret ballot of the members must be held at least once every ten years if a union wished to use funds for political purposes. Ever since 1913 unions have had the right to maintain special political funds, separate from their general funds, but holding a ballot to establish such a political fund had been a once-for-all requirement. The 1988 Act provided for the appointment of a Commissioner for the Rights of Trade Union Members. The Commissioner's job is to give advice and support to any union member who wishes to take action against his or her union for failing in its statutory obligations and who might otherwise be deterred because of the difficulty of pursuing a case through the courts.

The power of trade unions depends partly on whether or not employers are forced to recognise and bargain with them and, consequently, the early repeal of the previous government's legislation on union recognition was highly significant. Part of the Employment Protection Act of 1975 had empowered the Advisory, Conciliation and Arbitration Service (ACAS) to investigate and pronounce upon applications by unions that specific employers should negotiate with them. If an employer refused to comply with an ACAS recommendation in favour of union recognition, the union concerned could apply for a binding arbitration award on pay and conditions for the employees involved. These provisions were repealed by the Employment Act of 1980.

The government also decided during the 1980s to reduce the powers of wages councils. It took the view that the councils made the unemployment situation worse by fixing minimum wage rates above the levels at which people, especially young people, would be prepared to work. The Wages Act of 1986 therefore removed employees under the age of 21 from the protection of wages councils, so that employers could offer them jobs at lower wages to reflect their level of training and experience. The Act also limited the powers of the councils to setting a single minimum hourly rate, an overtime rate and the point at which overtime should start. This limitation meant that the councils were no longer able to set different minimum rates for different grades of workers within an industry or to fix holiday entitlements.

The wages council system, which covered more than two million employees, mainly in retail distribution and the hotel, catering and clothing industries, was eventually abolished by the Trade Union Reform and Employment Rights Act of 1993. The government claimed that 80 per cent of those employed in wages council industries lived in households with at least one other source of income and argued that, where the councils forced firms to pay more than they could afford, jobs were destroyed.

5.5   Impact of the legislation

It is important to assess the effects that changes in the law relating to industrial relations matters have had. As far as strike activity is concerned, Table 5.2 shows that both the number of strikes and working days lost through strikes

Table 5.2 Stoppages of work due to industrial disputes in the
United Kingdom, 1965–93

Years	Average number of stoppages per year	Average number of working days lost per year (1000s)
1965–9	2 380	3 929
1970–4	2 885	14 077
1975–9	2 310	11 663
1980–4	1 351	10 486
1985–9	881	3 940
1990–3	355	960

Source: Calculated from annual data in various issues of the
Employment Gazette.

have fallen considerably since the 1970s. The main reasons for this fall appear
to have been economic. Rising unemployment between 1979 and 1986 and
again between 1989 and 1992 had a dampening effect on strike activity. This
was accompanied by a significant restructuring of the economy in favour of the
less strike-prone service sector. Furthermore, Britain's declining strike record
after 1979 was part of an international trend.

Nevertheless, legislative changes appear to have had an influence on strike
activity. The restrictions on what constitutes a trade dispute, on picketing and
on secondary industrial action all had some impact, but the most significant
change in the law was undoubtedly the strike ballot requirement introduced in
1984. Since then ballots have become an increasingly common feature of the
negotiating process, with union members in general now regarding them as a
prerequisite for industrial action. Indeed, ballots have sometimes been used to
put pressure on an employer to make an improved offer which is then
accepted. The use of ballots has thus reduced the number of strikes, not only
by making it less likely that a stoppage will take place without the support of
the majority of employees affected, but also because employers often respond
to a positive ballot result by making further concessions which lead to a
settlement of the dispute without a strike actually occurring.

The legislation dealing with the closed shop has helped to reduce its
coverage significantly, although in the early 1980s the number of employees in
closed shops fell mainly because of job losses in establishments that had
compulsory union membership arrangements. The introduction in 1982 of the
5-year ballot for the maintenance of existing closed shops turned out to be
extremely important. Relatively few employers and unions decided to hold
ballots and a number of major employers either ended their closed shops or
gave a commitment that no one would be dismissed for non-membership of a
union. By the end of 1986 ACAS estimated that no more than 30 000 employees
were covered by legally approved closed shops. However, despite dismissal

for non-membership of a union being made automatically unfair in 1988, some post-entry closed shops continued to operate on an informal basis. A National Opinion Poll (NOP) survey in 1989 suggested that the total number of people in closed shops of all kinds was still of the order of 2.5 million. Of these, 1.3 million workers were in jobs where they had to be union members before being considered for employment or before starting work, and this led the government to legislate against the pre-entry closed shop in 1990. Informal pressures on employees to be trade union members no doubt continue in many workplaces with a long closed shop tradition.

The ballot requirements for the election of the members of a trade union's main executive committee have forced unions to tighten up their internal organisation. Indeed, some unions had to make significant changes to their constitutions because they have previously held such an election at the annual conference or at local branch meetings. Many unions, however, already elected their leaders by a full ballot of the membership. Whether or not greater membership participation makes unions more responsive to external economic circumstances is, as Brown and Wadhwani (1990) have remarked, difficult to assess. They argue that direct election in unions whose membership is geographically dispersed tends to favour whichever faction within the union is the best organised, irrespective of its moderation or radical nature. Ironically, the legal requirement to hold a periodic 'political fund ballot' has resulted in more unions being entitled to spend money for political purposes than was the case in the early 1980s.

The repeal of the earlier legislation on union recognition, along with other statutory restrictions on union activity and also the government's decision in 1984 to ban trade unions at its Communications Headquarters (GCHQ) in Cheltenham, encouraged some employers to limit or push back union recognition. This may be significant in explaining why the membership of trade unions continued to fall after 1986, even though unemployment was also falling. There was an increase between 1987 and 1989 in the number of employers withdrawing union recognition for certain grades of staff, and this was sometimes accompanied by pressure from the employer for staff to drop their union membership. However, derecognition of unions was not common and, overall, affected only a relatively small number of employees. It usually occurred in situations where, for whatever reason, union membership had fallen to relatively low levels. Nevertheless, there were some well-publicised exceptions, notably in the newspaper industry and the P&O Ferries dispute. In the early 1990s the number of union derecognition cases continued to grow, but the number of workers affected was still quite small and according to Gall and McKay (1994) derecognition was not a major problem for the majority of trade unions.

Finally, the effects of the reform and eventual abolition of the wages council system must be considered. One of the reasons for limiting the powers of wages councils to setting a single minimum hourly rate was to make the orders issued by the councils easier for employers to understand. It was hoped that this would reduce the problem of underpayment, which had become a serious one. There was, as Simpson and Paterson (1992) have shown, a substantial fall in both the number of workers underpaid and the number of establishments found to be underpaying after 1986. Following the abolition of all the wages councils in 1993 downward pressure on pay was soon apparent. In a survey published early in 1994 by the Low Pay Network, nearly one-fifth of all vacancies in industries that had been covered by wages councils were offering a rate of pay that would have been illegal before the councils were abolished.

5.6   European Union directives

It is not surprising that a British government committed to greater labour market flexibility and reducing trade union power was unwilling to see that course of action obstructed by industrial relations policies at the European Union level. As a result, Britain has blocked a number of proposals put forward by the European Commission. During the early 1980s, for example, a proposed directive granting part-time and temporary workers the same rights as full-time employees, and another dealing with parental leave for family reasons, were both vetoed by Britain in the Council of Ministers. Britain later blocked the so-called Fifth Directive on Company Law, which would have required transnational companies to establish one of three forms of employee participation as part of their decision-making processes. The Vredeling Directive was also obstructed by British opposition. This Directive would have required large companies to inform and consult employees on matters ranging from the company's structure and financial situation to its business developments and likely trends in investment and employment. More recently, during the early 1990s, Britain prevented the adoption of a directive on the establishment of European Works Councils to inform and consult employees in large enterprises operating across two or more EU countries.

The British government has also been alone in voting against the European Commission's Charter of Fundamental Social Rights, which first appeared in 1989. The Social Charter, as it became known, was the culmination of the Commission's attempts to provide a social dimension for the European Union as it progressed towards the creation of a single internal market. The Charter listed a series of labour and social rights to be guaranteed across member states, addressing such issues as working conditions, freedom of movement of labour, fair remuneration, social welfare schemes, freedom of association and collective bargaining, vocational training, equal treatment for men and women, health and safety at work, child labour, and information, consultation and participation. The follow-on development to the Charter was a legislative action programme for implementing most of its provisions. This programme originally contained 47 proposals, 17 of which were draft directives – mostly in the area of health and safety. Key industrial relations issues, however, such as trade union recognition and the right to strike, were excluded from the action programme, partly because of their sensitive nature in certain countries.

At the Maastricht summit in December 1991 the 12 EU member states reached agreement on a European Union Treaty, but only after a so-called 'social chapter' was excluded from one of its two constituent parts – the Treaty of Political Union. The 'social chapter' provided, among other things, for a wider range of employment-related issues to require only a qualified majority vote in the Council of Ministers and the establishment of a mechanism that would enable European-level employers' organisations and trade unions to play a greater part in formulating and implementing EU social policy. The British government declined to sign any treaty containing provisions in these areas, maintaining that it would result in regulations being imposed on Britain which could harm its competitiveness and increase unemployment. Deregulation of employment and the decline in trade union influence in Britain would, the government claimed, be threatened by the proposed 'social chapter'. To enable the Treaty on European Union to be signed by all EU member states, the 'social chapter' was dropped. Instead, a protocol was added to the treaty stating that all countries except Britain wished to proceed along the path laid down in the Social Charter of 1989 and had reached an agreement among themselves to this end. The protocol allowed the 11 to establish common social legislation through EU procedures and mechanisms, but outside its legal framework. Once the Treaty on European Union came into force in November 1993 the proposal, referred to above, for a directive on European Works Councils was relaunched under the 'protocol provisions' and was adopted in September 1994. Britain, of course, is not covered by the directive.

However, the British government has been obliged to amend some employment legislation to bring it into line with EU directives, most notably in the area of equal opportunities. The Equal Pay Directive of 1975 provided for 'equal pay for work of equal value', a feature that had not been included in the British Equal Pay Act of 1970. Following a decision of the European Court of Justice in 1982, the right of men and women working for the same employer to 'equal pay for work of equal value' was added to British law. Additional changes in British law have been made as a result of two other rulings by the European Court in connection with the Equal Treatment Directive of 1976. The Sex Discrimination (Amendment) Act of 1986 brought private households and firms with fewer than six employees within the scope of the law and, more significantly, prohibited retirement age discrimination so that an employer cannot require female employees to retire at an earlier age than male employees. Furthermore, as a consequence of the 1986 Single European Act, which was designed to remove remaining obstacles to the free movement of goods, services, capital and labour within the EU, the British government may be required to accept certain changes in employment law in order to harmonise regulations affecting health and safety at work. The 1993 Directive on Working

Time is a case in point. It restricts the length of the working week (including overtime) to a maximum of 48 hours and insists on a minimum of four weeks paid holiday a year. The British government, however, is challenging its validity, as a measure relating to health and safety, in the European Court of Justice and will not implement any part of the Directive until the Court gives its ruling.

5.7 Conclusion

Industrial relations legislation since 1979 has been a major plank of government economic and social policy. In addition, pay bargaining has become more decentralised. Since the mid-1980s a growing number of industries have ceased participating in national pay bargaining. In some cases this has accompanied deregulation or privatisation, for example in the water, electricity and bus industries. However, it has also occurred in industries that have historically been in the private sector, such as engineering and banking. These developments will have pleased the government, but the main driving force behind them may well have been competitive pressures rather than government encouragement.

Although derecognition of trade unions by employers has not yet become a serious problem, government hostility towards unions has encouraged more and more employers to adopt an overtly anti-union position. The growth of the service sector, an influx of American-owned companies and falling union membership have also been factors at work. The anti-union stance of what has become a considerable number of employers may not have led to widespread union derecognition, but it has resulted in a frequent refusal to recognise unions on new (greenfield) employment sites. Thus a problem the British trade union movement faces is that when older unionised establishments close down they are often being replaced by non-union establishments in different industries. This only serves to reinforce the decline in the membership of trade unions, which continued in the early 1990s as unemployment again rose sharply. As Table 5.1 shows, by the end of 1992 total union membership had fallen to little more than 9 million, its lowest level since 1946.

There can be no doubt that the wide-ranging changes in industrial relations legislation since 1979 have had an impact on trade unions and the labour market. The government's main intentions were to curb the power of unions and to make them more responsive to their members' wishes. This was expected to have beneficial economic consequences. The assault on trade unions, however, appears to have done little to improve overall economic performance. It may have slightly increased wage responsiveness to market conditions, but it has not led to lower levels of unemployment being sustained. Perhaps the impact of trade unions on both wages and employment is rather less than the government had assumed.

Questions for discussion

1. On what methods does the power of trade unions to raise wage rates depend?
2. In what circumstances would a trade union be able to raise the wage rate of its members without reducing their employment prospects?
3. What factors are likely to influence the size of the mark-up of union over non-union wages?
4. Do trade unions in general have a negative or a positive effect on productivity levels?
5. Why did the government decide to embark on a programme of industrial relations legislation after 1979?
6. Was the abolition of the wages councils justified?
7. Assess the impact on trade unions of the industrial relations legislation enacted since 1979.
8. Why has the level of strike activity declined so markedly since the 1970s?
9. For what reasons did the government oppose the Social Charter and several draft directives affecting industrial relations drawn up by the European Commission?
10. Has the legislative assault on trade unions since 1979 done anything to improve Britain's economic performance?

References and further reading

Blanchflower, D.G., Millward, N. and Oswald, A.J. (1991) 'Unionism and employment behaviour' *Economic Journal* 101 July pp. 815–34.

Blanchflower, D. G. and Oswald, A. (1988) 'The economic effects of Britain's trade unions', *London School of Economics, Centre for Labour Economics*, Discussion Paper No. 324.

Brown, W. and Wadhwani, S. (1990) 'The economic effects of industrial relations legislation since 1979' *National Institute Economic Review* February pp. 57–70.

Dunn, N.S. and Gennard, J. (1984) *The Closed Shop in British Industry*, London: Macmillan.

Edwards, P. (1987) *Managing the Factory*, Oxford: Blackwell.

Freeman, R. and Medoff, J. (1984) *What do Unions Do?*, New York: Basic Books.

Gall, G. and McKay, S. (1994) 'Trade union derecognition in Britain, 1988–1994' *British Journal of Industrial Relations*, 32 September pp. 433–48.

Gill, C. (1992) 'British industrial relations and the European Community' in *A Handbook of Industrial Relations Practice* Towers, B. (ed.), London: Kogan Page.

Gregg, P. and Machin, S. (1992) 'Unions, the demise of the closed shop and wage growth in the 1980s' *Oxford Bulletin of Economics and Statistics* 54 February pp. 53–71.

HMSO (1981) *Trade Union Immunities* Cmnd. 8128, London: HMSO.

HMSO (1983) *Democracy in Trade Unions* Cmnd. 8778, London: HMSO.

HMSO (1987) *Trade Unions and their Members* Cm. 95, London: HMSO.

HMSO (1989) *Unofficial Action and the Law* Cm. 821, London: HMSO.

HMSO (1991) *Industrial Relations in the 1990s* Cm. 1602, London: HMSO.

Ingram, P. and Lindop, E. (1990) 'Can unions and productivity ever be compatible?' *Personnel Management* July pp. 32–5.

Machin, S. (1991) 'The productivity effects of unionisation and firm size in British engineering firms' *Economica* 58 November pp. 479–90.

Machin, S. and Wadhwani, S. (1991) 'The effects of unions on organisational change and employment' *Economic Journal* 101 July pp. 835–54.

Millward, N., Stevens, M., Smart, D. and Hawes, W. (1992) *Workplace Industrial Relations in Transition*, Aldershot: Dartmouth.

Nickell, S., Wadhwani, S. and Wall, M. (1992) 'Productivity growth in UK companies,1975–86', *European Economic Review* 36 June pp. 1055–85.

Simpson, L. and Paterson, I. (1992) 'A national minimum wage for Britain?' *Economics* XXVIII (1) (117) pp. 12–18.

Stewart, M. (1991) 'Union wage differentials in the face of changes in the economic and legal environment' *Economica* 58 May pp. 155–72.

Wilson, N. (1987) 'Unionisation, wages and productivity, some British evidence' *University of Bradford Management Centre Discussion Paper*, February.

CHAPTER 6

Pollution control policy

■

LESLIE SIMPSON

6.1 Introduction

The emission of waste products is a continuing source of environmental pollution. Although the environment has the ability to assimilate a certain level of waste, this is not unlimited. Where the assimilative capacity is exceeded pollution problems arise resulting in a wide range of environmental damage. A paper mill may discharge waste products into a river and cause damage to fish stocks and hence losses to fishermen operating downstream. If the paper mill is not required to compensate the fishermen for their losses and no action is taken to control the firm's polluting activities, then the waste emissions will continue regardless of the damage done. Environmental pollution involves costs to society as a whole over and above the private costs of production and consumption of individuals and firms. Such costs are called external costs and occur in this situation because producers and consumers have free and unrestricted access to environmental resources, for waste disposal purposes. Over time the damage will increase as air, water and land are degraded and depleted. In these circumstances there is clearly a need for policy to control pollution.

Every activity involves an opportunity cost. Pollution control is no exception to this and, while significant benefits may result from reducing the emission of waste products, control can only be achieved by incurring abatement costs. This is the basis of the pollution control controversy, for although many would argue that any action which reduces the level of environmental pollution is to be supported, others would argue that the benefits from a reduction in pollution damage must justify the costs incurred in achieving it.

6.2 The optimal level of pollution control

Figure 6.1 brings together the damage and abatement costs associated with different waste emission levels for two profit maximising firms operating in a competitive economy. MDC is the marginal damage curve which measures the monetary value of the additional damage done by increasing waste emissions

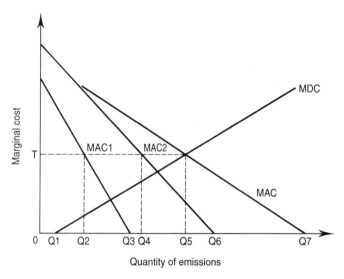

Figure 6.1 Optimal pollution control.

by one unit. Initially, it is assumed that the assimilative capacity of the environment is able to cope with the discharges. When the total quantity of emissions discharged by the two firms exceeds Q1, however, pollution costs are incurred. As the amount of emissions rises, the harm done by each additional unit of waste increases. Hence the MDC schedule slopes upward as the quantity of emissions becomes larger.

The marginal abatement cost schedule, MAC, shows the opportunity cost of reducing waste emissions by one unit. It is the horizontal summation of the marginal abatement cost schedules for two firms, MAC1 and MAC2. Initially, pollution abatement is relatively inexpensive. However, as the level of emissions is reduced the marginal abatement cost increases. The range of options for waste reduction available to the two firms may be quite extensive including a change of production process (technology or inputs), recycling, waste treatment and reduced output. In order to obtain the least cost combination of options for each successive reduction in the quantity of emissions, each firm must equate the marginal cost of all available pollution control strategies.

In the absence of any regulation or incentive for the firms to reduce waste disposal, the quantity of emissions will be at Q3 for firm 1 and Q6 for firm 2. For both firms marginal abatement cost will be zero. The total level of emissions will be Q7 (Q3+Q6), where MAC is also equal to zero. However, this is very inefficient in terms of economic welfare. If the quantity of emissions was cut by one unit, society would gain more from the reduced environmental damage than it would lose from increased abatement costs. The optimal quantity of emissions is at Q5, where MAC and MDC are equal. Between Q7 and Q5 the marginal benefits from reduced environmental damage exceed the marginal costs for each unit reduction in emissions. However, reducing the quantity of emissions below Q5 would involve marginal costs in excess of marginal benefits.

How should a pollution control agency distribute the total reduction in emissions, Q7–Q5, between the two polluting firms? For any given quantity of emissions reduction, the agency should reduce the emissions of the polluter for whom the additional unit of emissions reduction adds least to the total abatement costs. This amounts to saying that the agency should distribute the emission reductions among the waste dischargers in such a way that the marginal abatement costs of each discharger is equal to the marginal abatement cost of all other dischargers. This will give the lowest possible monetary value of total abatement costs. In Figure 6.1 the most cost effective distribution of emission reductions will be Q3–Q2 for firm 1 and Q6–Q4 for firm 2. Firm 1 will continue to discharge Q2 units of waste and firm 2 will continue to discharge Q4 units of waste. The total quantity of emissions will be at the optimal level, Q5. With this distribution of emissions the marginal abatement costs are equal for both firms. If this condition did not hold, an increase in emission by the firm with the higher marginal abatement cost, matched by a reduction in emissions by the firm with the lower marginal abatement cost, would achieve the optimal quantity of emissions at a lower total abatement cost.

The model usefully highlights the economic principles involved in pollution control management and can be more generally applied to situations involving any number of polluters. However, establishing the optimal level of pollution control in practice will be extremely difficult. Where many firms are involved in contributing to the discharge of a pollutant, and each firm has a range of options available for reducing emissions, establishing the least cost combination of abatement alternatives at each emission level with any degree of accuracy, raises many problems. The difficulties involved with measuring and evaluating the marginal damage associated with each level of emissions are even more daunting. These involve establishing the relationship between different emission levels and the harm done, and putting a monetary value on the damage. Estimating the monetary value of damage resulting from air pollution, for example, would involve calculating damages to health, property, agriculture and the natural environment. Although economists have made considerable advances in dealing with these issues, many gaps still remain.

In view of the major problems involved in determining the optimal level of pollution control, it is perhaps not surprising that the optimal approach to setting emission levels has not been adopted. In practice pollution control agencies in Britain have tended to use a pollution standards approach to policy-making. It is very unlikely that the resulting emission level would coincide with the optimal level of pollution control. Nevertheless, in the absence of an accurate knowledge of MAC and MDC, a pollution standards approach to environmental management can give rise to a net increase in economic welfare, as long as the total benefits arising from the implementation of the standards set exceed the total costs. For air pollution control this has involved a case-by-case specification of the production technology and pollution control equipment that is required. The emission level for each process is effectively determined by the production and abatement technology which is installed. An alternative approach, which has been used for water pollution control, concentrates on the benefits of emission reductions. Data relating the concentration of pollution in the environment to its physical effects is used to set a minimum ambient environmental quality objective. Appropriate action is then taken to reduce emission levels in order to achieve the standard set. Direct controls have been the most popular policy instruments for achieving environmental quality objectives in the past. These have included regulations limiting emission levels from individual firms and industries, and the specification of production processes and abatement technology as referred to above.

6.3 Economic incentives

In recent years there has been a growing awareness of the potential advantages of using economic incentives to achieve pollution control objectives:

- economic incentives achieve reductions in the emission of pollutants at the lowest possible total abatement cost;
- economic incentives can provide a continuing inducement for dischargers of pollutants to find new and more cost effective ways of reducing emission levels whereas regulations may encourage only minimum compliance;
- economic incentives are perceived to be the most appropriate means of pollution prevention because they encourage the development of cleaner technology; and
- economic incentives remove the necessity for regulators to acquire a comprehensive understanding of production processes and costs.

To achieve pollution control objectives at the lowest total cost, reduction in emission levels should be undertaken by those operators with the lowest marginal abatement cost. Consider the case in Figure 6.1 where MDC and MAC are known and the optimal quantity of emissions is Q5. If a pollution charge per unit of emission is introduced, equal to MDC at Q5, pollutant emissions will fall to Q5. When the charge, T, is introduced polluters have the option of reducing emissions or paying the pollution charge. Figure 6.1 shows that between Q3 and Q2 for firm 1, and between Q6 and Q4 for firm 2 the marginal abatement cost is less than the pollution charge. Firm 1 and firm 2 will reduce emissions to Q2 and Q4, respectively, to the point where the marginal abatement cost is equal to the pollution charge. Because both polluters are subject to the same pollution charge, it follows that their marginal abatement costs will be the same and that total abatement costs will be minimised.

The total quantity of emissions will be at the optimal level Q5 (Q2+Q4). The pollution charge could also be used to achieve a specified ambient environmental quality objective. Each polluter would have an incentive to reduce the amount of waste discharged until the marginal abatement cost had increased to the level of the pollution charge. By fixing the pollution charge at the appropriate level an environmental agency would be able to implement whatever degree of emission control it required at the lowest possible abatement cost. This contrasts with the regulatory approach, where only by chance could the environmental agency hope to achieve the most cost effective allocation of emission quotas.

A pollution charge per unit of emissions may be impracticable where there are many sources of emissions with no obvious point where they can be monitored. In these circumstances an alternative would be to add a pollution tax to the price of the materials used or the products and services sold. This is done on the presumption that the environmental damage caused by the pollutant is proportional to the quantity of the good consumed. The tax would raise the price of the final product, reducing the quantity demanded and hence reducing the level of pollution. In Figure 6.2, the industry demand curve, D, indicates the benefits consumers receive from a product in a perfectly competitive industry. S1 is the industry supply curve which shows the marginal cost of production at each level of output. The quantity of the product purchased will be Q2 and the price paid by consumers will be P1. By requiring the firms to include external costs in their costs of production the supply curve would move upward, for example, to S2. Equilibrium price would then rise to P2 and output would fall to Q1. In terms of Figure 6.2, the ideal tax would be just enough to encourage producers to view their supply curve as S2 instead of S1. However, the size of the tax can be adjusted to achieve whatever level of pollution control is judged acceptable. The additional tax charged on leaded petrol, first introduced in Britain in 1986, has encouraged a switch by customers to unleaded petrol, thereby reducing the emissions of lead to the atmosphere. See Chapter 10 for an application of these ideas to issues of traffic congestion and road pricing.

The European Commission proposals for introducing a European carbon-tax has run into difficulty because of the potential impact on international competitiveness. The objective of the tax is to reduce the emissions of carbon dioxide as part of a programme of controlling greenhouse gas emissions to counter the problems of global warming. All EU member states have agreed to stabilise carbon dioxide emissions at 1990 levels by the year 2000. The proposed tax, which would be introduced in stages, combines a tax on the carbon content of fuels and a tax on all non-renewable forms of energy. It would encourage energy conservation and fuel substitution from carbon intensive fuels to those which generate less carbon dioxide per unit of energy. Pearson and Smith (1991) suggest that there is considerable scope for fuel substitution

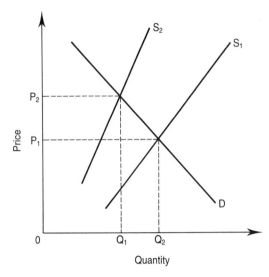

Figure 6.2   Pollution tax.

in response to relative price changes. However, the low price elasticity of demand for energy means that relatively high taxes would be required in order to have any significant impact on the overall demand for energy. The main objection to this tax is that it would reduce competitiveness on a worldwide basis. Because of this objection the European Commission argued that the EU should only implement the tax if its main industrial competitors act similarly. At the end of 1994, the EU was still without a strategy for reducing carbon dioxide emissions because of continuing objections to the use of Community taxes on carbon dioxide or energy.

In 1985 member countries of the Organisation for Economic Cooperation and Development (OECD) adopted the Declaration on Environmental Resources for the Future. By doing so they reaffirmed their acceptance of the Polluter Pays Principle (PPP[1]) first adopted in 1972, and undertook to introduce more flexible, efficient and cost-effective pollution control measures, through a consistent application of PPP and a more effective use of economic instruments. The PPP, as defined by OECD in 1972, simply requires that polluters should bear the costs of pollution prevention and control measures decided upon by public authorities to ensure that the environment is in an 'acceptable state'. It does not imply an acceptance of the pollution charge or tax approach described above, where polluters pay a charge on unabated pollution. However, in May 1993 the European Commission adopted a Green Paper on Civil Liability for Environmental Damage. The objective was to find ways of dealing with the costs of restoring the environment after damage which will also provide an incentive for pollution prevention.

In accordance with PPP, pollution charges are used in Britain to recover the costs of services provided by pollution control authorities, and the treatment of industrial effluents at sewage works. The emphasis is on revenue collection rather than providing an incentive for pollution abatement. There are exceptions such as the tax differential designed to encourage consumers to switch to unleaded petrol.

Despite the arguments supporting the use of economic incentives, such approaches to pollution control are seldom used. The emphasis is placed on the use of standards and regulations as discussed below in the case of air, water and land pollution. Nevertheless, the Department of Environment has made it clear that, 'for the future, the Government's policy is to reduce our reliance on regulation and instead to make increasing use of economic instruments' (*Making Markets Work for the Environment*, Department of the Environment, 1993).

6.4   Air pollution

Responsibility for air pollution control in Britain has traditionally been shared between central and local government. Central government agencies, operating under the Alkali and Works Regulation Act 1906 and the Health and Safety Act 1974, have regulated 'scheduled' industrial processes and plant with the greatest pollution potential. Until 1987 'scheduled' processes in England and Wales were the responsibility of the Industrial Air Pollution Inspectorate. In 1987, control transferred to Her Majesty's Inspectorate of Pollution (HMIP) as part of a policy of integrated pollution control. In Scotland, Her Majesty's Industrial Pollution Inspectorate (HMIPI) has similar responsibilities.

The approach to pollution control adopted by these central government agencies is based on the specification of production and abatement technology. Prior approval is required from the inspectorate before any new plant or process can be operated. Before the introduction of new legislation in 1990, operators and inspectors had a duty to ensure that production processes made use of 'best practicable means for preventing the escape of noxious or offensive gasses . . . and for rendering such gases where discharged harmless and inoffensive'. 'Practicable' was defined as: 'reasonably practicable, having regard amongst other things to local conditions and circumstances, to the current state of technical knowledge and to the financial implications'. The approach to establishing best practicable means (BPM) was pragmatic and involved discussions between the inspectorate and the industry concerned. The conclusions were published in BPM notes which prescribed agreed production technology and abatement techniques and specified the emission limits achievable. Supporters of the BPM approach to environmental pollution control argued that its main advantage was its flexibility, and the opportunity it allowed for regulatory officials to take account of the varying circumstances of different plants. Furthermore, it was claimed that the process of negotiation between polluters and regulatory officials increased the likelihood of polluter compliance. However, critics argued that BPM was too flexible and that too much weight was given to the costs of pollution abatement and insufficient attention given to benefits from reduced environmental damage.

Local authority powers have been more limited. Under the provision of the Clean Air Acts of 1956 and 1968, it was possible for local authorities to require operators of non-scheduled combustion processes to adopt appropriate abatement equipment before commencement of operations. However, in the case of other processes local authorities were unable to take action until some offence had occurred, effectively precluding any application of BPM to most activities under local authority control.

The Environmental Protection Act 1990 introduced radical changes to the control of air pollution. This was the result of two important influences. First, Britain was required to implement the European Union Directive on Emissions from Industrial Plant (see Section 6.7). Secondly, the Government decided in 1987 to introduce integrated pollution control (see Section 6.8). Under the 1990 Act all production processes which cause environmental damage are designated 'prescribed processes'. Each category of 'prescribed process' is divided into two parts. Part A covers plants with the potential for creating pollution damage in more than one environmental medium. They are subject to the control of central government agencies, HMIP in England and Wales and HMIPI or the River Purification Boards in Scotland. These agencies will be responsible for emissions to air, water and land with the overall objective of minimising the pollution of the environment as a whole. Part B processes are controlled by local authorities for air pollution purposes only. For the first time, local authorities will give prior written authorisation for the prescribed processes under their care. Operators of all prescribed processes are required to use 'best available techniques not entailing excessive cost' (BATNEEC) to prevent or minimise pollution. Processes under the control of central government agencies are also required to adopt the 'best practicable environmental option' (BPEO).

The Department of the Environment has issued guidance on the meaning of BATNEEC. 'Techniques' refers both to the process used and the way in which it is operated, 'available' refers to obtainable processes and 'best' means the most effective for dealing with pollution. However, best available techniques need not be used if they involve excessive cost. For new processes, whether or not costs are excessive depends upon the environmental benefits that result, thus implying a balance of costs and benefits of pollution control. For existing plant, what is excessive depends on the particular operating circumstances of the plant. Plant inefficiency and financial exigency are not acceptable excessive cost arguments.

6.5　Water pollution

Before 1989 the principal legislation for the prevention of water pollution was Part II of the 1974 Control of Pollution Act. Under this legislation effluent discharges into rivers, estuaries and coastal waters in England and Wales, were controlled by ten Regional Water Authorities (RWAs) as part of a programme of integrated river basin management. In addition to water quality management and conservation, RWAs were responsible for several related services, including the supply of water and the collection, treatment and disposal of sewage. The approach to water pollution control adopted by the RWAs was based on environmental quality objectives related to the assimilative capacity of the receiving waters. To achieve these objectives, emissions were regulated by consents issued by the RWAs. The RWAs issued their own consents for discharges from sewage treatment works. This conflict of interests between water quality management and sewage disposal led critics to argue that RWAs themselves were major water polluters who did not give sufficient priority to pollution control relative to their other responsibilities.

The 1989 Water Act separated sewage disposal and water quality management. Private water service companies, set up under the Act, were given responsibility for the provision of water supply and the collection, treatment and disposal of sewage. Overall responsibility for water quality management was given to a regulatory body called the National Rivers Authority (NRA). The government had initially planned to privatise the RWAs in their original form, making them responsible for water supply, sewage disposal and pollution control. However, EC intervention prevented this. It was pointed out that the EC Directive on the Discharge of Dangerous Substances to Water required a 'competent authority' to authorise the discharge and the question was asked whether a private company could act as a 'competent authority'. Under the new arrangements statutory water quality objectives will be set by the Secretary of State for the Environment on the advice of the NRA subject to meeting the quality standards required by EC water pollution directives.

In Scotland seven mainland River Purification Boards and three Island Councils are responsible for controlling pollution of inland and coastal waters and conserving the water resources of their areas. They have the duty of ensuring that specified water quality objectives are achieved and issue consents for the discharge of trade and sewage effluent.

From April 1991, discharges to water from 'scheduled' industrial processes came under the control of HMIP in England and Wales and HMIPI or River Purification Boards in Scotland under the system of integrated pollution control introduced in the 1990 Environmental Protection Act. The most hazardous substances are subject to strict environmental quality objectives, and producers are required to adopt BATNEEC and BPEO. These developments represent a significant move in Britain's water pollution control policy towards the stricter, precautionary, EU approach to pollution standards.

6.6   Land pollution

The problem of land pollution is closely associated with policy on waste management. In 1985, the 11th Report of the Royal Commission on Environmental Pollution identified four principal routes by which waste can cause pollution of the ground and soil:

- landfill disposal of toxic and hazardous waste which seriously constrains future use of the site;
- landspreading of treated waste, e.g. water and sewage sludge, which can lead to a build up in the soil of contaminates such as heavy metal;
- the disposal of particulate emissions from waste incineration; and
- the disposal on industrial sites of potentially contaminating material used in or generated by industry.

In addition to being a source of land pollution waste disposal is also a potential source of water and air pollution. The stricter controls over emissions to air and water discussed in the previous sections will affect the quantity and quality of waste disposal on land providing a strong argument for the use of integrated pollution control.

The control and disposal of industrial commercial and household waste ('controlled waste') is governed by the Control of Pollution Act 1974 and the Environmental Protection Act 1990. Under this legislation local authorities, predominantly district councils (plus island councils in Scotland), operate as waste collection, disposal and regulation authorities. County councils have waste disposal duties in rural England. The regulation of waste disposal involves production and periodic revision of waste disposal plans and the issue of licences to the operators of waste disposal sites, treatment plants and waste storage facilities. The most hazardous wastes e.g. PCBs, dioxins and heavy metals, are subject to the most intensive control systems. Following the 1990 Environmental Protection Act the waste disposal duties of local authorities in England and Wales are to be transferred to private contractors leaving the councils with planning, regulation and enforcement responsibilities.

At present approximately 70 per cent of 'controlled waste' is disposed of in landfill sites and between 2.5 per cent and 5 per cent is incinerated. The remainder is reused or recycled. In April 1992, a recycling credits scheme was introduced in England and Wales to provide an economic incentive for reclamation in waste disposal. From April 1994, the credit which is payable to recyclers of waste is equivalent to the marginal cost of disposal which would otherwise have been incurred. Because of the growing shortage of suitable landfill sites and the increasing environmental standards being imposed on them incineration will become an increasingly important disposal option. However, from December 1990 new incinerators require authorisation under the policy of integrated pollution control to ensure BATNEEC, BPEO and to meet the EU directives on incineration plant emissions which take full effect in December 1996. The recent Report by the Centre for Social and Economic

Research for the Global Environment (HMSO, 1993), which investigated the environmental impacts of landfill and incineration, concluded that incineration *with energy recovery* resulted in a net environmental gain because of the consequent pollution reduction from alternative systems of energy generation. Similar conclusions supporting incineration *with energy recovery* are reached in the 17th Report of the Royal Commission on Environmental Pollution. Consequently, it is expected that 'All new incineration plants are likely to be able to utilise heat from the incineration process in some way to generate energy' (*Sustainable Development: The UK Strategy*, 1994).

6.7   European Union directives

EU environmental legislation is now very extensive and covers a wide range of issues. Consequently it has had a significant impact on the environmental programmes of member states. The first action programme on the environment was adopted by the EU Council in 1973; the fifth, which emphasises the use of economic incentives to achieve sustainable development, was implemented in 1993. Over 200 EU environmental directives are now in force. Furthermore, under the 1988 Single European Act 'environmental protection requirements shall be a component of the Community's other policies', thereby raising the profile of the environmental consequences of other EU programmes. New practices adopted since the launch of the fifth environment programme require that: 'Henceforth, any project liable to have an impact on the environment will have to be the subject of a strategic environmental impact assessment and each year the Commission's 23 Directors General will provide a report on their activities with regard to the environment.' These EU developments and the establishment of a European Environment Agency in 1994, reflect the increasing public interest in the environment, and the recognition by member states that environmental issues are an important factor in EU development.

EU air pollution directives can usefully be divided into three categories. The first, aimed at avoiding non-tariff barriers to trade, include directives which set uniform pollution standards for products, such as those limiting the amount of sulphur in gas oil, lead in petrol and the emission of carbon monoxide, unburned hydrocarbons and nitrogen oxides from vehicles. Secondly, there is a set of directives controlling ground level air quality standards including smoke, sulphur dioxide, nitrogen dioxide and lead. In each case the primary objective has been to protect human health. The third category of directives sets emission standards for industrial plant. In 1987 the EU Council adopted a Framework Directive on Emissions from Industrial Plant. This was the first significant response of the EU to the problem of acid rain. Member states must ensure that authorisation is obtained by all plant causing air pollution before commencing operations.

By far the most interesting and important Daughter Directive to date, deals with power station emissions of sulphur dioxide, nitrogen oxide and dust. The directive, adopted in November 1988, which is known as the Large Combustion Plant Directive (LCPD), deals with combustion plant of over 50 megawatts. All new plant is required to incorporate BATNEEC and is subject to uniform emission limits. Existing plant must be modified to conform with the agreed overall national reductions in sulphur dioxide set out in the directive. The British reductions are 20 per cent by 1992, 40 per cent by 1998 and 60 per cent by 2003 compared with 1980 emissions (see Table 6.1). The LCPD is due for review in 1994 when it is expected that further emission reductions will be agreed. It is estimated that Britain should be able to achieve reductions of 80 per cent by 2010–15 as a result of changes in fuel use and the adoption of cleaner technology.

EU water pollution directives can similarly be divided into three categories. The first involves the implementation of exposure standards with the primary objective of protecting human health. The Directive on Drinking Water falls into this category. Secondly, there are several directives which set quality objectives to protect public health and amenities. These include the directives relating to bathing, fresh water fish and shellfish, and water from which drinking water is to be abstracted. The third category of directives set emission limits for dangerous substances. The Framework Directive on Dangerous Substances in Water was adopted in 1976, but not without controversy.

A major policy problem affecting the EU environmental programme has been the long-running dispute between Britain and the other member states over the use of uniform emission limits for the control of water pollution. There

Table 6.1 Ceilings and reduction targets for emission of SO_2 from existing plant (1000 tonnes)

	Emissions	Emission ceilings			% reduction over 1980		
	1980	1993	1998	2003	1993	1998	2003
Belgium	530	318	212	159	−40	−60	−70
Denmark	323	213	141	106	−34	−56	−67
Germany	2225	1335	890	668	−40	−60	−70
Greece	303	320	320	320	+6	+6	+6
Spain	2290	2290	1730	1440	0	−24	−37
France	1910	1146	764	573	−40	−60	−70
Ireland	99	124	124	124	+25	+25	+25
Italy	2450	1800	1500	900	−27	−39	−63
Luxembourg	3	1.8	1.5	1.5	−40	−50	−60
Netherlands	299	180	120	90	−40	−60	−70
Portugal	115	232	270	206	−102	+135	+79
United Kingdom	3883	3106	2330	1553	−20	−40	−60
EC	14430	14430	8402	6140	−23	−42	−58

Source: Official Journal of the European Communities (1988).

has been general agreement that uniform pollution standards should be specified for products as part of product harmonisation – to avoid a situation where different national pollution standards might operate as non-tariff barriers to trade. However, there has not been comparable agreement over the wider use of uniform emission limits. The British position was that emission limits were the means of implementing environmental quality objectives and, as such, they should reflect local circumstances. It was quite logical, therefore, that emission limits would vary from place to place. Countries such as Britain with an extensive coastline and fast-flowing rivers and estuaries would be in a position to achieve environmental quality objectives with higher pollutant emission levels than other countries lacking in such geographical advantages. Those member states which were supporting the use of uniform emission limits argued that if some countries had lower standards than others, this would result in unfair competition. Britain's response was that this was no more than an application of comparative advantage.

Under the Framework Directive two lists of substances have been compiled on the basis of their toxicity, persistence and bio-accumulation. For List 1, which includes such substances as mercury, cadmium and lindane, subsequent Daughter Directives are used to specify emission limits based on BATNEEC to which all dischargers must conform. Because of Britain's objection to this uniform emission limits approach, member states were given the option of choosing an alternative means of control based on environmental quality objectives. Under this arrangement it is possible to use different emission limits to reflect different environmental conditions as long as the environmental quality objectives are met. For List 2, which includes possibly less dangerous substances such as copper, lead, zinc and chromium, member states are required to organise pollution reduction programmes based on emission limits linked with environmental quality objectives.

The application of the Framework Directive, and the subsequent Daughter Directives on Dangerous Substances in Water, continue to be controversial. The majority of member states would like to extend the uniform emission limits approach to List 2 substances. Others, including Britain, prefer the environmental quality objectives approach. The recent developments in Britain where the Environmental Protection Act requires the use of BATNEEC coupled with environmental quality objectives can be seen as an attempt by Britain to come more into line with her EU partners. However, the fifth environment programme proposes that member states should be free to choose their own system of pollution control, provided that they comply with the objectives set at Community level and the rules of the internal market.

In contrast, the Framework Directive on Waste which was adopted in 1975 raised little controversy in Britain. This can be explained by the fact that the 1973 Control of Pollution Act had, according to the responsible Minister, been a model for the directive. The uncontroversial directive required EC member states 'to take the necessary measures to ensure that waste is disposed of without endangering human health and without harming the environment'. To accomplish this, EU member states were required to designate authorities that would prepare plans for waste disposal and issue permits to waste disposal installations. In addition, governments were required to encourage recycling and apply PPP. More recently, however, the draft Directive on Waste Disposal and Landfill Sites has been delayed by arguments favouring more flexibility at local, regional and national level.

6.8   Integrated pollution control

In November 1993, the European Commission published its proposal for an Integrated Pollution Control Directive. The proposal applies to emissions from industrial installations mainly in the manufacturing sector but also covers waste management and energy production. Eight of the EU member states, Belgium, Denmark, France, Greece, Ireland, Luxembourg, Portugal and Britain, already operate an integrated pollution control policy.

The case for integrated pollution control in Britain was first put forward in the 5th Report of the Royal Commission on Environmental Pollution in 1976. The Commission argued that in view of the close connection between different types of industrial pollution, the lack of cooperation between pollution control authorities was unsatisfactory. It was evident to the Commission that pollution control in one medium was giving rise to increased pollution in another, with the possibility that the overall impact was worsened. The Royal Commission recommended an integrated approach to the most difficult pollution problems. The objective was to minimise the damage to the environment as a whole, by selecting the best practicable environmental option. It was not until 1986 that the government announced that a new unified pollution inspectorate, Her Majesty's Inspectorate of Pollution, would be set up for England and Wales. The Environmental Protection Act 1990 established the legislative basis for HMIP and integrated pollution control. In Scotland responsibility will go either to HMIPI or to the River Purification Boards.

In 1988 the Royal Commission's 12th Report set out to define BPEO. The concept is concerned not only with the optimal combination of waste disposal methods in order to minimise environmental damage, but also incorporates production technology, operating procedures and control equipment. Paragraph 2.1 of the 12th Report states:

> A BPEO is the outcome of a systematic and consultative decision-making procedure which emphasises the protection and conservation of the environment across land, air and water. The BPEO procedure establishes, for a given set of objectives, the option that provides the most benefit or least damage to the environment as a whole, at acceptable cost, in the long term as well as in the short term.

Establishing a BPEO will involve the identification, quantification and evaluation of the environmental impact of polluting processes, taking account of the alternative emission disposal options. Recognising this challenge, paragraph 3.20 of the 12th Report comments:

> The advice of experts may be sufficient to ensure that best results for the environment are secured. However, where trade-offs are difficult or controversial, the selection of a BPEO cannot be left to scientists, industrialists and regulatory experts alone. Public involvement is needed so that the public values underlying the choice of a BPEO are identified and clearly understood.

These developments in integrated pollution control represent major changes in Britain's pollution control policy. Recent announcements by the government envisage further developments. These will come in the form of two independent environmental protection agencies, one for England and Wales and the other for Scotland. In each case these new agencies will bring together the key pollution control functions affecting air, water, and land under a single organisation.

There are several reasons cited for the proposals. First, the agencies will resolve the problems of overlap and potential conflict between pollution control authorities. Secondly, they will be able to ensure that full consideration is given to achieving BPEO. Thirdly, environmental monitoring will be undertaken on a coordinated basis and finally, the new organisations will be independent. The precise role and functions of the proposed agencies are at present under consideration.

6.9 Conclusion

The development of integrated pollution control in Britain is based on the argument that there are important links between pollution in different media. In so far as these linkages exist, the proposed Environmental Agency for England and Wales, and the Scottish Environmental Protection Agency will be better placed than existing agencies to ensure that the social costs of environmental pollution are minimised. Nevertheless, it is not unreasonable to question the extent to which the new agencies will be in any better position to establish the relationship between the costs and benefits of pollution control, or to achieve pollution control objectives at the lowest cost. The White Paper, *This Common Inheritance* (1990), identifies two broad approaches to the future control of pollution in Britain. These are, the use of regulation, so that agreed standards can be applied, and economic incentives including taxes and prices which can be used to influence producers and consumers. Subsequent annual reports have monitored progress towards meeting environmental objectives.

Pollution control policies adopted in the United Kingdom during the next decade and beyond will be influenced by EU environmental legislation and the global policies emerging from the United Nations Conference on Environment and Development, known as the Earth Summit, which took place in Brazil during June 1992.

The Earth Summit brought together political leaders from all over the world in an attempt to establish a global strategy for dealing with global environmental issues such as the greenhouse effect, ozone holes and deforestation. At the end of the Summit the Rio Declaration on Environment and Development set out agreed principles and Agenda 21 set out a comprehensive programme for the achievement of sustainable development in the twenty-first century. Included in Agenda 21 is a proposal to establish a United Nations Commission on Sustainable Development, the first meeting of which was held in June 1993. Government leaders were also invited to sign two binding conventions on climate change and biodiversity (Pearce, 1992; Cockburn and Hecht, 1992). Britain ratified the Climate Change Convention at the end of 1993 and intends to ratify the Biodiversity Convention, subject to certain financial assurances, in the near future. Furthermore Britain has become a member of the newly established United Nations Commission on Sustainable Development.

Questions for discussion

1. Explain the concept of an optimal level of pollution control.
2. What are the advantages of pollution taxes over other means of controlling environmental pollution?
3. How should pollution control authorities allocate the total reduction of emissions between polluting firms?
4. Compare the regulatory approach to air and water pollution control used in Britain. To what extent do these adopt the principles of pollution control advocated by economists?
5. Why do economists prefer economic incentives to regulatory controls?
6. Why does the Royal Commission on Environmental Pollution advocate the adoption of the Best Practicable Environmental Option?
7. In what circumstances might different national pollution standards operate as non-tariff barriers to trade?
8. What arrangements exist in the United Kingdom to control:
   (a) atmospheric pollution?
   (b) water pollution?
   (c) land pollution?
9. 'There were three main influences on the 1990 Environmental Protection Act, namely integrated pollution control (including BPEO), BATNEEC and EC directives.' Discuss.
10. What are the advantages and disadvantages of integrated pollution control?

Note

1. Not to be confused with the alternative meaning of PPP – purchasing power parity – discussed in Chapter 15.

References and further reading

Central Office of Information (1993) *Pollution Control*, London: HMSO.

Central Statistical Office, *UK National Accounts* (1980), London: HMSO.

Central Statistical Office, *UK National Accounts* (1994), London: HMSO.

Centre for Social and Economic Research of the Global Environment (1993) *Externalities from Landfill and Incineration*, London: HMSO.

Cockburn, A. and Hecht, S. (1992) 'Up a blind alley' *New Statesman* 5 (204) pp. 18–19.

Department of the Environment (1990) *This Common Inheritance: Britain's environmental strategy*, Cm. 1200, London: HMSO (and subsequent annual reports).

Department of the Environment (1993) *Making Markets Work for the Environment*, London: HMSO.

Department of the Environment (1994) *Sustainable Development, The UK Strategy*, Cm. 2426, London: HMSO.

Department of the Environment (1994a) *Climate Change: The UK programme*, Cm. 2427, London: HMSO.

Department of the Environment (1994) *Biodiversity: The UK action plan*, Cm. 2428, London: HMSO.

Department of the Environment (1994) *Sustainable Development: The UK strategy*, London: HMSO.

Haigh, N. (1990) *EEC Environmental Policy and Britain*, Longman: Essex.

Official Journal of the European Communities (1988) L336, 31, 7 December.

Organisation for Economic Co-operation and Development (1989) *Economic Instruments for Environmental Protection*, Paris: OECD.

Owens, S. (1990) 'The unified pollution inspectorate and best practicable environmental option in the United Kingdom' in Haigh, N. and Irwin, F. (eds) *Integrated Pollution Control in Europe and North America*, London: Conservation Foundation, Institute for European Environmental Policy.

Pearce, F. (1992) 'Last chance to save the planet?' *New Scientist* 134 (1823) pp. 24–8.

Pearce, D., Markandya, A. and Barbier, E.B. (1989) *Blueprint for a Green Economy*, London: Earthscan.

Pearson, M. and Smith, S. (1991) *The European Carbon Tax: An assessment of the European Commission's proposals*, London: Institute for Fiscal Studies.

Royal Commision on Environmental Pollution, 5th report (1976) *Air Pollution Control: An integrated approach*, London: HMSO.

Royal Commission on Environmental Pollution, 11th Report (1985) *Managing Waste: The duty of care*, London: HMSO.

Royal Commission on Environmental Pollution, 12th Report (1988), *Best Practicable Environmental Option*, London: HMSO.

Royal Commission on Environmental Pollution, 17th Report (1993) *Incinerating Waste*, London: HMSO.

CHAPTER 7

Public expenditure and taxation

PHILIP WELHAM

7.1 Introduction

Should governments intervene in markets at all? Adam Smith's 'invisible hand' suggests that efficiency is maximised where people pursue their own interests. Consumers maximise utility, equating marginal utility with price by purchasing goods up to the point where the utility derived from the last unit consumed is just equal to the price paid. Firms maximise profits by equating marginal cost with marginal revenue which, under conditions of perfect competition, is the same as price. Thus economic efficiency is achieved; that is, the marginal utility that consumers derive from a good equals the marginal cost of providing it. However, this holds in perfectly competitive markets only and ignores problems of external costs such as pollution (see Chapter 6), problems of acquiring information and the unequal distribution of income and wealth (see Chapter 8). Whenever market failures occur governments may intervene in an attempt to improve the allocation of resources. The scope of the public sector for this chapter covers central and local government spending on goods, services and transfer payments and the raising of revenue to finance the expenditure by central government. Local government taxation is covered in Chapter 9.

'Public goods' (goods that are indivisible and consumed by everyone, such as defence) cannot readily be supplied by private markets because consumers cannot be prevented from deriving the benefits of the good once it exists. The benefits from defence, public sanitation, prevention of spread of infectious diseases and policing, for example, accrue to society in general. If some people pay for these goods others (so-called free-riders) derive benefits also and thus do not have to pay at all or can contribute less than the benefits they derive. The economic characteristics of public goods are developed more fully in the next section. Externalities (effects on the utility of people other than the producer or consumer of the good) are another area where market failure occurs. While markets take into account the costs and benefits of the two parties to the transaction, buyer and seller, the benefits and costs to third parties, such as benefits from attractive landscaping or costs such as noise pollution or chemical waste damage caused by firms, are not taken account of by the market mechanism. Unless the state intervenes to legislate, tax or subsidise so that externalities do influence the output level of the industry, economic efficiency will not be achieved.

Market failure also occurs when information is less than perfect. Many people are likely to underestimate their needs in old age and make insufficient provision. Others cannot calculate their risks of being unemployed, or might prove to be bad risks for private insurance purposes. There is a general agreement, therefore, that the state should provide retirement and unemploy-ment benefits as well as sickness, single parent and other benefits. Lack of information, at least on one side of the market, leads the state to regulate work conditions and the quality of consumer products, and also to require information to be published about the nature and composition of many products. Finally a category of goods called 'merit goods' (goods or services that society thinks everyone should consume) gives rise to state intervention not in order to deliver efficiency as has so far been defined – but because the state wishes to 'improve on' consumer preferences. The state takes a paternalistic line and requires consumption of certain goods (e.g. education is compulsory up to the age of 16 years), or bans other goods (e.g. drugs).

The economics of public expenditure and taxation, or Public Finance as it is called, covers three main areas. The first area is macroeconomic, involving issues such as stabilisation and growth of the whole economy. This will be covered in Chapter 11. The second area involves equity. Taxes and expenditure affect the distribution of income and wealth. These issues are the subject of the next chapter. The final area concerns the allocation of resources. Public spending and taxation affect the efficient use of resources. In this chapter we will be discussing the appropriate size of the public sector, the components of government expenditure and the ways in which the tax base and tax rates affect firms' and households' decisions. We will cover central and local government together. The term General Government Expenditure (GGE) is used when central and local spending are considered jointly.

7.2 The public sector share of national income

To understand the economic ideas behind the division of national income into public and private sectors we present a two-person model of the economy to show how demands for public goods and private goods should be aggregated.

In Figure 7.1 the demands of two individuals for public and private sector goods are shown. O is the origin for public goods and Y is the origin for private goods. OY (the horizontal axis) represents the potential of the economy for producing public or private goods and is equivalent to national income for our two-person economy. As the output of public goods is increased, less resources are available to produce private goods and consequently the output of private goods falls. Individual A's demand for public sector goods is DA and

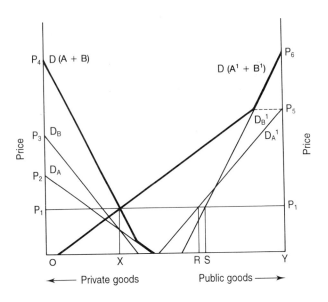

Figure 7.1 Demand for public and private goods.

is shown as starting at P_2, the maximum valuation A places on one unit of public goods. A's demand for private goods is DA^1 which slopes down to the left from P_5 and obeys the normal properties of demand curves apart from being plotted to the left from Y instead of to the right. Similarly B's demand for public goods is shown as DB, starting at P_3, and for private sector goods is DB^1.

Since public goods are non-rival in consumption, i.e. A's consumption of defence or the benefits of a lighthouse do not diminish the amount of the good or service available for B, their two demand curves are summed vertically, giving a joint demand for public goods $D(A+B)$ (note, therefore, that $P_2 + P_3 = P_4$). Private goods are removed from the market when purchased so a good consumed by A is not available to B. The two demands for private goods have to be added horizontally giving $D(A^1+B^1)$. The opportunity cost of public sector goods is the foregone private sector production and the value placed on the private goods by A and B. $D(A^1+B^1)$ is thus the marginal cost or supply curve for public goods as well as the demand of the two individuals for private goods. Thus the diagram shows the optimal division of national income into a public (OX) and private (XY) sector, with the marginal valuation of the last unit produced of public goods OP_1 being equal to the value placed on the last unit produced of private sector goods. Both A and B consume OX of public goods but A consumes YR and B consumes YS of private sector goods. This approach appears to provide a sound theoretical basis for dividing national income between private and public goods.

Unfortunately, although we can get good information for private sector demand, shown by the prices people are willing to pay, there is almost no good information about the demand for public goods. People do not have to pay directly for public goods and even if they did the free-rider problem would lead them to under-declare their preferences and hope that others would pay for the public good. The basic rule that public goods in total, and for each component of public spending, should be produced up to the point where the marginal benefit of an additional unit of supply equals marginal cost is the correct principle but lack of adequate information means that its implementation in practice is highly unlikely. The rule does draw attention to the fact that utility is maximised when attention is paid to estimates of demand (benefits) as well as costs. It is not sufficient to consider costs only.

We now turn from general principles to look at one of the major concerns of the government after 1979, namely control of the growth of total public expenditure including transfer payments as well as spending on goods and services. It is of interest to look at the system of planning used. (For a fuller, year-by-year, account see Johnson, 1991). The key issue is whether future plans for government expenditure are made in cash terms, that is the amount of money to be spent (cash limits), or in volume terms, that is expressed in current prices with future adjustments to be made to allow for any rise in prices. From 1961 to 1976 plans had been made in volume terms (also called 'survey prices' or, less reverently, 'funny money'). Between 1976 and 1982 plans were made in cash terms for 1 year and volume terms for 3 years. After 1982 spending was planned in cash terms only. Cash terms provide a better guide to the finances needed and for macroeconomic purposes. However, volume plans are necessary if efficiency objectives are important since they give a better guide to the real resources being provided. Volume plans place greater emphasis on the needs for government spending. Limiting the amount that could be spent in cash terms, i.e. cash limits, was not applied initially to demand-determined spending like social security payments but attempts were made in the late 1980s to make all spending subject to cash limits.

Turning to the path of actual government expenditure, we can see from Table 7.1 that in cash terms GGE grew from £75 billion in 1978–9 to £269 billion in 1992–3. The real change was from £208 billion for 1978–9 expressed in 1992–3 prices. The ratio of GGE (including transfer payments) to gross domestic product (GGE/GDP) showed an increase from 37 per cent in 1963 to 49 per cent by 1975 and a fall to 43 per cent in 1977 (data sources as for Table 7.1). The fall was partly accounted for by the exclusion of nationalised industries' investment after 1976 but also reflected a sharp cut in public sector investment advised by the International Monetary Fund. In 1979, the incoming Conservative government set out to reduce GGE/GDP but the opposite happened, so the target was revised in 1980. Real government spending was planned to fall for the next four years. As can be seen from Table 7.1, this did not happen either. Real expenditure was roughly constant in the mid-1980s, after which it started to rise again. GGE/GDP fell from 1983 to 1990 mainly reflecting the rise in GDP. The fall in income in 1991, together with the rise in government expenditure,

Table 7.1   General government expenditure 1978–9 to 1992–3 (£bn except for row 4)

	1978–9	1981–2	1984–6	1987–8	1990–1	1992–3
1. GGE excluding privatisation proceeds of which:	75	121	153	178	222	269
2. GGE on services	65	104	132	154	197	242
3. debt interest	7	13	16	18	18	18
4. (1) as % of GDP[1]	44	47	47	42	40	45
5. GGE in real terms[2]	208	222	238	243	247	269
6. Privatisation proceeds	0	0.5	2	5	5	8

Notes: [1] The figures for GDP have been adjusted (down by *c.* 1.8%) before 1990 to allow for the effects of the community charge.
[2] Cash figures adjusted to 1992–3 price levels by excluding the effects of general inflation.
Note that row 5 figures have been reduced by privatisation proceeds. Cash terms for rows 1, 2, 3, 6.
Source: HMSO (1994–5), Tables 1.2, 1.3, 1.4.

raised the ratio sharply in the early 1990s. The United Kingdom was about at the OECD average in 1986 for the size of the public sector. It should be noted that almost half the expenditure is on transfer payments which influence spending decisions in the private sector, but do not require the transfer to and use of factors of production in the public sector other than the cost of administering the transfers. The absorption of factors of production directly into the public sector represents just over 20 per cent of gross domestic product.

A very worrying aspect of the growth of GGE concerns the low ratio of capital to current spending in the public sector. From 1974 to 1979 capital spending divided by GGE had fallen by 40 per cent. Gross domestic capital formation, before subtracting sales of assets, increased from £8 billion in 1980 to £12 billion in 1992 (figures in 1985 prices from the *Blue Books* (the UK's National Accounts), table 9.3) but public sector capital formation has still not returned to 1974 levels in real terms. Much of the public sector capital stock is in a bad state of repair. For example, a National Audit Office report (quoted in the *Observer* of 22.3.92) said that £3 billion was needed for repairs to schools alone. This issue is not pursued further here, since it will be referred to in Chapter 11.

7.3   Components of government expenditure

It is useful to distinguish four main reasons why an item of government spending might grow. The first is because of a demand for increased quality. The demands for health and education are thought to grow as income increases. There is some dispute about whether the income elasticity is above or below one. Above one would indicate an increasing proportion of income going on that item. For health and education the income elasticity of demand is certainly greater than zero, indicating increased real expenditure through time to satisfy the demand for increased quality of service. Examples of increased quality would be lower pupil to teacher ratios, improved forms of treatment for medical conditions and longer patient time with doctors. The second reason for growth of expenditure is also connected with demand, namely to satisfy an increased need due to a structural change in the economy. An ageing population means that the demands on the health service increase and more pensions have to be paid. Similarly, a rise in the birth rate would, in five years, give rise to a need for more primary school places and teachers. Although each pensioner or pupil would be getting the same quality of service as before, the increased numbers push up government spending.

On the cost side we get the other two reasons for an increase in GGE – increases in the costs of inputs and increases in the prices of inputs. A good example of the former comes from defence. External defence is regarded as successful if potential aggressors can be deterred. The increasing sophistication of military equipment drives up the cost of achieving external defence without deriving any extra benefits (ignoring spillover effects of research for non-military purposes). The price of inputs increases whenever salaries rise relative to productivity and, as many forms of government spending are labour-intensive, the scope for productivity gains is often less than in industries that set the lead in wage bargaining. The price of inputs also rises if bureaucratic factors expand the personnel employed in producing a given public service without giving an increased ouput.

In the 1980s, government White Papers on expenditure put much more emphasis on restraining costs than on estimating the needs for government services. Formally, the objectives of the Financial Management Initiative (FMI) that was introduced in 1982 covered assessment of outputs and performance in relation to objectives, which would involve demand assessment. But the White Papers seemed to stress the other objectives of FMI, namely making the best use of resources ('value for money') and acquiring information, particularly about costs. Costing of programmes had been done on a regular basis since 1961 under the Public Expenditure Survey Committee system (PESC) which provides the basis for the public expenditure White Papers. Demand studies had been conducted under Programme Analysis and Review (PAR) although the information was never published. The Heath government introduced PAR in 1970 but it was abandoned in 1980, in line with the emphasis that was going to be placed on costs and the introduction of market system influences into the public sector. In addition the National Audit Office was set up in 1984 to provide independent advice to the government and suggestions for improving efficiency and effectiveness.

It is extremely difficult to define and measure efficiency in most areas of public spending. The level of health or education of the nation cannot be measured directly and evaluation of the benefits from health and education is problematical, therefore. Some benefits, like those from defence, are impossible to assess in a monetary sense and thus value of benefits cannot be equated with costs. To try to deal with these difficulties, in the 1980s performance indicators were developed. Targets for output, costs and dates for achieving programmes were set. Performance indicators rarely involve a final output measure. Various alternatives are used, such as intermediate output, or the gap between supply and demand, or input use. The difficulty with intermediate and input yardsticks is that when a change in output is linked to a single input change the effect may have been caused by substitution of extra inputs of some other factor or efficiency gains from all inputs together. The scope for performance indicator gains can be pushed too far if other measures are not used to check reliability. For example, gains from hospital bed turnover could be offset by re-entry of newly discharged patients.

Better information about demands and needs would help analysis about what are reasonable levels of public provision of a good or service. Some areas obviously should not have queues forming, examples being emergency medical treatment or response of a fire engine; but how many emergencies should it be possible to deal with simultaneously? There cannot be provision for all eventualities. Costs of provision are positive but a zero price charged to users means that no demand is choked off by the price mechanism. Thus in some situations economic efficiency requires that not all demand be satisfied and possibly queues form. Not satisfying demand and long waiting times can be carried too far; for instance, there would be no point in a 1-year waiting list for abortions.

Government expenditure is made up of the items shown in Table 7.2 together with interest payments on the national debt, which are shown in Table 7.1. Debt interest was approximately 10 per cent of total GGE in the 1980s but is now a smaller fraction. Apart from debt interest the main components of GGE are social security payments, the NHS, education and defence. The largest fall in Table 7.2 occurred for housing. The fall was not quite as dramatic as it appears since the value of house sales is subtracted from the expenditure figures. The other area to show a significant fall was trade and industry. Defence increased its share of GGE in the early 1980s. The government objective had been for a real rate of growth for defence of 3 per cent per annum, but this objective was dropped in the late 1980s and the share of defence fell back again. In the 1990s defence expenditure may decline further if the 'peace dividend' materialises. However, careful planning is needed if benefits are to ensue – with unemployment high a large reduction in defence personnel would not yield immediate dividends. Education formed a marginally smaller proportion of total spending in 1992–3 than it did in 1978–9.

Table 7.2   General government expenditure on services (% of total)

	1978–9	1984–5	1990–1	1992–3
1. Defence	11.5	13.0	11.2	9.8
2. Trade and industry	4.7	3.9	2.3	2.2
3. Employment and training	1.7	2.3	1.5	1.4
4. Transport	4.6	4.3	4.1	4.4
5. Housing	7.0	3.7	2.5	2.6
6. Other environmental services	3.8	3.0	3.7	3.7
7. Law and order	3.9	4.7	5.8	5.9
8. Education and science	14.0	13.3	14.5	13.3
9. Health	12.0	12.7	14.2	14.4
10. Social security	26.0	30.2	30.1	33.0
11. Other	9.8	8.9	10.1	9.3
Total	100.0	100.0	100.0	100.0

Notes: 1. The share of housing is reduced by sales of dwellings being subtracted from the actual expenditure for 1984–5, 1990–1 and 1992–3.
2. The table excludes debt interest.
Sources: HMSO (1994–5b) Table 2.4 for the first three columns; HMSO (1994–5a) Table 1.2 for 1992–3.

Social security had the largest increase, mainly in the earlier part of the period. The change was due to an increase in the number of pensioners (not the value of the basic pension, though outgoings on the State Earnings-Related Pension increased) and to an increase in the number of people unemployed. The increase in the number of low income households led to greater spending on housing and supplementary benefits (see the next chapter for a fuller discussion of social security issues). Government expenditure on the NHS increased as a proportion of the total, as is shown in Table 7.2, and it increased in real terms from £22 billion in 1978–9 to £35 billion in 1992–3 (figures in 1992–3 prices). But such figures do not tell enough about the true trends in health expenditure since relative price effects (RPE) are excluded.[1] Nor do they tell us about the demand for health provision.

Total spending in real terms (based on data in the government White Paper, Cm. 2519) increased by 3 per cent for defence, 44 per cent for health and 25 per cent for education between 1980–1 and 1992–3. These figures can be compared with information from Table 9.3 of the 1993 *Blue Book* which gives changes in real terms adjusted for the RPE. On this basis, the volume of real spending for the same period fell by 2 per cent for defence and increased by 2 per cent for education and 24 per cent for health. The figures are for final consumption only but this was the major component of expenditure. (Gross domestic capital formation divided by current expenditure in 1990 was 3% for defence and 6% for both health and education – data from *Blue Book*, 1994a, Table 9.4.)

Unfortunately, a more complete picture of the volume of real spending is not provided in official sources. Patchy information is given in the White Papers but a systematic examination of the volume of spending and the need for it is not provided. Specific research inquiries are needed to get a better picture. One such study is provided by Le Grand, Winter and Woolley in Hills (1990). They point out that not all spending on health is funded by the government. Private health spending was equivalent to 3 per cent of NHS expenditure in the late 1980s and prescription charges were about 3 per cent. Also patients bear indirect costs of travel and waiting time; but government expenditure is still the main component of health spending. Le Grand *et al.* compare the annual growth rates for the NHS for the period 1973–4 to 1978–9 with the period 1978–9 to 1987–8. For the latter period the annual rate of growth in real terms was 2.8 per cent and in volume terms, i.e. allowing for the RPE, it was 0.9 per cent, while need grew at 0.8 per cent. (The earlier period figures were volume growth of 4.4% against need of 0.2%). These figures ignore any change in demand, as opposed to need, and also any efficiency gains – which are estimated by Le Grand *et al.* to be about 2 per cent of the budget in the late 1980s. The probability is, however, that demand was outstripping provision in the 1980s. Spending on the NHS has increased since 1990 in connection with the market-style changes that have been introduced but it is too early yet to judge how significant the changes have been. Market-style reforms may improve efficiency and lead to a greater awareness of consumer preferences but Le Grand in Hills (1990) argues that the cost savings claimed for the introduction of quasi-markets into the public sector may not materialise. Higher administrative costs may result from the procedures, and higher labour costs may occur if unions bargain with smaller units instead of a large monopsonist.

GGE on housing consists mainly of new house building and subsidies to tenants. The figures are usually presented net of privatisation proceeds so appear to be lower than a comparison with, for instance, the 1970s would indicate (since no privatisation was going on then). A dramatic fall took place in capital formation. Public sector completions in Great Britain were 131 000 in 1978 (stock was 6.5 m) and 4000 in 1992 (stock was 4.8 m). In that time 1.8 m council houses were sold. Originally the sales were meant to provide funds for new building, but central government restrictions meant that new building in the public sector continued to decline throughout the 1980s. Private rented plus housing association stock fell by 0.5 m. The lack of sufficient rental accommodation developed into a more serious problem in the 1980s with increases in homelessness and people in temporary accommodation (see Hills and Mullings in Hills (1990)). Between 1978 and 1992 the total housing stock increased by 2 m and owner-occupier stock by 4 m. Over-encouragement of the latter led in the 1991–2 recession to a large number of repossessions.

The subsidy component of local authorities' housing revenue account (HRA) expenditure (data from the *Blue Book*) was 58 per cent of the total in 1978 and 61 per cent in 1992. Rents were increased but there was a larger concentration of low income tenants, as only the better-off had been able to purchase their house. The form of the subsidy changed away from general contributions from central and local government to the HRA (which reduce rents on average) towards benefits for individual tenants. (Local authority subsidies, called 'Rate Fund Contribution', were stopped on central government instruction after 1990.) Rent rebates, re-named housing benefits after 1982, formed 12 per cent of HRA in 1978 and 49 per cent in 1992. Housing benefits depend negatively on income and positively on rent paid. Thus the structure has good features but the benefit rates became less generous in the period under consideration. If we ignore ownership of dwellings as being of mainly political interest, and judge housing expenditure against the two objectives of increasing the number of dwellings and providing housing assistance to the poor, it can be seen that policy has been only partly successful. The number of public sector houses built (and the total for all sectors) has been very low by post-war standards but the subsidy system overall improved, in that a greater proportion of the subsidies became progressive.

7.4 Taxation

Income and expenditure are the main bases for taxation in the United Kingdom, with taxes on income including income tax, national insurance contributions and corporation tax and taxes on expenditure including value added tax and excise tax. The primary object of taxation is to raise revenue to finance government expenditure. So one criterion for a successful tax is whether it can yield a substantial revenue net of collection costs. Two main principles have been proposed to justify an individual's contribution; these are the ability to pay and benefits received. Ability to pay involves horizontal equity, namely that people in identical circumstances should pay the same amount of tax ('equal treatment of equals') and vertical equity, namely that people should pay according to their means ('the rich should pay more than the poor'). In the UK tax system, the ideas behind horizontal equity give rise to different allowances to reflect different family circumstances. When considering vertical equity it is useful to classify taxes into poll, regressive, proportional and progressive taxes. With a poll tax each person pays the same amount. A tax is regressive when the proportion of income paid in tax declines as income increases. A poll tax is the extreme form of regressive tax, other forms having the absolute amount paid in tax increasing as income increases. Under a progressive tax the proportion of income paid in tax increases as income increases. A regressive tax could, therefore, satisfy the criterion of 'the rich pay more than the poor', if the phrase is interpreted in an absolute sense; but usually ability to pay is associated with a progressive tax in the sense just defined.

The benefit principle tries to bring market ideas into the public sector. Under it people should pay taxes in accordance with the benefits they receive from public expenditure. The benefit principle appears to have a certain plausibility. However, as we saw in the previous section, it is almost impossible to establish just how much people value public goods and services. If it were the only guide for taxation, the benefit principle would deny a redistributive role for the government budget. In practice it provides a justification for few of the UK taxes. The tax on petrol can be thought of as a tax on a complement in lieu of a user charge for roads. Employees' national insurance contributions (NICs) can be regarded on average as paying for pensions (but other taxes also help the 'fund'). At the individual level, contributions do not match amounts received in pensions or unemployment benefits. Local rates provided a residue of the benefit principle in that taxes rose with the rental value of property as did consumption of some but not all local services. The largest item of local expenditure is education, so the link behind the benefit principle relating to local rates is very tenuous.

Neither the benefit nor ability-to-pay approaches to taxation get us very far in examining economic issues. It is better to turn to the effects of taxes on the level of activity of the economy, the distribution of well-being and the allocation of resources. The first two areas are dealt with elsewhere (especially in Part 1, and Chapter 8). This chapter concentrates on efficiency although we need to bring in distributional aspects also.

Taxes affect three sets of choices in markets. Labour market effects are discussed in Chapter 11. Choices about which current goods or services to buy and hence the relative sizes of different industries and choices about whether to consume now or in the future are discussed here. Figure 7.2 shows two

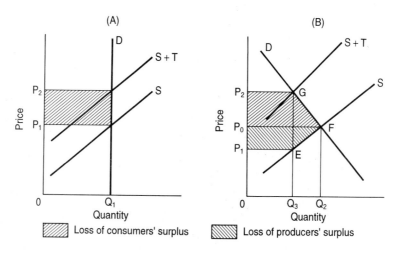

Figure 7.2   Effect of tax on a good.

cases of the effect of a unit tax on a good. In case A, demand for the product is completely inelastic. Supply without the tax is S, giving equilibrium at P_1Q_1, and with the tax it is $S + T$, giving P_2Q_1. Revenue is the shaded area. In case B, demand is more elastic and the effect of the tax is to reduce the amount traded from Q_2 to Q_3 and push up price from P_0 to P_2 (tax revenue in case B is $(OP_2 - OP_1) \times OQ_3$). In case A there is no loss of producer surplus and the loss of consumer surplus is equal to the tax revenue. In case B the combined loss of producer and consumer surplus is greater than tax revenue by area EFG, which is called an 'excess burden', a form of efficiency loss. Excess burdens increase as demand or supply becomes more elastic as Figure 7.2 shows. Similar arguments hold for choices between consuming goods now and goods in the future, i.e. for decisions about consumption or asset accumulation.

There are two types of taxes on commodities – unit taxes and *ad valorem* taxes. A unit tax is constant per unit of output and an *ad valorem* tax is proportional to the price or value of the commodity. Figure 7.2 shows the effect of a unit tax such as the UK excise duties. An *ad valorem* tax such as value added tax (VAT) is most conveniently shown in a diagram as a downwards movement of the demand curve in a wedge-shaped manner, the demand curves before and after tax coinciding at zero price, i.e. where value is zero. Subsidies can be dealt with as negative taxes and exemptions from any tax base act like subsidies.

Where resource allocation is originally efficient, taxes have harmful effects which are greater the higher the elasticities of supply and demand. If, however, there are existing inefficiencies in resource allocation, taxes may be used to counter the inefficiencies in market provision. The use of taxes to restrict output has been proposed to counteract too rapid a depletion of natural resources, e.g. fossil fuels. The argument that markets are inefficient rests on the view that people underestimate the benefits to themselves and future generations. Not all economists concur with this view. There is more general agreement that external costs can justify taxes since markets would otherwise be producing too much of that good (see Chapter 6). External costs to the health service could justify some taxation of alcohol and tobacco and pollution costs could justify taxes on petrol. Taxes have also been advocated for harmful products which would be an additional reason for taxing alcohol and tobacco. This paternalistic argument does not correspond to economic efficiency as consumers' preferences would not be determining the optimal level of output. Nevertheless, many people would agree with taxes on betting, alcohol and tobacco on these grounds. Note that one argument for taxing tobacco, namely that demand is relatively inelastic, is inconsistent with the paternalistic argument. Also, because tobacco expenditure forms a high proportion of low income budgets, there is an adverse effect on income distribution.

Taxes have effects in many areas simultaneously; therefore, it is worth looking at the trade-off between efficiency and equity. The standard argument is that the higher taxes needed to reduce higher incomes in order to improve equity lead to greater distortions in the market or reduced supply of resources and thus have greater efficiency costs. We look at exceptions to the standard rule in relation to the tax base and tax rates. Distortions to choices are introduced by exemptions from the tax base. If one form of income is taxed, there are stronger allocative effects than could occur if all income were taxed. Exemptions from income tax for superannuation contributions and Personal Equity Plans (PEPs) introduce distortions into the choices made about future income. Their removal would be a progressive measure since the benefits accrue primarily to higher income groups. The exemption of housing income and capital gains for owner occupiers is a good example of a system which achieves neither of the two main objectives of successive governments' housing policy since 1945. The objectives were to provide more dwellings and to assist poorer households to acquire satisfactory accommodation. Rather than the provision of more units, tax relief for housing has encouraged the production of larger dwellings since the subsidy increases with the value of the dwelling. The largest subsidies accrue to higher income ranges so the second objective is not achieved either. For further discussion of this issue, see Welham (1982).

Equity and efficiency do not necessarily conflict when the effect of a tax change is separated into average and marginal rate effects. The change in the average rate equates to the income effect of a price change and the marginal rate to the substitution effect. A higher average rate of tax on income makes people worse off and they take less leisure. A higher marginal rate reduces the reward for working an extra hour and people take more leisure. So, if a progressive tax change increased the average rather than the marginal rate, there would be an increase in labour supply and a gain in equity.

Finally, before we look at the tax changes since 1979, let us look at the main base for tax purposes. Wealth could serve as a tax base but its role in the UK system has never been very important; however, it is discussed more fully in Chapter 8. The main base could be either income or expenditure. As we do not have a personal expenditure tax in the United Kingdom (i.e. a tax based on the aggregation of all of a person's expenditure in a period and possibly on a progressive scale), we will proceed on the assumption that a comprehensive measure of income is the appropriate yardstick for a neutral tax system. A neutral tax on either income or expenditure would treat all forms of saving equally (the former taxing all savings, the latter taxing none) and thus would not introduce distortions into capital markets. A comprehensive income tax (CIT) would tax all forms of real income equally. Any compensation for decline in real capital values due to inflation is not an appropriate part of the base. Interest receipts should therefore be included on a real not a nominal basis. Particular forms of income should not be exempt for tax purposes although personal exemptions can be justified for removing a subsistence element from income and for administrative convenience in removing very low income people from the tax net.

The total tax burden in the United Kingdom increased between 1980 and 1990 from 36 per cent to 43 per cent of gross national income at factor cost and the United Kingdom changed from ninth highest to eleventh ranking out of 16 OECD countries (source of data, *Economic Trends*, 1992). Thus there was no dramatic shift by international standards.

Changes in the proportions of total revenue contributed by the main taxes in 1978 and 1993 are shown in Table 7.3. The taxes that showed the largest increase were VAT, up from 9 per cent to 21 per cent and corporation tax, up 2 per cent. Taxes that declined in relative importance were income tax (down 6%), social security contributions and alcohol duties. Petroleum revenue tax (PRT) appeared relatively small in 1978 and 1993 but contributed £7.4 billion in 1985. Overall, the table suggests a relatively stable tax structure, but this hides a large number of tax changes in budgets from July 1979 onwards.

The broad thrust of the Conservatives' fiscal strategy was to reduce the importance of income taxes because they believed income taxes had strong disincentive effects. They also sought to reduce the tax burden on higher incomes. The resulting reduction in the redistributive power of the budget is discussed in Chapter 8. There is not space here to give all the tax changes after

Table 7.3 Government revenue from taxation

	1978		1993	
	£bn	% of total	£bn	% of total
1. *Taxes on income* of which	22	39	73	35
income tax	19	33	58	27
corporation tax	3	5	15	7
petroleum revenue tax	0.2	—	0	—
2. *Taxes on expenditure*[1] of which	16	28	78	37
VAT	5	9	44	21
tobacco	2	4	6	3
oil	2	4	12	6
alcohol	2	4	5	2
3. *Taxes on capital* of which	1	2	2	1
death duties	0.3		1	
capital gains	0.5		1	
4. Social security contributions	12	21	39	18
5. Rates/community charge/council tax	6	11	21	10
Total	57	101	211	101

Notes: [1] Excludes national insurance surcharge in 1978 – it is included in row 4 and exludes business rates in 1992 which are included in row 5.

Sources: for 1993, *UK National Accounts (1994)* Tables 7.2, 7.3, 8.1, 9.6.
  for 1978, *National Income and Expenditure (1980)* Tables 7.2, 8.1, 9.7.

1979 but some of the major changes are noted below (see Johnson (1991) for fuller details).

Income is taxed in the following way. Most income is liable but some forms of income are not included on the tax forms, e.g. imputed rent from owner-occupier housing, some interest on government securities and superannuation contributions. From income that is declared certain allowances, such as the single person, married and age-related allowances, are offset to establish taxable income, which is then taxed at different rates. In 1995–6 the rates are 20 per cent on the first £3200 of taxable income, 25 per cent on the next £21 100 and 40 per cent on the rest. In 1978–9 the rates varied from 25 per cent on the first £750 of taxable income through 33 per cent on the next £7250 and eight more intermediate steps, until 83 per cent was paid on taxable income above £24 000. In addition, in 1978–9 there was an investment income surcharge of 10 per cent or 15 per cent with its own allowance. Investment income could thus be liable for a maximum rate of tax of 98 per cent. It can be seen that the income tax structure has been greatly simplified. The higher rates were removed in stages and the investment income surcharge was abolished in 1980.

Much of the simplification and the removal of the highest rates can be regarded as worthwhile. However, a highest rate of 40 per cent is too low from an equity viewpoint and is low by international standards. The removal of the investment income surcharge leaves earned income paying a higher rate when the combined effects of income tax and NICs are taken into account. An investment income surcharge can be justified on the grounds that labour income lasts until retirement, but asset income can run in perpetuity, and also on a second best argument, namely as a proxy for a tax on wealth. The investment incomes of husband and wife were no longer aggregated for tax purposes after 1990 – a move that has mainly benefited higher income couples. Separate taxation of husband and wife is to be welcomed in principle though it has had little impact as yet, apart from the one mentioned.

Other income tax changes of note were the removal of mortgage interest deductions at the higher rate of relief in 1991 and phasing the standard rate of relief down to 20 per cent in 1994–5 and down subsequently in 5 per cent annual stages. The ceiling has been held at £30 000 since 1983, thus reducing the real value of housing subsidies to the individual. Three changes shifted the income tax system in the direction of a CIT, namely removing the relief for new life insurances premiums after 1984, increased taxation of fringe benefits and the merging of capital gains tax (CGT) and income tax in 1988. (Features of CGT that do not conform to a CIT are the exemption of gains occurring before 1982; it is payable on realisation not accrual of gains; there are large allowances; and liability is removed on death.) However, there were also moves away from a CIT, with increased exemptions for income tax and/or capital gains tax for the Business Expansion Scheme (1983), Personal Equity Plans (1986), profit related pay (1987) and tax exempt special savings accounts (1990). The net cost of these four items in 1992–3 is estimated at £950 million (data from *Inland Revenue*

Statistics, HMSO, 1993.) The same source gives tax relief for housing as £6 billion, for occupational pensions as £8 billion and personal allowances as £25 billion. Erosion of the tax base drives up the marginal rates of tax on what base is left and thus magnifies efficiency costs of taxation. Choices about which assets to save are strongly affected by the exemptions from the income tax system. The assets favoured include housing, pensions and schemes such as the formalised ones just mentioned. What is not subsidised is straightforward purchase of shares in companies.

NICs are paid by employers and employees. The employee rate used to have several bands but in 1995–6 there are two – a small 2 per cent band and 10 per cent for earnings up to £22 880 per annum. (An 8.2% rate replaces the 10% one for employees contributing to occupational pension schemes.) When income tax is combined with the standard NIC rates, an employee's marginal rate of tax varies from 2 per cent through 10 per cent, 30 per cent, 35 per cent, 25 per cent and finally 40 per cent. In other words there was a dip in the marginal rate at the ceiling for NICs. The ceiling for employers' contributions was abolished in 1985. The maximum rate in 1995–6 is 10.2 per cent. Together employer and employee NICs introduce a wedge of about 20 per cent between what a firm pays and what the employee receives in pre-income-tax earnings.

For low-income people, the combined effects of NICs, income tax and loss of social security benefits gives rise to very high marginal rates of 'tax', sometimes over 100 per cent. The situation whereby a considerable increase in gross earned income leaves a person almost no better off or even worse off is called the poverty trap. The reductions in income tax rates after 1979 helped to lower the marginal rates but NICs were increased and this partially offset the income tax effect. In 1985 lower bands for NICs of 5 per cent and 7 per cent were brought in but at each new band the higher rate applied to all earnings. This effect was unchanged in 1989 with a 2 per cent band that applied to everyone's earnings, and the other lower bands were removed. In the mid-1980s the effective marginal rate of tax was between 94 per cent and 127 per cent (comprising income tax, NICs, loss of family income supplement (FIS) of 50% and loss of housing benefits of 9–38%). In 1985 a married couple with two children could not increase their net income despite a gross income increase from £60 to £140 per week.

In 1988 family credit replaced FIS and housing benefit was reformed. Anyone with measurable wealth greater than £6000 was ineligible. Tapers (the rate of benefit loss) of 70 per cent for family credit and 85 per cent for housing benefit applied after 1988 but they related to net income not gross income. The poverty trap rates could no longer be above 100 per cent. For the income range £60–120 the marginal rate was effectively 97 per cent in 1989–90 (made up of income tax 25%, NIC 9%, family credit loss 46.2% and housing benefit loss 16.8%; see Brown and Jackson (1990) for fuller details). The worst features of the poverty trap had been reduced but there still remained a serious problem of marginal rates very near 100 per cent.

There are problems in trying to devise a scheme for reducing the poverty trap for working people with low incomes. To do so would mean creating a greater difference in net income between the bottom and the top of the trap. Lowering net income below the trap would reduce living standards for families already in poverty. This is the cheap but nasty way. However, it was the basis of the 1988 reform. Increasing net income at the top of the trap could be achieved by lowering either the rate of tax or the rate of benefit loss. Tax threshold increases tend to push the whole poverty trap higher up the income scale unless the threshold occurs in the trap. Tax changes apply to all taxpayers and cost too much unless offsetting tax increases are brought in higher up the income scale. Tax changes have relatively little effect on the poverty trap rates because benefit tapers now depend on net income. The 1992 budget introduction of a 20 per cent income tax band for the first £2000 of taxable income reduced poverty trap marginal rates not by the 5 per cent drop in income tax rates but by 0.3 per cent. Even if taxes in the trap were zero, the current tapers combine to yield a marginal rate of 95.5 per cent! Thus, reform needs to come on the benefit side if the trap is to be modified; but reducing benefit rate loss would be costly. It would increase the number of people eligible for benefits and would spread the poverty trap higher up the income scale.

A significant change in the taxation of corporate income started in 1984. Corporation tax had been 52 per cent (42% for smaller companies) but many allowances existed, particularly for investment in plant and equipment. These investment allowances were scaled down drastically and the rate of tax was cut to 33 per cent (25% for smaller firms). Thus over the period the base broadened and the rates were cut. Although this is generally a move in the right direction, there is dispute about whether investment allowances are important devices for encouraging growth of the economy.

The main tax increase in the period after 1979 was in VAT. The base remained broadly the same until 1989 when water, fuel and construction were included. The rate of tax, however, jumped from a range of 8–12.5 per cent to 15 per cent in 1979 and increased again in 1991 to 17.5 per cent. The moves could have been regarded as a move towards an expenditure tax system but both changes occurred in an attempt to find revenue to replace other taxes which were cut (income tax in 1979, community charge in 1991). VAT was extended to energy in the 1993 budget, to be phased in in two stages (the second stage, however, was rejected by Parliament in late 1994). The objective was to assist in the process of reducing the budget deficits. Membership of the European Union imposed conditions on the VAT system but this has not had an undue effect on the UK government's strategy with regard to taxation. However, EU proposals for indirect taxes appeared at one stage to involve significant changes for the United Kingdom. Such items as food, transport and books were to become liable for VAT instead of being zero-rated. The imposition of VAT on food would have an adverse effect on low income families unless it was offset by an increase in benefits. The EU's June 1991 position on tax harmonisation accepted zero rating for a limited range of goods and required a normal minimum of 15 per cent for VAT. These details and the EU harmonisation rates for excise duties have yet to be finalised.

Overall the tax changes of 1979–91 had a mixture of items of merit and of demerit from an efficiency point of view. Many tax changes are not desirable, especially if they are to be subsequently reversed. 'An old tax is no tax' is a saying which illustrates that adjustments occur after a new tax, which then become less noticed and sometimes less harmful. Changes in the system always impose adjustment costs, which depend on economic agents' expectations about the likely future course of tax policy. This issue of adjustment costs, however, is outside the scope of the present chapter.

7.5   Summary and future trends

Almost certainly there has been too little government spending in many areas, for example, on education, health and housing. In particular capital expenditure is far too low. Better information about the demand for, and benefits of, public expenditure should be provided. The benefits from public expenditure are the opportunity costs of tax cuts.

Despite the impression created by the switch away from the personal income tax towards indirect taxes, the overall burden of taxation increased in the 1980s. The 1990s are likely to reinforce this trend away from income taxes because of an ideological view that it would encourage incentives to work.

Changes in government expenditure and taxes in the next few years are likely to be dominated by the attempt to reduce government borrowing. The government started the process in November 1993 with the extension of VAT to energy from 1994. Even if the political commitment to lowering – or at least not raising – income tax rates is kept, broadening the base to include items currently exempt, such as owner-occupier housing, superannuation payments and many savings schemes, would provide revenue to reduce the amount of borrowing and increase efficiency by standardising the tax treatment of savings. The phased reduction of mortgage interest relief is a step in this direction.

Questions for discussion

1. Which goods and services should the public sector provide?
2. Are changes in the ratio (GGE/GDP) important?
3. How can the appropriate level of government expenditure on health be determined?
4. What are the main reasons for the growth of government expenditure?
5. How do taxes impair economic efficiency?

6. Under what circumstances can the allocative effects of taxes be justified?
7. Explain the basic structure of the UK income tax system.
8. Have the Conservative government's tax changes improved resource allocation?
9. Were government's housing objectives achieved in the 1980s?
10. What is the poverty trap? How can it be reduced?

Notes

1. Notice that these volume changes are not the same thing as the real GGE changes discussed later (Table 7.1) since the GDP deflator is used then. What is needed for volume planning is the appropriate price index for each spending department which may be higher or lower than a general price index. The difference between the GDP deflator and the price index for a particular form of expenditure is called the 'relative price effect' (RPE).
2. In simple macroeconomic models, it is this that we usually refer to as G, rather than the broader concept of public spending used in this chapter.

References and further reading

Brown, C.V. and Jackson, P.M. (1990) *Public Sector Economics*, 4th edn (especially Chapters 6 and 18) Oxford: Blackwell.

Ermisch, J. (1991) 'Housing policy and resource allocation' *Oxford Review of Economic Policy* Autumn.

Hills, J. and Mullings, B. (1990) 'Housing: A decent home for all at a price within their means?' in *The State of Welfare* Hills, J. (ed.), Oxford: Oxford University Press.

HMSO (1980) *National Income and Expenditure*, London: HMSO.

HMSO (1992) 'International comparisons of taxes and social security contributions in 20 OECD countries 1979–1989' *Economic Trends* London: HMSO.

HMSO (1993) *Inland Revenue Statistics 1993*, London: HMSO.

HMSO (1994a), 'United Kingdom national accounts' *Blue Book*, London: HMSO.

HMSO (1994b) *Public Expenditure: Statistical supplement to the financial statement and budget report 1994–95*, Cm. 2519, London: HMSO.

Johnson, C. (1991) *The Economy Under Mrs. Thatcher* Chapters 3 and 4, London: Penguin.

Keen, M. (1991) 'Tax reform' *Oxford Review of Economic Policy*, Autumn.

Le Grand, J., Winter, D. and Woolley, F. (1990) 'The national health service: safe in whose hands?' in *The State of Welfare* Hills, J. (ed.), Oxford: Oxford University Press.

Likierman, A. (1988) *Public Expenditure* (especially Chapter 5), London: Penguin.

Welham, P.J. (1982) 'The tax treatment of owner-occupier housing in the UK' *Scottish Journal of Political Economy*, 29 (2).

Wilkinson, M. (1992) *Taxation* Chapters 6, 7 and 9, London: Macmillan.

CHAPTER 8

The distribution of income and wealth

PHILIP WELHAM

8.1 Introduction

Income in any period is the flow of earnings which results from the employment of a nation's factors of production. Wealth is a stock and is measured at a moment in time. Wealth is the value of two of the factors of production, namely land and capital. The relevant measure of wealth for our purposes is marketable wealth of the personal sector and corresponds broadly to the nation's land and capital outside the government sector. Public sector assets also yield welfare but the benefits cannot easily be attributed to particular individuals. Thus distributional studies focus on marketable wealth. Both income and wealth contribute to a person's welfare.

The welfare or wellbeing of an economy depends not just on total income or wealth but also on the distribution of income and wealth between different households or individuals. Welfare involves both efficiency and equity aspects. Economists agree that more income is preferable to less income and can thus study efficiency issues objectively. Equity is more difficult to assess since it involves comparisons between individuals and thus value judgements have to be made. Equity issues require decisions about whether welfare has increased when one person gains while another loses and hence whether more or less inequality is desirable. More equality usually, although not always, involves less efficiency. Glyn and Miliband (1994) argue that the extent to which more equality leads to inefficiency has been greatly overstated and in many areas more equality could accompany increased efficiency. Different economists rarely agree on what is a desirable degree of inequality. However, most would regard a move towards greater equality as being desirable provided the efficiency losses were not too severe. Most people would also accept the value judgement that households should have sufficient means to avoid poverty.

When we come to measure the distribution of income and wealth we meet the difficulty of trying to summarise a large number of observations by means of a single indicator, or a short list of statistical indicators. The usual ways in which distributions are shown in official studies are by means of a Lorenz curve, showing the percentage shares in income or wealth of different groups of the population, e.g. the top 1 per cent or 20 per cent, or by a Gini coefficient. The Lorenz curve (see Figure 8.1) plots the cumulative percentage of households (ranked usually from the lowest income to the highest) against the cumulative share of their income. If every household had the same income the bottom 20 per cent, for instance, would have 20 per cent of total income and the Lorenz curve would be the central diagonal of the diagram or the 'line of complete equality'. The further the Lorenz curve lies from this line, the greater is the degree of inequality. Lorenz curves can be regarded as showing greater or less equality in an unambiguous way provided that they do not intersect. If the Lorenz curves do intersect, part of the distribution reflects a move to greater inequality and the rest shows a move in the opposite direction.

The Gini coefficient appears to offer a solution to this problem. The Gini coefficient measures the degree of inequality by dividing the area between the Lorenz curve and the line of complete equality (area G in the figure – the shaded area) by the total area under the line of complete equality (area OAB in the figure). A Gini value of zero means complete equality, a value of 1 means one household has all the income (sometimes the figures are expressed as percentages). The Gini coefficient provides a useful summary of degrees of inequality in general, although it has limitations even when the Lorenz curves do not intersect (see Atkinson, 1983, Chapter 3). Where the Lorenz curves do intersect it is important to know what has happened to different parts of the distributions and not to regard the Gini value as sufficient. The best way to proceed is by looking at estimates of several different quantile shares of the total. Quantiles, the generic term, can be examined for different sections of the population with, e.g. quartiles showing the shares of the four quarters, quintiles each fifth, deciles each tenth.

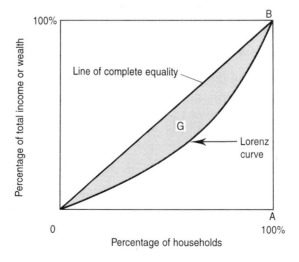

Figure 8.1 A Lorenz curve.

The sequence in this chapter is as follows. Section 8.2 looks at the broad trends in the distribution of income. Section 8.3 deals with the effect the government budget has on the distribution of income. Government expenditure yields benefits to households and taxes impose burdens so wellbeing between households is redistributed as a result of the budget. In Section 8.4 changes in the patterns of wealth holdings are presented together with a brief discussion of policy measures that redistribute wealth. In Section 8.5 poverty trends in recent years are discussed. Section 8.6 provides a summary and brief speculation about trends in the 1990s.

8.2 The distribution of income

The most comprehensive measure of the distribution of income in the United Kingdom combines data from the Survey of Personal Income (SPI) based on Inland Revenue statistics together with Family Expenditure Survey (FES) information. Income includes transfer payments from the government as well as earned and investment income. The unit for this series is the family (a single person or a married couple). Data from selected years are presented in Table 8.1 to provide a broad picture of the trends in the distribution. Care must be taken in interpreting the trends as the data are not consistent over time. The years 1938–9 and 1948–9 are based on SPI data only. The exclusion of non-taxpayers leads to an underestimate of inequality, as can be seen by the jump in the Gini coefficient in 1949 compared to 1948–9. For 1949 and 1964 mortgage interest tax relief is excluded from income – but it is included for 1978–9 and 1984–5; exclusion leads to underestimating income particularly in the top half of the distribution. It appears from Table 8.1, together with the above points about coverage, that inequality of incomes fell during the Second World War and, to a lesser degree, between 1949 and 1978–9 but increased after 1978–9. This finding holds both for the Gini coefficient and for the shares of the top 1 per cent, 5 per cent or 10 per cent of the population. As can be seen from the share of the top 50 per cent, most of the gains from the trend towards greater equality were confined to this half of the distribution.

Unfortunately, we do not have more recent data. The series was produced annually while the Royal Commission existed but the incoming Conservative government abolished the Commission in 1979. The series on family incomes was then to have been produced on a 3-year basis but it is now more than 6 years since anything was published (see *Economic Trends*, HMSO, 1987).

The data in Table 8.1 probably underestimate the degree of inequality. Inland Revenue data excluded income not declared for tax purposes, most fringe benefits and capital gains. The FES is known to be unrepresentative of certain groups like the elderly, the self-employed and those on higher incomes, and under-records casual earnings.

We can bring part of the picture more up to date by looking at the distribution of earnings data provided by the New Earnings Survey given in

Table 8.1 Distribution of family income before tax

Shares of:	1938–9	1948–9	1949	1964	1978–9	1984–5
Top 1%	17	11	11	8	5	6
Top 5%	32	23	24	20	16	19
Top 10%	41	32	33	29	26	30
Top 50%	75	73	76	77	77	78
Gini coefficient	42	36	41	40	37	41

Notes: 1. 1938–9 and 1948–9 from *Royal Commision on the Distribution of Income and Wealth* 1, Table 10.
Data based on SPI only (covers taxpayers only).
2. 1949 and 1964 ibid. Table 15. Based on SPI and FES (covers taxpayers and non-taxpayers). Data exclude mortgage interest tax relief.
3. 1978/79 and 1984/5 from HMSO (1987). Data based on SPI and FES and include mortgage interest tax relief.

Social Trends (1994). The pattern is one of a move to more unequal earnings, with the gap between the top and bottom deciles increasing through time. By April 1993 the figure for median male earnings for the top decile was £567 per week and for the bottom decile was £175 per week.

More recent data on the distribution of income are also provided by the FES alone. The FES provides five different measures of income, corresponding to various stages in the redistribution of income which we will be looking at in the next section. The nearest to the measure given in Table 8.1 is 'gross income'. The Gini coefficient for gross income was 38 per cent in 1985 and 40 per cent in 1987 (see *Economic Trends*, HMSO, 1990a). Thus it can be seen that inequality has continued to increase.

This is also confirmed by the alternative measure now used by the Central Statistical Office, namely equivalised income (equivalised income is income adjusted for household size). The Gini coefficient on this basis for gross income was 32 per cent in 1985 and 37 per cent in 1992 (see *Economic Trends*, HMSO, 1994). The unit for the FES is the household, defined as one person living alone or a group of people living at the same address and having common needs. Both the 'household' and the 'family' suffer, therefore, in having varying numbers of people in a single unit. 'Equivalised income' attempts to circumvent this problem by weighting the income by a factor reflecting the different number of adults and different ages of children in an attempt to standardise for the size of the household (for details of weights see *Economic Trends*, HMSO, 1994).

8.3 The redistribution of income

In order to assess the impact of the government's budget on the distribution of income we need to compare the before and after situations. Ideally the comparison would be between the distribution of income as it would exist in the country without a government sector – the 'counterfactual' – and the actual distribution of income after adding the benefits households get from government expenditure and subtracting the burdens ('incidence') households suffer from taxes. We cannot estimate the counterfactual because the starting point, or 'original income' as the CSO study calls it, has been affected by taxes and government benefits. There will have been, for example, effects of the budget on labour supply and on wage rates. Also, because unemployment and retirement benefits exist, households need to acquire less investment income. Original income therefore has to be the starting point.

The second set of difficulties lies in trying to assess the incidence of taxes and government expenditure. There are two types of problem, data availability and assessing economic incidence. Sufficient information on household incomes and expenditures is not available for a complete study. The FES provides the best dataset available for the United Kingdom but it has limitations, some of which have been mentioned earlier in this chapter. Economic incidence issues concern only who loses from a particular tax and how much welfare is gained by a household from government expenditures. Who gains most from defence expenditure? Is it mainly people with high income or large wealth or does everyone benefit equally? The difficulty of answering such questions has led the CSO to ignore defence expenditure in their analysis. Even for items which are included broad assumptions are made. The CSO attitude is that it will only include an item if there is a clear idea of where incidence lies. This is misleading because, as we shall see, we are also uncertain even about the items that are included. A better way to proceed would be to see how sensitive results are to alternative assumptions.

Figure 8.2 shows the effect of a tax on income under two different conditions of labour supply. The schedules labelled D in Figure 8.2 (A and B) show the

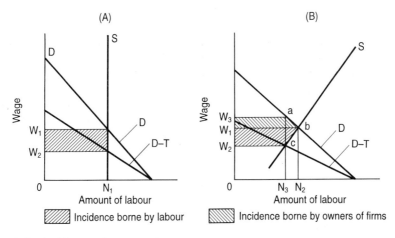

Figure 8.2   Incidence of a tax on income.

quantities of labour that firms are willing to employ at each (pre-tax) wage rate. They correspond to the conventional demand for labour schedule. The schedules labelled D–T show the after-tax wages at each level of employment, as perceived by the workers, following the introduction of a progressive income tax.

In part A labour supply (S) is completely inflexible. Prior to the introduction of the income tax, the equilibrium wage is W_1 and the amount of labour employed is N_1. The effect of the progressive income tax is to reduce the net wage rate to W_2, the level of employment remaining at N_1. In this case, the full burden of the tax is borne by the employees in the form of reduced net wages. Employees' surplus is reduced by $ON_1 \times (W_1 - W_2)$ which is exactly the same as the tax revenue.

In part B the labour supply schedule is more flexible. Initially, the equilibrium is at W_1 and N_2. Following the introduction of the tax, however, both net wages and the level of employment fall to W_2 and N_3, respectively. The pre-tax wage rate paid by the firms is driven up to W_3. In this case workers bear part of the burden of the tax, as do the owners of firms in the form of reduced employers' surplus. Employees' surplus is reduced by an amount equal to area W_1bcW_2 and employers' surplus is reduced by W_3abW_1. Tax revenue is just $ON_3 \times (W_3 - W_2)$. The two shaded triangles to the right of N_3 (area abc) represent an excess burden, i.e. a loss of surplus over and above the tax revenue. The two cases illustrate the importance of assumptions made about the incidence of taxes (similar arguments apply to taxes other than income tax).

Empirical evidence suggests that the inflexible labour supply case is more likely in competitive markets and the CSO study makes this assumption for the incidence of all income taxes. In fact both flexibility of supply and of demand affect economic incidence. The burdens of taxation are assessed by allocating tax revenue to particular groups. The excess burdens are not included because of the difficulties of trying to measure them.

In the CSO study, the burden of indirect taxes is allocated to consumers on the assumption that prices of products are raised by the amount of tax. To the extent that sales fall as a result of higher prices owners of firms will get lower profits, but this possibility is not allowed for. The benefits from government transfer payments are attributed to the recipients and the benefits of health and education spending (measured as costs of providing the service) are allocated on a pattern-of-use basis. Some items, e.g. defence and debt interest, are not included, as indicated above. The CSO study allocates approximately half of total expenditure and two-thirds of taxes, so it can be seen to be an incomplete budget that is being examined. The main taxes missing are employers' national insurance contributions, corporation taxes and business rates. One study (O'Higgins and Ruggles, 1981), includes the missing items of the CSO budget and shows the effect of alternative assumptions about incidence of some of the key budget items.

The CSO study shows that the budget leads to a reduction in inequality in all years shown in Table 8.2. The effect can be seen when original income is compared with final income, e.g. in 1979 the Gini coefficient falling from 45 per cent to 32 per cent. Note that final income is not provided by the CSO for equivalised income, four stages only to post-tax income being given. Alternatively, the redistribution can be seen by the change in the share of the bottom quintile from 0.5 per cent of original income to 7 per cent of final income in 1979. Generally the bottom 40 per cent gains and the top 40 per cent loses as a result of the budget.

Other patterns that can be seen from Table 8.2 are that inequality of original income increased in the 1980s, as noted in Section 8.2. Redistribution, measured as the change in the Gini coefficient between original and final unadjusted income increased between 1979 and 1987; but the measure using equivalised income had the gap narrowing from a difference of 15 points between original and post-tax income in 1979 to 14 points in 1992. Consequently, the change over the period of the extent to which the budget reduces inequality is ambiguous. A large number of tax and benefit changes during the 1980s shifted the balance between rich and poor in favour of higher incomes (e.g. reduction in higher income tax rates, removal of investment income surcharge and increased investment income exemptions) and away from lower incomes (e.g. linking pensions to price changes rather than changes in average earnings). Thus one would expect the budget to play a somewhat less redistributive role in 1989 than it did in 1979 for a constant distribution of original income. The shifts towards less redistribution appear clear from the majority of changes made but it was not a publicly claimed policy by the government. Finally, Table 8.2 shows that income distribution net of taxes and benefits was more unequal in 1987 (or 1992) than it was in 1979.

The various stages in the process of redistributing income are shown in Table 8.3. Two years are shown but the pattern of change can be seen to be in the same direction for both years. The major redistribution occurs between original and gross income. The adjustments made at this stage are to add in the benefits from government transfer payments, particularly the retirement pension. A further move towards greater equality occurs between gross and disposable income and is caused by allowing for the burdens of income tax, employees' national insurance contributions and rates. (Rates had been included at the next stage in earlier editions of the CSO study.) Direct taxes on income are thus broadly progressive but indirect taxes, as can be seen by the difference between disposable and post-tax income, are regressive. The net effect of the tax system is to leave the Gini coefficient unaffected.

Economists writing on other issues usually assume that the UK tax system is progressive, presumably because they are thinking primarily of the effect of direct taxes, but Table 8.3 shows the same inequality measure for both gross and post-tax income. The tax system is proportional. The rich contribute the same proportion of their income as the poor to pay for public services. Other

Table 8.2 Effects of taxes and benefits on the distribution of household income in the United Kingdom

	Unadjusted income				Equivalised income			
	Original income		Final income		Original income		Post-tax income	
Share of quintile group	1979	1987	1979	1987	1979	1992	1979	1992
Bottom	0.5	0.3	7	6	2.4	2.1	10	6.5
2nd	9	6	12	11	10	6	13	11
3rd	19	16	18	17	18	15	18	16
4th	27	27	24	24	27	26	23	23
Top	45	51	38	42	43	50	37	44
Gini coefficient (%)	45	52	32	36	44	52	29	38

Notes: (1) Equivalised income attempts to standardise for different family size; see HMSO (1994) for weights.
    (2) The income unit is the household.
Sources: 1979, 1987 unadjusted income, HMSO (1990a), p. 118.
    1979, 1992 equivalised income, HMSO (1994) pp. 122–3.

Table 8.3 Gini coefficients for the distribution of income at each stage of the tax-benefit system

Gini coefficient (%)	1979	1987
Original income	45	52
Gross income	35	40
Disposable income	33	36
Post-tax income	35	40
Final income	32	36

Source: HMSO (1990a) p. 118.

studies for other countries have reached the broad conclusion that their tax systems are neutral (i.e. roughly proportional). The final stage of the budget process – the allocation of benefits in kind such as health and education expenditure – leads to further redistribution to lower income groups. Overall, therefore, the budget does lead to a redistribution of income but it is due to the expenditure side of the budget not the tax side, with the major component of redistribution being the old age pension. O'Higgins and Ruggles (1981) conclude that the CSO study overestimates the degree of redistribution somewhat but their overall conclusions were broadly similar.

However, an important point to consider is the time scale. All the results so far derive from studies of the annual impact of the budget. The largest single contribution to redistribution comes from the retirement pension. Retired households are predominantly in the lower half of the income range in annual studies; but they would be randomly scattered through the income scale if lifetime income was considered. Pensions would then accrue not only to low income ranges but throughout the income scale, with a possible bias towards the higher end because richer people live longer. The budget redistributes, but over the life cycle rather than from rich to poor, as Welham (1990) argues.

Policy measures to reduce inequality of incomes can be separated into those that would reduce the spread of original income and changes that would increase redistribution through the budget. A minimum wage would cut off the tail of lower earned incomes but any increased unemployment that may result could offset the effect. Reduction in remuneration for high income groups has been requested at times by governments with little apparent result. Incomes policies may temporarily achieve a narrowing of earnings but such policies do not usually last for long. Thus it is not easy to see how much could be done in the short run to reduce inequality of original income. In the longer term a change in social attitudes might narrow earnings differentials somewhat, but the change most likely to reduce inequality of original income would be a significant reduction in the level of unemployment.

Budget redistribution could be increased if the benefits from government expenditure accrued more to low-income groups and the burden of taxes fell more on higher incomes. Steps to increase the benefits to low-income ranges involve increasing the benefit rate and indexing benefits to average earnings instead of retail prices. Increasing eligibility for unemployment benefits and stopping cash limits on supplementary benefit payments would help, but in a minor way. Measures to increase the tax burden on high-income groups include shifting the balance away from indirect taxes and towards income taxes, increasing the exemption limit for taxable income and increasing the higher rates of income tax.

Taxing investment income at the same or a higher rate than earned income (at present earned income is liable for income tax and national insurance contributions) would hit higher income groups and the elderly – the two main groups with investment income. When the investment income surcharge of 15 per cent was removed in 1984 it was on the grounds that the elderly would benefit. No mention was made of where the greatest part of the benefits would accrue. However, a better way of assisting the elderly would be to increase allowances for the over 65s either for all income or for investment income. Finally, measures to increase the tax base such as including imputed rent for owner-occupiers or not allowing deduction for superannuation payments, would be progressive.

8.4 The distribution of wealth

Marketable wealth, as can be seen from Table 8.4, is distributed much more unequally than is income. The information for wealth holdings comes from

Table 8.4   The distribution of wealth

| Share of wealth owners | Marketable wealth | | | | Marketable wealth plus pension rights |
| | Old series | New series | | | |
	1976	1976	1979	1991[1]	1991[1]
Top 1%	24	21	20	18	11
Top 5%	45	38	37	37	25
Top 10%	60	50	50	50	36
Top 25%	84	71	72	71	58
Top 50%	95	92	92	92	82
Gini coefficient	76	66	65	66	49

Notes: Data refer to the adult population of the United Kingdom. The unit is the individual, not the family.

See text for discussion of revisions to the data. The 'New Series' was first published in 1990.

[1] Data provisional.

Sources: 1976 and 1979, HMSO (1990b).
1991, HMSO (1993).

Inland Revenue estimates based on the value of estates at death. It is an imperfect measure because of the small sample of estates in certain categories, e.g. for young people or for estates below the exemption limit for tax purposes. Estimates for the total population are calculated by using mortality rates of different groups to get the value of estates for the living. Adjustments have to be made for types of assets that have been excluded, e.g. by being handed on in a manner that avoids tax liability. CSO estimates of the personal sector 'balance sheets' (i.e. aggregates of assets minus liabilities) are used to modify the Inland Revenue data. The revised estimates of the importance of these adjustments to wealth distributions since 1976 were issued in *Economic Trends* of October, 1990 (HMSO, 1990b). Previously the levelling off of the long-term trend to greater equality in wealth holdings was thought to start at about 1980 but the date for levelling off is now given as 1976. The main causes of the revisions are reappraisals of the importance of joint property and new estimates of small estates.

The distribution of marketable wealth has had a Gini coefficient in the range 0.64–0.67 over the period 1976–91 showing a relatively stable distribution. The share of total wealth held by the top 1 per cent has declined slightly, from 21 per cent to 18 per cent but the share of the top 10 per cent has remained at 50 per cent.

The long-term trend in the distribution of wealth is difficult to quantify due to changes in the database, but Atkinson and Harrison (1978, table 6.5) suggest that the share of the top 1 per cent fell from 61 per cent of total wealth in 1923 to 32 per cent in 1972. However, the share of the next 2–5 per cent increased slightly. The share of the top 10 per cent fell from 89 per cent to 70 per cent. Note that these figures are not compatible with those in Table 8.4 because they relate to England and Wales and do not cover property missing from the estate data, though allowance is made for the excluded population. The Royal Commission on the Distribution of Income and Wealth (HMSO, 1975) suggested that the contrary movements in shares of the top 5 per cent were due partly to attempts to avoid estate duty, and that the general levelling of the bottom 95 per cent was probably the outcome of increased standard of living and greater equality of incomes.

The composition of marketable wealth changes through time due to the relative growth of different items in absolute amounts together with different relative price movements. The main trends have been a growth in the share of life insurance and pension funds from 15 per cent in 1971 to 31 per cent in 1992 and a decline in stocks and shares from 23 per cent to 9 per cent in that period. Other changes were the increase in dwellings (net of mortgage debt) from 26 per cent of net wealth of the personal sector in 1971 to 33 per cent in 1992. In 1992 consumer durables were 5 per cent of net wealth, building society shares, bank deposits, and cash and National Savings were 18 per cent. (see *Social Trends*, 1994, table 5.22).

There are interesting variations by size of estate. In 1986 the smallest estates (under £50 000) had almost half their net wealth in housing compared with only 20 per cent for the largest estates (over £300 000) (data derived from Stark, 1990, Table 38). Life insurance policies provided another 22 per cent for the smallest estates but only 9 per cent for the largest estates. Land and company shares, however, made up 46 per cent of the net wealth of the largest estates and only 2 per cent of the smallest estates. Mortgage debt as a proportion of gross wealth declined from 9 per cent for small estates to 2 per cent for larger estates but other debt increased from 4 per cent to 6 per cent. Total debt thus declines as the size of the estate increases.

Wider definitions of wealth would include the value of human capital (the present value of future earnings) and pension rights. There are no official estimates of the distribution of wealth including human capital but *Economic Trends* gives, in addition to marketable wealth ('Series C'), marketable wealth plus occupational pensions ('Series D') and marketable wealth plus occupational and state pensions ('Series E'). The three series paint broadly the same picture for trends over the last 15 years but the degree of inequality in 1992, as measured by the Gini coefficient, is reduced from 0.66 for Series C down to 0.58 for Series D and 0.49 for Series E.

8.4.1 Redistribution of wealth

An individual's total wealth includes marketable assets together with the value, discounted back to the present, of future real income such as future earnings and pension entitlements. Proposed taxes on wealth, however, usually relate to marketable wealth only. A tax on wealth could be levied on an individual's stock of wealth but the UK system, at present, is to tax the transfer of wealth. It is easier administratively to tax once per lifetime than to have an annual wealth tax and it is normally easier for the individual to pay tax on inheritance than to have to sell off some of his/her own assets. Of the two main causes of wealth inequality – inheritance and accumulation of one's own savings – it is the former that is usually regarded as the least justified or 'deserved', and hence more appropriately taxed.

Taxation of wealth and the transfer of wealth can be justified on the grounds of ability to pay. Thus if two people have equal incomes, but one has much greater wealth, the wealth holder has the greater ability to pay taxes. Wealth confers power, prestige and influence which are not affected by income or expenditure taxes. Taxation is one of the main ways whereby existing inequalities of wealth holding could be reduced. However, in the United Kingdom taxes on the transfer of wealth form a very small part of total tax revenue. Inheritance tax (IT) brought in 0.5 per cent of tax revenue in 1992 and Capital Transfer Tax (CTT), which it replaced in 1986, brought in about 0.5 per cent in 1980. Small as it is, the effect of taxes on the distribution of wealth has been reduced since 1986. CTT was levied on estates at death and on gifts between the living but IT removed the taxation of gifts between living people, and replaced a scale of ascending rates by a flat 40 per cent in 1988. There is also a tax threshold, with estates of less than £150 000 in 1994–5 paying no tax.

8.5   Poverty

There are severe problems involved in trying to define an absolute standard for poverty for the United Kingdom in the late twentieth century. The minimum food needed for existence depends on the type of work being done, e.g. a manual worker would need more food than an office worker. Dwellings in colder areas would require more heating. If an element is to be allowed for recreation, should it allow the purchase or rental of a radio – or a black-and-white TV – or even a colour TV? Even if some minimum could be established for food, clothing, shelter and recreation would the cost of, for instance, the calories and vitamins be priced at an expert's knowledge of nutritional values purchased at the cheapest retail outlet? These kinds of difficulties have led to poverty being studied in relative rather than absolute terms. While there is no single or generally accepted measure of what constitutes poverty, the problem is often resolved by using the income level for government supplementary benefits or, more recently, 50 per cent of average earnings, as a yardstick.

There was a fall in the real living standards of the poorest decile over the period 1979 to 1991–2. Data on *Households Below Average Income* (HMSO, 1994a) show that the real median income of the bottom decile was the same before housing costs (BHC) in 1991–2 as in 1979 but once housing costs were taken into account (AHC) it was 17 per cent lower in 1991–2. Using the AHC measure the next decile up had no increase in real income while the whole population had an average increase of 36 per cent and the top decile an increase of 62 per cent. The figures may be affected by the income reported by the self-employed. Excluding the self-employed gives a fall of 9 per cent (AHC) for the bottom decile between 1974 and 1991–2. Note that the measures rely on FES data which relate to households and exclude people in residential care and the homeless. A report by the Institute of Fiscal Studies (Goodman and Webb, 1994) corrects the FES data for two biases – incorrect family types and under-representation of the rich. It shows broadly similar conclusions to HBAI, giving a fall in real (1994) income (AHC) of the poorest decile from £73 per week in 1979 to £61 in 1990 but cautions about the influence of reported self-employment income mentioned above.

Using a relative standard of poverty, the number of households below half average incomes (AHC) changed from 5.2 m (or 9 per cent) of the total in 1979 to 13.9 m (25 per cent) in 1991/2. The increase was most marked for the unemployed (1.9 m), pensioners (1.7 m), lone parents (1.7 m) and full-time workers (1.3 m) (source of data, HBAI HMSO, 1994a, table 11.11).

A combination of demographic trends and government policy caused the increase in low incomes. The ageing population led to more pensioners and the benefit levels were reduced relative to average incomes by being linked to the retail price index instead of average earnings. Unemployment levels were considerably higher in the 1980s with government policy objectives emphasising inflation rather than unemployment. Also the value of benefits was eroded by the tightening of conditions of eligibility, the taxation of benefits and abandoning of statutory indexation. Social trends led to the increase in single parent families. Government policy emphasising free market forces and reducing the role of wages councils contributed to the increased numbers of low income earners.

The failure of private markets to provide adequate insurance for all contingencies is likely to require state provision of social security. Individuals are unlikely to purchase adequate insurance against unemployment even if they have entered the labour market, nor is everyone likely to purchase adequate pension arrangements for retirement. The growth of private occupational pensions may in time reduce the amounts that the state would need to provide, but many households are likely to need a state-provided safety net at some stage during their life cycle. As we have seen, the fall in levels of state provision has contributed to increased poverty since 1979.

Government policy concentrated on incentive effects of benefits rather than the implications for household living standards. A reflection of this can be seen in the trend of replacement ratios – i.e. the ratio of income when unemployed to income when working. For a single person the figure was 22.3 per cent in 1974, 24 per cent in the later 1970s and 18.9 per cent by 1988. Similar patterns were displayed for other sizes of households. Barr and Coulter (see Hills, 1990) insist that the argument that higher replacement ratios lead to work disincentives is 'to put it no more strongly, not proven', nor is reducing the living standard of unemployed families a policy with which everyone agrees.

Perhaps the most serious aspect of the government's concentration on reducing spending rather than proving an adequate safety net can be seen in the arrangements introduced in 1988 through the Social Fund which replaced the previous discretionary payments under Supplementary Benefits for certain specific expenses or debts of low income households. Maternity payments for low income mothers and funeral expenses remained as grants but other payments such as for a cooker, bed or pair of shoes were changed to a loan repayable from future benefits. Up to 40 per cent of a single person's benefit can be deducted (there was no overall limit but limits on individual items) to meet such expenses as poll tax, gas and electricity and water bills and later for mortgage interest payments. Two major problems are that the fund is cash limited and there is no legal right of appeal against the decisions of the Social Fund officers. A National Audit Office report in February 1991 said that in 1989–90 780 000, or 34 per cent, of applicants were turned down, 23 000 of whom were refused because the applicant was too poor (!) and 195 000 because there was insufficient money in the scheme.

Policy measures to reduce poverty involve reducing the incidence of particular events occurring or increasing the payments made to low income households. We cannot, short of euthanasia, reduce the numbers of the elderly but the basic pension value can be increased. The rise in the number of single parent families is the result of social trends but increased availability of part-time work together with more adequate and better funded child-care facilities could enable single parents to enter the labour market. Low incomes from earnings could be increased by expanding rather than contracting the role of wages councils. Perhaps the single most effective measure would be to reduce unemployment (as indicated above), but for those still without a job less restrictive rules for benefits and more generously funded training schemes would lower the incidence of poverty. In addition, attention needs to be paid to increasing the take-up rate for benefits.

8.6 Summary and future trends

From 1945 to 1979 there was a reduction in the inequality of income in the United Kingdom, but income inequality increased again in the 1980s. Continued emphasis on market forces and the increased level of unemployment are likely to increase income inequality further in the 1990s. The tax system as a whole has little impact on the distribution of income but transfer payments redistribute annual income in favour of the poor. Redistribution is mainly over an individual's life cycle rather than from rich to poor (defined in terms of lifetime income). The distribution of income measured after taxes and benefits became more unequal in the 1980s and early 90s and this trend is likely to continue in the 1990s. Poverty also increased in the period, and with current government policy there does not appear to be any major reduction likely in the next few years. Falling unemployment may lead to some reduction but the overall level of unemployment is likely to remain very high. The long-term reduction in wealth inequality ceased in about 1976. Current taxation levels on wealth transfers are unlikely to cause significant redistribution of wealth and the best guess is that the stable wealth distribution since 1976 will continue.

Increased inequality of both pre- and post-budget income and the halting of the trend to lower inequality of wealth are bad news for people who desire a more egalitarian economy. What the government's attitude to inequality has been since 1979 can only be deduced from the accumulation of evidence on policy actions since pronouncements on policy towards inequality have not been forthcoming. The likelihood is that despite Mr Major's stated desire for a classless society, recent Conservative governments have not been unhappy with what has been happening to the distribution of income and wealth.

Questions for discussion

1. Explain how an increase in equality can be measured using:
   (a) Lorenz curves;
   (b) percentile shares;
   (c) Gini coefficients.
2. What problems arise in trying to measure changes in the distribution of income through time?
3. What have been the recent trends in the distribution of income and wealth?
4. How can we measure the extent to which the budget redistributes income?
5. What light does economic analysis throw on the question of who bears the burden of particular taxes?
6. 'Government expenditure has been paid for by income taxes raised from the rich.' Discuss.
7. Are taxes on wealth important in the United Kingdom? Should they be more important?
8. Is poverty a major problem in the United Kingdom?
9. What have been the main causes of the increase in poverty since 1979?
10. What can be done to reduce poverty?

References and further reading

Atkinson, A.B. (1983) *The Economics of Inequality* 2nd edn, Chapter 3, Oxford: Oxford University Press.

Atkinson, A.B. and Harrison, A.J. (1978) *Distribution of Personal Wealth in Britain* (especially Chapter 6), London: Cambridge University Press.

Barr, N. and Coulter, F. (1990) 'Social security: solution or problem?' in *The State of Welfare* Hills, J. (ed.), Oxford: Oxford University Press.

Brown, C.V. and Jackson, P.M. (1990), *Public Sector Economics* 4th edn, Chapters 15, 18 and 22, Oxford: Blackwell.

Glyn, A. and Miliband, D. (1994) *Paying for Inequality* Chapters 7 and 8, Introduction, London: IPPR/Rivers Oran Press.

Goodman, A. and Webb, S. (1994) *For Richer for Poorer; The changing distribution of income in the United Kingdom, 1961–91*, London: Institute for Fiscal Studies.

Hills, J. (1990c) *The State of Welfare* (especially Chapter 7), Oxford: Oxford University Press.

HMSO (1975) *Royal Commission on the Distribution of Income and Wealth*, Report No. 1, Cmnd. 6171, London: HMSO.

HMSO (1987) 'The distribution of income in the United Kingdom 1984/5' in *Economic Trends*, London: HMSO, November.

HMSO (1990a) 'The effects of taxes and benefits on household income 1987' in *Economic Trends*, London: HMSO, May.

HMSO (1990b) 'Estimates of the distribution of personal wealth' in *Economic Trends*, London: HMSO, October.

HMSO (1991) 'Estimates of the distribution of personal wealth II: Marketable wealth and pension rights of individuals 1976 to 1989' in *Economic Trends*, London: HMSO, November.

HMSO (1993) *Inland Revenue Statistics*, London: HMSO.

HMSO (1994) 'The effects of taxes and benefits on household income 1992' in *Economic Trends*, London: HMSO, January.

HMSO (1994a) *Households Below Average Income: A statistical analysis 1979–1991/92*, London: HMSO.

HMSO (1994b) *Social Trends*, London: HMSO.

O'Higgins, M. and Ruggles, P. (1981) 'The distribution of public expenditure and taxes among households in the U.K.' *Review of Income and Wealth* 27 pp. 298–326.

Pond, C. (1989) in *Restructuring Britain; The Changing Social Structure* Hamnett, C., McDowell, L. and Sarre, P. (eds), London: Sage.

Pond, C. (1989) 'The changing distribution of income, wealth and poverty' in *Restructuring Britain: The changing social structure*, Hamnett, C., McDowell, L. and Sarre, P. (eds), London: Sage.

Stark, T. (1990) *Income and Wealth in the 1980s* 2nd edn, London: Fabian Society, Working group papers.

Welham, P. (1990), 'The impact of the budget on lifetime income: A survey' *Journal of Economic Studies* pp. 66–84.

CHAPTER 9

Local government services and finance

GLEN BRAMLEY

9.1 Introduction

This chapter is concerned with some key contemporary policy issues affecting a particular part of the public sector, local government. It picks up some of the themes identified in the previous two chapters as they apply in this particular context. Local government is a particular institutional structure which has evolved to provide a range of public services and interventions on a decentralised basis and subject to a mechanism of local democratic accountability. As such, it raises a number of issues about the way the public sector can finance and provide public services efficiently and fairly, as well as examples of some dysfunctional aspects of public decision-making.

The three current policy issues considered relate to the reforms in the funding of local government, changes in methods of service provision involving more market-like arrangements, and reform of the structure of local government. Before looking specifically at these, this chapter briefly reviews some of the principal insights from economic theory into the role and financing of decentralised government. It also presents some basic data on trends in the size and composition of the local government sector.

9.2 Theoretical perspectives

Chapter 7 sketched out the economic theory of 'public goods', showing that although these provide a primary example of market failure calling for some form of collective or state intervention, the problem of deciding how much public goods to provide to meet the preferences of members of society was a knotty one. Public goods are central to the economic function of local government.

It has long been recognised that many public goods have the characteristic of providing benefits in a finite geographical area, rather than to the whole nation. First, there are services of the 'public utility' kind which take services directly to people's doorstep: water, energy, streets and refuse collection are all examples. Historically, most of these were developed originally by local government, although some are now operated as free-standing commercial utility companies. Secondly, there are services which are provided from a central facility to which people travel in order to make use of them: information bureaux, theatres, old people's day centres, schools and sports centres are some examples. Here the time and cost of travel limits usage and benefits to local residents. Thirdly, there are interventions which provide general environmental benefits to people within a locality, for example policing of health regulations, planning, or the provision of open space and landscaping.

Organising the provision of this class of local public goods through a decentralised structure of local government helps to solve the efficiency problem posed in Chapter 7 in a number of ways. First, local conditions vary and locally controlled provision can help to tailor what is provided to suit those local conditions in a way which is informed by local knowledge. Secondly, with democratic control over local services, decision-making can be expected broadly to reflect local preferences. Thirdly, where services are funded by local taxes or charges, that decision-making can explicitly balance the marginal perceived benefits against the marginal costs in the way that economists would regard as highly desirable on efficiency grounds. Fourthly, local government in Britain is generally open and accountable in its operations, which receive extensive coverage in the local media, and this can help to ensure that waste is kept in check. Fifthly, having multiple local agencies providing similar services enables comparisons of units costs and performance to be made on a regular basis, sometimes known as 'yardstick competition'. This practice has been promoted by the Audit Commission, which has a brief of overseeing efficiency in local government, and has been further encouraged by initiatives such as the Citizens' Charter.

Lastly, a different mechanism is also available to encourage efficiency in the 'allocative' sense (i.e. producing the right mix of services to reflect preferences) as well as widening choice. In a mobile society, people may move around from one local authority area to another, choosing localities that produce the mixture of service quantities and qualities that they prefer at different local tax rates. This mechanism, first proposed in a famous article by Tiebout (1956) has some limitations and possibly adverse side effects, but nevertheless operates to some extent to reinforce the efficiency properties of a decentralised system.

What does economics have to say about the appropriate functions of local government? The discussion so far has emphasised local public goods, but in practice local government concerns itself with a wider range of things. The standard economic view is associated with Musgrave and Musgrave (1980), who classified the economic functions of government as falling into three 'branches':

1. Stabilisation of the macro economy, through instruments of fiscal and monetary policy.

2. Redistribution of income and wealth, mainly through taxation and benefits but also through particular services like education.
3. Allocation of resources, mainly concerned with microeconomic measures to improve efficiency by correcting 'market failures'; these would include public goods, and also problems of externalities, information limitations on markets, and monopoly/imperfect competition.

Within this framework, it is generally argued that the appropriate functions of local government lie in the third (allocation) branch of policy, particularly in relation to the provision of local public goods and the regulation or correction of externalities. Where public goods or external effects spread across a wider area, so-called 'spillover effects', local decision-making alone may not be efficient. For example, major transport infrastructure generally has effects across the boundaries of individual local authorities. Solutions to these problems can involve cooperative arrangements between local authorities, higher tier county or regional authorities, or the payment of grants by central government to encourage provision for the wider good (illustrated by Figure 9.1).

Why are the first two branches of policy, stabilisation and redistribution, considered unsuitable for local government involvement? So far as stabilisation is concerned, the scope of action even for national governments is seen nowadays as rather constricted in a very globalised economy. At a local level economies are very open indeed, with flows of trade and income across local boundaries being massive. Any local fiscal policy would quickly leak out into the wider economy and be ineffective. It is impossible to operate monetary policy at any level below the nation state. Major taxes are not suitable as instruments which could vary between localities, and while local authorities might aspire to pursue policies to promote local economic development, there are serious dangers of wasteful competition between local authorities trying to attract industry.

It is also argued that redistribution is not an appropriate function for local governments (Stigler, 1957). First, this could give rise to very different levels of services, benefits and tax rates between different localities, which would be an example of the problem of horizontal inequity. Secondly, this could lead in turn to people and businesses moving from one jurisdiction to another, so-called 'fiscal migration'. For example, rich people and mobile firms would tend to move away from areas with extensive redistribution programmes and high tax rates to localities which did little and kept taxes low. In this way, local redistribution would be ultimately self-defeating, as local authorities competed to retain their taxpayers.

In the real world, local government does still engage in substantial redistributive activity. For example, education redistributes in favour of families with children, social services target frail elderly and handicapped people, and public housing is aimed mainly at low-income groups. Part of the reason for this may be historical, and it is somewhat arbitrary that some services of this kind are provided in local government while others, such as the health service, are nationally controlled. In general, redistributive local services have some characteristics which mean that local decisions and administration of service delivery still bring some of the advantages enumerated above. For example, 'community care' of frail elderly people is best organised in a way that relates to the local community that is providing much of the care. Often these services are closely linked to other naturally local functions, for example housing being linked to planning, urban redevelopment, environmental health regulation and social services.

Thus, in practice local government does provide redistributive services, so the system of financing and control must take account of this. In some cases, there is close regulation of standards so that these do not vary too much around the country. In general, grants are used to even out the costs so that these do not create an excessive burden in particular areas.

The view just presented of what local government should do (its functions) also has implications for how it should be financed. First, the efficiency benefits of local decision-making are more likely to be attained where services are predominantly funded by local taxes rather than by grants from central government. Local councillors will then have to weigh the cost of extra local taxes (possibly translated into votes) against the benefits of extra services, rather than just regarding grants as 'free money'. This discipline will be reinforced if, as in Britain, local governments are obliged to operate on balanced budget rules. Local authorities may not borrow to finance current deficits, and borrowing for capital investment is strictly controlled. These rules also largely rule out attempts by local authorities to operate their own local fiscal policies, as argued above.

If the main function of local government is to provide local public goods rather than engage in redistribution, there is a case that the local taxes used to finance them should be 'benefit taxes'. The traditional reliance on a local property tax was partly justified in these terms. However, in modern conditions with local government engaged in significant redistribution this is a more difficult argument to sustain, and there is no single suitable benefit tax available (Bramley, Le Grand and Low, 1989; Coopers and Lybrand Deloitte, 1990). Nevertheless, this remains an argument against a local tax which would be highly redistributive, such as a progressive income tax.

Some economists have argued that local government should make more use of user charges rather than general taxes, at least for 'facility-based services' (Coopers and Lybrand 1990; Foster, Jackman and Perlman, 1980). The overall potential for charges is rather limited owing to the importance of public goods and redistributive services. There is some scope for charging fees for some regulatory functions (as in 'the polluter pays' principle), including charges against land development profits which can be used to pay for infrastructure and community facilities to support new developments when planning permission is given (Healey, 1993). Also, some facility-based services (sports, libraries) tend to be used more by the better-off and charges could be acceptable in distributional terms, especially where concessionary rates can be given to groups such as the retired and unemployed (Bramley *et al.*, 1989).

What role is there for government grants in this scheme? Five distinct roles can be identified in both theory and practice (general normative theories of the role of grants may be found in Oates, 1972; Foster *et al.*, 1980 or King, 1984). First, grants can be used to correct or compensate for spillover effects which go beyond the boundaries of individual authorities. In Figure 9.1, a local authority would tend to underprovide the service at point A, where marginal local benefits equal costs, unless a grant such as BC per unit were provided, so raising output to the socially optimal level.

Secondly, grants can be used to share with local government the revenues derived from major taxes (e.g. income tax, VAT) which cannot easily be operated at local level. Thirdly, specific grants can be used to pay for services which central government has a strong interest in either controlling or promoting, including cases where local government essentially acts in an agency role (e.g. police, housing benefit). Fourthly, grants can be used as a general regulator on the propensity of authorities to spend, to enable central government to exert a general influence on the levels of spending and taxation in the economy as a whole.

Finally, grants can be used to 'equalise' the financial position of different authorities which face differences in the cost of providing services due to factors outside their control like wage rates or the number of children or old people to be catered for (Bramley, 1990). Equalisation can also be used to compensate authorities that have smaller tax bases on which to levy their local taxes (e.g. poorer residents, lower property values, less business). Figure 9.2 illustrates this equalisation process, with the vertical axis measuring the local tax base and the horizontal axis showing the expenditure required to finance a

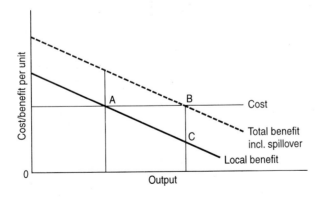

Figure 9.1 Marginal benefit, cost and output of local service with spillover.

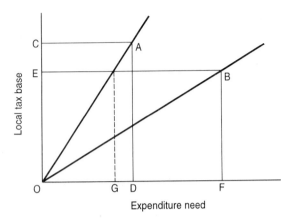

Figure 9.2 Equalisation for differing needs and resources.

level of service provision. A local authority at position B with a small tax base (e.g. because property values are low) and more needs (e.g. more school-age children) will need a higher rate of tax to finance a given level of service at point B (given by BE/BF) than the more favoured authority at point A (tax rate given by AC/AD). An equalisation grant would be used to fill some or all of the gap GF so as to enable authority A to spend what it needs to spend without having a higher tax rate than authority B.

The picture just painted portrays local government, with appropriate functions and financing, as a benevolent, effective institution for delivering necessary services. However, particularly since the 1980s, local government (along with other parts of the state apparatus) has been the target for a more critical stance. One important source of such criticism has been the 'public choice' school, which applies some of the analytical concepts and assumptions of economics (e.g. rational, maximising individual behaviour) to political and organisational behaviour. Some classic works in this tradition include Downs (1957) and Buchanan and Tullock (1962) on democratic politics and Niskanen (1971) on bureaucratic behaviour, and the field is surveyed by Mueller (1989) and Le Grand (1991).

The first main area of criticism concerns the possibility of failures of voting mechanisms (local elections, council committees) to produce decisions which reflect the preferences of the local electorate at large. People do not vote on particular issues but for political parties, who package together policies in ways which suit them rather than the voters. Producer interests may be more strongly represented than consumer interests, because producers have a stronger interest in political activism; at the same time, redistributive policies may be followed which favour majorities at the expense of minorities. People are alleged to vote more on national than on local issues, and electoral turnouts are often low in local polls, and the financial system may not give the right 'price signals' about the cost of policies; for example, before 1986 it was normal for local residents to have to pay less than half of the marginal cost of extra spending commitments, because of the 'subsidy' provided by business ratepayers and government grants (Foster *et al.*, 1980; Department of the Environment, 1986).

The second main area of criticism concerns the role of the 'bureaucratic' organisations which administer and deliver services on behalf of local elected representatives. It is alleged that these organisations exploit their greater detailed knowledge to use the resources provided by the council to pursue their own goals rather than the public interest (Niskanen, 1970; Jackson, 1982). The result may be both 'allocative inefficiency' – too much spending on local public services – and 'productive inefficiency' or, in more common parlance, waste. In general this critique leads to the view that what is needed is more information, more competition and more choice.

9.3   The changing profile of local government activity

Before going on to look at three particular contemporary areas of policy reform and controversy arising in part out of this critique, it is useful to put the discussion in context by providing a brief statistical picture of local government activity in Britain. In practice, because of the way the government is organised and data collected, most of this information refers to England and Wales; a broadly similar picture applies in Scotland.

Despite attempts at curbing local government spending and some reductions in its powers, this remains a substantial part of the public sector and indeed of the economy as a whole. Table 9.1 shows that local government spends £75 bn. in a year, about a quarter of all government spending. This spending is equivalent to 10–11 per cent of the economy as measured by GDP, although if you deduct transfer payments the share of output is about 8 per cent. This share rose rapidly from the end of the Second World War to about 1976, since when it has fluctuated somewhat. Capital spending fell sharply after the 1970s, but current spending still tends to rise despite tightening controls. What is the money spent on? Table 9.2 looks at real current expenditure trends for the main services for which local government is responsible, while Table 9.3 contrasts the pattern of current and capital spending. Education is by far the largest component, with local government still responsible for the bulk of schooling although higher and further education have been removed from local control.

Falling numbers of school-aged children account for some of the lower growth since 1981 in this sector. Personal social services, including social work and care for children, elderly and handicapped people, have been one of the fastest-growing sectors. There are more elderly people needing care and more of this care is now provided 'in the community' rather than in hospitals. Police and other services associated with 'law and order' have also grown greatly, reflecting higher crime rates in society. Public housing has been a major

Table 9.1 Local government expenditure and the economy

United Kingdom	1981–2	1985–6	1990–1	1994–5
Actual expenditure £bn				
Total local government expenditure	26.6	35.2	57.8	73.3
Exhaustive local government expenditure	23.2	29.8	44.1	53.4
Locally financed expenditure	12.9	18.2	15.3	11.8
Real expenditure £bn				
Total local government expenditure	50.3	53.7	65.8	71.9
Exhaustive local agreement expenditure	43.9	45.4	50.2	52.4
Locally financed expenditure	24.4	27.7	17.4	11.6
Percentage of general government expenditure				
Total local government expenditure	22.0	21.8	25.9	24.8
Exhaustive local government expenditure	19.2	18.5	19.7	18.1
Locally financed expenditure	10.7	11.3	6.8	4.0
Percentage of GDP				
Total local government expenditure	10.2	9.6	10.4	10.8
Exhaustive local government expenditure	8.9	8.2	7.9	7.9
Locally financed expenditure	4.9	5.0	2.7	1.7

Source: HM Treasury (1995), Tables 1.1, 4.1, 4.3; HM Treasury (1987), Tables 2.3, 2.7, 4.1, 4.8.

Table 9.2 Real net current expenditure by service (England and Wales, £m., 1993–4 prices)

	1981–2	1985–6	1990–1	1994–5
Education	17 756	17 948	21 235	19 278
Personal social services	3 471	3 637	4 727	6 870
Police, fire, courts	4 919	5 591	6 645	8 025
Highways & transport	3 261	2 768	3 443	2 044
Housing	1 641	1 076	521	490
Libraries, museums	611	614	721	750
Recreation, parks, sports	1 060	976	1 097	1 115
Environmental health, waste	1 586	1 427	1 671	1 792
Planning, development	707	502	559	673
Revenue collection	263	238	720	524
Other	1 193	1 538	3 741	2 896
Total	41 561	40 753	50 692	49 695

Source: CIPFA *Financial and General Statistics* (annual).

Table 9.3 Percentage shares of net revenue and gross capital expenditure by main services

	Net Revenue		Capital	
	1985–6	1994–5	1985–6	1994–5
Education	51.3	43.0	10.4	10.4
Personal social services	10.4	15.3	2.5	2.7
Police, fire, courts	16.0	17.9	1.1	4.3
Highways & transport	7.9	4.6	10.4	19.1
Housing	3.1	1.1	54.2	32.3
Libraries, museums	1.8	1.7	na	na
Recreation, parks, sports	2.8	2.5	na	na
Environmental health, waste	4.1	4.0	na	na
Planning, development	1.4	1.5	na	na
Revenue collection	0.7	1.2	na	na
Other	4.4	6.5	21.5	22.1
Urban regeneration	na	na	na	9.1
Total	100.0	100.0	100.0	100.0

Sources: CIPFA *Financial and General Statistics*, 1985/6 and 1994/5, CIPFA *Capital Expenditure and Debt Financing Statistics* 1985/6; HM Treasury (1995) Tables 4.8–4.10.

responsibility for councils in Britain, but this is one sector where government policies have brought about a large reduction in both investment and subsidy expenditure, partly associated with the large privatisation policy of encouraging council tenants to buy their homes. However, expenditure on 'housing benefits' to low income tenants (most of which is not shown in these tables) has increased. Expenditure on collecting local taxes increased sharply in 1990 at the time of the reform of finance which introduced the ill-fated poll tax, discussed below. This change also saw a large increase in the general level of expenditure, as shown in the last row of the table. The pattern of capital spending across services is significantly different from the pattern of revenue spending. Services such as education and social care are predominantly labour-intensive, whereas housing and transport (including roads) are more capital-intensive. A high proportion of all local government spending is on staff wages and salaries (71% of exhaustive expenditure). A significant chunk of the diminished total of local capital spending is targeted on urban regeneration under the new 'Single Regeneration Budget' arrangements, which seek to coordinate spending on different services within particular deprived urban areas.

Table 9.4 traces changes in the pattern of funding sources used for local government current expenditure since 1981 (this presentation somewhat understates the role of specific grants, some of which are counted separately, e.g. housing benefit, student awards). Up to 1990 the government was deliberately trying to reduce the volume of grant support, partly in an unsuccessful attempt to discourage local authority spending. Consequently,

Table 9.4 Financing of local government current expenditure (England and Wales

	1981–2	1985–6	1990–1	1994–5
Percentage shares of financial support				
Specific grants	11	13	9	12
Rate/revenue support grant	45	38	28	43
Non-domestic rate	24	26	28	24
Local domestic tax	20	23	35	21
Total	100	100	100	100
Locally variable taxes	43	49	35	21
of which LDT rebates, etc.	na	na	6	4
Real local domestic tax bill per household per year (before rebate, 1993/4 prices, £)	440	521	750	453

Sources: as for Tables 9.1, 9.2.

the contribution of local taxpayers through the rating system (a local property tax) tended to increase. The last line of the table shows that the average household bill for rates (or, in 1990, the Community Charge or 'poll tax') increased substantially in real terms, from £440 per year to £750 per year. This increase had much to do with the controversy surrounding local government finance in this period. Local businesses and other users of property also paid a growing share through the Non-Domestic Rate. As part of the reform in 1990, this tax was effectively nationalised, with the proceeds redistributed to local authorities as a per capita grant. From 1990 onwards this contribution has been pegged to the rate of general inflation, which is why its share is now falling again.

The nationalisation of this tax also accounts for the fall in the share of 'locally variable taxes'. A further major fall in this element was engineered in the 1991 budget, as a response to the political crisis brought on by the poll tax experience. Grants were increased, funded by an increase in the rate of VAT, and the poll tax contribution (since replaced by the Council Tax) was reduced by a corresponding amount. A byproduct of these changes which has been much criticised by some analysts (e.g. Travers, 1995) is the problem that the locally variable tax is now a such a small proportion of the total that it is unduly sensitive to changes in expenditure or grants. For example, if local authorities find they have to spend 5 per cent more than the government assumes, they have to raise their local tax by nearly 24 per cent to compensate. This is known as the 'gearing effect'.

Although capital expenditure is now a small part of total local authority expenditure, its control and financing is quite an important issue in the relationship between central and local government. Traditionally, capital investment was mainly financed by borrowing, and central government controlled local borrowing in order to regulate public sector debt and macro-economic conditions. In the 1980s, with increased sale of local government assets, particularly council housing, authorities found themselves with increasing amounts of capital receipts on their books, which they often wished to reinvest despite government attempts at control. In 1990, for example, capital receipts (£3.5 bn) represented more than half of the total of new capital spending (£6.5 bn).

9.4 Reform of funding

In the last five years local government finance in Britain has gone through the major upheaval of two reforms. The first in 1990 was comprehensive and fundamental, while the second in 1993 was a necessary response to the manifest failure of part of the first reform. The reforms followed a period in the 1980s of major instability in the system and serious political conflict between central and local government.

The 1990 reform was foreshadowed in a Green Paper (Department of the Environment, 1986) which proposed three major changes in the way local government was financed (see also Bailey & Paddison, 1988; Travers, 1995).

1. Domestic rates were replaced by an adult poll tax, known as the Community Charge; means-tested benefits were also modified so that everyone had to pay at least 20 per cent of the tax.
2. Non-Domestic Rates were nationalised, with a new 'uniform business rate' determined centrally applied to revalued property and the proceeds redistributed to local authorities by a per capita addition to the grant.
3. Grants were changed so that a fixed Revenue Support Grant was distributed on the basis of a simplified needs assessment known as the Standard Spending Assessment (SSA) with the effective ending of 'resource equalisation' grants for poorer areas.

What were the reasons for these major changes? Rates had for long been controversial, with problems of outdated valuations and perceived unfairness for some groups like elderly householders living alone. As the level and burden of rates rose in the 1980s (see Table 9.4) these problems came to a head. Businesses became more vocal about the burden they were carrying, particularly in recession, and it was argued that business location decisions might be distorted by rate levels. The most important arguments for change had to do with accountability, following the arguments of Foster *et al.* (1980) and others, that the mechanism of efficient local decision-making outlined in Section 9.1 was being distorted by the system. Local voters were paying too small a share of the marginal cost of extra spending, because much of it was being met by grants (which increased with expenditure), by businesses through the Non-Domestic Rate, and by rate rebates for poorer households. Instability and complexity in the grant arrangement further confused the accountability relationship. It was argued that local taxes should be more like 'benefit taxes', although some commentators suggested that the poll tax was little better in this respect (Bramley *et al.*, 1989). The politics of central–local relations also played a part, with an 'inverse electoral cycle' meaning that many local authorities were controlled by Labour and Liberal Democrat councillors who took a different view of spending priorities from the Conservative central government. The 1980s was a period of particular ideological polarisation between the main political parties. There had also been a long-running debate over whether central government had a legitimate macroeconomic policy interest in the general level of local government spending. It is arguable whether that interest is that strong, so long as local spending is balanced by local revenue-raising, but the Treasury generally takes the view that it should regulate the overall level of public spending, including local government's share.

The 1990 reform was undoubtedly a failure, both financially and politically. One important manifestation of this failure was the fact that in 1990 local authorities increased their spending by the largest amount in 1 year for well over a decade. Accountability was crucially blurred in the year of transition, and authorities correctly guessed that central government would take the blame for higher local tax bills. The second problem was that the poll tax proved extraordinarily expensive and difficult to collect. Quite apart from the large number of people who objected to paying it on principle, it was inherently difficult because of the much larger number of individual taxpayers, some with little or no income to pay with, who displayed an alarming tendency to move around (unlike houses and factories). It became apparent that many people regarded a poll tax as unacceptably unfair and regressive, even people who themselves stood to gain from the change. At the same time, a large number of people were worse off, and many of these were potentially marginal voters (Travers, 1995). The 'gearing effect' mentioned earlier was another problem, with local tax levels too sensitive to changes or errors in grant calculations. A longer, more gradual transition, might have made the changes more acceptable, as originally proposed in 1986, but the government opted for a wholesale change and had to live with the consequences.

Following the change of Conservative leadership and Prime Minister at the end of 1990, the government moved quickly to limit the damage and find a more acceptable system. First, VAT was increased to finance a shift of funding from the poll tax to grant. Secondly, powers in the existing legislation to 'cap' the spending of individual local authorities were applied across the board rather than selectively. From 1991 onwards, most local authorities have effectively lost the power to determine their overall budget. Thirdly, it was decided to abandon the poll tax and revert to a system of local domestic taxation which was based primarily on domestic property. The new tax known as the Council Tax was introduced from 1993. Houses and flats are placed in one of eight bands according to their assessed capital value in 1991 (the old rates were based on notional rental values) and the tax liability rises with higher bands, although at about half the proportionate rate (so a £200 000 house pays 50 per cent more than a £100 000 one). The basic tax liability is subject to discounts, so that in particular a single adult pays less than two or more adults. Rebates are available for low income occupiers, and the system reverts to the pre-1989 situation of providing full 100 per cent rebates for the poorest households. As argued by Hills and Sutherland (1992), the Council Tax is thus a hybrid, containing elements of a property, household, individual and (via the rebates) income tax.

The second element of the 1990 reform, the uniform national Non-Domestic Rate, has been retained, as this aspect had wider support although the Labour Party still proposes to reintroduce an element of local variation in this tax. The third element, the fixed Revenue Support Grant, has also been retained but with some modification. The needs calculations (SSAs) have been modified somewhat, following considerable criticism (see Audit Commission, 1993a) which flows in considerable measure from the greater impact that these figures have because of the gearing effect and the general use of capping (capping is partly based on SSAs). Resource equalisation has also been reintroduced, so that areas which have lower valued properties for Council Tax purposes get more grant, but the grant remains fixed, unlike the pre-1990 situation.

How should we evaluate the system which is now in place, in the light of the general criteria set out in the initial theoretical discussion? The system may now be more stable and acceptable, providing a firmer basis for local government to go about its business of delivering local services. The Council Tax was introduced with relatively little trouble and is clearly much easier to administer than the poll tax, as well as being somewhat fairer and more up-to-date than the old rates. The crudeness of the valuation and banding exercise is still causing problems, with many householders appealing for different bandings, and this problem may not go away given the volatility of the housing market.

The fundamental problem with the system as it now exists centres on the fact that the government has found it necessary to impose a general regime of capping. This fatally undermines the basic economic logic of local government set out in the opening section. The allocative efficiency benefits of local budgetary decision-making are lost, and accountability remains very blurred if the overall level of the budget is essentially determined by central government. Why have a local tax, if its level is set by central government? It can be argued that local authorities have a stronger incentive to reduce productive ineffici-ency under a capping regime, and they still make allocative decisions as between different services. Capping is also creating a growing technical problem with the SSA system. It has led to a rapid convergence of expenditure levels on the levels set by SSAs, but the methods used to calculate SSAs rely heavily on statistical analysis of expenditure patterns. This is clearly now a circular process, which cannot go on indefinitely.

Nationalisation of the Non-Domestic Rate has some undesirable side effects that are becoming more apparent over time. Local government no longer has such a clear rationale for engaging in a dialogue with local business about what kind of services should be provided of relevance to the local economy and at what cost. Such dialogues were one of the healthier features of the mid-1980s. Local authorities still collect this tax, but they no longer have any incentive to maximise the revenue, and it is apparent that the yield of the tax is falling off as a consequence.

The fixed grant system is easier to operate and should generate more certainty. Although there is still an equalisation element, because it is a fixed lump sum grant it does not help poorer or more needy authorities at the margin; they have to raise taxes more to achieve a given improvement in services than more favoured ones. SSAs are not completely stable, and even small changes can have a major effect because of the gearing factor. Local authorities have an incentive to put effort into trying to secure changes in the formula, rather than trying to improve their service provision and efficiency which should be their major concern.

Part of the problem with local finance may be to do with the diversity of functions which local authorities perform. Economic theory suggests that different solutions may be appropriate for different kinds of services, in terms of differing kinds of local tax or charge, differing rates of grant support and differing degrees of central control. This kind of 'horses for courses' approach is exemplified in Coopers and Lybrand (1990).

9.5   Devolution, contracting and competition

Financing is not the only aspect of local government which has been subject to radical change and questioning. Since the mid-1980s, the basic mechanisms used to procure, organise and deliver local public services have been exposed to radical reform in many cases. A range of interconnected changes have been applied, with or without prior testing, across many services. Although the models vary a good deal, what they have in common is a move away from the traditional public sector bureaucracy model with its top–down hierarchy of command and control. Instead, decision-making is devolved down to operating units, the role of service provider is separated from the role of purchaser by the use of formal contracts, elements of competition are introduced, including some involvement of private sector providers, and consumers may be given more choice. In some cases what is involved is full privatisation, but this is less common than various intermediate models where the local government retains the role of purchasing, regulating and perhaps planning the service on behalf of the general public (Bartlett and Le Grand,

1993; Hill and Bramley, 1986, chapter 6). The changes parallel substantial reform in other parts of the public sector discussed elsewhere in this book, including Health Service reform and so-called 'Next Steps' and 'Market Testing' reforms in the civil service.

It is useful to distinguish the main alternative models conceptually, although in some cases elements of different models may be combined.

1. *Devolution/decentralisation* of detailed control to local operating units, e.g. schools, housing estates, area offices.
2. *Purchaser–provider separation* in organisational and accounting terms, with formal contractual arrangements specifying service levels in exchange for budgets, as in NHS reforms, Direct Labour Organisation (DLO) regulations, some Community Care services.
3. *Competitive tendering* for contracts, with outside providers (public, private, or voluntary/non-profit) able to compete for work; LAs may adopt this approach voluntarily but generally government has felt it necessary to make this approach compulsory for some services (CCT) and to regulate the terms of the competition strictly.
4. *Consumer choice* may be introduced, within the public sector (a 'quasi' or internal market) or across public and private sector providers; this could involve direct consumer choice, as under the system of open enrolment and formula funding for schools, or else choice mediated through a professional adviser such as a doctor or social worker.
5. *Opting out* by provider units may be an element in the process, whereby schools for example can 'opt' to go out of local authority control and receive their funding directly from the government.
6. *Deregulation* may be a significant feature for some services already provided substantially on a trading basis albeit with some subsidy, as in the case of the bus industry; for many services, such as care for elderly people, regulation is likely to remain an important issue.
7. *Withdrawal/privatisation* may occur in the case of non-statutory services, with the local authority making no provision and potential users having to rely on self, voluntary or private market provision; this is the approach of some authorities to nursery education and school meals, for example.

A number of forces are driving these changes. Perhaps most obvious, in a British context, is the fact that we have had a government with an ideology which favours rolling back the boundaries of state and local government activity wherever possible and promoting competition and choice. However, changes of this kind are being applied in many other countries too, with different political profiles. This suggests that there are strong underlying forces or arguments for such changes.

First, the arguments of the public choice school reviewed briefly in the opening section, have been taken increasingly seriously. Neither electoral democracy nor public bureaucracy can be relied upon to produce the right services (allocative inefficiency) at minimum cost (productive inefficiency). Long-standing awareness of market failure has been joined by a newer awareness of potential 'state failure' (Le Grand, 1991; Wolff, 1988). Secondly, there has been a general move towards people demanding more choice and control over services, rather than passively receiving a standard product, rather in parallel with the move towards product differentiation and more diverse consumer lifestyles evident in the private market sector. Thirdly, we have already seen that local public services are often labour-intensive ('people processing') activities, and one consequence is that the scope for productivity improvements associated with technological change are much less than those found in other sectors of the economy. Consequently, as general living standards and wages rise the real cost of local public services tends to rise as well (Hill and Bramley, 1986 chapters 5, 10). In other words, it is a constant battle even to contain expenditure while maintaining service levels, which is what the evidence in Table 9.2 above suggested.

There is no doubt that since the 1980s a range of reforms involving different combinations of the above elements have affected most of the activities of local government and that cumulatively they have had a major impact. This is certainly true as far as the internal organisational structure and culture of local government is concerned. Managers are much more preoccupied with competition and competitiveness, with contractual relationships, and with performance indicators and standards. In some instances the withdrawal of the local authority from the role of direct service provision is substantial and the role of the local authority is reformulated as being one of 'enabling'.

Lack of space prevents description of all of the relevant changes in particular services. One major example, schools, provides a good picture of the potentially far-reaching changes involved. Under the 1988 Education Reform Act substantial managerial and budgetary responsibility was devolved to most school governing bodies. Funds were to be distributed by formula which, although locally determined, had to distribute most money on the basis of numbers and ages of children. 'Open enrolment' enabled parents to choose to send their children to particular schools, so long as space was available. Schools had to teach a new national curriculum and standard tests of attainment were to be undertaken at various ages, with information about the performance of schools on tests and other indicators (e.g. truancy) becoming publicly available. This is clearly a fairly fully fledged quasi-market model, which comes close to the concept of the educational 'voucher' proposed in the past to give more consumer choice. Under this model, the role of the local education authority becomes much circumscribed, and even some of the collectively provided specialist services (e.g. inspection, maintenance) have become subject to competitive tendering. It is difficult to plan provision, since demand and resource allocation is driven by the choices of parents. This problem is further complicated by the ability of schools to 'opt out', further encouraged by more recent policies and legislation. The future role of local authorities in what has hitherto been their major activity, education, is thus very problematic.

The quasi-market model has been tried to varying degrees in other services, including housing and community care (see Bartlett and Le Grand, 1993). However, perhaps the other most important model which has been applied across much of local government has been Compulsory Competitive Tendering (CCT). This is a more narrowly conceived model, comprising items (2) and (3) on the above list, which is clearly directed at increasing productive efficiency, reducing cost, and scaling down local government. It does not of itself have much bearing on consumer choice, service levels or standards and their regulation. Walsh (1995) provides a useful review of the experience with CCT.

The first major application of the CCT model was to building and roads construction and maintenance under 1981 legislation, following concern during the 1970s about the efficiency of 'Direct Labour Organisations' in this field. The main features of the model, then and now, are: (a) the specification of classes of work to which the rules apply; (b) requirements to put work out to competitive tender; (c) rules to limit 'anticompetitive behaviour'; (d) separation of accounts for direct service provision organisation; (e) requirement for these accounts to show breakeven or minimum rate of return on capital; (f) powers to close down organisations failing to win enough work or undertake it profitably enough to meet this target. This legislation applied a competitive contractual model to a sector where there was already a well-established private market.

The next wave of CCT came with legislation in 1988 which extended the principle to a number of services which, unlike building, were essentially public sector services without an established private market: refuse collection, street cleaning, building cleaning, catering, vehicle maintenance, sport and leisure management. It should be noted that these are mainly routine, blue-collar activities, often providing an input to a wider service rather than a whole service (the last being an exception to this). Some authorities had already tried competitive tendering and contracting out for some of these, particularly refuse collection, in the 1980s (Domberger, Meadowcroft and Thompson, 1986). The third wave, characteristic of the 1990s, applies the model to services which involve a greater input of professional and managerial staff and which involve more policy issues, including some central functions such as finance and legal services as well as the major function of housing management. Indirect financial pressures are also being used to require much more contracting out of services like residential care homes for elderly people.

CCT has had a substantial impact, in a number of respects, including as mentioned on organisation and culture. Some work has actually gone out to private contract and this tends to build up over time (Walsh, 1995, pp. 35–6). A wider section of local government jobs and spending is affected (over 300 000 and £6 bn respectively). Even where the in-house team wins the contract, the threat of competition has been very effective in forcing changes in working practices, reductions in staffing and often in rates of pay. While earlier studies following voluntary completion showed quite large savings (10–20%), the savings from compulsory competition may be less (Walsh, 1995, pp. 37–8). Some part of these 'savings' may result from lower pay and poorer conditions, essentially a redistributional effect, and some part may be offset for the public sector by higher unemployment among unskilled workers. Some have speculated that competition will not be maintained in these markets once the private sector has taken over, but Walsh argues that this is not convincing, because of inherent contestability of the market.

The need to specify the output levels and standards which are to be provided is unavoidable under CCT and contractual models generally, whereas these things may not have been well-defined in the past. This is generally regarded as a beneficial effect, but it is not without a cost. The Audit Commission (1993b, p.17) estimate the 'client side' costs of administering and monitoring contracts as lying between 1 per cent and 9 per cent of annual contract value, depending on the service. They also suggest ways in which the client role could be played more effectively, including through better specifications with more emphasis on results and through more customer involvement. How far CCT makes sense depends on the level of these 'transactions costs', and also on how far the provider has better access to information than the client and may be motivated to behave 'opportunistically' (Walsh, 1995; Bartlett and Le Grand, 1993; Williamson, 1975). Arguably these problems may be more serious in the more complex, professionally based services featuring in the third wave of CCT and some of the quasi-market developments.

Most of the discussion of these changes focuses on the primary goal of efficiency, although consumer choice also gets some consideration (CCT may make little difference to consumer choice). In evaluating public policies it is also appropriate to consider equity and redistributional effects. For both quasi-markets and CCT, the general conclusion so far would be that there are some efficiency gains but at the same time there are some generally adverse or regressive distributional effects (Bartlett and Le Grand, 1993). We have already mentioned some labour market effects of this kind stemming from CCT. Another example would be the adverse effect of the quasi-market in schools on the schools which are competitively weakest, usually in areas of deprivation with falling rolls; local authorities are less able to support such schools and stem their decline. While in some cases closure might be the best option, communities will lose a local resource and children will have to travel further and have their schooling disrupted. Popular schools, particularly those which have opted out, will increasingly use means of selection which will almost certainly disadvantage children from working class, low income or deprived backgrounds.

9.6   Structural reorganisation

The other major area of change and debate at the moment is the issue of local government structure and boundaries. The present British structure was established in 1974–5, with a system of two-tier local government throughout the country. In most of the country, county councils (Regions in Scotland) provided a range of important and expensive services, including education, roads and social services, while districts provided housing and local environmental services. In London and other metropolitan conurbations, the districts also took the major spending functions such as education and social services. In 1986 this structure was modified with the abolition of the upper tier county authorities in London and the six metropolitan areas. Nevertheless, this has been a period of relative stability during which there has been a relatively coherent structure with functions allocated in a well-understood way. Two-tier structures are common in other countries and if the British system is unusual it is mainly in the relatively small number (366 in England) and consequent large size of lower tier district councils, whose average population exceeds 130 000.

A complex and long-drawn-out process of review of structure was instituted in 1991 by the then Secretary of State for the Environment, Michael Heseltine. In England this took the form of setting up a Commission to examine arrangements area by area (excluding London and metropolitan areas) and recommending revised structural and boundary arrangements which would take account of (a) the identities and interests of local communities, and (b) how to secure effective and convenient local government. The Commission would undertake some research (on costs and local opinions) as well as consulting in each locality before making recommendations. Government guidelines in the process leave open the continuance of the status quo, but generally tend to favour single tier (unitary) local authorities which are intermediate in size between present districts on the one hand and larger cities and county authorities on the other hand (Department of the Environment, 1991, 1992, 1993). In weighing alternatives the Commission are asked to consider the criteria of 'identity', 'accessibility', 'responsiveness' and 'demo-cracy'. The government have also expressed approval of the concept of the 'enabling authority', which can be taken as code for favouring maximal use of contracting out mechanisms for service provision. This means that traditional arguments about economies of scale in production of local services no longer carry so much weight. A simplified version of the same process has been set in train in Scotland and Wales; here Secretaries of State have determined the new structure, after some consultation, and this takes the form of a single tier structure with intermediate-sized (albeit very unevenly sized) unitary authorities.

It is not at all clear why this reform has been instituted and where, in the case of England, it is going (Leach, 1995). There had been a degree of dissatisfaction with two-tier local government in some areas, particularly in big cities such as Bristol which had unitary status before 1974. Where functions overlap (e.g. planning) there was inevitably some scope for duplication and conflict. Some of the new creations of 1974, such as Avon and Humberside, were not widely loved. Presumably the underlying assumption must have been that single-tier local government should be cheaper to administer than two-tier, and as local government slimmed down in its new enabling role, with major functions such as schooling increasingly devolved or contracted out, one tier should be enough. It is also clear that the process was instituted by a particular minister with a particular agenda, and has then been influenced by other particular political considerations at each stage. The Local Government Commission, with its perhaps not well-defined brief, has not, in the view of a range of expert commentators, distinguished itself. It has not defined its own operating principles and has produced a range of apparently inconsistent recommendations. The government has then intervened to try and change the outcomes, and there have been legal and political challenges to the whole process.

This is not to say that there are not a range of arguments of principle or questions susceptible to being answered on the basis of empirical evidence, which might better inform such a process of structural review. A range of arguments can be considered in relation to the economic functions of local government as discussed at the beginning of this chapter. Further arguments of principle can be adduced from concepts of political democracy and the constitutional role of local government. However, many of these arguments do not seem to have been taken into account in this process of local government review.

The traditional argument for larger local authorities was one of economies of scale in the production of local services. In fact, the evidence for this at the level of size at issue here (e.g. populations in the range 50 000–500 000) has never been very convincing (Watt, 1994; Bramley, 1990, chapter 5; Travers, Jones and Burnham, 1993). Only in the provision of very specialised services is size a factor here. The Commission make use of evidence from a (somewhat hypothetical) study by Ernst and Young on the indirect costs of different sizes of authority, which do show unlimited scale economies, but within the general administrative support functions that account for only 10 per cent of total service costs in all. In addition, with the enabling/contracting out approach favoured, it would seem that production costs can be largely separated from size of purchasing authority.

'Local identity' is emphasised as a criterion by the government, but it is not easy to interpret all of the opinion survey evidence collected on this issue. If anything, it seems to show a great deal of identification with quite a local level of neighbourhood or town, rather than the larger units characteristic of British local government (Leach, 1995). Taken in conjunction with the point about enabling/contracting, this would suggest that the government and the Commission should have looked more seriously at *smaller* units rather than bigger ones. This could then have been allied to some of the basic economic arguments for local government rehearsed in the opening section. With smaller units, there can be more diverse levels and mixes of service provision between areas and more similarity of people and conditions within areas. This means that more people can get a package of services similar to what they would prefer. In other words, the system would generate more allocative efficiency. This is an argument which the Local Government Commission has conspicuously ignored.

The other important economic/geographical argument which the Commission has also completely ignored is one which points in a rather different direction. This argument emphasises the more strategic planning and regulatory roles of local government, including its functions in relation to land use and transport. For these functions the logical areal basis is undoubtedly the 'functional region', that is, the major focal employment/shopping/leisure centres (mainly cities, but sometimes transport nodes) and their surrounding hinterland with which they are strongly connected in terms of day to day travel and economic linkages. Authorities based on this principle have been early targets for abolition, including the Greater London Council in 1986 and Avon County Council (and in Scotland the regions based on main cities) in the current review. Without such regional bodies, awkward arrangements for coordination and planning of such areas have to be made. Alternatively, there is chaos rather than coordination, with major developments in one district not meshing closely with what is going on next door; or else central government does the job without consulting local interests. The strategic planning and regulation argument for functional regions is perhaps one important example of how there is not one single solution for all functions. Two-tier local government may in fact make sense, although it might make more sense with smaller districts and larger regions than it does in its present form.

There are also arguments for larger units connected with the redistributional role of some major local services, again little considered by the review Commission. Needs and resources for such services vary more sharply between small areas, and the old county/regional authorities performed an important equalisation function. Moving to smaller unitary authorities increases the job to be performed by the imperfect grant system, including SSAs.

There are also political and constitutional arguments for larger unitary local authorities. These are more likely to attract able people to lead them, politically and managerially, and have the resources to support intelligent decision-making. Such authorities would provide a firmer platform for the articulation of local needs and strategies for the development of local economies and communities.

9.7 Conclusions

Local government in Britain has been through a turbulent period, culminating in major reforms on the three fronts of finance, service delivery mechanisms and structure. The three sets of reforms have not been closely coordinated, although the current review of structure pays some attention to the shift of local government from a direct provision towards more of an enabling role. It can be argued that neither the financial nor the structural reforms pay sufficient attention to the very different characteristics of different local services. It is also apparent that these reforms, particularly the first and third, pay scant attention to the underlying economic rationale for local government. Consequently, it is difficult to be optimistic that the system in place in the late 1990s will provide an adequate solution to the problems confronting it.

Questions for discussion

1. To what extent can local government services be classified as 'public goods'?
2. What are the advantages, if any, of local rather than central government provision of public services?
3. How should the economic functions of government be divided between central and local government?
4. Should local government make more use of user charges and less use of local taxes?
5. How far is the mechanism of local political accountability for budgetary decisions as a means for promoting efficient service provision compromised by the present capping of local authority budgets by central government?
6. What is the most suitable way of raising local finance for local services, and how well have the systems of local taxation employed since 1980 met these requirements?
7. Contrast the pattern of current and capital expenditure undertaken by local government in England and Wales.
8. Examine the ways in which local government finance has changed in recent years. What are the reasons for these changes?
9. Given the changes in the way local services are provided, with more use of contracting and quasi-market mechanisms, what type of structure would be most suitable for local government in the future?

10. Does the economies of scale argument provide a sufficient case for the move towards single tier (unitary) local authorities?

References and further reading

Audit Commission (1993a) *Passing the Bucks: The impact of standard spending assessments on economy, efficiency and effectiveness* Vol. 1, London: HMSO.

Audit Commission (1993b) *Making Markets: A review of the audits of the client role for contracted services*, London: HMSO.

Bailey, S. and Paddison, R. (1988) *The Reform of Local Government Finance in Britain*, London: Routledge.

Bartlett, W. and Le Grand, J. (1993) *Quasi Markets and Social Policy*, Basingstoke, London: Macmillan.

Bramley, G. (1990) *Equalisation Grants and Local Expenditure Needs: The price of equality*, Aldershot: Avebury.

Bramley, G., Le Grand, J. and Low, W. (1989) 'How far is the poll tax a "Community Charge"? The implications of service usage evidence' *Policy & Politics* 17(3) pp. 187–206.

Buchanan, J. and Tullock, G. (1962) *The Calculus of Consent*, Ann Arbor: University of Michigan Press.

Chartered Institute of Public Finance and Accountancy (Annual) *Financial and General Statistics*, London: CIPFA.

Coopers and Lybrand Deloitte (1990) *Alternatives to the Community Charge* A contribution to the debate commissioned by the Joseph Rowntree Foundation from Coopers and Lybrand Deloitte, York: Joseph Rowntree Foundation.

Department of the Environment (1986) *Paying for Local Government* Cmnd. 9714, London: HMSO.

Department of the Environment (1991) *Local Government Review: The structure of local government in England* Consultation Paper, London: DOE.

Department of the Environment (1992) *Policy guidance to the Local Government Commission for England*, London: DOE.

Department of the Environment (1993) *Draft Revised: Policy Guidance to the Local Government Commission for England*, London: DOE.

Domberger, S., Meadowcroft, S. and Thompson, D. (1986) 'Competitive tendering and efficiency: the case of refuse collection' *Fiscal Studies* 7(4) pp. 69–87.

Downs, A. (1957) *An Economic Theory of Democracy*, New York: Harper & Row.

Foster, C., Jackman, R. and Perlman, M. (1980) *Local Government Finance in a Unitary State*, London: Allen & Unwin.

Healey, P. (1993) *Gains from Planning: Dealing with the impacts of development*, York: Joseph Rowntree Foundation.

Hill, M. and Bramley, G. (1986) *Analysing Social Policy*, Oxford: Blackwell.

Hills, J. and Sutherland, H. (1992) *Banding, Tilting, Gearing, Gaining and Losing: An anatomy of the proposed Council Tax* Welfare State Programme Discussion Paper WSP/63, London: London School of Economics.

HM Treasury (1987) *The Government's Expenditure Plans 1987–88 to 1989–90*. Vol. ii, Cm. 56–II, London: HMSO.

HM Treasury (1995) *Public Expenditure: Statistical supplement to the Financial Statement and Budget Report 1995–96* Cm. 2821, London: HMSO.

Jackson, P. (1982) *The Political Economy of Bureaucracy*, Oxford: Philip Allan.

King, D. (1984) *Fiscal Tiers: The economics of multi-level government*, London: Allen & Unwin.

Leach, S. (1995) 'The strange case of the Local Government Review' in *Local Government in the 1990s* Stewart, J. and Stoker, G. (eds), Basingstoke, London: Macmillan.

Le Grand, J. (1991) *The Theory of State Failure* Studies in Decentralisation and Quasi Markets, Bristol: School for Advanced Urban Studies.

Mueller, D. C. (1989) *Public Choice II* revised edn, Cambridge: Cambridge University Press.

Musgrave, R. and Musgrave, P. (1980) *Public Finance in Theory and Practice* 3rd edn, New York: McGraw-Hill.

Niskanen, W. (1971) *Bureaucracy and Representative Government*, Chicago: Aldine.

Oates, W. (1972) *Fiscal Federalism*, New York: Harcourt Brace.

Stigler, G. (1957) 'The tenable range of functions of local government' in *Federal Expenditure Policy for Economic Growth and Stability*, Washington DC: Joint Economic Committee.

Tiebout, C. (1956), 'A pure theory of local expenditures' *Journal of Political Economy* 64(5) pp. 416–24.

Travers, T. (1995) 'Finance' in *Local Government in the 1990s* Stewart, J. and Stoker, G. (eds), Basingstoke, London: Macmillan.

Travers, T., Jones, G. and Burnham, J. (1993) *The Impact of Population Size on Local Authority Costs and Effectiveness*, York: Joseph Rowntree Foundation.

Walsh, K. (1995) 'Competition and public service delivery' in *Local Government in the 1990s* Stewart, J. and Stoker, G. (eds), Basingstoke, London: Macmillan.

Watt, P. (1994) 'Cost and size of authority in the local government review' in *The Local Government Review: Key issues and choices* Leach, S. (ed.), Birmingham University: INLOGOV.

Williamson, O. (1975) *Markets and Hierarchies: Analysis and anti-trust implications*, New York: Free Press.

Wolff, C. (1988) *Markets or Governments: Choose between imperfect alternatives*, Cambridge, Mass: MIT Press.

CHAPTER 10

Transport

DAVID BEGG

10.1 Introduction

Transport is one of the most important sectors in the economy. It accounts for 16 per cent of consumer expenditure and employs 7 per cent of the total labour force! It is therefore of vital importance to the economy as well as the environment. In the last few decades the relentless growth in car use has produced unacceptable levels of traffic congestion and atmospheric air pollution which has increased public awareness and concern. This has resulted in transport becoming a crucial political issue.

10.2 Why transport is different

10.2.1 Derived demand

It is important to appreciate what makes transport different from other sectors in the economy. Transport is rarely demanded for its own sake. It is a derived demand. We demand transport because we want to travel for work, leisure and social purposes. Only transport enthusiasts travel for the pleasure travel itself gives. Goods require to be transported from the point of production to the point of consumption. The demand for transport is inextricably linked with the level of economic activity in the economy. The demand for transport as a whole is often viewed as being a necessity and this results in the product being very price inelastic. This has important implications for policy-makers because during periods of rising economic prosperity significant price increases are required to constrain the demand for transport.

10.2.2 Externalities

The external costs imposed by transport on the rest of society are far greater than any other sector. In the United Kingdom, transport accounts for 24 per cent of the carbon dioxide (CO_2) emitted and worldwide is the fastest-growing contributor to global warming (Department of Environment, 1993). It is also one of the main sources of noise and visual intrusion and is responsible for almost 4000 fatal accidents per annum in the United Kingdom. Transport is responsible for nearly two-fifths of accidental deaths in Britain: in 1992, 39 per cent of accidental deaths took place on the roads, and a further 2 per cent in connection with other forms of transport (CSO, 1994). A road accident is the most likely cause of death in Britain for anyone under the age of 30 years (Davis, 1993). The relentless growth in car use has also resulted in growing traffic congestion. The study by the British Roads Federation in 1988 estimated that traffic congestion cost the UK conurbations £3 bn a year (British Roads Federation, 1988). A 1989 survey by the Confederation of British Industry estimated that traffic congestion cost the UK economy £15 bn per annum. Congestion costs imposed by one road user on other road users are also an external cost. The market does not take account of these externalities and that is why it is crucial that there is government intervention in the form of regulation, quality control and taxation to ensure that these external costs are taken into account.

10.2.3   Location decisions

Location decisions are heavily influenced by transport and the demand for transport is heavily influenced by location decisions. In past centuries towns were built around a port; in the nineteenth century the railway station became the focal point, but in the twentieth century the road network has been critical in influencing location decisions. Over the last 25 years the average distance travelled per person in Britain each day has risen by around 75 per cent from 10 miles, to nearly 18 miles (Department of Transport, 1993). People now make more journeys and the average length of their journeys has increased. The growth in travel has taken the form of an enormous increase in the distances travelled by car: a 10-fold increase over the last 40 years. Seven out of 10 journeys of a mile or more are now by car and these account for over 86 per cent of the total distance travelled. The proliferation of out-of-town shopping centres, leisure and business parks has resulted in people travelling further each time they step into their cars. This has important implications for decision-makers because planning and transport are inextricably linked and if the demand for transport is to be constrained then planning policies should attempt to ensure that facilities are located nearer to where people live.

10.2.4   Perishable product

Transport is immediately perishable. If a bus runs from A to B and no passengers board it, scarce resources such as fuel, labour, etc. have been consumed and yet no demand has been satisfied. This output cannot be stored and utilised at a future point. If a car manufacturer overproduces one year, the product can be stored and sold at a future point. This is impossible in transport and it is, therefore, especially important in this sector that efforts are made to match supply with demand. The 1985 Transport Act which introduced bus deregulation has resulted in excessive competition on profitable routes. There is, as a result, significant spare capacity and a substantial volume of transport services has been, in effect, wasted. This apparently contradicts conventional economic theory which portrays the market as being an efficient allocator of resources, with government intervention to regulate the market being more than likely to distort resource allocation and generate inefficiency. However, transport is different from other sectors in the economy, and so conclusions that might be valid for a typical consumer goods market may not apply: this should be borne in mind by decision-makers when formulating transport policy.

10.3 Theory of congestion

Traffic congestion is caused because the demand for road space outstrips the available supply. There are almost 22 m cars on Britain's roads and the Department of Transport has forecast that car use will increase by between 83 per cent and 142 per cent between 1989 and 2025 (Department of Transport, 1989).

Traffic congestion is a major contributor to economic inefficiency, imposing substantial costs in terms of both increased journey time and increased fuel consumption. The problem has manifested itself in falling traffic speeds, particularly in our city centres. In London, peak hour speeds have fallen to 11 m.p.h. which is not much different from the speed at which a horse and cart travelled a century ago.

If traffic is moving at an average speed of 10 m.p.h., every additional car driving for 1 minute imposes 2 minutes' additional delay on the other vehicles. If traffic is moving at an average speed of 5 m.p.h. every additional car driving for 1 minute imposes 10 minutes' additional delay on the other vehicles. The theory of congestion is illustrated in Figure 10.1. The demand line (DD) represents the marginal benefit derived by a motorist from making a journey on a particular road. F_0 is the free flow traffic capacity of the road; when traffic volume increases beyond this point the road becomes congested and there is a divergence between the marginal social costs (MSC) and the marginal private cost (MPC) of additional traffic. The MPC is the cost which the motorist takes into account when deciding whether to make the journey or not (internal costs) while the MSC takes into account these internal costs plus external costs such as congestion. (It would also include other externalities such as pollution, accidents, etc.) F_1 is the unconstrained traffic flow. Motorists will use this road up to the point where their marginal benefit from the journey, represented by the demand line DD, is equal to the MPC. However, this is not an optimum position and represents a misallocation of resources because the marginal benefit of the journey is significantly less than the marginal social cost. If a

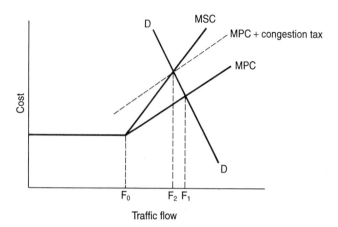

Figure 10.1 Illustrating the theory of congestion.

congestion tax was imposed, then this could shift the MPC line up to MPC plus congestion tax and reduce the traffic flow on the road from F_1 to F_2. This would represent an optimum traffic flow as marginal benefit would then be equal to the marginal social cost. A congestion tax is now commonly referred to as road pricing.

10.3.1 Road pricing in practice

Road pricing was recommended in the United Kingdom as early as 1964 by the government-commissioned Smeed report. It recommended that motorists should be charged according to the level of congestion on the road they were using. Two types of electronic road pricing were suggested: on-vehicle and off-vehicle systems. Both involved a magnet on the road which picked up the registration of the vehicle from the electronic number plate. The on-vehicle technology consisted of a meter inside the car (similar to a taxi meter) which clocked up units of road space. The more congested the road, the longer the journey would take and the more units would be used. The off-vehicle technology is compatible with the charging system which is common for telephones and could have resulted in the motorist being billed every quarter.

Although road pricing was originally proposed as a solution to congestion, it could also be used as a method of reducing road traffic for environmental reasons or as a way of ensuring that road users make payments which reflect the cost of the damage they cause to the environment or other social costs they impose. It could also be used to raise money for the building of new roads to make public transport a more attractive alternative to car use, or as a contribution to the government's general revenue. The objectives of a road pricing scheme determine what structure and levels of charges are appropriate.

The most successful existing road pricing scheme is in Singapore. One important factor contributing to its success is that Singapore is geographically isolated, as are the three Norwegian cities (Oslo, Bergen and Trondheim) which have introduced charges for entry. The success of the Singapore scheme is also related to the fact that they have introduced a predetermined number of permits for car ownership which are auctioned each year, and there is also a high annual tax on cars. In other countries, the political unattractiveness of road pricing has prevented progress towards it: a scheme in Hong Kong was never implemented, even though the pilot stage had been reasonably successful.

Road pricing has not been implemented in the United Kingdom mainly for political reasons. There is a very strong roads lobby and charging for the use of road space is seen as being a very draconian and unpopular measure.

10.3.2 *Arguments against road pricing*

1. *The motorist already pays too much in taxation*

This is an argument which is frequently advanced by the Automobile Association and the RAC. Figures for the fiscal year 1994–5 show that the government collected over £20 bn in tax from road users and yet central and local government only spent just under £7 bn on roads (capital cost of new construction plus maintenance). Therefore, if road users are already paying almost three times as much in tax for the infrastructure they use as it costs to provide and maintain it, why should they be asked to pay more?

The above is a very superficial argument which fails to take account of the significant external costs that we have already identified. Estimates of the environmental cost of road transport (air pollution, climatic change, noise and vibration and accidents) range from between £10.9 bn per annum and £20.5 bn per annum (Royal Commission on Environmental Pollution, 1994). If the accurate figure for environmental costs of transport is nearer the upper estimate then road users are not fully covering their true costs and therefore there is a strong case for increasing the tax burden on them. However, if the lower estimate proves to be accurate then it could be argued that road pricing would result in an added and unfair tax burden on road users. If this was the case then road pricing could still be introduced and other taxes, such as vehicle licence duty, could be reduced or abolished.

2. *It would be unfair on low income motorists*

Someone with a high income would be able to pay to access the congested road, while someone with a low income would be unable to pay and would, therefore, be priced off the road. There is clearly an equity issue to be dealt with here, although it is far from evident that road pricing is the proper way to deal with it. Moreover, there is a more important equity issue concerning how we ensure mobility and access for those people in society who do not have access to a car at all. Such people are becoming increasingly marginalised as public transport deteriorates and location decisions for work, leisure and shopping are tending to be made on the basis that people do have access to a car. Only 20 per cent of those in the lowest income quartile in the United Kingdom have access to a car; 57 per cent of this income group are women and 32 per cent are senior citizens (Department of Transport, 1986). A tax on motoring is a progressive tax because the number of cars per household increases with income as does the mileage travelled. If the significant sums of revenue that could be raised from road pricing were hypothecated and used to improve public transport then this would represent an extremely progressive taxation policy.

3.   *It would be simpler to increase fuel tax*

While the vehicle licence duty is a tax on car ownership and not related to car use, taxes on fuel are directly related to the mileage travelled. The external costs imposed by road users on the rest of society are directly related to miles travelled and a fuel tax is an effective way of internalising these costs.

The Royal Commission on Environmental Pollution recommended increasing the duty on fuel by 10 per cent per annum in real terms which would double the price of petrol by 2005. The Commission also supported road pricing in urban areas. The rationale behind these recommendations is that fuel tax is an effective tax on the air pollution emitted by road vehicles and is directly related to vehicle use, while road pricing is a more efficient way of taxing congestion. If the fuel tax were to be utilised as a congestion tax as well as a pollution tax, then it would be unfair to people in rural areas who are usually driving on uncongested roads.

10.4   Government transport policies since 1979

The election of the Conservative government in 1979 heralded the end of the political consensus on transport policy that had existed since 1945. The full weight of the 'Thatcher Revolution' was felt by the transport sector, with three main policies being pursued: deregulation, commercialisation and privatisation.

10.4.1   *Bus deregulation*

The government believed that the regulated framework which had dominated transport since the 1930s severely restricted competition, leading to inefficiencies and higher costs and fares.

The market for express bus services was deregulated by the 1980 Transport Act. This saw the birth of successful bus companies such as Stagecoach and the increased competition did result in lower fares and higher patronage. The government viewed the 1980 Transport Act as being very successful and this led them to introduce the 1985 Transport Act which deregulated local bus services. This Act was the most controversial and radical change in transport policy during the 1980s. Road service licensing, which was introduced in the 1930 Transport Act, was abolished for all parts of the United Kingdom except London. In justifying the legislation the government argued that bus services were inefficient and that the lack of competition increased operating costs with passengers being forced to pay higher fares for a deteriorating service.

Most local bus services are run on a commercial basis but local authorities do have the power to go out to tender and subsidise uneconomic services.

The government hoped that deregulation would arrest the decline in bus patronage which has been evident since the early 1950s. However, judging by the evidence shown in Figure 10.2, the 1985 Transport Act has actually accentuated the decline in patronage.

While bus kilometres have increased by 20 per cent since 1985, the number of passenger journeys has declined by 28 per cent and fares have increased in real terms by 10 per cent. The fall in the number of passengers, coupled with the increase in capacity has resulted in bus occupancy falling to only 8.7 per cent per vehicle (Department of Transport, 1992). While the proliferation in the number of minibuses has contributed to the fall in vehicle occupancies there has been an increase in the number of empty seats provided which is being paid for by passengers through higher fares.

However, bus operating costs have fallen by more than one-third in real terms since 1985. While there is evidence to suggest that bus companies are operating more efficiently, not all of the cost savings can be viewed as virtuous: staff wages have been cut by 9 per cent in real terms, there have been drastic

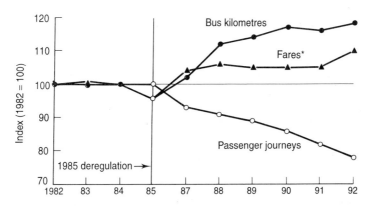

Figure 10.2 More empty seats, buses outside London. * Deflated by increase in retail prices.
Source: Department of Transport.

cuts in investment in new buses, maintenance standards have fallen and expensive parts of the operation (Sundays, evenings, and public holidays, etc.) have been cut.

It is the lack of investment in new buses which gives most cause for concern. An industry which is not investing is an unhealthy industry with an uncertain future. Competition has resulted in uncertainty and has squeezed profit margins. This has led to a fall in investment. Since 1985 the average age of a bus in the United Kingdom has increased from 7.2 years to 10.2 years, with the proportion of buses over 12 years old trebling since 1985 (Transport Operations Research Group, 1993). This trend, if continued, will lead to a deterioration in the quality of service and accentuate the decline in patronage. Proponents of the 1985 Transport Act would argue that it is not operating in the way it was intended to. They would point to increased concentration in the industry as a result of the high number of buyouts and non-competitive agreements between operators as factors which have stifled the level of competition. The fundamental question which needs to be addressed is whether competition is desirable in the long run for passengers and, if the conclusion is positive, whether the Office of Fair Trading and the Monopolies and Mergers Commission can be effective in enforcing it. The ever-increasing number of acquisitions in the UK bus industry will eventually result in a handful of large and powerful operators dominating the market. They could ensure that barriers to entry prohibit potential new operators from entering the market. The large operators have the necessary resources to engage in a fares war and/ or flood the market with buses to force new entrants out of the market. In most cases new entrants will not appear because of this competitive threat.

10.4.2   The changing structure of the bus industry

Privatisation and deregulation have resulted in a significant increase in concentration in the UK bus industry. Seven major operating groups control more than half of the local bus markets. Stagecoach, Badgerline, British Bus, the Go Ahead Group, Grampian Region Transport, MTL Trust Holdings (Merseybus) and West Midlands Travel took their combined share of the market to 53.3 per cent based on 1992–3 turnover. Of the remaining 46.7 per cent of the market, the smaller groups control only 10.5 per cent, management-controlled companies account for 20.6 per cent, while those owned by their employees and the remaining municipal companies control just 7.9 per cent and 8 per cent.

There has been a significant number of mergers and takeovers in the bus industry and management/employee shareholders around the country have joined in the rush to get the best deal possible for their businesses rather than be left in the position of being forced to sell on poorer terms at a later stage.

This trend underlines the long-held scepticism of many bus industry observers towards the government's insistence that deregulation would foster competition. Promises that deregulation would herald a new era of healthy competition have proved unfounded. It would appear that monopoly is the natural state of the bus industry. The private groups now dominating the market do so without the controls and accountability that existed when they were in the public sector. The higher profitability reflects not only economies of scale but also reductions in staff wages and conditions that have seen bus drivers slipping further and further down the pay league table. With no sign of any easing of the current merger mania – and despite the interest shown by the Monopolies and Mergers Commission in some recent deals – the trend is firmly towards increased concentration in the industry.

10.4.3 *The 1993 Railways Act*

The above piece of legislation is commonly referred to as railway privatisation. However, the Act concentrated more on deregulating the railways, with services being put out to franchise. The government's proposals have put the future of our railways into the hands of four main players: Railtrack, the Franchising Director, the Regulator, and British Rail Operations and Infrastructure Services (BRIS).

Railtrack will operate, maintain and invest in a fixed infrastructure, principally track and signalling. It will be responsible for defining train paths and timetabling them. It will be given the financial objective to break even after earning a defined rate of return on capital, recovering the bulk of its costs through charges to users of all kinds. The government initially announced that Railtrack would stay within the public sector. However, in December 1994 the Secretary of State for Transport, Brian Mawhinney, announced that the government would privatise Railtrack.

The Franchising Director will define services, singly or in bundles, which will be offered to independent train operators under competitive tender. The successful bid may be positive or negative, depending upon the view the market takes of the profitability of the bundle. It would generally be up to the bidder to decide the scale of charges to passengers, although the Franchising Director may control fares in certain circumstances. The contract for which a bid is made will specify the services to be offered; the Franchising Director will have 'booked' the appropriate train path with Railtrack in advance on known terms. The tariff will have two parts: a fixed access charge and a charge related to the volume of usage. The government intends that eventually it will pass all financial subsidies for the railways through the Franchising Director with the exception of certain capital grants. It will be the Franchising Director's responsibility to determine the level of the subsidy required to maintain each service.

The Regulator is to be established as an independent entity, with several functions. He or she will issue licences to operators, resolve disputes, prevent anticompetitive practices and be responsible for setting charges and making agreements between the active parties. He or she will oversee the agreements giving train service operators access to infrastructure, the agreements between the franchised service operators and the Franchising Director, and the operation of fares control. The Regulator will also approve the charging regime set by Railtrack for the use of the infrastructure. The Regulator can insist on an independent operator gaining access to the track on reasonable terms, including services in direct competition with those on franchise contracts – although the government has said that it may wish to restrict this direct competition in the early stages to ease the letting of the first franchises (Department of Transport, 1993, para. 5.1). Under an amendment to the original bill, the Regulator will also be under a duty to take into account any guidance given by the Secretary of State until the end of 1996.

British Rail Operations and Infrastructure Services will continue for a period – possibly for several years – while services are progressively franchised and the infrastructure is transferred. The government is keen to have complete franchising as soon as possible. Operations will be separate from Railtrack and will have a new and separate management structure. Railtrack will 'buy in' most of its services such as infrastructure maintenance, signalling repairs, investment, etc., initially from British Rail and, over time, from the private sector as these activities are transferred from British Rail ownership. Rail privatisation is extremely complex and is proving to be a sensitive political issue. There is a major difference between what the government is currently attempting to do to the railways and the privatisation of water or electricity. The latter are profitable industries whereas British Rail continues to enjoy significant public sector subsidy. This has meant that opposition parties have been able to question whether certain services will continue to be provided in the future. There is a clear risk that the openness of the franchising process will generate economic pressure to close lines and reduce services. While ministers have tended to exaggerate the degree of change and the possible benefits of change, opponents of rail privatisation have overplayed many potential difficulties of reforming the railways. The process of publishing the costs of operating particular services will lead to new pressures on the railway. Most of these pressures will arise because of increased openness about the condition, costs and benefits of the railway which may, in turn, lead to a debate about whether less (or more) should be spent on Britain's railway system (Glaister and Travers, 1993). The Regulator, Railtrack, and the director of franchising will each operate in a highly public and highly political environment where their decisions could lead to difficulties for the government.

10.5 Transport and the environment

Sustainable development, and in particular the goal of curbing 'greenhouse' gas emissions is nowhere more elusive than in the field of transport. The much-publicised 'Earth Summit' held in Rio in 1992 resulted in participating governments giving a commitment to draw up a strategy for sustainable development. The UK government set an objective of returning emissions of carbon dioxide (CO_2) to 1990 levels by the year 2000 (see Chapter 6). The consumption of fossil fuels is the prime culprit in the build up of CO_2, which along with a handful of other gases is thought to be warming the planet through its accumulation in the atmosphere.

The government's action, as outlined in *Sustainable Development: The UK strategy* (Department of Environment, 1994), sets a target for the transport sector to contribute around a quarter of the saving in CO_2 emissions by the end of the decade. The movement of people and goods currently represents almost a quarter of the UK CO_2 emissions and is the fastest growing source of this gas. Any strategy for tackling emissions of CO_2 must therefore take account of future trends in transport demands – in particular the approximate doubling in road traffic that is currently forecast to take place by the year 2025.

As far as the year 2000 target is concerned, the Department of Environment appears to have fought shy of tackling traffic growth head-on. Instead, improving the fuel efficiency of vehicles is identified as the most promising avenue for securing reductions in CO_2 emissions, encouraged by sustained increases in fuel duties. In the spring budget of 1993, the government proposed an annual 3 per cent real increase in fuel tax as well as a one-off fuel tax increase of 10 per cent. The government portrayed this strategy as an alternative to the 'carbon tax' on fossil fuels proposed by the European Commission. In the November budget of 1993 the government set a target of increasing the price of fuel by 5 per cent per annum in real terms until the end of the decade.

The Department of Transport's preference for fuel pricing as a means of curbing CO_2 emissions stems from the broad based influence that taxation is known to exert on fuel consumption. If signalled well in advance, fuel taxation does give a clear message to vehicle manufacturers to develop more fuel-efficient models. It also allows greater flexibility in the response that individuals make. They can choose to reduce car travel by switching to other transport modes or go in for car sharing, making shorter journeys or not make some journeys at all. They can drive more carefully, they can improve the maintenance of their vehicle or they can choose a more fuel-efficient car.

There is certainly evidence to suggest that fuel pricing measures, if introduced with sufficient vigour, could eliminate many of the inefficiencies which currently exist in the movement of people and goods. Numerous examples exist of energy wasting practices in freight distribution, where internal economies of centralisation may lead to goods travelling many hundreds of miles to a central depot. Similarly, in the personal travel sector, higher fuel costs could exert pressure for shopping and leisure trips to be shortened.

The Department of Transport's enthusiasm for technological solutions, and particularly for fuel efficiency improvements, could, however, be regarded as over optimistic. Improved energy efficiency (in the form of more economical cars and trucks) together with alternative fuels, could certainly deliver some reduction in emissions but this would be dependent on holding down overall vehicle kilometres travelled, for otherwise the savings will be more than cancelled out by increases elsewhere. Research has shown that the most significant influence on transport-related CO_2 emissions over the next 30 years will be the rate at which traffic is allowed to grow, rather than the characteristics of individual vehicles.

10.5.1 *Royal Commission on Environmental Pollution*

The government was challenged by the Royal Commission on Environmental Pollution to make dramatic changes in its transport priorities, with targets for reducing the environmental damage caused by the rising volume of movement and increasing the role of public transport and other alternatives to motor vehicles (Royal Commission on Environmental Pollution, 1994).

In a radical agenda covering a wide range of impacts caused by transport, the Commission calls for almost all new road building to be halted and for fuel prices to be doubled in real terms over the next 10 years. This is an increase which is twice as high as the target set by the government. The Commission recommended that the proportion of urban journeys undertaken by cars should be reduced from its current level of around 65 per cent to 50 per cent by the year 2020, with cycle use quadrupling to 10 per cent of urban trips by 2005. A goal of 30 per cent of passenger–kilometres for public transport was suggested, compared with the 12 per cent share at present. Corresponding targets were proposed for the freight sector, where the Commission calls for rail's share of tonne–kilometres to be increased from 6.5 per cent to 20 per cent over the next 15 years.

The Commission addressed the growing contribution of transport to CO_2 emissions by suggesting that the current target of stabilising emissions at 1990 levels (across all sectors) by the year 2000 be strengthened with a commitment to cut CO_2 emissions from transport to no more than 80 per cent of their 1990 level by the year 2020. The report suggests that the average mile per gallon of new cars should be increased by 40 per cent between 1990 and 2025. Excise duty on cars should be varied according to their official fuel economy rating, to promote sales of more economical cars. The Commission also called for local transport 'package' funding to be increased by easing the restrictions on the use of different types of grant. New Passenger Transport Authorities were proposed – including one for London – to ensure a coordinated approach in large urban areas.

The Royal Commission Report was a damning indictment of government transport policy and its recommendation that there should be more integration and coordination of transport as well as a halt to most new road building would, if implemented, represent a dramatic change in policy.

10.6 Conclusion

The report by the Royal Commission on Environmental Pollution (1994) included a comprehensive critique of government transport policy. The policy of introducing competition through deregulation and privatisation since 1979 may have been successful in other sectors in the economy, but transport must be viewed in a different light because the externalities are so great. The market mechanism leads to a misallocation of resources when there are substantial external costs which are not reflected in the price paid for a product. This is the case in the transport sector, where external costs in the form of congestion, air pollution, noise and accidents are borne by the rest of society and not the individual road user. There is a case for strong government intervention through fiscal and regulatory policies to ensure that the market does not distort resource allocation.

The government's free market approach to transport policy has encouraged the relentless growth in car use and resulted in severe traffic congestion problems, particularly in our cities, with growing medical concerns about the impact of car exhaust emissions on health. While private transport continues to grow rapidly, the number of people using public transport continues to decline. Although the growth in incomes must be a major factor in explaining this trend, it has been exacerbated by government transport policy. The significant cuts that have taken place in subsidies to British Rail (public service obligation) have increased fares in real terms and the 1985 Transport Act, which deregulated and privatised bus services, has accentuated the decline in bus patronage.

While it is widely acknowledged that improvements to public transport are essential if the growth in car use is to be contained there is also a need for other, more draconian measures, such as higher fuel tax, road pricing and possibly motorway tolling, if car use is to be reduced. The government have grasped the nettle as far as the higher tax on fuel is concerned, but road pricing and motorway tolling are still viewed as being too politically contentious. It is difficult to avoid the conclusion that until we charge directly for the use of road space then we will always face problems of excess demand and unacceptable levels of traffic congestion.

The language used by government ministers has changed in the 1990s when compared with the 1980s. There is an acceptance that we cannot continue to build roads as this could prove to be counter-productive, that we must reduce the damaging impact of transport on the environment and that public transport should be encouraged. Hopefully, the change in language will prove to be a precursor for a change in policy.

Questions for discussion

1. Explain why an understanding of what makes transport different from other sectors in the economy would be of assistance to decision-makers when formulating transport policy.
2. Discuss the economic and environmental case for introducing urban road pricing.
3. How successful has the 1985 Transport Act been in achieving the government's objective of arresting the decline in bus patronage?
4. Why is the privatisation of British Rail proving to be more complex and politically difficult than other privatisations?
5. Discuss government policies to contain the transport sector's environmental impact in the light of the 1994 report from the Royal Commission on Environmental Pollution.

References and further reading

British Roads Federation (1988) *The Way Ahead: The cost of congestion*, London: British Roads Federation.

Central Statistical Office (1994) *Social Trends 24*, London: HMSO.

Davis, R. (1993) *Death on the Streets*, Yorkshire: Leading Edge Press.

Department of Environment (1993) 'Road transport and the environment: the future agenda in the UK: air pollution' *The UK Environmental Foresight Project 2*, London: HMSO.

Department of Environment (1994) *Sustainable Development*, London: HMSO.

Department of Transport (1989) *Roads to Prosperity*, London: HMSO.

Department of Transport (1992) *Transport Statistics Great Britain*, London: HMSO.

Department of Transport (1993a) *National Travel Survey 1989/91*, London: HMSO.

Department of Transport (1993b) *Gaining Access to the Railway Network*, London: HMSO.

Glaister, S. and Travers, T. (1993) *New Directions for British Railways*, London: Institute of Economic Affairs.

Department of Transport (1985) *An Analysis of Personal Travel*, London: HMSO.

HMSO (1994) *Annual Abstract of Statistics*, London: HMSO.

Royal Commission on Environmental Pollution, 18th Report (1994) *Transport and the Environment*, London: HMSO.

Transport Operations Research Group (1993) 'The effect of bus deregulation and privatisation in the Scottish bus group' *Research Report No. 84*, Newcastle-upon-Tyne: University of Newcastle-upon-Tyne.

PART 2

Macroeconomic policy

CHAPTER 11

Fiscal policy and the public sector deficit

STUART SAYER

11.1 Introduction

Fiscal policy directly concerns taxation, government expenditure on goods and services, and transfer payments such as welfare benefits paid to the unemployed or poor. As such, it has many facets that cannot be adequately dealt with in a short chapter. The focus of this chapter is on broad macroeconomic aspects of fiscal policy and its financial implications, centring on the Public Sector Deficit (PSD). It is somewhat similar in spirit to the opening sections of an annual budget speech. Section 11.2 explains the PSD and provides a summary review of its behaviour in recent years. To assess this behaviour it is helpful to distinguish between long-run and short-run aspects, and these are considered in Sections 11.3 and 11.4, respectively. Section 11.5 addresses some specific issues to do with political pressures and expectations, that provide an interesting perspective on recent fiscal history. Finally, Section 11.6 concludes with a summary check-list that can be used to review the macroeconomic aspects of the annual budget.

11.2 The public sector deficit

In simple terms the public sector deficit arises from the difference between public sector outgoings and income over an accounting period. There are a number of different measures of the deficit based on different ways of measuring outgoings and income.

The most commonly used measure in the United Kingdom is the Public Sector Borrowing Requirement (PSBR). The PSBR directly measures the extent to which the public sector borrows from other sectors of the domestic economy or overseas. From 1987 to 1991 the PSBR was negative, so that instead of borrowing, the public sector was repaying previous borrowing, This negative PSBR was sometimes referred to as a (positive) Public Sector Debt Repayment. Many discussions, particularly in the media and political circles, treat the PSBR as the primary indicator of the state of the government's finances. This was formalised in the original version of the Medium Term Financial Strategy

(MTFS) introduced in 1980, which set out explicit targets for reducing PSBR/ GDP, and more recently the Maastricht treaty of the European Community set a guideline for PSBR/GDP (see Section 11.5).

One problem with the PSBR as a measure of the underlying state of the public sector's finances concerns its treatment of the sale of public sector assets, such as the sale of publicly owned corporations (e.g. British Telecom) or the sale of council houses. The proceeds raised from public sector asset sales directly reduce the need for the public sector to borrow and hence reduce the PSBR, at least in the accounting period in which the sale takes place. When assessing the state of the public sector's finances, however, public sector asset sales are best thought of as a means of *financing* the public sector deficit rather than as a means of *reducing* it (see the discussion in Section 11.3). To take account of this the proceeds from public sector asset sales ('privatisation proceeds') need to be added to the PSBR. This measure, referred to in official statistics as the PSBR excluding privatisation proceeds, is the measure of the PSD used below.

Figure 11.1 shows the actual behaviour of the PSD between 1970 and 1993 and the plans announced in the 1993 budget. It is presented as a percentage of GDP, since this provides a more meaningful scale than the basic numbers.

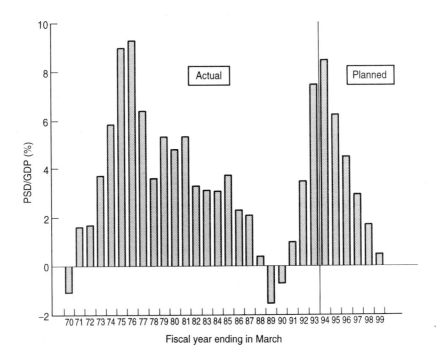

Figure 11.1 Public sector deficit as a percentage of GDP.
Sources: Financial Statement and Budget Report and *Annual Abstract of Statistics.*

Reading too much into these raw figures can be dangerous. The remaining sections of this chapter aim to elucidate this behaviour and, as should become apparent, first impressions may be misleading. Two features of Figure 11.1 are worth highlighting. First, PSD/GDP has varied markedly, ranging from a high of 9.3 per cent in the fiscal year 1975–6, to a surplus (i.e. a negative PSD/GDP) of 1.6 per cent in 1988–9. Secondly, in contrast to party-political rhetoric, there does not appear to have been a particularly dramatic change in the state of public sector finances under the Conservative administrations that have been in power since 1979.

A more detailed picture of what underlies the behaviour of PSD/GDP can be obtained by considering the behaviour of the public sector outgoings and income that give rise to the PSD. The main source of public sector income is tax revenues. The behaviour of tax revenues as a percentage of GDP (T/GDP) is shown in Figure 11.2. An important point to note is that, despite the much publicised cuts in rates of personal income taxation, the tax share of GDP was consistently higher throughout the 1980s than it was in the previous decade. This partly stems from 'fiscal drag' since tax thresholds, at which one starts to pay basic or higher rates of tax, have not risen in line with GDP, as well as from changes in the structure of taxation, notably increases in the rate of VAT. In addition to tax revenue, public sector income includes revenue from assets

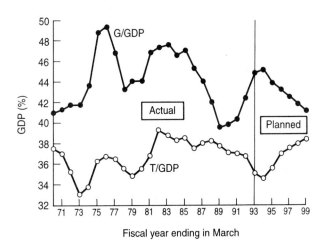

Fiscal year ending in March

Figure 11.2   Tax revenues and general government expenditure as a percentage of GDP.
Notes: G/GDP, general government expenditure as a percentage of GDP; T/GDP, tax revenue (including social security contributions but excluding North Sea taxes) as a percentage of GDP.
Source: Financial Statement and Budget Report.

owned by the public sector. Although this makes a relatively small contribution to public sector income, it is of some importance when considering public sector asset sales as a source of finance for the deficit. The sale of public sector assets straightforwardly reduces the flow of revenue that the public sector would have received from these assets in future periods.

Turning to public sector outgoings, the main outgoings are classified as General Government Expenditure (GGE), which comprises expenditure by central and local government on consumption, capital investment, transfer payments and interest payments on public sector debt. Figure 11.2 shows the behaviour of this measure of government expenditure as a percentage of GDP (G/GDP). Comparing Figures 11.1 and 11.2 there is a clear relationship between the behaviour of PSD/GDP and G/GDP. Both peak in 1974–6, fall in the latter part of the 1970s under the Labour government, rise in the early 1980s under the Conservatives, fall substantially in the latter part of the 1980s, and rise again in the early 1990s.

Breaking down GGE into the four components listed above provides further insight (see Figures 11.3a, 11.3b). One important feature of Figure 11.3b that is worth highlighting is the very low level of general government investment expenditure throughout the 1980s. This is a potential cause for concern to which we return later.

Returning to the more aggregated picture provided by Figure 11.2, actual and planned G/GDP is now substantially lower than it was throughout much of the 1970s and early 1980s. The consideration of whether this change has been wholly or partly desirable raises complex and important issues to do with the scale and scope of government that we do not address directly in this

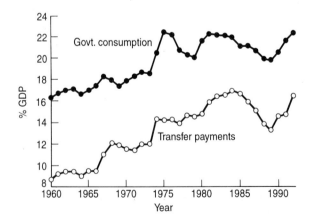

Figure 11.3a   Public sector consumption and transfer payments as a percentage of GDP.
Source: Economic Trends.

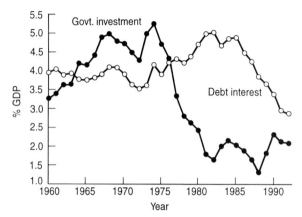

Figure 11.3b   Public sector investment and debt interest as a percentage of GDP.
Note: Government investment is measured by GGE on gross domestic fixed capital formation.
Source: Economic Trends.

chapter (but see Chapters 1, 3 and 7).[1] Our concern is primarily with the broader picture provided by the overall PSD, though the component parts that make up the PSD do, at times, have an important bearing on our discussion.

11.3   Deficits, money and debt in the long run

When assessing the PSD/GDP ratio from a long-run perspective the key issues concern the consequences of financing the PSD. Three main ways of financing the PSD can be distinguished, which we consider in turn.

11.3.1   *Public sector asset sales*

Public sector asset sales, related to privatisation, have provided a significant source of finance during the 1980s (see Figure 11.4). As noted in Section 11.2, the proceeds from public sector asset sales constitute the difference between our measure of the PSD and the PSBR, so that subtracting public sector asset sales from the PSD gives the PSBR. Since public sector asset sales reduce the PSBR, at least in the accounting period in which the sale takes place, they have the attraction of improving the appearance of the government's finances as well as making it easier to meet targets for PSBR/GDP. This appearance is, at least for the most part, cosmetic and misleading. In the first place, public sector asset sales can normally only provide a temporary rather than sustainable source of finance. Once the asset sales programme is completed, this source of finance dries up.[2] When this occurs the PSD will either have to be reduced or financed by some other means. Secondly, the current reduction of the PSBR

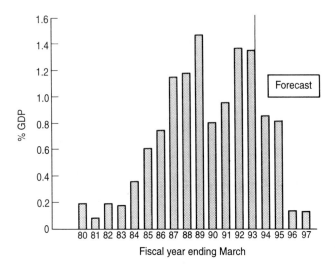

Figure 11.4 Public sector asset sales as a percentage of GDP.
Sources: Annual Abstract of Statistics and Financial Statement and Budget Report.

resulting from an asset sale is offset by the increase in the PSD and PSBR in all future time periods that results from the loss to the public sector of the income stream from the asset. Thirdly, public sector asset sales absorb private sector savings in much the same way as the sale of interest bearing government debt. Somewhat simplistically, since the adjustments to savings behaviour are more complex than this, individuals or institutions who might otherwise have purchased interest bearing government debt to finance a given amount of the PSD, may use the identical funds to purchase public sector assets and finance the PSD by an equivalent amount. Moreover, the loss in the public sector's revenue stream resulting from the asset sale is, in essence, similar to the interest stream payable on government debt.

11.3.2 *Increasing the monetary base or high powered money (money finance)*

In simple terms this can be thought of as printing new money to finance the PSD, though the monetary base also includes bankers' balances at the Bank of England in addition to notes and coin. This method of financing the PSD utilises the seignorage gain that accrues to the issuer of money. 'Seignorage' reflects the difference between the direct costs of creating new money which, particularly for notes and bankers' balances, are relatively trivial, and the value of the goods and services for which the new money can be exchanged (see also Chapter 12). At first sight this might seem an attractive and painless way of financing the PSD. However, there are potentially serious drawbacks that stem from the inflationary consequences of excessive money creation.

11.3.3 The sale of interest-bearing government debt

The key feature of financing the current PSD by the sale of interest-bearing government debt is that this will result in a time stream of interest payments raising the PSD in all future time periods. The consequences of this depend on whether or not the rate of interest on government debt exceeds the rate of growth of GDP. If the interest rate is less than the growth rate, then it is possible for all the interest payments on outstanding debt to be financed by new debt issue, without any increase in government debt as a proportion of GDP (GD/GDP). This condition appeared to be satisfied in the mid- to late 1970s when inflation was unexpectedly high, but care needs to be taken when considering this episode since unexpectedly high inflation is not sustainable. In more recent years the interest rate on government debt has exceeded the growth rate of GDP, and we focus on this case here. In this case financing the interest payments on outstanding debt by new debt issue is potentially explosive, the GD/GDP ratio would become larger and larger, and ultimately this is not sustainable.

However, far from exploding, the actual GD/GDP ratio in the United Kingdom declined significantly from 1976 to 1991. Despite the recent rise in GD/GDP during the recession of the early 1990s it remains substantially lower than in the mid-1970s (see Figure 11.5). Whether this decline has been altogether desirable is a complex and contentious issue. Reducing the GD/GDP ratio has transitional effects which we discuss in Section 11.4. The precise nature of these effects depends on circumstances, but in general they can be

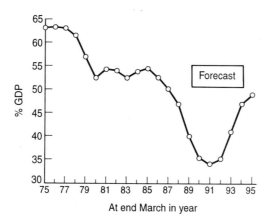

Figure 11.5   Government debt as a percentage of GDP.
Sources: Annual Abstract of Statistics and *Financial Statement and Budget Report.*

thought of as requiring taxes to be higher or government expenditure lower than they would otherwise be. If we could start from scratch, or rewrite history, we might prefer a lower GD/GDP ratio. But given the GD/GDP ratio we have inherited from the past, the current cost of reducing it may outweigh any (suitably discounted) future benefits. This argument applies with particular force to the current situation in the United Kingdom, since the UK's GD/GDP ratio is now low by both historical and international standards.

Comparing Figures 11.1 and 11.5 suggests a puzzle. Even though the PSD/GDP ratio was substantially positive for most of the period the GD/GDP ratio fell from 63 per cent in 1975 to 35 per cent in 1990. To a very limited extent this can be explained by other means of financing the PSD – e.g. public sector asset sales – but this by no means provides a complete explanation. The solution to the puzzle hinges on the fact that the capital value of most government debt is fixed in money terms. In consequence the value of outstanding debt does not rise automatically in line with either real GDP growth or inflation, so that the GD/GDP ratio automatically falls as nominal GDP grows unless new debt is issued. In order to maintain a stable GD/GDP ratio new debt has to be issued in proportion to nominal GDP growth, and this has implications for the PSD/GDP needed to maintain a stable GD/GDP ratio.

A simple calculation, set out in Buiter (1985), gives a rough guide to the numbers involved. Suppose the GD/GDP ratio is to remain stable at 50 per cent, and the annual real growth rate of GDP is 2.5 per cent. With zero inflation, new debt issues of 1.25 per cent of GDP would be required (i.e. the 50% GD/GDP ratio times the real growth rate of 2.5%). Whereas, if the stable inflation target were 5 per cent, there would need to be additional new debt issues of 2.5 per cent of GDP to offset the effects of inflation (i.e. the 50% GD/GDP ratio times the 5% inflation rate). Overall, new debt issues amounting to 3.75 per cent of GDP would be needed to maintain the stable GD/GDP ratio in the 5 per cent inflation case. The PSD/GDP ratio that this warrants depends on the seignorage revenue from increasing the monetary base. Using Buiter's estimates, the 5 per cent inflation case allows a sustainable PSD/GDP ratio of 4.1 per cent, while the zero inflation case allows 1.4 per cent. (See Buiter, 1985, for further elaboration and a discussion of alternative approaches to estimating the sustainable PSD/GDP ratio.)

This analysis sheds an interesting light on the medium-term plans of the current government. These plans envisage maintaining a zero PSBR/GDP on average over the medium term. The consequences of this strategy depend on inflation. Even assuming a zero inflation rate, this strategy may involve further reductions in the GD/GDP ratio. A more realistic assumption about inflation is that it will be low but positive (e.g. between 2% and 5%). This implies even more strongly that the medium-term strategy set out by the government involves further reductions in the GD/GDP ratio. Given that the GD/GDP ratio is already low, the merits of this strategy are questionable.

11.4   Short-term variations in PSD/GDP

Relative to some benchmark level of a stable GD/GDP ratio, a reduction in GD/GDP requires the current PSD/GDP to be lower than it would otherwise be. In future periods the reduced GD/GDP ratio will mean that interest payments on outstanding debt are lower, so that a given PSD/GDP target allows for either lower revenues or some other component of public sector outgoings to be greater. For simplicity we will concentrate on tax revenues, so that a reduction in GD/GDP involves an increase in current tax revenues and a reduction in future tax revenues, relative to the benchmark. Conversely, an increase in GD/GDP involves a cut in current tax revenues and an increase in future tax revenues. In effect changes in the GD/GDP ratio redistribute the tax burden over time.

How should the government make use of this ability to redistribute the tax burden over time? We focus on two broad cases that serve to illustrate the basic principles and shed light on recent fiscal policy in the United Kingdom (e.g. the increase in PSD/GDP in the early 1990s shown in Figure 11.1).

11.4.1.   *Exceptional public sector investment*

The focus on exceptional investment is important. 'Normal' public sector investment should take place at a more or less even rate over time. Exceptional situations may, however, arise from time to time. Two pertinent examples are unforeseen disasters, such as an environmental catastrophe or war, and the cumulative effect of past under-investment by the public sector, which may have stemmed from the political pressures for short-sightedness that are considered in Section 11.5. Assuming that the exception is genuine, then some increase in the GD/GDP ratio to provide at least partial finance for the investment would normally be justified. One simple justification is that the timing of the tax burden should be related to the timing of the benefits that accrue in the future from the investment. Further, by smoothing the tax burden over time, rather than wholly financing the exceptional expenditure by a rise in current taxation, debt financing can reduce the distortions arising from taxation and help the private sector to even out consumption over time (this is spelled out in more detail in the second case below).

A key difficulty of applying this prescription is identifying genuine exceptions. In some cases this may be relatively straightforward, e.g. (thankfully) war. In others, particularly specific cases of alleged under-investment, for example in transport, prisons, the sewage system, health, training and education, this can be more problematic. Those making the case may have a natural tendency to regard their interests as exceptional. On the other hand, it may be politically convenient to dismiss genuine exceptions as the product of vested interests at least until some crisis is experienced. We return to this issue in Section 11.5.

Consideration of this case can provide interesting insights into the arguments surrounding cutting rates of income tax. One beguiling argument runs as follows. Cutting income tax rates improves incentives, so although the impact effect of a cut in income tax rates will be to reduce revenue, at a given level of economic activity, over time the improvement of incentives will raise the level of activity to offset this effect, or even generate higher tax revenues from lower tax rates. If this argument were true, cutting income tax rates has obvious attractions. It effectively raises the size of the national cake in the long run, giving scope for both higher public and private sector expenditure. However, in the short run, until incentive effects have raised the tax base sufficiently, tax revenues will fall and this temporary fall in tax revenues will need to be financed. One approach is to allow PSD/GDP to rise and use debt finance, and this can be justified along the lines discussed above by thinking of the tax cut as an exceptional investment.

Although this argument, in various guises, has received widespread currency in recent years, it suffers from a fundamental weakness. There is no evidence to support the belief that cutting income tax rates has the substantial effects on incentives envisaged by the above argument. Cuts in the basic rate of income tax appear to have no significant effects on the incentive to work and unambiguously reduce tax revenues. The effect of cuts in higher rates of income tax is less clear, partly because the available information on higher rate tax payers is limited. Again the balance of the evidence suggests that there is little or no effect on work incentives, though the revenue effects are more complex since, for example, cuts in higher rates of taxes may alter the way in which taxpayers choose to be compensated (see Brown, 1988; and Dilnot and Kell, 1988).

Some exponents of tax cuts argue that this evidence is limited because it neglects longer-term changes to the work and risk-taking culture, which they regard as important. The weight of the evidence seems clear that, at least at the rates that have prevailed in the United Kingdom, cutting the basic rate of income tax produces a permanent reduction in tax revenue below what it would otherwise have been. If the tax rate cut is to be sustained, there must be a permanent change to some other component of the public sector finances: for example, an increase in some other form of taxation (e.g. taxes on expenditure such as VAT) or a permanent reduction in government outgoings below what they otherwise would have been. Tax rate cuts do not provide a magic solution that allow us to have our cake and eat it, though the attractions of this magic solution can be important in the context of the political issues introduced in Section 11.5.

11.4.2   *Stabilisation over an economic cycle*

The second case concerns an economic cycle in which GDP fluctuates about its trend path. Standard economic analysis suggests that consumers plan to even out their consumption over the cycle. In a recession, where GDP is below its trend, they would choose to increase the proportion of current income devoted to consumption and finance this by borrowing or dissaving against the expectation of higher future income. Conversely, in a boom where GDP is above trend, they would reduce the proportion of income consumed and increase savings. The ability of the private sector to smooth their consumption in this way is limited by the operation of financial and credit markets. The spread (i.e. difference) between borrowing and lending rates available to private sector agents – particularly individuals and small- to medium-sized corporations – is often large. This can make it unattractive to borrow when times are bad and lend when times are good. In some cases individuals may be unable to obtain any credit at all (e.g. the unemployed in a recession) or be required to pay exorbitant rates of interest. Recent theroretical work on the operation of financial and credit markets suggests that there are good reasons, to do with information and risk, for these limitations on private sector borrowing and lending. For our purpose they have the important implication that it is generally easier for the government to reallocate income or spending power over time, by varying PSD/GDP, than it is for at least most private sector agents.

This argument suggests that PSD/GDP should be higher than normal in a cyclical recession. In effect the public sector increases its borrowing in a recession, and the tax payments made by the private sector are lower than they would need to be to maintain the normal PSD/GDP ratio. Since tax payments take a smaller share of current income, private sector agents can afford to devote a larger share of current income to consumption, limiting their need to borrow to finance consumption smoothing. Conversely, in a boom PSD/GDP should be lower than normal or even negative, with the tax payments made by the private sector being higher than they would need to be to maintain the normal PSD/GDP ratio.

At least loosely, this is reflected in the behaviour of PSD/GDP in the late 1980s and early 1990s (see Figure 11.1). PSD/GDP was low or negative in the boom phase of the late 1980s, followed by a substantial increase in PSD/GDP in the recession of the early 1990s. Although this might appear to validate the fiscal policy of the period, this simple observation needs to be treated with considerable caution.

In addition to the pure consumption smoothing argument just outlined, resources may also be utilised inefficiently over the economic cycle, for instance as a result of various frictions inhibiting the operation of market forces. If resources are used inefficiently then a judicious use of fiscal policy may be able to improve efficiency. A relatively simple example is an economy where frictions result in underutilised or unemployed resources in a recession. One possible response might be to use current fiscal policy to improve the efficiency of resource use. For example, taxation might be increased on those in work, whose income might be little affected by the recession, in order to finance an increase in public sector expenditure that uses unemployed resources for some socially useful purpose. In general, however, it is more efficient to spread this tax burden over time by increasing PSD/GDP, since this enables both tax and consumption smoothing.

Although these arguments establish a broad case for varying the PSD/GDP ratio over the cycle, they sidestep a number of important practical problems to do with the timing, size and structure of fiscal policy actions.

Ideally the timing of PSD/GDP changes should coincide with the timing of the income changes that they are designed to smooth. In practice, at least when the underlying disturbance that causes the income change is unpredicted, there is likely to be a lag before the PSD/GDP ratio can be adjusted. Further, it may take time for the change in fiscal policy to take effect, particularly in the presence of frictions. In the extreme, if this lag is sufficiently long relative to the length of the cycle, the policy may itself be destabilising.

With regard to the appropriate size of PSD/GDP changes it is difficult to generalise. The ideal size depends on the nature of the cycle, the significance of impediments to borrowing and lending in the private sector, the timing and structure of the PSD/GDP change, as well as other components of the policy package notably monetary, interest rate and exchange rate policy.

The question of structure concerns the need for the underlying changes in government outgoings or taxation to be appropriately directed to those whose income or employment is affected by the cycle in order for variations in PSD/GDP to actually bring about income or employment smoothing. This question is often neglected in simple macro economic models which focus on aggregate income or employment. In practice the main effects of disturbances are commonly localised, either geographically or in particular industrial or employment sectors, or some sector or region may gain while others lose. Where the disturbance is localised a general fiscal stimulus, such as a cut in income taxes, can exacerbate rather than dampen the fluctuations in income since the majority of the beneficiaries of the tax cut are unaffected by the disturbance. Some attempt at targeting, e.g. by subsidies or tax cuts directed at specific industries or regions, would normally be worthwhile, though information and administrative difficulties make it difficult for fiscal policy to be perfectly targeted.

A more specific, but important, complication concerns the distinction between temporary cyclical variations in income and employment, and permanent shocks that cause a permanent shift in the trend path of income and employment. The smoothing argument outlined above only applies straightforwardly to cyclical movements. By contrast a permanent shock requires a permanent adjustment to consumption. The practical problem is that at the time they occur it may be difficult or impossible to distinguish between a temporary and a permanent shock. If a permanent shock is mistakenly thought to be temporary, a mistake that may be made by both public and private sectors, then both private sector borrowing and PSD/GDP may be set inappropriately high.

This scenario can provide some insight into recent fiscal history in the United Kingdom and elsewhere (see Roubini and Sachs, 1989). A widespread view is that the United Kingdom suffered from a permanent downward shock, or series of shocks, to potential output and employment in the late 1960s and early 1970s, reflected in a permanent increase in the Non-Accelerating-Inflation-Rate-of-Unemployment (NAIRU) (see Chapter 12 for further discussion). The initial response was to treat this permanent shock as if it were a temporary cyclical downturn in activity and increase PSD/GDP, most notably in the so-called Barber boom in 1973–4. In addition a substantial portion of the PSD was financed by money rather than debt. The consequences were high inflation and a depreciating exchange rate. Eventually, in the later 1970s and early 1980s, uncomfortable fiscal adjustments had to be made to take account of the permanent nature of the shock. The initially inappropriate response made these adjustments more uncomfortable than would have otherwise been the case, and at least some would argue that the adjustments were more painful than was strictly necessary.

It is also misleading to think of the PSD/GDP ratio as directly under the control of the government. In practice both the PSD and GDP may differ quite markedly from the government's offical projections set out in the budget. Further, the PSD will tend to be higher than expected when GDP is lower than expected, since lower GDP reduces tax revenues by reducing the tax base on which given rates of income and expenditure taxes are charged, and also tends to increase those who qualify for transfer payments (e.g. unemployment benefits, income supplement). In consequence, the effect of forecasting errors on the PSD/GDP ratio can be quite dramatic. For example, in recent years the average error in the forecast for the coming year's PSD has been around 1 per cent of GDP.

This automatic variation of the PSD/GDP ratio has some attractions when viewed as a response to an unforeseen cyclical disturbance. It is likely to be fairly well directed to the extent that those who suffer an unforeseen income loss pay lower taxes or receive transfer payments. The delays associated with legislative action to change tax rates or outgoings are avoided. Although it should be noted that the automatic response of tax and transfer payments to an income disturbance is not immediate, as is clear from the estimates cited below, there are various administrative delays in practice and some tax payments in particular are paid substantially in arrears. The key problem with this automatic effect is that its size is an essentially arbitrary feature of the tax and transfer system and there is no guarantee that it produces the right size of response to a particular disturbance. A rough guide, based on recent Treasury estimates, is that a 1 per cent decline in GDP relative to trend will 'automatically' increase PSD/GDP by 0.3 per cent in the first year and 0.7 per cent in the second year (see Davies, 1991).[3] Naturally, this automatic response does not distinguish between temporary and permanent movements in GDP, and for the latter it is likely to be inappropriate. Thus, despite their prominence in recent budget speeches, 'automatic stabilisers' need to be treated with caution. The need for discretionary judgements about the appropriate stance of fiscal policy remains.

11.5   Government failure, political pressures and expectations

For a variety of reasons governments may tend to set the PSD/GDP ratio at an inappropriate level, or the underlying components of fiscal policy that give rise to the PSD may be poorly structured to deal with the current economic situation. This may result from more or less understandable errors of judgement; for example, misinterpreting a permanent shock as a transitory shock as discussed in Section 11.4; or anticipating a down-turn in economic activity that does not materialise, e.g. following the October 1987 Stock Exchange crash. The consequences of inappropriate policy tend to be asymmetric. A prodigal policy – i.e. an excessive or poorly structured PSD/ GDP – tends to generate a nominal boom, with higher inflation and a depreciating exchange rate, especially if a significant part of the PSD is money financed so that fiscal policy is reinforced by an 'accomodating' monetary policy. In contrast, an excessively tight fiscal policy tends to induce a real recession. Specific examples depend on one's underlying judgements about the appropriateness of policy. Many commentators regard the early 1980s as illustrating an excessively tight fiscal policy with an associated real recession, although see below for a subtly different view of this period. Similarly, many regard the 'Lawson boom' of 1987–8 as illustrating a prodigal policy with an associated resurgence of inflation.

The problems can be more serious if fiscal policy is subject to a systematic bias. To illustrate, we concentrate on one fairly general and simple story that has been applied to recent fiscal history in the United Kingdom and elsewhere. The basis of the story is that decisions in practice are boundedly rational, i.e. they are based on limited information and a relatively short time horizon. In 'normal' times attention is focused on the immediate benefits of an increase in the GD/GDP ratio in terms of the current reduction in taxes or increase in government outgoings. Although at some future date the PSD/GDP ratio will have to be cut, for the long-run reasons discussed above this does not cross information thresholds. In effect, people act as if tomorrow never comes, or at least does not come in their own lifetime, so that the burden of cutting the PSD/ GDP ratio will be borne by future generations and is not of immediate concern.

These perceptions give rise to political pressures, both from the electorate and interest groups, for a high and possibly rising PSD/GDP ratio, and policy-makers, who are also subject to bounded rationality, succumb to these pressures. Although for appearances' sake they may attempt to disguise this fiscal prodigality as a prudent response to the current economic situation (see

Buchanan, Burton and Wagner, 1978, who also consider other aspects of the political system that may add to these pressures). As well as affecting the overall level of PSD/GDP, boundedly rational (and other) political pressures may also bias the fiscal components that give rise to the PSD. For example, policy may be focused on changes that give immediate and obvious benefits – e.g. cuts in income tax or increases in outgoings directed at powerful interest groups – at the expense of other areas, e.g. less visible taxes on expenditure, and public sector investment, especially where it yields indirect and long-term benefits. A further influential variant of this story argues that the pressures to increase the PSD/GDP ratio are particularly pronounced in the run-up to an election, giving rise to the notion of give-away election budgets and the political business cycle. Despite the popular attention given to political business cycles, however, the evidence in support of this notion, at least in a simple form, is at best weak (see Alesina, 1989).

Periodically, normal times are interrupted by crises, when some key indicator, notably the rate of inflation, balance of payments and/or exchange rate, moves outside its accepted limits. The cause of the crisis may be the cumulative effects of an excessive PSD/GDP, but other factors may also be at work, e.g. major disturbances such as oil price shocks and excessive monetary growth. In some cases crises may even arise as a result of disturbances in financial markets that have little or no basis in fundamental economic activity (see Sayer, 1992). Once a crisis is perceived, fiscal policy is focused on responding to the crisis. Crisis rhetoric may emphasise a concern with long-run fiscal prudence, although the boundedly rational focus on the immediate crisis, allied to feelings of guilt about past profligacy and the need for harsh medicine, may give rise to a tougher fiscal stance than long-run fiscal prudence requires. Once the key indicators have fallen back below their information thresholds and feelings of guilt have receded normal times return, until the next crisis unfolds.

This simple story has a certain intuitive appeal, though it is difficult to formulate and test in a rigorous fashion. One problem is that boundedly rational perceptions and pressures appear to change over time. In part this may reflect increasing recognition of and desire to avert the type of fiscal cycle that the story describes; but there are other apparent changes. For example, in comparison to the 1970s unemployment appears to have become more politically acceptable and inflation less (i.e. their respective crisis thresholds appear to have shifted), and the perceived benefits of income tax cuts, at the expense of other components of the PSD, appears to have increased. A further important issue concerns the increasing scale and sophistication of financial markets (partly related to the regulatory changes discussed in Chapter 13), which has made the reaction of financial markets to fiscal policy increasingly significant. Some argue that financial markets help to check fiscal prodigality. Others take a less benign view, arguing that the reactions of financial markets may be biased or unrelated to fundamental economic behaviour.

The consideration of expectations, whether in financial markets or elsewhere, adds a subtle twist to the above story. If fiscal policy is expected to be prodigal, which may be a reasonable expectation in the light of the above story, this expectation will itself tend to put upward pressure on inflation and interest rates and downward pressure on the exchange rate. Moreover, given the expectation that policy will be prodigal, the best short-term response of the government may be to pursue a prodigal fiscal policy. Failure to do so would cause a surprise or expectational error, which would be likely to depress output and employment. In effect the government may become caught in a trap where expectations of prodigality become self-fulfilling. In order to escape this trap, expectations of fiscal prodigality need to be revised downwards. We briefly consider three approaches, which can also be interpreted more broadly in terms of the basic bounded rationality story.

First, despite the costs to output and employment, the government may pursue a tighter than expected fiscal policy in order to establish a reputation for fiscal prudence. This may be difficult if expectations of prodigality are firmly entrenched, and there may remain a lurking suspicion that at some point the government will revert to its prodigal ways. A variant of this approach is to tighten fiscal policy dramatically to try to signal a clear break with the past. The immediate effects of such a regime shift on output and employment may be severe, but this may serve to reinforce the signal and allay suspicions, since a government that was not firmly committed to fiscal prudence might be thought to be unwilling to countenance these effects. This provides an interesting interpretation of the controversial 1981 budget, where in the depths of a recession the budget changes were aimed at increasing tax revenues by about 1.6 per cent of GDP. This interpretation needs to be treated with a certain amount of care, since there are other aspects of the 1981 budget that need to be considered to tell a complete story (see Budd, 1991; or Allsopp, 1985). It can also be of interest to consider the sequel to this budget. Having administered this sharp shock to expectations (or crisis response), did subsequent administrations maintain fiscal prudence or revert to prodigality in a manner similar to that suggested by the bounded rationality story outlined above?

Secondly, the government may enter into a commitment that indirectly limits the scope for fiscal prodigality. The Exchange Rate Mechanism (ERM) of the European Monetary System provided an example of such a commitment. The key feature of the ERM was that, while the United Kingdom remained a full member of the ERM, it limited the permitted normal movement of the exchange rate for sterling against other member currencies to within a fairly narrow band (see Chapter 14 for further details). The commitment was not, however, fully binding. The ERM allowed for the possibility of the target band being adusted in exceptional circumstances and there was the option of withdrawing from the ERM, as was illustrated by the withdrawal of sterling by the United Kingdom in September 1992. These options weakened the force of the commitment, since they allowed member governments to choose to adjust or abandon their target exchange rate rather than make the other adjustments needed to maintain the exchange rate. The proposed moves towards European Monetary Union (EMU), outlined in the Maastricht treaty, envisage a stronger commitment to fixed exchange rates, as well as removing the scope for individual nations to decide unilaterally to increase monetary growth to provide more seignorage revenue to finance the deficit. Following the events of 1992 the planned progression towards EMU has been put on hold. One interesting, though difficult, question that arises from these events is whether the speculative attacks on sterling and other currencies could have been avoided had there been a firmer commitment to maintaining fixed exchange rates.

Attempting to answer this question and provide a full consideration of the ERM and EMU would involve a number of important political and economic issues that would take us too far afield. We focus here on one relatively simple implication of the ERM, and more generally fixed exchange rate targets, for fiscal policy. That is, that if fiscal policy puts downward pressure on the exchange rate, this will need to be offset by higher domestic interest rates (i.e. tighter monetary or interest rate policy) in order to maintain the exchange rate within its target band. In a sense the effects of a prodigal fiscal policy under the ERM become more concentrated on high domestic interest rates, and can no longer be dissipated in an exchange rate depreciation. The political and economic consequences of high interest rates may dampen the government's enthusiasm for fiscal prodigality, although the effectiveness of this mechanism is questionable. In the eyes of a number of critics, fiscal policy in the late 1980s and early 1990s was prodigal (at least in the sense of being poorly structured, even if the overall PSD/GDP ratio was more or less right). The resulting exchange rate pressures meant that interest rates had to be maintained at undesirably high levels (see e.g. Vines, 1989), and ultimately led to sterling's withdrawal from the ERM in September 1992.

Thirdly, the government may enter into a commitment that directly limits the scope for fiscal prodigality. A topical example is the guideline agreed as part of the EC Maastricht treaty of a PSBR/GDP ratio of 3 per cent. Again there are important wider aspects of this guideline that relate to the conduct of fiscal policy under full EMU, although we focus here on the narrower merits of such a guideline as a credible check on fiscal prodigality. One basic point links back to the discussion of Section 11.3; that is, since the target is expressed in terms of the PSBR rather than the PSD, this may encourage inappropriate public sector asset sales, to finance a prodigal fiscal policy within the 3 per cent guideline. However, even if the guideline had been stated in terms of PSD/ GDP, problems would remain since the 3 per cent guideline may not always be appropriate. Explicitly if, in the light of the underlying economic situation, the appropriate PSBR/GDP were less than 3 per cent, this leaves some scope for fiscal prodigality without breaching the guideline. On the other hand, situations may arise where the appropriate PSBR/GDP exceeds 3 per cent, so that if the guideline were strictly interpreted as an upper limit fiscal policy would be tighter than the underlying situation warrants. To avoid the latter problem exceptions may be allowed, and provision for this was made in the Maastricht treaty. Provided that the exceptions are genuine there is a clear sense to this provision. However, there is a corresponding danger that more dubious exceptions will be allowed, or be expected to be allowed, and this effectively weakens the credibility of the commitment.

11.6   Conclusions

A basic point that emerges from the foregoing discussion is that fiscal policy is complex. Simple prescriptions, such as maintaining a zero PSD on average over the medium term, or raising PSD/GDP in response to any down-turn in economic activity, are too simple. Moreover, things are not always what they seem. 'Automatic stabilisers' may not always be stabilising, and a deficit may be consistent with a falling GD/GDP ratio. While it is important to recognise this complexity, and be sceptical of simplistic answers, it would be wrong to conclude that fiscal policy is an incomprehensible morass. At least as far as the macroeconomic aspects of fiscal policy are concerned, it is relatively easy to understand the main issues that should and do affect budget judgements. The following check-list provides a guide that is roughly based on the structure of this chapter.

11.6.1   *Budget check-list*

1. Assess the long-run target for PSD/GDP, taking into account the target for inflation.
2. Assess the components of PSD/GDP from a long-run perspective. What should be the long-run levels of different components of outgoings and revenue (as a proportion of GDP)? Is the tax share too high? Or is it too low to provide funding for adequate public sector expenditures and transfer payments? Is public sector investment too low?
3. Assess the underlying state of the economy at the time of the budget and over the future when budgetary actions will have their effects. Particular issues to consider include the following: the nature of disturbances and their consequences – e.g. are they temporary or permanent? Domestic or global? Supply or demand shocks? Concentrated on particular industries or regions, or general? Are resources unemployed or under-utilised? Are there any genuine cases for exceptional public sector investment?
4. In the light of your assessment of Points 1 – 3, what is the appropriate fiscal response? This should take into account your judgements about timing, size and structure. The relationship with other areas of policy, notably monetary policy and the exchange rate, should also be considered.

5. If the actual budget differs from your assessment do not be surprised, but consider how these differences might be explained. Can they be explained by 'reasonable' differences in opinion about the above issues – e.g. different forecasts, different views about policy effects, etc.? In particular, when viewing a budget retrospectively, to what extent is your judgement affected by hindsight, e.g. were forecasting errors understandable?

6. Consider the extent to which the actual budget judgement might have been affected by the issues raised in Section 11.5. For example: political pressures for prodigality, a crisis reaction, concern to establish a credible reputation for fiscal prudence, or more general concerns about the reaction of financial markets.

Assessing these issues, with regard to a particular budget or a longer period of fiscal history, is not easy, even with the benefit of hindsight. The study of economics certainly helps to clarify the issues and expose quack cures but it does not, at least at present, provide all the answers. There remains considerable scope for differing judgements about the state of the economy and the appropriate stance of fiscal policy, as well as scope for further study to refine these judgements.

In broad terms my own judgements at the time of writing are the following:

(i)   The medium term objective of a zero PSD, and the implied further reduction of GD/GDP (especially as inflation is likely to remain somewhere in excess of 2%) is inappropriate.

(ii)   More contentiously, cuts in personal income tax rates have gone too far to provide adequate funding for an appropriately sized public sector. The belief in significant incentive effects from lowering income tax rates (given their current level) is mistaken. Given the visibility of personal income taxes, and the associated political pressures, it may be difficult to reverse this process. Other less visible forms of taxation may be more politically attractive, although they may be less effective at raising the revenue needed.

(iii) Due to the low levels of public sector investment since the mid-1970s there is an incipient crisis in many areas of the public sector. There is a case for exceptional public sector investment expenditure, along the lines discussed in Section 11.4. Care needs to be taken to smooth this over time to avoid a major demand disturbance.

(iv)   More imaginative, less blunt and better directed, use of fiscal instruments could be used to stimulate economic activity in recessions. Again there has been an excessive emphasis on personal income taxation.

(v)   A tighter fiscal policy should have been adopted to dampen the Lawson boom (e.g. an increase in personal income taxation), reducing the emphasis placed on interest rates. Similarly, there are concerns that fiscal policy will remain too loose as the economy recovers from the recession of the early 1990s.

(vi) There are long-run structural problems in the United Kingdom (linked to the 'permanent' shock and rise in the NAIRU discussed in Section 11.4), which might be addressed by more imaginative use of fiscal policy.

(vii) The scope for the use of fiscal policy is constrained by political pressures and the reaction of financial markets (as discussed in Section 11.5), and this needs to be borne in mind when drawing up a feasible fiscal programme. There is a need to be seen to be getting PSD/GDP back under control, to restore a reputation for fiscal prudence. Re-establishing this reputation may be difficult in the absence of an anchor or commitment to influence expectations, although designing an effective and credible commitment to take the place of the ERM is itself fraught with difficulties.

Questions for discussion

1. Why may the PSBR be a misleading indicator of the state of public sector finances when there is a major 'privatisation' sale of a public sector asset?
2. Assess critically the objective of maintaining a zero PSD over the medium term.
3. Use the check-list set out in Section 11.6.1 to assess the latest budget.
4. Use the check-list set out in Section 11.6.1 to assess the controversial budget of 1981.
5. Use the check-list set out in Section 11.6.1 to assess the differing fiscal responses to recession reflected in the 1971, 1981 and 1991 budgets (see Budd, 1991).
6. Assess critically the argument that the incentive effects of lower rates of income tax will enable us to afford improvements in public sector services.
7. Why might 'automatic stabilisers' be destabilising?
8. Is a cut in the basic rate of income tax an appropriate response to a (temporary) negative shock that has its primary impact on a particular industrial sector or region? Can you think of a better fiscal response?
9. Is there a genuine case for 'exceptional' public sector investment that it would be appropriate to debt finance, in: (a) education and training; (b) the Health Service; (c) transport; (d) any other area?
10. 'The British government tends to run excessively high budget deficits particularly in the run-up to general elections.' Discuss.

Notes

1. It is interesting to consider these issues in an international perspective. Most industrial countries have gone through a broadly similar period of retrenchment in the public sector as the United Kingdom (see Roubini and Sachs, 1989). In

broad terms government outgoings and income as proportions of GDP in the United Kingdom are not out of line with those of other industrialised countries, nor were they in the 1970s. Space prevents a more detailed analysis, which is really needed for an adequate comparative study.

2. In principle some asset sales might be sustainable, e.g. ongoing public sector investment in housing which is subsequently sold to the private sector. However, the potential contribution of such sustainable asset sales is relatively small, particularly in comparison to the one-off asset sales that have taken place in the 1980s.

3. Estimates of the size of automatic effects are sometimes used to calculate the 'structural public sector deficit'. This purports to measure what the PSD would be if the economy were operating at some measure of potential output. In addition to the problems of estimating the size of automatic effects, estimates of the structural PSD also depend on what potential output is assumed to be. In consequence measures of the structural PSD are model dependent. They should be treated with considerable caution unless the underlying assumptions are clearly spelled out, and this is best done in the context of a macroeconomic model (see Buiter, 1985).

References and further reading

Alesina, A. (1989) 'Politics and business cycles in industrial democracies' *Economic Policy* April pp. 56–98.

Allsopp, C. (1985) 'The assessment: monetary and fiscal policy in the 1980s' *Oxford Review of Economic Policy* March pp.1–20.

Allsopp, C. (1993) 'The assessment: strategic policy dilemmas for the 1990s' *Oxford Review of Economic Policy* September pp. 1–25.

Allsopp, C., Jenkinson, T, and Morris, D. (1991) 'The assessment: macroeconomic policy in the 1980s' *Oxford Review of Economic Policy* September pp. 68–80.

Brown, C. (1988) 'Will the 1988 income tax cuts either increase work incentives or raise more revenue?' *Fiscal Studies* May pp. 93–107.

Buchanan, J., Burton, J. and Wagner, R. (1978) *The Consequences of Mr Keynes* (Hobart Paper 78), London: Institute of Economic Affairs.

Budd, A. (1991) 'The 1991 budget in its historical context' *Fiscal Studies* May pp. 1–8.

Buiter, W. (1985) 'A guide to public sector debt and deficits' *Economic Policy* November pp. 13–79.

Central Statistical Office (1995) *Annual Abstract of Statistics*, London: HMSO.

Central Statistical Office (1995) *Economic Trends*, Annual Supplement 1995 Edition, London: HMSO.

Davies, G. (1991) 'The 1991 budget: fiscal policy inside the ERM' *Fiscal Studies* May pp. 9–22.

Dilnot, A. and Kell, M. (1988) 'Top-rate tax cuts and incentives: some empirical evidence' *Fiscal Studies* May pp. 70–92.

Her Majesty's Treasury (1994) *Financial Statement and Budget Report 1995–1996*, London: HMSO.

Roubini, N. and Sachs, J. (1989) 'Government spending and budget deficits in the industrial countries' *Economic Policy* April pp. 99–132.

Sayer, S. (1992) 'The city, power and economic policy in the UK' *International Review of Applied Economics* May pp. 125–51.

Vines, D. (1989) 'Is the "Thatcher Experiment" still on course' *The Royal Bank of Scotland Review* December pp. 3–14.

CHAPTER 12

Inflation and monetary policy

GEOFFREY WYATT

12.1 Introduction and historical overview

Inflation is a persistent tendency for prices in general to rise. This has occurred in the United Kingdom throughout the second half of the twentieth century, as is evident in Figure 12.1 which charts the percentage rate of change of the general price level since 1950. The point to note is that inflation has almost always been above zero in this period. Inflation is not inevitable. In earlier times price falls were as frequent and as severe as price rises, and on average the general level of prices was roughly constant.[1] However, it seems that inflation is a distinguishing feature of the post-war economy.

The general level of prices has normally risen sharply at times of war with the shortage of raw materials that it brings. This can be seen in the 'blips' on the chart in 1951, 1974 and 1979, which correspond to the Korean war of 1950, the 6-day war in the Middle East in 1973 and the Islamic revolution in Iran in 1979, respectively. However, despite the dramatic appearance of the blips on the chart of inflation this chapter is mainly concerned with the general tendency for prices to rise, what causes both the strength and the fluctuations

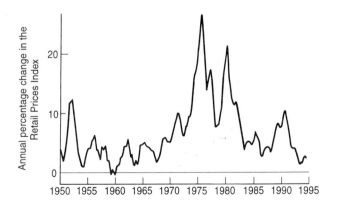

Figure 12.1 Inflation since 1950.

in inflation and the impact of monetary policy on inflation. It appears that the post-war era has an inflationary bias, and it is legitimate to ask whether this was induced by the new post-war approach to economic management, with its macroeconomic focus. The pre-war era had assumed the macro economy to be self-regulating, and in terms of inflation it regulated itself around the zero mark. If government intervention by demand management has really regulated the economy, we might also ask whether the post-war inflation is an expression of public choice or an accidental side effect.

Whatever the reasons for the inflationary tendency in the post-war era, it has surely affected the behaviour of all sorts of actors in the economy: individuals as consumers, workers, savers and investors, and businesses, as well as government itself. This in turn has affected the way that economists think the economy functions. Nowadays it is quite impossible to analyse the state of the macro economy without taking expectations about inflation into account.

12.2   The measurement of inflation

Since inflation is a rise in the general level of prices, in order to measure it we need to measure the general level of prices. This is done by constructing an appropriate price index. Generally, it is the prices faced by consumers that are considered to be relevant, so inflation is appropriately measured by the rate of change of the consumer price index (CPI). The CPI is the price deflator of consumers' expenditure in the National Accounts – nominal consumers' expenditure is converted to real consumers' expenditure by dividing by the CPI. This converts consumers' expenditure in current prices to consumers' expenditure in constant 1985 (or 1990 or 1995) prices, depending on the base year of the CPI.

In practice the CPI, or consumer expenditure deflator, is not the only available measure of the general price level. Another possibility would be the GDP deflator, which is the price index for national output, although this is less commonly quoted than the CPI. A further possible index, and actually the one that is most frequently quoted, is the retail price index (RPI). The RPI has the great advantage that it is published monthly rather than quarterly like the CPI, and it is published more rapidly too – about 2 weeks after the end of the month concerned. However, the RPI is conceived as a measure of the 'cost of living', which is a concept somewhat removed from that of a price index for consumers' expenditure. Thus it ignores the expenditure patterns both of wealthy individuals and of certain pensioner households, and more seriously it incorporates the interest cost of servicing a typical house mortgage. This last feature is particularly troublesome for an index measuring inflation. Of course housing has a cost, but that is better approximated by its rental value rather than the cost of servicing a debt. For that reason, the official monthly indicator of inflation has become a version of the RPI which excludes the mortgage servicing component. It is known as RPIX.

The construction of a general price index such as the RPI or the CPI involves two types of data: the first determining the composition of the 'basket' of goods and services that consumers actually consume, and the second being the prices of the individual items in the 'basket'. In the United Kingdom the first component is determined from the Family Expenditure Survey, which asks a stratified random sample of about 7000 households to record their outgoings over a particular fortnight. The second component involves getting the prices of some 130 000 goods and services every month. These two components are combined in a chained index which accurately reflects the changing composition of peoples' spending.

The rate of inflation at a given date is usually quoted as the percentage change of the relevant price index from its value a year earlier. This is of course a backward-looking measure, and does not necessarily capture the current rate of change, let alone peoples' expectation about how it will develop in the future. However, it is expected future inflation which is relevant for most decisions, and this is reflected in various contracts such as wage agreements, rentals and loans. Expectations are notoriously difficult to measure, but one possibility is to use the data in the rates of interest quoted on nominal and real bonds (known as 'index-linked' bonds in the United Kingdom) to extract the implicit expectation of future inflation.

12.3   Inflation control as an objective of policy

The principal macroeconomic target of policy since 1979, when Mrs Thatcher was first elected as prime minister, has been the rate of inflation. The other targets of macroeconomic policy, namely the levels and rates of growth of wealth, output, consumption and unemployment have all been subordinated to the control of inflation, largely because low and stable inflation has been thought of as a precondition for the achievement of these other goals. However, in terms of their contribution to peoples' wellbeing, those other goals are generally of more direct relevance than the rate of inflation. Inflation and unemployment are highly interconnected, and reducing one is likely to increase the other in the short run (a year or two), although they are much less closely coupled in the long run. Once inflation is in the system, it seems that a period of relatively high unemployment is an inevitable consequence of policies to eliminate it.

Because it is not at all obvious that inflation should rank so high among the objectives of economic policy, it is worth considering the matter further. To do so, we distinguish between anticipated and unanticipated inflation. If inflation is steady and predictable, we would expect people to allow for it in the decisions they make concerning their income and expenditure. Thus it should be reflected in wage agreements, pension arrangement, tax thresholds, interest rates, company dividends and so on. In effect, all sources of income should be indexed to the rate of inflation and real incomes, in terms of command over consumption goods, should be unaffected by fully anticipated inflation.

Why then should any particular rate of fully anticipated inflation be a cause for concern? There are some rather minor costs to note. One is the need to change price tags, and the faster the rate of anticipated inflation the more often such changes would be needed. Another cost of high inflation is the erosion in the value of nominal assets – assets whose value is expressed in money terms. Where inflation is fully anticipated, we should expect the price of all assets to be indexed to it; except, that is, money itself. So the higher the rate of anticipated inflation, the greater the incentive for people to reduce their holdings of money. This induces the so-called 'shoe leather cost' of anticipated inflation, as people are encouraged to make more frequent trips to the bank. The proportion of money in peoples' portfolios of assets tends thereby to diminish, and this general loss of liquidity inhibits people from making quick responses to buying opportunities. Thus the usefulness of money in making transactions and as a store of value is impaired. These costs are not trivial, but they pale in significance when set against the costs of unanticipated inflation.

When people are taken unawares by an increase in the general price level there are several consequences. To begin with, there is a redistribution of real income from savers to borrowers which comes about because the expected rate of inflation incorporated in the nominal interest rate is lower than the inflation that actually occurs. When inflation is less than people had anticipated, the transfer is from borrowers to savers. Since there is a systematic pattern of saving and borrowing over the life cycle, the redistributive consequences of unanticipated inflation (or its converse) tend to fall on particular age groups. Thus young adults, who are generally borrowers, possibly with recently acquired mortgages on their houses, tend to benefit from unanticipated inflation, and older people with accumulated savings tend to lose out.

Another effect of unexpected inflation is that it engenders confusion about relative price changes, and a consequent misallocation of resources due to decisions taken on misleading price signals. In an effort to avoid making costly mistakes, decision-makers may expend substantial effort on forecasting inflation, or by taking steps to mitigate possible errors. Higher rates of inflation are associated with greater variability, and hence greater unpredictability, of inflation, so the costs associated with unanticipated price changes tend to be more important in circumstances of high inflation. Even when it is clear that an erroneous assumption about inflation has been made it may be difficult to correct quickly. Particularly important examples of this include wage contracts, which may be revised annually or biennially, and property rentals which may only be revised at even longer intervals of time – five years is not uncommon. Such 'sticky' prices tend to prolong misallocations of resources in times of high inflation.

It is clear from the foregoing that the consequences of inflation can badly damage the functioning of an economy. Since, as will be argued shortly, inflation can be controlled by government action, this would seem to be a proper objective of policy, but first we should consider a different angle on the subject, namely how it is that government may stimulate inflation by opting for a particular mode of financing its activities.

Governments can finance their spending in three ways: taxation, borrowing from the general public and 'printing money', which is shorthand for the process of borrowing from banks and thereby expanding the stock of money. Government revenue from taxes is normally by far the most important source of funding for its expenditure, and the other sources of finance are usually considered as devices to cover a deficit occasioned by a tax shortfall. While taxation and borrowing from the general public entail a direct transfer of resources from the private sector to the government (involuntary and voluntary respectively), the process of printing money appears to give the government control over real resources without a corresponding sacrifice by the private sector. This command over real resources derived from printing money is known as 'seigniorage' (see also Chapter 11). However, unless the resources claimed by the government would otherwise be unused, as might be the case in a recession, this seigniorage adds to the general pressure of aggregate demand and eventually results in higher prices. To reflect this, the financing of government spending by printing money is sometimes called the 'inflation tax'. The tax is paid by people who had not anticipated the monetary expansion, and consequently suffer in the general transfer of real income from savers to borrowers that occurs with unanticipated inflation. Thus nominal interest rates are too low as they do not yet reflect the coming inflation due to the new pressure on resources, and the inflation tax falls on income from saving. The major beneficiaries are future taxpayers, for whom the real burden of the National Debt is eroded by the unanticipated inflation.

12.4 Money and inflation in the long run

'Inflation is too much money chasing too few goods.' This suggestive aphorism lends itself to both monetarist and Keynesian explanations of inflation. Monetarist explanations are couched in terms of the supply and demand for money, with an insistence that the supply of money is controlled by the government. Keynesian explanations centre on excessive aggregate expenditure. The monetarist view of inflation emphasises the long run, and would not deny that in the short term there can be reasons for aggregate price changes other than money. Keynesian explanations apply to short-term fluctuations in the price level which are ironed out in the long run.

If the money price of all goods and services were doubled there would be no change in any relative price, but the general level of prices would clearly have doubled and the purchasing power of a unit of currency would have halved. If this had happened over the course of a year the rate of inflation that year would have been 100 per cent. It is conceivable that this could have happened without any change in the amount of money in general circulation or the amount of goods and services purchased with that money, so that the given stock of money was being transferred from buyer to seller twice as fast. Conceivable, but not plausible. It is more likely that neither the velocity of circulation (the value of all transactions divided by the stock of money) nor the volume of sales were much different, but that roughly twice as much money was in general circulation. This is the usual experience in inflations, so much so that Milton Friedman's dictum that 'inflation is always and everywhere a monetary phenomenon', is not seriously disputed as holding true over long periods of time, or in rapid inflations as in this example. In such circumstances inflation is always associated with an expansion in the stock of money held by the public. However, over shorter periods of time more modest inflation can occur without much change in the stock of money, but with a fall in the volume of transactions or a rise in the velocity of circulation.

The 'quantity equation' is a famous tautology connecting the stock of money (M), the price level (P), the number of transactions (T) and the velocity of circulation (V) in the following equation: $MV = PT$. All of the variables in this identity may change over time, and the equation is only of serious empirical validity if the velocity of circulation of money is predictable. On the assumption that it is, a further step of reasoning is to assert that since the stock of money can be controlled by the government, this provides a mechanism through which it can influence the general level of prices and the rate of inflation. This is the beginnings of the doctrine of 'monetarism' which assumed considerable importance for the first term of the Thatcher administration, from 1979 to 1983.

In the money market, if the supply of money is fixed the demand for money is brought into equality with it by changes in the short-term interest rate. On the other hand, if the interest rate is fixed which means that the central bank stands ready to meet whatever level of demand for cash that emerges, the supply of money becomes perfectly elastic at that rate of interest. If, as monetarists suppose, the demand for money is well determined as a stable and predictable function of a set of variables including the rate of interest and the level of income, and the interest elasticity of demand for money is low, then it should be possible to control the stock of money by central bank control of the interest rate. The monetarist view of the purpose of such control over the stock of money is not that it should be used to influence the level of demand in the economy in the short run, but that it should set a framework designed to lead to a steady and low rate of inflation in the longer term. Thus discretionary monetary policy should be eschewed in favour of a publicly declared rule of a constant, low rate of monetary growth, to which the central bank is committed.

The monetary authorities may control the money supply either directly, by open market operations which change the reserves of the commercial banks, or indirectly by changing the discount rate at which commercial banks can borrow from the central bank, which in turn influences short-term interest rates generally. Whichever method they adopt, they must be prepared for wide fluctuations in short-term interest rates as the demand for money fluctuates, because of the low interest elasticity of demand for money. Most empirical studies before the 1980s confirmed the assumed low elasticity. However, financial innovation and liberalisation has since then produced a spectrum of different forms of money, and differences in rates of return between them influence the form in which people hold their money if not the total amount of money-like liquid assets.

The transmission mechanism by which expansion in the money supply eventually translates into increased prices may take many paths, and it may vary from time to time and from country to country. The most direct route is the stimulation of expenditures through lower interest rates. This, of course, depends on the interest elasticity of such expenditure, and one would expect it to be confined to durable and investment goods. Prices generally are pushed upwards as aggregate demand presses on aggregate supply, which is determined by real variables such as the availability of factors of production and technological change.

Another channel of monetary influence is by a fall in the exchange rate which is brought about by the downward pressure on interest rates. Lower domestic interest rates induce people to sell UK bonds and buy foreign bonds, reducing the demand for sterling in the process. The resulting fall in the exchange rate pushes up the price of imported goods. It also stimulates the demand for exports, which adds to the pressure of total demand and tends to pull prices up.

A further channel of monetary influence, and one which monetarists tend to emphasise, is through adjustments in the composition of wealth. Although money is only a small fraction of peoples' tangible wealth, as can be seen from Table 12.1, the monetary expansion which pulls down short-term interest rates – interest rates on 3-month Treasury Bills – tends to drag down other interest rates too, and as the implied interest rates on all sorts of assets, both financial and non-financial, drift down in sympathy, so the prices of those assets tend to rise. Thus peoples' nominal wealth rises, and thereby also aggregate demand. Another way of looking at this is in terms of the composition of wealth portfolios directly. When the central bank purchases gilt-edged stock from the public in an open market operation, the proportion of money in the aggregate portfolio of the private sector increases, and now exceeds the desired level. The people with excess cash will try to turn it into other assets, bidding up their price in the process. Thus there is an increase in the wealth of those who hold the substitute assets, some of which translates into spending.

Financial wealth accounts for roughly one-third of total tangible wealth of the personal sector in the United Kingdom, as is shown in Table 12.1, and most of the remaining two-thirds is in the form of house ownership or tenancy rights. A steep and steady decline in the proportion of notes and coin in total tangible wealth has occurred, so that by 1993 it was less than two-fifths of the

Table 12.1 Personal sector wealth composition

	1975	1980	1985	1990	1993
Net wealth (£bn)					
of which (%):	303	694	1196	2170	2581
Non-financial assets	67.9	69.0	63.5	68.0	55.1
Housing	56.4	57.8	55.7	61.9	50.5
Net financial wealth	32.1	31.0	36.5	32.0	44.9
Notes and coin	1.6	1.2	0.9	0.6	0.6
Bank deposits	6.4	5.3	5.3	7.2	6.5
Building society deposits	7.4	7.2	8.7	7.3	7.6
Shareholdings	9.1	6.6	6.9	6.9	9.8
Pension & insurance funds	11.5	15.4	24.3	24.3	32.9
Mortgages (liability)	−8.3	−7.6	−10.6	−13.5	−13.7
Bank lending (liability)	−1.9	−2.2	−3.4	−4.0	−3.0

Source: United Kingdom National Accounts (Blue Book), 1994 and earlier editions, CSO, HMSO.

1975 proportion. Over the same period the proportions of tangible wealth held in bank and building society deposits fluctuated, but in 1993 these proportions were very similar to what they had been in 1975. Traditionally bank deposits were considered as money available for transactions, whereas building society deposits were mostly in savings accounts. In the first half of the 1980s, however, the building societies substantially increased their share of deposits as they entered into competition with the banks by offering very similar services. The banks responded by offering interest-bearing current accounts and improved services, and recaptured the market share they had lost. In the process of such competition, the earlier distinctions between banks and building societies were eroded and the inclusion of bank deposits, but not building society deposits, in a wide definition of the money stock became questionable. On the other hand, assigning all deposits, of both banks and building societies, to a measure of the money stock is also inappropriate since an unknown proportion of both are really savings accounts.

The effects of financial innovation and competition between different forms of liquid assets is evident in Figure 12.2 which charts the velocity of circulation of two measures of the money stock. M0, or 'narrow money', mainly comprises notes and coins in circulation with the general public, although it also includes the commercial banks' reserves held at the Bank of England. Its velocity of circulation is calculated as the ratio of some measure of the total value of transactions during a period to the stock of M0. The velocity shown in Figure 12.2 uses the value of consumers' expenditure as numerator and the average of the stock of M0 at the beginning and at the end of each year as denominator. M1 is a wider definition of money that includes demand deposits in banks and building societies in addition to notes and coin. Its velocity of circulation is calculated in the same way as that for M0. The two measures of velocity have

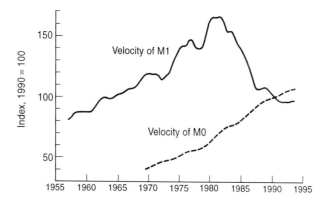

Figure 12.2 Velocities of circulation* of M0 and M1. *Consumers' expenditure divided by money stock, smoothed.

been converted into indexes so that movements in them can be compared easily.

It is clear from Figure 12.2 that there are strong trends in the velocities of M0 and M1. The steady upward trend in M0 velocity since 1969 is consistent with the decline in notes and coin as a proportion of financial wealth shown in Table 12.1. People are using less cash for their spending for a number of reasons, among which are the following trends: growth in the use of bank accounts and payments by cheque; wages paid straight into bank accounts; the use of credit cards and other forms of plastic payments; and the availability and use of cash dispensing machines. All these trends make token money less necessary.

The trend in the velocity of M1 is a little more complex. Ignoring cycles, the trend was one of rapid growth until 1980 since when velocity has fallen even more rapidly, although it seems to be levelling out in the 1990s. Given this pattern, it is perhaps not surprising that estimated money demand functions based on historical data were found to be an unreliable basis for the conduct of monetary policy in the 1980s, when control of wider monetary aggregates became a cornerstone of government policy. The decline in velocity in the 1980s is probably due in large part to the competition between banks and building societies for deposits, and the attractive terms, such as interest on demand deposits and free banking for larger deposits, that such accounts offered as a result. In addition many of the trends which made cash less attractive, outlined above, encouraged a tendency to switch to current accounts. This is discussed further in Section 12.7 below.

12.5 Aggregate demand and inflation

Part of any explanation of inflation is the pressure of aggregate demand on resources. Inflation can only be controlled by relieving this pressure. A convenient way to measure the pressure of demand is to compare the level of

GDP with its trend value. Figure 12.3 plots GDP and its trend since 1950. The trend rate of growth has been allowed to vary gradually over this period. The recessions of 1975, 1981 and 1991 are clearly visible.

Now let us examine the relation between the pressure of demand and inflation. We measure the pressure of demand as the percentage deviation of GDP from its trend level, derived from Figure 12.3. A measure of this sort is sometimes referred to as the 'output gap'. Inflation is measured by the annual percentage change of the RPI, centred in the middle of the year to which it relates. These two variables are smoothed and plotted in Figure 12.4 in which the common cyclical movement between inflation and the pressure of demand is quite evident. However, while the cyclical phasing of the series is remarkably similar, changes in the amplitude of inflation do not appear to be

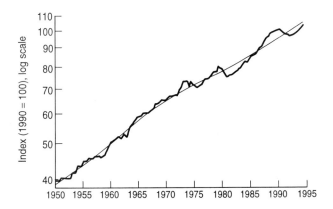

Figure 12.3   Growth of GDP with trend.

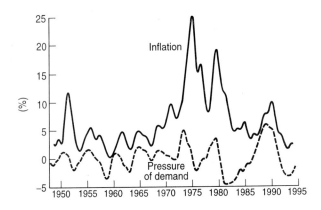

Figure 12.4   Inflation and the pressure of demand.

explained by the pressure of demand. We might, however, suspect them to be related to variations in monetary growth.

Comparing the peaks and troughs of the two series we see that fluctuations in the pressure of demand appear to be followed after a year or two by fluctuations in inflation. It is perhaps noteworthy that the lag between the two series began to lengthen in the mid-1970s. At that time an 'incomes policy' was in place to control inflation. Its ineffectiveness is evident from the height of the inflation curve, but its main effect may have been to delay the reaction of inflation to variations in the pressure of demand, which came through in the end anyway. Another feature of note is the greater extension of the inflation-output cycle in the 1980s and 1990s compared to earlier decades. It seems possible that inflationary expectations became more firmly embedded and more difficult to eradicate after the historically unprecedented inflation experience of the 1970s. Such entrenched inflationary expectations would have the effect of deepening and prolonging the recessionary period of slack demand necessary to bring inflation down by any given amount.

Since fluctuations in the pressure of demand generally precede, and never lag behind, fluctuations in inflation it seems reasonable to suppose that they are the proximate cause of fluctuations in inflation. This is consistent with both a monetarist and a Keynesian view of the inflation process. However, not all the fluctuations in the pressure of demand are caused by public policy. While some of them are surely due to monetary and fiscal policy, others have their origins in other exogenous factors impinging on both aggregate demand and aggregate supply.

12.6 Interest rates and inflationary expectations

Interest is both the cost of borrowing and the reward for lending. In a world without inflation there would be just one interest rate.[2] This is the 'real rate of interest'. Optimising behaviour on the part of savers and borrowers tends to make the real rate of interest equal to both consumers' marginal rate of time preference and producers' marginal product of capital. A higher real rate of interest encourages consumers to postpone their consumption and to lend more instead. Equally, producers are discouraged from borrowing to make certain investments. Thus, the real interest rate plays a vital role in determining saving and investment.

Matters become more complicated in the presence of inflation. Now the actual or 'nominal' rate of interest i is equal to the sum of the real rate of interest r and the rate of inflation expected to prevail over the lifetime of the loan, π^e:

$$i = r + \pi^e.$$

If inflation is steady and expected to remain so then it is easy to see what the real rate of interest is, given any particular nominal rate; but if inflation is varying it becomes difficult to assess and agree on the real rate of interest. This uncertainty about the real rate of interest becomes worse the higher the inflation because the variability of inflation also tends to be higher then.

The interest rate on a loan may depend on how long the loan is to last. Thus we may need to distinguish between a 'short-term' interest rate and a 'long-term' interest rate, and obviously there can be a continuous range of interest rates depending on the duration of the loan. This is referred to as the 'term structure of interest rates' or, in the financial press, as the 'yield curve'. Let us suppose that the shortest duration of a loan is for 1 day only. Then the interest rate on a loan of 1 year's duration will depend on what is expected for the 1-day interest rate during the course of the year in question since it could be substituted with 365 1-day loans. This gives us a way to interpret the term structure of interest rates. If long-term rates exceed short-term rates, then short-term rates of interest are expected to rise, and if real rates of interest are roughly constant then we may assume that inflation is expected to rise. Conversely, if long-term rates are lower than short-term rates, then short-term interest rates are expected to fall, probably implying that inflation is expected to fall.

The market for government bonds in the United Kingdom is unusual in that there are real bonds, i.e. bonds whose nominal value is indexed to inflation, which coexist with nominal bonds. This makes it possible to analyse inflationary expectations in the bond market in a novel and unique way. By comparing the term structure of real and nominal interest rates it is possible to extract an implied term structure of 'forward' – i.e. expected – inflation rates. Figure 12.5 shows such derived forward inflation rates at the ends of 4 particular days: the day before and the day of entry to the ERM, the Exchange Rate Mechanism of the European Community, and the day before and the day

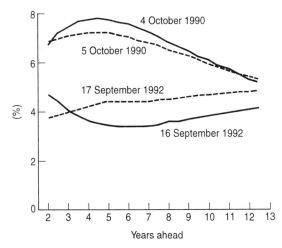

Figure 12.5 Implied forward inflation rates on entry to and exit from the ERM. *Source:* King, 1995

of exit from the ERM. On 5 October 1990 it was announced that the United Kingdom would join the ERM. Immediately prior to this announcement it had been expected that inflation would rise in the next 4 years to just under 8 per cent before gradually declining thereafter. Entry into the ERM seems to have reduced inflationary expectations by a maximum of about half of 1 per cent after 4 or 5 years, as shown by the implied forward rates at the end of 5 October 1990. By the time the United Kingdom left the ERM on 16 September 1992, the general level of inflationary expectations had come down substantially, and implied forward inflation rates just prior to exit showed that inflation was expected to fall further. The term structure of expected inflation immediately after exit from the ERM shows that future inflation rates were expected to shift upwards and show a rising pattern over time. This is discussed further in Section 12.8 below.

Whereas long-term interest rates are determined by supply and demand in the market for long-term loans, short-term interest rates are mainly determined by the stance of monetary policy. Indeed, it is by setting 'base rate', the rate of interest at which the discount houses (which in turn serve as 'lender of last resort' to the commercial banks) can borrow from the Bank of England, that the government actually carries out its monetary policies, including those that involve controlling some monetary aggregate. Thus long-term interest rates do not necessarily move in parallel with short-term rates, although there will be some tendency for them to move together since a long-term rate is an average of expected future short-term rates, including the current short-term rate at one end of the range from which the average is derived.

A switch in the monetary stance which involves a progressive slowing down of both the rate of monetary expansion and the rate of inflation over the medium term should therefore imply a widening gap between short-term and long-term interest rates as the short-term rates rise in response to monetary tightness, while the tendency of long-term rates to rise in sympathy is offset by a downward tendency reflecting an expectation of lower inflation in the future. This can be seen in the graph of the differential between short- and long-term rates of interest shown in Figure 12.6. Consider two periods as illustrations: first the period 1977–80, and secondly the period 1987–94.

In 1977 when the economy was recovering from the depression that followed the first great oil price shock, monetary policy was easy, with short-term interest rates in the region of 5 per cent while long-term rates reflecting inflationary expectations were around 12 per cent. Policy was very significantly tightened in the next 3 years as short-term rates were pushed up, reaching record levels in 1980. Meanwhile, long-term rates edged up only slightly, reflecting the attenuated inflationary expectations. Despite the considerable tightening of monetary policy, it seems that people were not fully convinced that future inflation would fall, so it took a further 2 years of a tight monetary (and fiscal) stance, producing an unsustainably high exchange rate and the most severe recession since the 1930s, before long-term rates came down

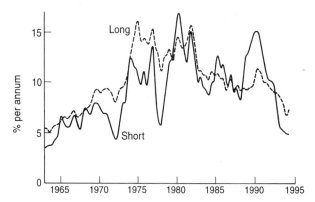

Figure 12.6 Short- and long-term interest rates (yields on Treasury bills and 20-year government bonds).

significantly, moving in parallel with both short-term rates and inflation in 1981 and 1982. Inflation appeared to be under control at around 5 per cent between 1983 and 1987, with both long- and short-term interest rates in the region of 10 per cent.

In 1987 the target of monetary policy switched from the monetary aggregates to the exchange rate as a prelude to the United Kingdom joining the ERM in 1990. Although it was not officially articulated thus, monetary policy was aimed at stabilising sterling to an exchange rate of 3 German marks; but since inflation in the United Kingdom was significantly in excess of German inflation, this could only be maintained by higher short-term interest rates, well above long-term rates. The resulting high exchange rate together with income tax reductions at first encouraged a consumer boom, burgeoning imports and an acceleration in inflation. By 1990 the artificially high exchange rate had made domestic industry quite uncompetitive, and this, together with the high cost of short-term borrowing to finance accumulating inventories, created a severe recession (see Figure 12.3). Throughout this period, however, it seems that expectations of future inflation in the bond market were rather sanguine, judging from the relative stability of long-term interest rates. Indeed, inflation subsequently fell from around 10 per cent in 1990 to around 2 per cent in 1994. By 1994 long rates were above short rates, implying that short rates were expected to rise to contain any inflationary tendency in the strong recovery of 1994.

12.7 Monetary policy in the 1980s

The new Conservative government of 1979 had inherited a high and rising rate of inflation, and its main goal was to correct it. To do so, it adopted the previous Callaghan administration's practice of setting monetary targets, expressed as a range of growth rates for sterling M3 (£M3), which is currency in circulation plus bank deposits denominated in sterling. Such £M3 target ranges were intended to exert a gradual squeeze on the economy, forcing inflation down. However, direct control of the monetary base was eschewed in favour of manipulating short-term interest rates via the government's official discount rate, known then as minimum lending rate (MLR). This decision stemmed from a judgment that direct control of the monetary base, which would have left interest rates to be determined entirely by market forces, would have implied very large fluctuations in interest rates, more than could be tolerated. Instead, the government set interest rates and allowed the money stock to respond indirectly, via the money demand function. In choosing greater stability for short-term interest rates, it sacrificed stability in its ostensible target indicator, the money stock.

In 1979 and 1980 the monetary squeeze, which required high interest rates, combined with both a sharp rise in the price of oil and the emergent self-sufficiency of the United Kingdom in oil to push the exchange value of sterling sharply upwards. Although the rise in sterling was attenuated by the abolition of exchange controls in October 1979, which encouraged a net outflow of portfolio capital, it was nevertheless the main factor leading to the severe recession of 1980 and 1981.

The formal expression of the Thatcher government's monetary policy was the 'Medium Term Financial Strategy' (MTFS) which was launched in the 1980 budget. This initiated a programme of rolling targets for monetary growth and the public sector borrowing requirement (PSBR) expressed as a proportion of GDP, over 3–5-year horizons from each annual budget. The aim of the MTFS was clearly to create an environment of relatively stable and predictable monetary conditions; but it only partially succeeded in doing so. The success was with regard to the PSBR, which by 1987 had turned into a surplus. However, the monetary aggregates stubbornly refused to comply with the government's targets throughout most of the period up to 1990, when monetary targeting was effectively abandoned (see Table 12.2).

In order to succeed in monetary targeting through the indirect channel of interest rates, it is necessary to have reliable knowledge about the money demand function, or the determinants of the velocity of money circulation. This was the subject of considerable research at the Bank of England and in the Treasury during the 1970s and 1980s, but the forecasting accuracy of the estimated money demand functions tended to be rather poor. This was particularly true for the wider definitions of money such as £M3, and it was partly due to this that £M3 tended to systematically overshoot its MTFS targets. A further factor is that the government wished to target a measure of the personal sector's stock of liquid assets that would be used for expenditures as opposed to savings, but financial innovations made it difficult to maintain this

Table 12.2 Medium term financial strategy; out-turn of key variables and their targets 1 year ahead

| | Monetary growth, % change | | | | PSBR, % of GDP | |
| | £m3 | | M0 | | | |
	Target, range	Out-turn	Target,[1] range	Out-turn	Target[2]	Out-turn[3]
1979–80	7–11	16.5			4.5	4.8
1980–1	7–11	19.5			3.8	5.5
1981–2	6–10	12.8			4.3	3.5
1982–3	8–12	10			3.5	3.3
1983–4	7–11	9.8			2.8	3.3
1984–5	6–10	9.5	4–8	5.4	2.3	3
1985–6	5–9	14.8	3–7	3.6	2	1.5
1986–7	11–15		2–6	4.6	1.8	1
1987–8			2–6	5.8	1	−0.8
1988–9			1–5	6.2	−0.8	−3
1989–90			1–5	6.2	−2.8	−1.5
1990–1			1–5	2.4	−1.3	0
1991–2			0–4	2.1	1.3	2.3
1992–3			0–4	4.7	4.5	5.8
1993–4			0–4	6.2	8.0	7.8
1994–5			0–4		5.5	5.0
1995–6			0–4		3.0	

Notes: [1] Referred to as a 'monitoring range' since 1990.
[2] PSBR projected for the year after the Budget Statement.
[3] Out-turn for the fiscal year as reported in the Budget *Red Book* of the following year.

Sources: Financial Statement and Budget Report (Red Book) (1995–6) and earlier years, London, HMSO; *Economic Trends, Annual Supplement* (1994) London, CSO, HMSO.

distinction between different kinds of bank or building society accounts. As a consequence, after some experimentation with different definitions of money, both wide and narrow, the monetary focus for the MTFS switched in the mid-1980s from £M3 to the narrow definition of money stock as notes and coins in circulation plus commercial banks' deposits at the Bank of England, M0. However, M0 was treated less as a target than as an indicator of monetary conditions. It was not the sole indicator – the exchange rate and short- and long-term interest rates were also used in that capacity. The underlying target became the growth of nominal GDP in 1987.

The government's systematic inability to keep its chosen definition of money within the target range was probably due to a number of factors. Foremost among these were the rapid financial and technological innovations that took place in the 1980s, the removal of constraints on bank lending (the 'corset') and on international capital movements at the beginning of the period, and the changing behaviour of the stock of money when it becomes a target indicator.

The 1980s was a decade of worldwide financial liberalisation and innovation, much of the demand for which was generated by the global monetary regime of fluctuating exchange rates and interest rates. Although institutions such as offshore banks, eurocurrency markets and derivative asset exchanges already existed at the beginning of the decade, they grew rapidly during the 1980s and activities that had hitherto been the preserve of banks were for the first time engaged in by other financial institutions and also by the finance departments of large companies. This was enabled to a large extent by the developments in information technology and electronic communications. Commercial banks competed more vigorously than ever before for business, and were also forced to compete with other non-bank financial companies. A consequence of this competition was the blurring of the distinction between demand deposits and time deposits. Formerly only the latter paid interest, whereas by the 1990s nearly all bank deposit accounts earned interest. The volume of demand deposits, which are the most liquid type of bank account, was revealed to be quite sensitive to interest rate differentials, and increased substantially as a result of switching both from time deposits and from cash as the opportunity cost of holding liquid assets in these forms rose. Thus the demand for checking accounts increased and their velocity of circulation fell, as is evident from Figure 12.2. See the discussion in Section 12.4 for more detail. All of these developments had an influence on the demand for monetary aggregates and, therefore, given the indirect method of control, on the stocks of those self-same aggregates.

As an identity, any increase in the stock of narrow money is equal to the PSBR plus the overall balance of payments surplus minus sales of government debt to the non-bank public, so reducing the PSBR, which was the successful aspect of the MTFS of the 1980s, does not necessarily imply a reduced growth of the narrow money stock. It is largely a matter of how the deficit is financed. However, narrow money (M0) was reasonably well under control in the 1980s, so the failure to keep to the announced targets for wider money (£M3) can be attributed in large part to the government's failure to foresee the changes in the competitive behaviour of banks and of the general public who switched their financial assets into interest-bearing bank deposits.

By the end of the 1980s, after several years of quite fast economic growth which boosted tax revenue and reduced the level of unemployment and related benefit payments, the deficit (PSBR) was transformed into a surplus. With the onset of recession in 1990, however, these trends reversed and the PSBR emerged once more. Soon, monetary policy would be assigned the task of maintaining the sterling exchange rate within the European Community's

Exchange Rate Mechanism and monetary policy would take a rear seat in the operation of the MTFS.

12.8 Monetary policy in the 1990s: 'Black Wednesday' and after

The United Kingdom has been operating under two different exchange rate regimes in the 1990s. Between October 1990 and September 1992 the United Kingdom was a member of the ERM of the European Community in which sterling was operating within a quasi-fixed exchange rate system, tied to the other currencies of the ERM. After 'Black Wednesday', 16 September 1992, sterling reverted to the earlier floating regime, its value being freely determined in the global market for currencies.

With a freely floating exchange rate there is no need for the Central Bank to buy or sell foreign currency in order to offset the overall balance of payments position, and thus no need to change its reserves of foreign currency, which are part of the monetary base. Thus the effect of this exchange rate regime is to decouple domestic monetary conditions from external influences in the balance of payments. This means that the stock of money, and its rate of expansion, are determined solely by the government. Alternatively, the government's discount rate (base rate) can be set without reference to interest rates elsewhere, though it certainly has consequences for the exchange rate.

By contrast the ERM is a system of currency bands, in which each participating country undertakes to maintain the exchange value of its currency against all other participants' currencies within a specified margin. For the United Kingdom the margin was ±6 per cent, although the core group of ERM member states have narrow ±2.25 per cent bands. When the sterling exchange rate approached its lower limit against any other currency in the ERM (so that the other currency approached its upper limit against sterling), both central banks concerned stood ready to buy sterling on the currency markets. For the United Kingdom this implied a loss of reserves of foreign currency, and therefore a contraction of the money supply because foreign currency reserves held by the Bank of England are a component of the monetary base. The other European country, by contrast, would have experienced an expansion of its central bank's foreign currency reserves, and therefore of its money supply. Thus in the ERM an automatic monetary contraction is stimulated if the exchange rate depreciates to its floor, and an automatic monetary expansion is set in train if it appreciates to its ceiling. If the original reason for the depreciation of the exchange rate to its floor was a general expectation of higher inflation here than abroad, then the induced monetary contraction here and the monetary expansion abroad are appropriate offsetting responses. They should have the effect of narrowing the gap in inflationary expectations. Clearly, monetary policy is subservient to the need to contain the exchange rate within the specified band.

The ERM exchange rate regime is a hybrid, being neither purely floating nor rigidly fixed against some anchor. The monetary autonomy implied by the freedom of movement for the exchange rate within the allowed band is, at the most, of a short-run nature. Any divergent inflationary tendencies that it enables can only persist as long as the limits are not reached. It follows that in the medium to longer-term, the ERM system is in effect a rather sophisticated variation on a fixed exchange rate regime. Within this system the inflation rates of the participants must converge. It was this inevitable process of convergence, and the pain that it implies for countries that have to disinflate rapidly, that justified the initial wider 6 per cent band for the more inflation-prone countries.

In mid-September 1992 the currency markets were thrown into a state of turmoil as the divergent needs for higher interest rates in Germany after its reunification, and lower interest rates in a number of other European countries with the onset of recession, made adherence to the ERM currency bands unsustainable. First the Italian lira then the pound sterling came under pressure as huge volumes of speculative selling forced the central banks of both countries to buy their own currency in exchange for foreign currency reserves. The German central bank was obliged meanwhile to sell deutsch-marks for lira and sterling, thus adding to its reserves; but all this intervention proved futile as it was overwhelmed by the transactions of speculators convinced of impending changes in exchange rates, which duly transpired as Italy first devalued within the ERM, followed within days by the joint exit from the ERM of both Italy and the United Kingdom along with a devaluation of the Spanish peseta within the ERM. This dramatic episode ended the government's policy of fighting inflation by setting a high fixed exchange rate for sterling within the ERM.

A big issue in the fight against inflation has come to be seen as the credibility of anti-inflation policy. The reason for this is the interaction between the current actual rate of inflation and the future expected rate of inflation. The cost of reducing inflation is higher, in terms of foregone output or concomitant unemployment, the higher is the level of expected inflation. If it is believed that an announced anti-inflation policy will be effective, then that in itself will reduce expected future rates of inflation and hence make the fight against inflation easier. What will convince people of the effectiveness of anti-inflation policy? The problem here is that people can see a motive for the government not 'sticking to its guns' since disinflation is always painful in the short run. In the technical economics literature this is known as the problem of 'time consistency'. What is to guarantee that policy-makers will not renege on their long-term commitment to an anti-inflation policy in order to achieve a better outcome for unemployment in the short term?

One answer to this problem is to remove political discretion for anti-inflation policy from policy-makers. This, it is argued, has been achieved in Germany, which has an enviable record on inflation, by the fact that the Bundesbank conducts monetary policy with complete independence. This consideration stimulated a lively discussion on the need to make the Bank of England similarly independent of political control so as to achieve a credible anti-inflation policy. However, the ERM seemed to offer an alternative means to the same end. By making monetary policy subservient to the maintenance of sterling within the ERM, any discretion in the conduct of monetary policy would be removed and the credibility of anti-inflation policy would thereby be enhanced. With hindsight it is clear that this did not work, because the credibility of the United Kingdom's membership of the ERM was itself less than complete, essentially because the temptation to pursue a time-inconsistent policy was exacerbated by the diverging requirements of national economies within the ERM. Furthermore, in global currency speculation a mechanism exists to test a country's commitment to an exchange rate regime such as the ERM.

Exit from the ERM removed the 'nominal anchor' of the quasi-fixed exchange rate and required a new anti-inflation policy regime to be put in place. The government opted for flexibility and transparency by instituting a policy of setting base rate with reference to monetary conditions as given by a range of indicators, and by encouraging an open discussion of the monetary conditions that impinge on the decision. Having experimented in the past with several proxy targets – various measures of money, nominal GDP and the exchange rate – the government now sets an explicit target for underlying inflation itself, as measured by the annual percentage change in RPIX. The initial target range is 1–4 per cent, and below 2 per cent by the end of the current Parliament, which will be no later than April 1997.

As part of the policy, the Bank of England publishes a quarterly inflation report analysing monetary conditions. In addition, the minutes of the Chancellor's monthly meetings with the Governor of the Bank of England are published, with a delay of around six weeks. Furthermore, the Treasury now gives the reasons for any change in the base rate, and has set up a panel of independent forecasters to provide alternative forecasts and policy advice, which are published three times a year.[3]

The aim of the new policy seems to be to make inflationary expectations in the United Kingdom more elastic – better informed and more responsive to current developments – rather than to attempt to shift them significantly for all time by a credible commitment to an irrevocable policy stance. Although it is too early to judge the effectiveness of this policy since 'Black Wednesday', it is noteworthy that up to early 1995 there have been two years of economic recovery while inflation has shown no signs of being rekindled. Indeed, the adjective 'black' seems quite inappropriate when applied to an event that liberated the economy from its self-imposed uncompetitive straitjacket in the ERM. However, it still remains to be seen whether a commitment to greater openness and public discussion of the anti-inflation policy will produce the desired effect of attenuating inflationary expectations.

12.9 Conclusion

Controlling inflation has been the government's top priority since 1979 but policies for achieving that goal have varied, as indeed has the degree of success. The periods in which there were substantial reductions in inflation, that is the early 1980s and the early 1990s, coincided with periods of record unemployment. Thus the control of inflation appears to have been bought at substantial cost in terms of output and employment. This may have been an unavoidable consequence of the persistence of inflationary expectations, and that has to do with the credibility of anti-inflation policy.

The big difference between the 1980s and the 1990s is the monetary environment. Throughout the 1980s monetary targeting of one form or another was in sway, initially with full conviction but with little success in adhering to the targets, and finally merely as a monitoring device. In retrospect it seems that the wholehearted espousal of monetarism at that time was thwarted by the instabilities of an era of rapid financial innovation which made it virtually impossible for the authorities to read the runes. By contrast, independent monetary control having been abandoned while the United Kingdom was in the ERM, and then re-established after its peremptory exit in 1992, the authorities now try to influence the climate in which inflationary expectations are formed by stimulating an open and informed discussion about the appropriate level of short-term interest rates. The idea seems to be that, as a substitute for a truly independent central bank, the government is now seen to be doing its best to avoid inflation for fear of discipline by the electorate, as it will now be evident that lax policy is to blame for inflation. In view of recent history, however, it is perhaps not surprising that, on the evidence of the term structure of inflation implied by bond prices, the financial markets in 1995 remain somewhat sceptical. The proof of the pudding will be in the eating.

Questions for discussion

1. Why are asset prices inversely related to interest rates?
2. What are the strengths and weaknesses of the RPI as a basis for the measurement of inflation?
3. What are the 'costs of inflation'?
4. Describe three different mechanisms through which an expansion of the stock of money affects the general price level.
5. Why was it so difficult for the government to meet its monetary targets in the 1980s?
6. How are short- and long-term interest rates affected by an unforeseen monetary expansion?
7. Can you explain the behaviour of short- and long-term interest rates in the period from 1972 to 1976? (see Figure 12.5)

8. How have changes in the exchange rate regime affected the conduct of monetary policy in recent years?

Notes

1. See MacFarlane and Mortimer-Lee (1994) for a history of inflation since the founding of the Bank of England in 1694.
2. However, the interest cost on loans would vary if there were differences in the risk of default on repayments.
3. Most of the documentation thus made public is conveniently available on the Internet. It can be accessed on the World Wide Web (http://www.hm-treasury.gov.uk/).

References and further reading

Bank of England (various issues) *Quarterly Bulletin and Inflation Report*, London: Bank of England.

Central Statistical Office (annual) *Family Expenditure Survey*, London: HMSO.

Central Statistical Office (1987) *A Short Guide to the Retail Prices Index*, London: HMSO.

Central Statistical Office (1994 and earlier editions) *United Kingdom National Accounts* (Blue Book), London: HMSO.

Central Statistical Office (1994) *Economic Trends, Annual Supplement 1994 Edition*, London: HMSO.

Department of Employment (monthly) *Employment Gazette*, London: HMSO.

Her Majesty's Treasury (1994) *Financial Statement and Budget Report 1995–1996*, London: HMSO.

Johnson, C. (1991) *The Economy under Mrs. Thatcher, 1979 – 1990*, London: Penguin Books.

King, M. (1995) 'Credibility and monetary policy: theory and evidence' *Scottish Journal of Political Economy* 42(1) February, pp. 1–19.

Maynard, G. (1988) *The Economy under Mrs. Thatcher*, Oxford: Basil Blackwell.

MacFarlane, H. and Mortimer-Lee, P. (1994) 'Inflation over 300 years' *Quarterly Bulletin* Bank of England, May 1994.

Treasury and Civil Service Committee (1981) *Monetary Policy, Vol. II Minutes of Evidence* HC 163, London: HMSO.

Walters, A. (1990) *Sterling in Danger*, London: Fontana.

CHAPTER 13

Unemployment

PRABIR BHATTACHARYA

13.1 Definition and measurement

Unemployment is usually defined as the difference between the number of people willing and able to work at prevailing wage rates, and those who actually have jobs. The unemployment rate is the number unemployed expressed as a percentage of the labour force.

Unemployment in Britain has traditionally been measured as the number of people registered as unemployed at Job Centres on a particular day each month; since 1982 the measure used has been the number of people claiming Unemployment Benefit each month. There are a number of problems with this measure. First, it fails to take account of those who are registered as unemployed but are not eligible, or choose not to apply, for benefit. Secondly the new, like the old, method of counting fails to take account of workers out of work and seeking a job and hence economically active, but who choose not to register as unemployed. Thirdly, there is a large number of workers who are discouraged from entering the labour force because of the depressed labour market conditions. Since these individuals are *willing* to work at current real wages and job conditions but are deterred from doing so by the prospects of unsuccessful job search, they should be included in the total of those unemployed. In a more buoyant labour market this group of workers would be economically active and appear generally in the stock of unregistered unemployed.

As against these, however, the stock of claimants does include groups of workers who are not available for work and these should be excluded from the total. The 1983 Labour Force Survey, for example, showed that those who did not want to work for family or other reasons amounted to 6.1 per cent of the claimant total. Indeed by 1985, the benefit count was actually giving higher readings than labour-force surveys showing who was actively seeking work. Some benefit claimants were long-term unemployed discouraged from seeking work; others were doing part-time or even full-time jobs in the black economy. Not surprisingly these difficulties in obtaining precise estimates have encouraged commentators to exercise considerable latitude in their own calculations.

Those horrified at the scale of unemployment in Britain inevitably publish estimates much higher than the official figures while those more sanguine about the problem do the opposite.

Having indicated how unemployment is measured one might expect that we should regard full employment quite simply as that state of the economy where measured unemployment is zero (making suitable allowance both for those who do not register and for those not available for work). To do so, however, would be incorrect. Ours is a dynamic and mobile economy. Individuals quit jobs to look for better positions or to retrain for more attractive occupations. These phenomena, and many more, produce some minimal amount of unemployment. Economists call this the level of *frictional unemployment*. Frictional unemployment includes people who are temporarily between jobs because they are moving or changing occupations, or because their old firm went out of business, or for other similar reasons. A second type of unemployment – often difficult to distinguish from frictional unemployment – is called *structural unemployment*. This refers to situations where workers have lost their jobs because they have been displaced by automation, or because their skills are no longer in demand, or for other similar reasons. When the only unemployment is frictional and structural the economy is said to be at full employment, and the measured unemployment rate is then called the *natural rate of unemployment*. In much of the macro economics literature the term 'natural rate' is used interchangeably with the 'non-accelerating inflation rate of unemployment' (NAIRU), where the rate of unemployment is compatible with a stable rate of inflation (see Parkin and King, 1995, Chapter 29).

13.2   Costs of unemployment

When the level of employment is below the full employment level (i.e. the unemployment rate is above the natural rate), actual output will be below the economy's potential output, so that there is an economic cost of unemployment in terms of lost output. The relationship between output and employment is complex so that a 1 per cent reduction in employment is not necessarily associated with a 1 per cent reduction in output. Indeed, if actual employment is 1 per cent below the full employment level, then output may well be below potential output by 2 per cent or more. This is because firms are likely to respond to a slump in orders (i.e. a fall in demand for their products) in other ways besides reducing employment. For instance, when output is reduced by 2 per cent, firms may accomplish some part of this, perhaps 1 per cent, by abolishing overtime and cutting back the number of hours worked by employees. In that case, a drop in output of 2 per cent is accompanied by a fall in employment of only 1 per cent.

In other words, a given change in the level of unemployment might indicate a much greater change in the level of output. The American economist Arthur

Okun suggested a one-to-three ratio for the United States (i.e. a 1 percentage point rise in the unemployment rate indicating a 3 per cent fall in GNP) and formulated this into what became known as Okun's Law. Earlier, Godley and Shepherd had suggested the one-to-two ratio used above for the United Kingdom. It is of course difficult to estimate the true ratio and this may change over time, but it is clear that the value of output lost in periods when unemployment is well above the natural rate can be very large indeed.

However, there are other economists who think that the cost of unemployment in terms of lost output is not so high. They believe that the natural rate of unemployment itself varies (see Section 13.4). Thus, if rapid technological advances in a particular period lead to the growth of new industries (e.g. high-technology, computer orientated industries) and the decline of some old industries, then there would be a higher than normal amount of labour turnover. Unemployment would rise temporarily as many people lose their jobs in old industries. Lowering the unemployment rate in this case would prevent the necessary reallocation of labour. To reap the full advantage of the new technologies, workers need to relocate to new industries. If they do not, then both output and income would be lower than that which the new technologies could otherwise have achieved.

Apart from the lost-output cost of high unemployment, there are obvious and potentially substantial social costs. We live in a work-orientated society. A worker forced into idleness by a recession endures a psychological cost that is no less real for our inability to quantify it. High unemployment breeds mental anxiety and ill health and leads to a higher incidence of divorces, suicides, and so on. There is also growing evidence that high unemployment leads to increased crime and social disruption.

Another important cost of unemployment is the erosion of human capital that it causes. Accumulated work experience is a valuable asset. Those forced into idleness by unemployment not only cease to accumulate experience, but lengthy periods of unemployment have adverse effects on work habits, make workers 'rusty' and thus less productive when they are re-employed. Lengthy periods of unemployment also undermine the enthusiasm for training or relocation where that is a possibility. Short periods of unemployment exact different kinds of costs. A record of regular employment is important in applying for a new job, and a person who has frequently been laid off will lack this record of reliability.

13.3 The unemployment record

The unemployment record in the United Kingdom is set out in Figure 13.1. Unemployment, it will be noted, was extremely high during the inter-war years, the worst period being the Great Depression of the early 1930s, when over 20 per cent of the labour force was unemployed. By comparison, the post-war unemployment rate was very low until the late 1970s. By the early 1980s it

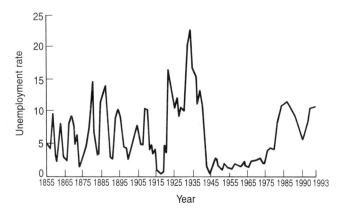

Figure 13.1 UK unemployment (%).
Sources: Mitchell (1962); Central Statistical Office (various).

was starting to return to pre-war levels and in 1985 and 1986 over 3 m people were seeking jobs. This basic pattern applies in many other industrialised countries. However, the United Kingdom was more successful than other countries, especially in Western Europe, in bringing unemployment down in the late 1980s, as indicated in Table 13.1.[1] From late 1990, however, unemployment started to rise again in the United Kingdom and by early 1993 the figure had once again approached 3 m. Since then it has fallen and at the time of writing stands at about 2.6 m.

It must be stressed that the UK unemployment rates for the years 1855-1990 illustrated in Figure 13.1 are not wholly comparable. There have been changes from time to time in the way the numbers unemployed are counted, with

Table 13.1 OECD standardised unemployment rates

Country	1979	1983	1985	1986	1987	1988	1989	1990	1991	1992	1993
United States	5.8	9.5	7.1	6.9	6.1	5.4	5.2	5.4	6.7	7.3	6.8
Japan	2.1	2.6	2.6	2.8	2.8	2.5	2.3	2.1	2.1	2.1	2.5
United Kingdom	5.0	12.4	11.2	11.2	10.3	8.5	6.9	6.9	8.8	9.9	10.3
Italy	7.5	8.8	9.6	10.5	10.9	11.0	10.9	9.8	9.8	9.8	10.2
France	5.9	8.3	10.2	10.4	10.5	10.0	9.6	8.9	9.4	10.3	11.7
West Germany	3.2	8.0	7.2	6.4	6.2	6.2	5.5	5.0	4.3	4.7	5.8
OECD Total	5.0	8.5	7.8	7.7	7.3	6.7	6.2	6.1	6.8	7.4	7.8

Sources: OECD Economic Outlook, OECD Labour Force Statistics.

several changes occurring in the 1980s. Before 1986, the unemployment rate referred to the percentage of the civilian labour force who were unemployed as a percentage of the total number of civilians employed plus the number regarded as unemployed. Since 1986, however, the unemployment rate refers to the number of people regarded as unemployed as a percentage of the total labour force, which includes not only the number of people employed and unemployed but also the self-employed and HM forces. The post-1986 approach reduces the measured unemployment rate since the number of people regarded as unemployed is divided by a larger number. It is difficult to be precise about the effects of these changes, but it has been suggested that the figures for the later years are probably at least 2 percentage points below what they would have been if the changes had not been made.

13.4   Labour market and unemployment

What explains the fluctuations in the rate of unemployment? What policies are needed to deal with high unemployment? How effective have the policies of the government been in dealing with high unemployment? Before we can answer these questions, it is necessary first to consider briefly the working of the labour market.

There are two leading theories of labour market equilibrium, one based on the assumption that money wages are flexible and the other based on the assumption that they are sticky (the former is often referred to as the 'neoclassical' view, the latter 'Keynesian'). Under the flexible money wage theory, the real wage rate (i.e. the money wage divided by an index of consumer prices) adjusts to ensure that the quantity of labour supplied equals the quantity demanded. The theory is illustrated in Figure 13.2. The demand for labour curve is LD and the supply of labour curve is LS. This market

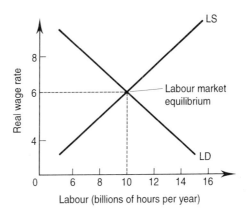

Figure 13.2   Equilibrium with flexible money wages.

determines an equilibrium real wage rate of £6.00 an hour and a quantity of labour employed of 10 bn hours. If the real wage rate is below this equilibrium level, the quantity of labour demanded exceeds the quantity supplied. In such a situation, given the price index, the money wage rate will rise since firms are willing to offer higher money wage rates in order to overcome their labour shortages. Consequently, the real wage rate will rise until it reaches £6.00 an hour, at which point there will be no shortage of labour.

Conversely, if the real wage is higher than its equilibrium level of £6.00 an hour, the quantity of labour supplied exceeds the quantity demanded. In this situation, firms will have an incentive to cut the money wage rate and households will accept the lower money wage to get a job. Given the price index, the real wage rate will fall until it reaches £6.00 an hour, at which point every household will be satisfied with the quantity of labour that it is supplying. Under the flexible money wage rate theory, changes in the money wage rate cause the real wage rate to adjust, ensuring that the quantity of labour supplied equals the quantity demanded.

According to the flexible money wage theory, the unemployment rate is always equal to the natural rate of unemployment. There is a balance between the quantity of labour demanded and the quantity of labour supplied; but the quantity of labour supplied is the number of hours of labour available for work at a given time without further search for a better job. The quantity of labour demanded is the number of hours of labour that firms wish to hire at a given time, given their knowledge of the individual skills and talents available. Households supply hours for work as well as time for job search. Those people who devote no time to working and specialise in job search are the ones who are unemployed. Additionally, unemployment may exist if the real wage rate is deliberately maintained above the level at which the labour supply and labour demand schedules intersect. It can be caused either by the exercise of trade union power or by minimum wage legislation which enforces a real wage rate in excess of the equilibrium real wage rate. Unemployment thus caused is known as *classical unemployment* and is usually included as part of the natural rate of unemployment (the natural rate of unemployment, in other words, strictly includes frictional, structural and classical unemployment).

In contrast to the flexible wage model, the sticky wage theory of the labour market emphasises that money wage rates are fixed by wage contracts for a year or more ahead and that they do not adjust freely minute by minute to enable changes in the real wage rate to maintain a balance between aggregate quantity of labour demanded and supplied. Real wage rates change more frequently than do money wage rates because of changes in the price level, but not with sufficient flexibility to achieve continuous full employment. In such a situation how is the wage determined? The money wage rate is set in the expectation or belief that, on the average, the quantity of labour demanded will equal the quantity supplied. However, when firms and workers agree to a money wage rate for a future contract, they do not know what the price level is going to be. All they can do is base the contract on their best forecast of future prices. If the price level turns out to be the same as expected, then the real wage rate is the same as in the flexible wage case and employment will also be the same. However, many other outcomes are possible. Consider what would happen to employment if the price level turns out to be different from what was expected.

The sticky wage theory assumes that it is the quantity of labour demanded which determines employment. Thus if the money wage rate is fixed and the price level turns out to be lower than what was expected, the real wage rate will be higher than the equilibrium real wage. Firms will, therefore, demand less labour than households wish to supply and employment will be below the labour market equilibrium. Conversely, when the money wage rate is fixed and the price level turns out to be higher than what was expected, the real wage rate will be lower, firms will demand more labour and employment will be higher.

According to the sticky wage theory, fluctuations in unemployment arise primarily from the mechanism just described, with the real wage deviating from its equilibrium level. Those economists who emphasise the role of sticky wages in causing fluctuations in unemployment commonly regard the natural rate of unemployment as constant – or slowly changing. Fluctuations in the actual unemployment rate are fluctuations around the natural rate. This interpretation of fluctuations in unemployment, it will be noted, contrasts sharply with that of the flexible money wage theory. The flexible money wage rate theory predicts that *all* changes in unemployment are fluctuations in the natural rate of unemployment.

This debate among economists about the causes of unemployment is not simply of academic interest and importance. It is critical for the design and conduct of macroeconomic stabilisation policy. If most of the fluctuations in unemployment do arise from sticky money wage rates, aggregate demand management can moderate the size of fluctuations in unemployment. By keeping aggregate demand (i.e. the sum of consumption, government expenditure and investment) steady so that the price level stays close to its expected level, the economy can be kept close to full employment. If, however, real wages are flexible enough to ensure that all unemployment is 'natural unemployment' and fluctuations in actual unemployment are fluctuations in natural unemployment, then aggregate demand policy has no role to play. Attempts by government to reduce unemployment below this natural rate by expansionary macro economic policies would then cause excess demand. This excess demand will lead to increases in wage and price inflation. In the short run workers are 'fooled' by the increase in money wages into believing that real wages have risen, and hence into supplying more labour, with less time being devoted to search and leisure activities. Consequently, unemployment falls. However, this deviation is only a short-run experience. In the long run workers realise that real wages have not risen, and their supply of labour therefore falls back again. As no government could contemplate a sustained acceleration in the rates of wage and price inflation, unemployment could not be permanently reduced below the natural rate. According to the flexible money wage rate model, to reduce the natural rate of unemployment permanently, the labour market has to be made more competitive and hence microeconomic policies (supply-side measures) are required. These may include the removal of labour market constraints caused by trade unions, minimum wages or wages councils (see Chapter 5), which maintain the real wage rate above its equilibrium level. Alternatively, reductions in marginal income tax rates (if not offset by higher indirect taxes – see Chapters 7 and 8) may provide the incentive for an increase in labour supply, while an increase in labour productivity would raise the demand for labour (LS and/or LD in Figure 13.2 would shift to the right).

13.5 Accounting for the rise in British unemployment

Economists remain a long way from agreement about the causes of unemployment and the reasons for its sometimes high and constantly fluctuating rate. In practice, however, Keynesian and neoclassical approaches to the determination of unemployment need not be mutually exclusive. A period of persistent high unemployment may reflect both unemployment above the natural rate and an increase in the rate over time. Thus all the recent attempts to estimate the natural rate for the United Kingdom suggest an upward trend over most of the last 20 years. Layard and Nickell (1985) have suggested that the natural rate of unemployment for male workers was around 2 per cent between 1955 and 1966, and then doubled by 1967–74 and doubled again between 1975 and 1979 to around 7.8 per cent. The rate then rose to 10.7 per cent by 1980–3. Davies' (1985) summary of three recent studies similarly suggested a rise of around 2–4 per cent between the late 1970s and the mid-1980s, that is, about half the actual rise in unemployment. This rise in the natural rate, it has been suggested, has been caused, among other things, by increases in trade union power, by the unemployed becoming less available for work due to higher replacement ratios (when unemployment benefit rises relative to wages from working, we say the replacement ratio has risen), by reduced pressure from benefit offices on recipients to find work and due to a general weakening of the work ethic.

The striking fact that estimates of the natural rate have moved up with the actual rate of unemployment suggests some form of 'hysteresis'. Pure hysteresis means that the current value of a variable depends upon history, the variable having no tendency to move towards any particular level. Therefore, there is hysteresis in unemployment if the natural rate of unemployment this year is affected by the unemployment level in previous years. Jenkinson (1987) investigates several possibilities for this influence and particularly important in this context appears to be the behaviour of the long-term unemployed. The long-term unemployed tend to become discouraged, they are not very active in looking for work, and their loss of skills make them less attractive to employers. They stop being part of the effective supply of labour and they therefore have little downward impact on wage pressure. The natural rate will increase as the proportion of long-term unemployed rises; support for this proposition has come from a wide range of models. Higher unemployment may also reduce labour market efficiency as on-the-job search is reduced and this results in lower labour market mobility among employed workers and increases mismatch between workers and jobs.

Any empirical investigation of the post-1979 unemployment experience must allow for both Keynesian and neoclassical mechanisms to operate. A good example is Layard (1986) and Layard and Nickell (1987). Results from their work suggest that demand factors played very little role in the growth of male unemployment (data on male unemployment is more comprehensively and reliably documented than data on the unemployment of women) in the 1960s and early 1970s, where union militancy and, in the 1970s, the rise in real import prices appear to be the dominant causes of that growth. The picture changes dramatically when we consider the rise in male unemployment in the late 1970s where contraction of aggregate demand alone accounted for 85 per cent of the rapid rise in male unemployment. Layard and Nickell conclude that although the influence of unions and replacement ratios may have caused an increase in unemployment in the 1960s and early 1970s, it is the contraction of aggregate demand which was mainly responsible for increases in subsequent years. McCallum (1986) reaches similar conclusions about the importance of restrictive fiscal and monetary policy as does Pissarides (1986). It would thus appear that the increase in UK unemployment in the 1960s and 1970s can be explained almost entirely by forces that had increased the natural rate.

The story, however, was very different in the late 1970s and the first half of the 1980s. Although the natural rate continued to increase, a substantial bout of Keynesian recession or deficient demand was overlaid. That is why unemployment rose so sharply. Conversely, UK unemployment fell rapidly in the late 1980s partly because the natural rate of unemployment fell due to supply-side measures of the government and partly because of a strong expansion of aggregate demand. Conditions for receiving unemployment benefit were made more stringent in 1986 under the Restart Programme and there was a crackdown on those registering for benefit. The dramatic fall in British unemployment after 1986 was partially due to these measures, which increased the effective labour supply so that, when demand surged ahead, there was initially only a limited increase in wage inflation.

The strong expansion of aggregate demand in the late 1980s was caused both by the fiscal stimulus of tax cuts and because the financial revolution (see Chapter 14) made available consumer credit to an extent never previously encountered. The growth of demand, which was initially hailed as a successful conclusion to the recession, eventually got out of hand because the government failed to appreciate its strength and did not believe in using fiscal policy to control it. The government greatly underestimated the growth of real demand in 1987 and 1988. This was due partly to deficiencies in the official statistical system and partly to a deterioration in the Treasury's previously impressive forecasting record. Thus, while the Treasury forecast that domestic demand would rise by 4 per cent in 1988, the actual increase turned out to be 8 per cent – so the forecast change in demand was wrong by a margin of 100 per cent!

The government's supply-side policies of tax-cutting and deregulation were not sufficient to stimulate the British economy to expand supply by as much as they stimulated demand. Inflation, which had come down in the mid-1980s, began to climb again, soon returning to double-digit rates. The government was forced to raise interest rates substantially. However, the use of interest rates rather than fiscal policy to control inflation slowed the growth of the economy and bore heavily on home-owners in spite of massive mortgage subsidies. The 1987–9 boom gave way to slump in 1991–2 and by early 1993 unemployment once again approached the 3 m figure. We are currently in the recovery phase of the cycle and unemployment is once again falling and capacity utilisation rising.

Macroeconomic policy became expansionary after sterling was forced to withdraw from the Exchange Rate Mechanism (see Chapter 18), and the impetus given by the depreciation of sterling and reduction in interest rates is still carrying the economy forward. There is some purely cyclical fall in unemployment due to demand expansion yet to come, but, on the basis of past experience, it is unlikely that the level of unemployment can be held much below 2 to 2.5 m without leading to fresh problems of inflation and for the balance of payments, unless the expansion were to be accompanied by substantially improved competitiveness and growth of capacity.

13.6 Government policies on unemployment

In the last 12 years there has been a remarkable turnabout in policies to deal with unemployment. During the Conservative government of Edward Heath in the early 1970s the then high levels of unemployment of 1971 and 1972 were greatly reduced in 1973 by a major increase in the aggregate demand for goods. Taxes were cut, public investment increased and there was a large expansion in the money supply. These were the instruments of the so-called 'Barber boom' which assumed that since unemployment was largely Keynesian in nature, such an expansion was all that was necessary. The only significant feature of policy that departed from this diagnosis was the emphasis placed on regional incentives to reduce 'structural' unemployment in certain regions in the country.

Since then much has changed and during the Callaghan government of the late 1970s, the need to control the public-sector borrowing requirement (PSBR) and the money supply became important objectives of economic policy. However, it was the Thatcher government after 1979 which became particularly identified with the re-emergence of conservative macroeconomics in Britain. In general, the government rejected the notion that a reflation of demand via increases in current public spending or public investment is a viable solution to high unemployment, and cuts in public investment and public spending programmes for a time reduced the PSBR as a share of GDP to one of the lowest in the industrial world (see Chapter 11). Instead the government has concentrated upon failures in the operation of the labour market and attempted to reduce wage pressure by various supply-side measures. The causes of unemployment, the government consistently argued, were high union density, an excessive ratio of benefits to wages and too much taxation of both employers and employees. Trade union reform, the reduction of earnings-related benefit, the crackdown on fraudulent benefit claimants, the abolition of the National Insurance Surcharge on employers, and income-tax cuts all became parts of a supply-side package for reducing it.

Other aspects of government policy also confirm this broadly classical perspective. The emphasis on the quality of the labour force, especially as far as education and training are concerned, and the degree to which this determines the speed with which workers and employers adapt to 'new products and processes and new competitive pressures which offer new challenges and opportunities' indicate this. The government believes that this adaptability has not been characteristic of the British labour market and that this has lowered the natural rates of output and employment.

With its emphasis on policies to reduce the natural rate of unemployment and its assertion that too high a level of real wages rather than a shortage of aggregate demand is the primary cause of unemployment above the natural rate, the government has clearly identified itself with the classical view of unemployment. Critics of the government position, however, would argue that demand management policies are not impotent and that the impact of the government's deflationary policy since 1979 confirms this conclusion. Given the rigidity of prices and wages in the short run, contractions of aggregate demand initially lead to reductions in levels of output and employment and cause unemployment to rise above the natural rate. Estimates from the models discussed above suggest that about a quarter of unemployment in 1985, and almost half of the rise in unemployment during the period 1979–85, were due to contractionary macroeconomic policies. When aggregate demand increased in 1987, unemployment too declined. It is the government's failure in managing this demand properly that subsequently led to demand expanding faster than output and to the problems of high and rising inflation. It is, however, now being claimed that the flexibility of the labour market brought about by the Thatcherite reforms is just beginning to have its effect, with the low growth in earnings and the fall in unemployment over the past 18 months or so being evidence of this.

However, one must be cautious in one's interpretation of the significance of the recent fall in unemployment, especially as there is not much evidence of an increase in jobs. In a flexible labour market one would expect to see those who lose their jobs to make a rapid transition back into employment, and for most of the population that would mean into full-time and 'permanent' employment. It is, however, the case that part-time employment as a proportion of total employment has increased from 16.4 per cent in 1979 to 21.8 per cent in 1990, to 23.5 per cent in 1992, and continues to rise. Similarly, in a flexible labour market one would expect the average duration of unemployment to be short. Yet, in 1993 the proportion of long-term unemployed (i.e. those unemployed for more than 12 months expressed as a proportion of total unemployment) was still as high as 36.9 per cent. Finally, in a flexible labour market one would not expect to find large numbers of 'discouraged' workers dropping out of the labour force altogether because they gave up hope of finding any suitable job at all. Additionally, in recent years there has been a devastating loss in full-time jobs for male workers. There has been a rapid rise in the share of output and employment accounted for by the service sector and this changing sectoral composition has resulted in a greater proportion of total employment being accounted for by part-time jobs predominantly filled by female workers. The fall in the female unemployment rate relative to male unemployment rate in recent years suggests the emergence of a growing mismatch between gender and jobs.[2] By all of these criteria, it is therefore too early to be sanguine about the significance of the recent fall in unemployment. As already noted, the greater part of this fall in unemployment probably relates to the expansionary phase of the cycle rather than being mainly a result of the labour market reforms of recent years.

One major aspect of government policy has been ignored so far and that is the use of special measures to reduce unemployment and to assist the unemployed. Certain types of unemployment and certain groups of unemployed people have been particularly selected for attention and various training programmes and work-sharing measures have been put into effect. In total there have been about twenty different, often short-lived, schemes. A brief outline of some of the more important of these schemes is presented below and their effectiveness examined.

13.6.1 *Special employment measures*

The first of the special measures was the introduction in 1975 of the Temporary Employment Subsidy and the Job Creation Programme. At its peak in May 1977, the Temporary Employment Subsidy (TES) covered about 200 000 workers, providing employers with a subsidy (£20 per week) to postpone redundancies. Although not directly targeted, TES was highly concentrated in manufacturing with 90 per cent of the jobs covered being in this sector, and half of these jobs being in the clothing and footwear industries. The scheme, however, fell foul of an EC ban on this kind of subsidy and was abandoned in 1979. It was replaced by the Temporary Short-Time Working Compensation Scheme (TSTWCS), a subsidy aimed at inducing employers to substitute work-sharing for redundancies; at its peak in March 1981, it covered nearly a million workers. Once again it was in practice highly selective, with 95 per cent of workers covered being in manufacturing. This scheme was abandoned in 1984. More recently, the Enterprise Allowance Scheme (EAS) provided a subsidy for unemployed workers to start up their own businesses; it covered an estimated 80 000 workers in 1986–7. Overall the Department of Employment estimated that the special measures reduced unemployment by about 450 000 in the middle of the 1980s.

An alternative to supporting employment levels in the private sector is to introduce 'public works' schemes to provide public sector employment opportunities for unemployed workers. The Community Programme (CP) was of this kind, the jobs being largely organised by public bodies and voluntary organisations. In October 1987 about 230 000 long-term unemployed adults were covered by this scheme, working on projects that promote general community interests, such as environmental or educational facilities' improvements. Although the scheme was open to all long-term unemployed over 18 years of age, its flat-rate pay provided no incentives for those over the age of 25 years to participate; from 1988, it was replaced by the Employment Training Programme, with trainees paid on a 'benefit-plus' basis which made it less attractive to young single workers but more attractive to family men.

The Community Programme did little to improve the supply side of the labour market. More serious efforts at improving the quality of labour force were made with the Youth Training Scheme (YTS) for school leavers and the Technical and Vocational Educational Initiative for 14–18-year-olds, starting in 1983 and 1984. The official inspectors of YTS found 'a high and growing proportion of schemes offering nationally recognised qualifications', but against this they also found that 'many trainers lacked the levels of knowledge and skill needed to guide trainees towards recognised qualifications or credits towards them' (*Employment Gazette*, July, 1990). In 1988, the Manpower Services Commission (MSC) was redesignated the Training Commission and given the responsibility for running a single unified programme, Employment Training (ET). This took the place of the Community Programme and the YTS.

The final type of scheme used is work-sharing, though such schemes have been rather less important in the United Kingdom than those just outlined. The Job Release Scheme begun in 1977 provides a financial incentive for older workers to retire early and release their jobs to unemployed people. The scheme peaked at 95 000 jobs and was withdrawn at the beginning of 1988; a short-lived version for part-time workers was introduced in 1983. Also in 1983 a Job Splitting Scheme was introduced and in 1987 extended as Jobshare; this provides employers with a grant to split a full-time job into two part-time ones or consolidate regular overtime hours into part-time employment. The long-term effects of all these schemes must be to reduce the size of the workforce and so permanently lower output.

To conclude, special employment measures would appear to be no more than a short-term palliative, providing only temporary relief for particular unemployment-prone groups. Since they do not affect the long-term re-employment probabilities of these groups they do not provide a long-run solution for participating individuals. It has also been argued that the deadweight loss of special measures is unacceptably high. The deadweight loss is the result of payments or expenditure to bring about an increase in jobs or prevent a reduction that would have happened anyway. The apparent success of the special measures would thus appear to be in terms of reducing official unemployment figures and there is no evidence that they represent an efficient response to improving the utilisation and allocation of labour.

13.7 Conclusion

Unemployment is an enormously costly economic and social problem. To reduce unemployment it is necessary to reduce wage pressure by supply-side policies while at the same time raising the level of real aggregate demand. If the stimulus to aggregate demand can be directed towards high-unemployment groups, then the inflation costs of raising employment can be reduced. In particular, expansion should be concentrated on producing job opportunities for long-term unemployed. Emphasis needs also to be placed on training and improvement in the supply of skills. The better the workers are trained, the better their outlook in the long term. Meanwhile, the retraining of workers in the middle age group, who become redundant, or who have left the labour market and wish to return, assumes greater urgency.

Questions for discussion

1. Do you think that the Department of Employment overestimates or underestimates the number of people that are unemployed? Why?
2. What are the costs of unemployment?
3. 'The natural rate of unemployment will increase as the proportion of long-term unemployed rises.' Discuss.
4. How would the high unemployment in the 1980s be explained by (a) a Keynesian, (b) a Classical economist?
5. What effect do special employment measures have on the rate of unemployment?
6. What should the links be between special employment measures on the one hand and the education system on the other?

Notes

1. International comparisons of unemployment rates are fraught with difficulties. In Table 13.1, unemployment rates in selected countries are presented on the OECD standard basis using labour force surveys which define unemployment in terms of seeking work.
2. The relative female unemployment rate (i.e. the female unemployment rate divided by male unemployment rate) has declined from 0.67 in 1979 to 0.39 in 1993.

References and further reading

Ashton, D. (1986) *Unemployment Under Capitalism*, Hemel Hempstead: Harvester Wheatsheaf.

Central Statistical Office *Economic Trends* (various issues), London: HMSO.

Davies, G. (1985) *Government Can Affect Unemployment*, London: Employment Institute.

Department of Employment (1990) *Employment Gazette* 98(7), London: Employment Department.

Jahoda, M. (1982) *Employment and Unemployment: A social–psychological analysis*, Cambridge: Cambridge University Press.

Jenkinson, T. (1987) 'The natural rate of unemployment: does it exist?' *Oxford Review of Economic Policy* 3 pp. 20–6.

Johnson, C. (1988) *Measuring the Economy*, London: Penguin Books.

Knight, K. (1987) *Unemployment: An economic analysis*, London: Croom Helm.

Layard, R. (1986) *How to Beat Unemployment?*, Oxford: Oxford University Press.

Layard, R. and Nickell, S. (1985)'The causes of British unemployment' *Economica (Supplement)* 210 pp. S121–70.

Layard, R. and Nickell, S. (1987) 'The performance of the British labour market' in *The Performance of the British Economy* Dornbusch, R. and Layard, R. (eds), Oxford: Oxford University Press.

Lindbeck, A. and Snower, D. (1986) 'Explanations of unemployment' *Oxford Review of Economic Policy* 1(2) pp. 34–59.

McCallum, J. (1986) 'Unemployment in OECD countries' *Economic Journal* 96 pp. 942–60.

Minford, A.P.L. (1983) *Unemployment: Cause and cure*, Oxford: Martin Robertson (2nd edn Oxford: Blackwell, 1985).

Mitchell, B.R. (1988) *Abstract of British Historical Statistics*, Cambridge: Cambridge University Press.

Parkin, M. and King, D. (1995) *Economics*, Woking: Addison-Wesley.

Pissarides, C. (1986), 'Unemployment and vacancies in Britain' *Economic Policy* 3 pp. 499–541.

Trinder, C. (1988) 'Special employment measures and employment' *National Institute Economic Review*, February 123 pp. 17–19.

CHAPTER 14

Financial markets and public policy

IAN HIRST

14.1 Introduction

The most visible evidence of public policy towards the financial markets in the United Kingdom is the imposition of new legislation and new regulations. The 1980s were an active period in this regard. A short list of the most prominent changes in the United Kingdom since the return of a Conservative government in 1979 would run as follows:

1979 Exchange controls abolished.

1980 Supplementary Special Deposits scheme ended. This scheme, known as the 'corset', restricted the rate of growth of UK banks' deposits.

1982 Controls on consumer instalment credit ended.

1985 Company Securities (Insider Dealing) Act made insider trading a criminal offence.

1986 The 'Big Bang' reforms to the operation of the Stock Exchange take effect.

1986 The Financial Services Act setting up a new regulatory structure for parts of the financial services industry.

1995 (proposed) Pensions Act in response to the recommendations of the Goode Report.

The main purpose of recent changes has been to make refinements and adjustments to a financial system whose basic features are long established. Many of the main features of the financial system in the United Kingdom have resulted from inflation, the tax system, the system of state benefits and the place of state ownership in the economy. The main aspects of public policy that have shaped the financial markets are not clearly labelled as such. Conversely, some of the changes in regulations which have received so much publicity have had comparatively little impact. The 1985 Act covering insider trading certainly created a new criminal offence; but insider trading was regarded as unethical before the Act, and leading financial institutions had their own house rules to prevent it. Since insider trading can be disguised in a number of ways, it is likely that a significant amount still goes on without detection. The new law was certainly welcome in principle, but it is not clear that it made any substantial change to the working of the financial markets in practice.

The 1986 Financial Services Act comes into the same category. This massive regulatory edifice was set up in response to financial scandals resulting from the operations of a few rogue companies. The great majority of reputable firms incurred the costs of a more formal and prescriptive environment without major changes in their activities.

The most significant regulatory change in the list, by a wide margin, was the abolition of exchange controls in 1979. This opened the UK financial markets to external competition in several areas. It made the Special Deposits Scheme ineffective and undermined the structure of the Stock Exchange. The new legislative and regulatory environment has been partly created by international agreements. The Banking Directives of the European Union (EU) have enabled European banks to open branches throughout the EU since 1993. An agreement reached under the auspices of the Bank for International Settlements (BIS) in 1988 established the capital requirements for international banks for twelve major industrialised countries.

This chapter will not attempt to chronicle recent modifications to financial market regulations. Its main concern will be the effectiveness of UK financial markets. Because there are so many different markets, we must be selective. Priority will be given to company finance and to the supporting structure of the savings industry.

One of the curious features of financial markets is that the major industrial economies have very different financial systems. This contrasts with other industries where similar systems can be expected. In the automobile industry, for example, there is a strong similarity in the way cars are built in different parts of the world. One assembly line looks much like another. Financial markets and financial systems do not seem to follow the same logic. There are very substantial differences, which do not appear to be diminishing with time, between the corporate finance systems in the G5 countries (United Kingdom, United States, Japan, Germany, France). Sometimes the poor industrial performance of the UK and US economies are attributed to their financial systems, but so many variables contribute to industrial performance that it is difficult to isolate their different effects. It can also be argued that the sophistication and variety of the financial markets in the United Kingdom tend to counteract other factors which are the roots of Britain's industrial problems.

14.2 The economics of financial markets

In this section we shall look at the basic forces that shape financial markets, both in the United Kingdom and elsewhere. We shall look at inflation, interest, risk, liquidity and information. It is only by reviewing these fundamental factors that we can identify the distinctive features of the UK market and the policies that have produced them.

The financial markets bring together savers and borrowers. Within the market sector of the economy, savers are economic agents who are willing to postpone the enjoyment (consumption) of their wealth in order to invest in financial assets. Borrowers are economic agents who wish to spend above the level that can be covered by their existing resources. The phrase 'economic agent' is carefully chosen. It covers both individuals and companies. Our discussion will centre on individuals as savers (in what follows, we commonly refer to such people, loosely, as investors) and companies as borrowers, although individuals can also be borrowers as in the consumer credit market.

14.2.1 *The interest rate*

The basic price in the financial markets is the interest rate. To invidual investors, the interest rate is a reward for postponing consumption. To businesses, the interest rate is a cost incurred when using a production process which involves time. Body panels for modern cars are not produced by taking a sheet of steel and hammering it into a shape that fits. They are formed in giant presses using very carefully shaped dies. The job of designing and manufacturing the dies takes place many months before the resulting cars come to market. The production process is a 'roundabout' one. There are large set-up costs before production takes place. The production process is time intensive. The workers who manufacture the dies will need to be paid long before customers will pay for the cars. Capital, from individual investors (i.e. savers, see above), is needed to bridge this time gap. Where time-intensive (capital using) methods of production are most efficient, capital adds value and the individuals who have supplied capital can expect to be rewarded with interest payments.

Offered a greater reward, a higher interest rate, individuals will normally be willing to save more and provide more capital. On the other hand, at a higher interest rate businesses will look for ways to use less time in their production processes. A market-clearing interest rate will emerge at which the supply of savings from individuals will just match the borrowing requirements of businesses.

Markets have no respect for international boundaries. In the absence of barriers or discriminatory taxes the interest rate will be set at a rate that will clear the global capital market. Countries which have within their borders an excess of savers over borrowers will export capital. Other countries will be net importers.

14.2.2 *Inflation*

The explanation of interest rates given above is only valid in a world without inflation. With inflation, growth in money and growth in purchasing power will no longer be the same thing. Economic agents will have to decide whether to evaluate projects on the basis of the money amounts they will generate in the future or the amounts of purchasing power. It is not a hard decision. Money is not desired for its own sake: it is purchasing power that counts. The analysis must be modified in an inflationary environment to run in purchasing power units rather than amounts of money.

An interest rate can be regarded as an exchange rate, between an amount an individual investor can enjoy now (through present consumption) and the amount he could enjoy in the future if he is prepared to wait. The equilibrium rate which reconciles saving and borrowing behaviour is not the exchange rate between money now and money next year but an exchange rate between purchasing power now and purchasing power next year. The money-to-money rate is known as the nominal interest rate and is the kind of interest rate normally quoted in financial deals. The purchasing power–purchasing power rate is known as the real interest rate. Real interest rates are not normally quoted but the concept is familiar to most people. If the bank is giving you an 8 per cent (nominal) interest rate on your savings at a time when inflation is 13 per cent, you are growing poorer. Putting it another way, you are receiving a negative real interest rate on your savings. It is real rates which tend to equality in different countries. Nominal rates will be different because of different levels of inflation.

14.2.3 *Risk*

The outcome of most business ventures is uncertain. A very simple business opportunity might involve a cash outflow of £100 now and an inflow of either £90 or £140 in 1 year's time, with each of these two possible outcomes being equally likely. The return, therefore, has a 50 per cent probability of being +40 per cent, and a 50 per cent probability of being −10 per cent. The expected return is simply the probability-weighted average of these two numbers, 15 per cent. The usual numerical measure of risk is the standard deviation, which is a measure of how far away from the expected return the actual return is likely to be. In the example, the return will either be 25 per cent above the expected return or 25 per cent below it. The standard deviation of return in this example is, not surprisingly, 25 per cent. Businesses cannot offer all investors a fixed rate of return on their investment. Someone must take the risk. One function of financial markets is to allocate risk efficiently.

A saver (i.e. an individual investor) will look at both the expected return of each project and its risk. Investors are risk averse. This means that, if two projects offer the same mean return, they will choose the one with the lower risk of return. They would prefer to receive a guaranteed return of 15 per cent rather than an equal chance of a return of 40 per cent or −10 per cent. If the projects offer different mean returns, an investor may choose the one with the lower return if this disadvantage is counteracted by a lower risk.

To enable financial investors to control the level of risk in their investments (and for other reasons that will be discussed later) companies will split up the cash flow from their activities into different types of claim with different levels of risk. A good analogy comes from considering a dairy farmer. The milk comes out of the cows with a certain proportion of cream naturally included. Not all consumers want this particular mix. Some will want low-fat milk with the cream removed. Others want to buy pure cream to pour onto their strawberries. The dairy industry will separate out the components of the raw milk to satisfy these different tastes.

It is the same with business projects. In the raw state they offer a mixture of return and risk, but these two elements can be separated out and savers can be offered both low-risk and high-risk opportunities. Consider our earlier example of the £100 cash outflow rewarded a year later by an inflow of either £90 or £140. This project might be financed by two different types of claim. One could be zero-risk. Investors who put in £50 on this basis could be guaranteed that they would get £55 back. Their investment would offer a return of 10 per cent and a standard deviation of zero. The investors who put in the other £50 would take the risk. They would get back either £35 or £85 depending on which way the project turned out. They would receive a mean return of 20 per cent and a standard deviation of return of 50 per cent. The risky investment will have to offer a higher mean return to attract investors.

A company is a legal entity which stands between individual investors and the business projects which they fund. Companies normally package the proceeds from projects into a very low risk stream in the form of interest-bearing securities and/or bank loans, and a risky stream which goes to shareholders.

14.2.4   Diversification

One of the most visible characteristics of risk averse behaviour by individual investors (savers) is that they will spread their holdings of shares over a wide range of different companies rather than plunging it all into one. By doing this the overall risk to which their investment is exposed will be reduced. Some shares will do well; some will do poorly but the overall return will not tend towards either extreme. The risk on a portfolio of shares can thus be less than the risk on any single share within the portfolio taken in isolation.

There are limits to what diversification can achieve. The economic cycle in the United Kingdom will affect almost all business activities. Shares will tend to go up and down together in response. All UK shares have their price movements linked to some extent to the rise and fall of the stock market index.

This component of risk cannot be diversified away other than by investing in non-UK based businesses.

The remaining risk, the part that is specific to the individual company and quite independent of developments outside it, can be diversified away very effectively. If an investor spreads his money evenly over the shares of 30 different companies, this type of risk will have disappeared almost completely.

The implication of this is a surprising but important one in the theory of financial markets. For risk averse investors, extra risk must be rewarded by extra return, but it is only the component of risk which is linked to the movement of the stock market as a whole which is rewarded. The remaining risk is diversified away by investors. It does not harm them and they do not require any extra return to persuade them to accept it.

A second important implication is that investors will not typically have close links with individual companies in the sense that they are likely to read financial reports in great detail, attend and ask questions at Annual Meetings, and use their shareholder's rights actively. Their money will typically be spread over several dozen firms. This follows the old adage: 'Don't put all your eggs in one basket'. There is another saying: 'Do put all your eggs in one basket, and then take very good care of the basket'. Investors follow the first maxim, not the second, and the danger is that, as a result, the baskets (i.e. the companies) may not be very carefully supervised.

14.2.5 *Liquidity*

Most business projects are long term. Once the initial investment has been made, the benefits will arise over a period of years and, sometimes, of decades. Investors often have a shorter time horizon. They often do not know, when they make an investment, how soon they will want to take their money out. They will be well aware that they might need to withdraw their money at almost any time, as a result of illness or unemployment, for example. In other words, they need their investments to be liquid. The liquidity of a financial asset is defined as the ability to turn it into cash quickly and cheaply.

There are two ways in which the financial markets can perform the conjuring trick of providing funds to borrowers on a long-term basis while simultaneously assuring savers that they can get their money back whenever they want. The first is the secondary market, such as that organised by the Stock Exchange. The second is financial intermediary organisations such as banks.

The Stock Exchange

A primary financial market is one in which investors provide funds to companies (and other bodies, such as governments) and receive financial assets such as shares or bonds in return. A secondary market is one in which investors trade these financial assets among themselves. Investor A wants to sell shares; Investor B is willing to buy; their advisers or brokers will negotiate a price for the exchange; and the company and its business are unaffected.

The Stock Exchange is mainly a secondary market. Because shares in most companies are traded many times a day, price negotiation between buyers and sellers is much simplified. The starting point will be the price for the last deal and the new price will not move very far in either direction. The natural tendency is for the trading of a particular company's shares to be concentrated in a single market and the London Stock Exchange has a virtual monopoly in the trading of shares for most UK public companies. This also enables the Stock Exchange to control the primary market for company securities. Investors will not buy securities in the primary market unless they are sure that there will be an adequate secondary market, i.e. that the Stock Exchange will list the security and supervise trading in it. The Stock Exchange is, therefore, in a position to set rules governing the issue of new securities which are supplementary to the legal requirements of the Prevention of Fraud Acts. It can change its rules to stop any emerging abuse much more quickly than the government can rewrite the law.

The secondary market in shares can only work well when companies are large and have a large number of shareholders who will generate a constant flow of orders to buy and sell. This will produce a continuous market with small price jumps between transactions. Anyone who wants to trade can be confident that there will be counterparties in the market. For small companies the system tends to break down; there can be buyers without sellers or sellers without buyers so that a shareholder can find either that he is 'locked in' to his shares or that he can only dispose of them at an unattractive price; so in a financial system which relies heavily on a stock exchange for company finance (and we shall see later that the United Kingdom falls into this category) there will be a tendency for large firms to flourish more than small ones.

Banks

A bank creates liquidity in a quite different way. The depositors are assured that they can get their money out on demand or at short notice; the borrowers, mainly companies, are assured that their loans only need to be repaid over a negotiated period which may be as long as 5 or 7 years. The bank is performing an asset transformation by taking in short-term deposits and giving out long-term loans. The system relies on the bank's ability to attract new depositors to replace those who withdraw. Under normal circumstances this can be achieved by judicious use of marketing campaigns and new, more attractive types of account for depositors.

A bank will also need its own risk capital so that if some of its loans to businesses go bad the loss can be absorbed by the shareholders in the bank rather than the depositors. Under the Basle Concordat, there is now international agreement that banks must have risk capital (reserves) equal to at least 8 per cent of their total assets (i.e. the risk-weighted value of their loan portfiolio).

In times of economic and financial crisis there remains the possibility that large losses on bad loans will undermine public confidence and a bank will not be able to keep its deposit base. Any banking system is, in this respect, inherently unstable. Implicitly or explicitly the government and the central bank will underpin the banking system by guaranteeing depositors against loss and by standing ready to buy high quality assets from a bank that needs to raise cash urgently. Clearly, however, this support must be provided in such a way that its availability does not give the banks an undue incentive to take foolish risks in the future. Although the relationship between banks and governments is often not written down in black and white, it is very important in influencing bank behaviour and later we shall compare the system in the United Kingdom with that in other industrial countries.

Notice that where a business is financed by shares quoted on the Stock Exchange, these shares will be actively traded and any adverse information about the success of the business will show up clearly and directly in a fall in the value of the shares. Where the finance comes from a bank loan, the loan will not be traded and there will be no open-market price which would give an objective measure of what the loan is worth. For this reason the bank finance system cannot provide business with risk capital. The system would not generate the information needed to operate effectively. Banks are best suited to providing business with safe loans where the problem of constant re-evaluation in the light of new information does not arise.

The conclusion of this section on the creation of liquidity is that risk capital for a business (other than that provided by the founders and directors) should ideally be provided through the Stock Exchange. However, low-risk capital can be provided either through an open market, on which the companies debt securities are traded, or through banks.

14.2.6 *Information*

It is a basic rule in financial markets that those who take the risk in a business venture shall have the ultimate decision-making power. Investors will be reluctant to put up risk capital if they are powerless to correct management errors that put their wealth at risk. Consequently shareholders have votes for the selection of the company directors, and the bondholders or banks who have provided the rest of the capital do not. The United Kingdom has a 'winner-take-all' system for the selection of directors; 51 per cent of the votes are enough to control all the seats on the board.

When shareholders accept risk they want to understand clearly what the risks are and they want to see how they can act to protect their investment if things go wrong. Generally, investors will prefer to invest in a 'pure play', a company that concentrates on a particular industrial sector, rather than a conglomerate company which has its finger in many pies and is, therefore, much harder for outsiders to understand. Investors will be less enthusiastic about buying shares in companies where there is a controlling shareholder, perhaps the founder of the business and his family. They will be suspicious that the controlling shareholder may find ways of benefiting himself at the expense of other shareholders. They will also be aware that a controlling shareholder can block a takeover bid, so no relief from that quarter could be expected if the business performed poorly. Investors also dislike, for similar reasons, companies which own non-controlling shareholdings in other companies. Shareholders will generally prefer to have the shares (and votes) in their own hands rather than own them indirectly at one remove.

How are shareholders to know what is going on in the business? The Companies Acts require that shareholders be given a Report and Accounts every year. In the judgement of the Stock Exchange this is insufficient. Quoted companies must provide half-yearly accounts and inform shareholders of any significant acquisitions or disposals which may change the nature of the business. For large changes and for any transaction between the company and one of its directors they must seek their shareholders' approval in a vote. These requirements will certainly improve shareholders' awareness of what is going on in their company. However, it will remain true that the directors and managers are likely to have much more detailed and up-to-date information than anyone relying on published accounts. Furthermore, if the information available to shareholders is seriously deficient, the financial markets cannot perform their resource allocation role effectively.

The inequality (or 'asymmetry') of information between shareholders and directors/managers has a number of consequences. If the directors know better than any outsiders what the company's shares are really worth, they will be able to make profits by trading the shares in the secondary market. This is known as insider trading and its consequence is that the market will become unfair. The losses will fall in the first instance on the market-makers whose function is to quote, on a continuous basis, prices at which they are prepared to buy and sell. They will find, for example, that they have been 'stuffed' with shares by insiders just before bad news about the company becomes publicly available, and the share price falls. The market-makers take a loss. The only way that they can stay in business is by widening the difference between their buying price for shares and their selling price (the 'spread'). This means in effect that ordinary investors pay a larger commission or charge whenever they trade in the market. In this way the ordinary investors pay the insiders' winnings. Unequal information is therefore potentially very damaging to the liquidity of shares and the effective operation of a stock exchange.

The wider price spread reduces the liquidity that the Stock Exchange exists to create. Investors will pay less for shares if the secondary market deteriorates and, in the end, the whole economy suffers because companies cannot raise new risk capital on such favourable terms.

As noted in the introduction, insider trading has always been unethical. Since 1985, as a result of the Insider Trading Act it has been illegal; but it is a difficult crime to prove and an easy crime to conceal by, for example, dealing through an offshore nominee company. Insider trading may have been reduced, but it would be naive to suggest that the new law has eliminated it.

14.2.7 *Moral hazard*

The opportunities for unjust self-enrichment by company directors and managers are not confined to trading on the stock market. There are also opportunities for these individuals to:

1. Pay themselves excessive salaries and pensions.
2. Provide themselves with excessive perks in the form of cars, yachts, corporate jets, luxurious corporate offices and other facilities.
3. Sell off corporate assets to companies that they own privately at low prices; to buy assets for the corporation from their own private interests at high prices.
4. To set an undemanding pace of work; to appoint staff on grounds other than fitness for the job; to keep colleagues in their jobs even when they have proved themselves incompetent.

In all these respects, shareholders are exposed to moral hazard, the risk of being cheated. It is clearly sensible for the shareholders to take whatever steps they can to prevent their wealth being damaged in these ways.

In economic theory this is known as the Principal–Agent problem. The shareholders are the Principals; the Directors and Managers are the Agents, appointed by the Principals to act in their interest, but who will still be tempted to promote their own interests rather than those of the Principal if they feel they can get away with it. The problem is fundamental, and cannot be eradicated. The best that can be done is to monitor management's activities (through the auditors) and to try and devise incentive schemes for managers which will link their interests closely with that of shareholders (e.g. through share option schemes).

There is a further problem. If management is identified as inefficient or dishonest, who is going to incur the costs of energy and effort needed to put together a new and better team to take their place? The natural tendency of shareholders, as we saw earlier, is to reduce risk by spreading their shareholdings across a wide range of companies. There are many companies where no individual shareholder has more than 1 or 2 per cent of the shares. An investor is not a businessman; he expects to take a passive role; he normally has no direct contact with other shareholders. Although shareholders have, collectively, the power to use their votes to replace poorly performing directors, in practice this power is almost always unusable. The shareholder body lacks coordination, leadership, and any method of sharing the burden of the costs incurred. Although it is within the power, and the collective interest, of the shareholders to act, the incentive for the individual shareholder is to sit tight and hope someone else will take the lead.

The consequence of this is that boards of directors tend to become self-perpetuating oligarchies. When one member steps down, the remainder of the group will choose his replacement. They will choose a congenial individual, one who will fit in with the mores of the group and who can be relied upon not to make waves.

In the absence of any controlling or large shareholding, therefore, the only effective sanction against poor management will be the takeover bid. The unsuccessful company will become a victim. Another company, the aggressor, will offer to buy shares in the victim at a price above the previous market level. If it succeeds in acquiring more than 50 per cent of the shares, it can sweep away the existing board and put in its own team. If, under UK law, it acquires 90 per cent it can buy the remaining shares compulsorily and absorb the victim company fully into its own operations.

14.3   The UK financial markets: selected statistics

Up to this point, our discussion of the forces operating in financial markets has been fairly general. We now turn to look at specific features of the UK markets, making some comparison with other major industrial ecomonies.

14.3.1   *Interest rates and other returns*

The first item to notice in Figure 14.1 is the high level of average inflation in the United Kingdom compared to other industrial countries. Not only is UK

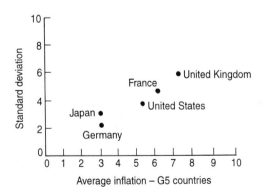

Figure 14.1   Average inflation and standard deviation of inflation, Q1 1976–Q4 1994. Quarterly data converted to annual rates.
Source: Datastream.

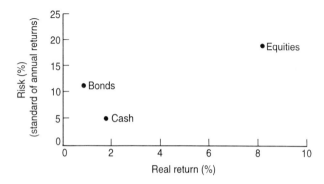

Figure 14.2   Risk and real return in the UK market for three classes of financial asset, 1967–90.
Source: Bank of England Quarterly Bulletin, 1991.

inflation high, but also the variability of inflation (measured by the standard deviation) has been higher. This variability has been largely unanticipated and has exacerbated the economic cycle in the United Kingdom.

Figure 14.2 shows the risk and return (both in real terms) for three classes of asset in the United Kingdom. Equities have offered high returns and high risk as would be expected. Short-term assets (near-cash) have offered low returns but still have a significant amount of risk because of the failure to control UK inflation over the period. Bonds (medium and long-term fixed interest securities) have offered an intermediate level of risk coupled with the lowest level of real return. This unattractive combination, again caused by inflation, has made bonds unattractive to both companies and investors. Companies cannot predict, in real terms, what their liabilities will be and investors have no certainty about how much they will receive.

14.3.2   *The size of the UK Stock Exchange*

The size of the Stock Exchange is perhaps the single most outstanding feature of the UK system. The comparison with Japan is misleading (see Figure 14.3). In the Japanese market cross-holdings between quoted companies are common. About 40 per cent of the capitalisation of the market is held in this way. A better comparison between the Japanese market and the other markets in the table is to multiply the Japanese figure by 0.6. With this adjustment, the UK stock market is substantially the largest in relative terms. In absolute terms it is as large as the German, French, Italian and Spanish markets added together. The size of the UK Stock Exchange made possible the privatisation of large state-owned companies such as British Telecom and British Gas in the 1980s.

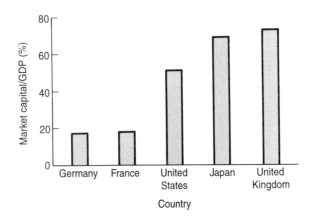

Figure 14.3 Ratios of stock market capitalisation of GDP, 31 December 1991. *Source: Datastream.*

14.3.3 Share ownership in the United Kingdom

The growth of institutional investors, especially pension funds and insurance companies, has transformed the stock exchange in the last three decades. Private individuals now account for less than a quarter of the market value of quoted shares, as shown in Table 14.1. Pension funds and insurance companies account for more than half. The policy of institutional investors is to avoid taking controlling stakes, nor do they ask for representation on boards of directors. They will keep their stakes in individual companies low. These small holdings can be quickly and easily sold. Institutional investors will switch their holdings from one company to another in accordance with their assessment of each company's prospects. They have no long-term commitment to the company or its management. They may not bother to use their voting rights. They will have no hesitation in selling their shares to support a takeover bid if the price is right but, short of a takeover, which is a very expensive and disruptive process, there is little pressure placed on management by shareholders in the UK system.

Table 14.1 Share ownership in the United Kingdom (%)

	1963	1969	1975	1981	1989	1993
Persons	54.0	47.4	37.5	28.2	21.3	17.7
Pension funds	6.4	9.0	16.8	26.7	30.4	34.2
Insurance companies	10.0	12.2	15.9	20.5	18.4	17.3
Unit and investment trusts	12.6	13.0	14.6	10.4	9.1	9.7
Other	17.0	18.4	15.2	14.2	20.8	21.1

This has been seen as a weakness. The Cadbury Committee report in 1992 recommended a code of best practice for boards of directors which has been widely followed. It is designed to deal, in part, with this problem. For example, one recommendation is that boards should include non-executive directors (i.e. directors who are not also involved in day to day management of the company) and that the pay and other conditions of service of the executive directors should be determined by a remuneration committee consisting wholly or mainly of non-executives. The intention is to prevent the executive directors awarding pay rises to themselves. There is some feeling that they tend to err on the side of generosity when they do so.

Because it is a code of practice and not a law, the Cadbury recommendations may well lead to improvements in companies which were already concerned with these ethical issues. It will have little effect on rogue companies which are determined to go their own way. Since it is normal that non-executive directors are, or have recently been, executive directors in other companies, it is sometimes suggested that the Cadbury approach may be flawed as a way of regulating top executives' pay and perks. The issue of the correct level for top managers pay is in any case economically and politically controversial. Practice varies widely in different developed economies. Payments in the United States, for example, are much higher than in Japan. Over recent years practice in the United Kingdom has been moving more towards the US model.

14.3.4 *Ownership structures in continental Europe*

Perrier, a French mineral water company, was the subject of a battle for control in 1992. The ownership pattern is typical of many other companies in continental Europe (see Figure 14.4). Many of the shares are held in large blocks on a long-term basis. If there is more than one such block, control will be exercised by an alliance between the interests involved. Banks and other commercial or industrial companies often hold blocks of shares. Cross-holdings of shares can be used to strengthen the grip of the controlling alliance. Members of the controlling alliance may have commercial links with the company they control, so that the benefit they get from their shareholding is not limited to the dividends and capital gains they receive. Any outsider who buys shares in the Stock Exchange cannot expect these extra benefits, and cannot expect that their voting rights will ever enable them to influence the management of the company. Notice the many differences between this structure and the usual situation in the United Kingdom described earlier.

14.3.5 *International comparisons of company gearing*

Gearing is the proportion of a company's capital which is in the form of debt. The implication of the large volume of share capital in the UK financial system is that the amount of debt will be correspondingly small. Figure 14.5 shows

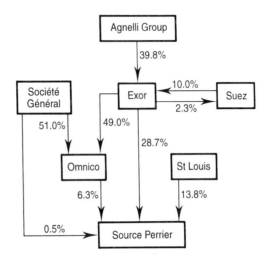

Figure 14.4 The network of major shareholdings relating to the French mineral water company, Source Perrier, in 1992.
Note: The numbers show the percentage of the shares in one company which are held by another company in the network. For example the Agnelli Group holds 39.8 per cent of the shares in Exor.
Source: The Economist.

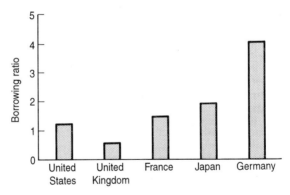

Figure 14.5 International comparisons of company gearing; average gearing 1987–91. The borrowing ratio is the ratio of total loan capital to total equity capital employed. *Source: Datastream.*

that this is the case. Companies in the United Kingdom have a conspicuously low level of gearing by international standards.

14.3.6 *New issues and takeovers in the UK stock market*

Figure 14.6 suggests that takeover activity, new issues of shares and the level of share prices tend to be linked. The state of the primary market for capital as

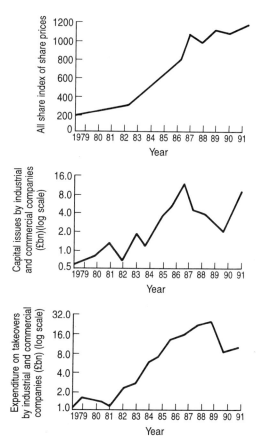

Figure 14.6 Share prices and takeovers.
Source: Bank of England.

measured by the capital issues of industrial and commercial companies follows the level of the stock market very closely. Both series show peaks in 1987 and 1991. The takeover series shows the same strong rise through the mid-1980s but sustained its growth through 1988 and 1989. It was not affected by the stock market crash of October 1987, largely because the government reacted to the crash by lowering interest rates and thus creating opportunities for profitable deal-making using borrowed money. The amount of takeover activity shown here greatly exceeds the level in any country in continental Europe.

The very large change in the level of new issues between, for example, 1979–80 and 1986–7 illustrates one of the main features of the Stock Exchange as a source of finance. It is unreliable: certainly it is less reliable than banks which are ready to lend, to creditworthy companies, throughout the economic cycle. At times the institutional investors are 'on feed' and willing to buy new issues.

At other times they are out of the market and even companies with a strong business case for raising more risk capital are turned away. UK companies tend to imitate camels as a result; fill up with share capital when you have the chance, it may be a long way to the next oasis, and until you get there you will have to rely on the support of your bankers. The figures also show that takeover activity in the United Kingdom is large and highly cyclical. If takeovers are really motivated by the low efficiency of existing management it is hard to see why the volume of takeovers should be so volatile.

14.3.7 *Foreign direct investment*

Backed by a plentiful supply of risk capital at home, UK companies have invested heavily overseas. Some of the investment is physical (setting up new factories, etc.) but a large part comes from overseas acquisitions. UK companies have shown a much stronger tendency to develop into international players in their respective industries than their continental equivalents. In this area, the UK financial system may be helping British companies to establish a competitive advantage. A cynic, of course, might suggest that British companies are so keen to expand abroad because the economic prospects look so poor at home.

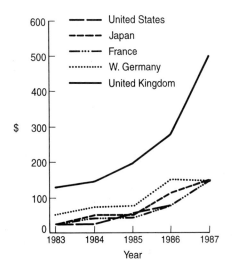

Figure 14.7 Foreign direct investment per capita, 1983–7 (1985 $US).
Source: D. Julius.

14.4 The logic of the UK markets

The statistics above have tended to show that the United Kingdom has a quite distinct system of corporate finance compared with other large industrial countries. The contrast between the United Kingdom and continental Europe is particularly marked. The purpose of this section is to explain how public policy decisions in the United Kingdom have produced the differences. We shall also discuss, briefly, how well public policy has served the public interest in the United Kingdom.

14.4.1 UK banks

Let us start with banks. Why do they play such a small role in corporate finance when compared, for example, to their German counterparts? There are three main reasons. The first is the uncertainty produced by inflation. Inflation in the United Kingdom has been high, highly variable and highly unpredictable in comparison with Germany. Inflation is, as we have seen, a major component of interest rates. High inflation leads to high interest rates; unpredictable inflation leads to unpredictable interest rates. The general disturbance to financial market equilibrium resulting from this means that real interest rates will also be volatile.

All this is bad for banks. Depositors will not commit themselves to 3- or 5-year deposits at fixed interest rates if this exposes them to considerable risk from unforeseen inflation. If bank deposits are on a short-term basis with interest rates linked to short-term market rates, then loans to businesses must also be on a variable interest rate basis. A company which agrees a 5-year loan may start paying at 8 per cent; if economic conditions change it may find the cost rises to 14 per cent, and this extra interest rate burden will come on top of a decline in orders as high interest rates tip the economy into recession.

For many purposes, companies would prefer to borrow money at fixed interest rates. If loans on this basis are not available they are likely to take their business away from the banks altogether and issue shares. This leaves a smaller role for UK banks to play. One indication of the restricted role of UK banks is that they are inferior to building societies in the level of deposits they attract from investors.

A second reason for the weakness of UK banks comes from the interaction between inflation and the tax system. Because their assets are monetary (rather than real assets like factories, machinery and stocks) the effective (i.e. inflation corrected) rate of tax can be considerably higher than the stated rate; so high, in fact, that no matter how hard the banks run, they find it difficult to avoid slipping backwards.

This point can be illustrated with a highly simplified example. Suppose the bank has the following four items on its balance sheet. Each item, other than shareholders' capital, has a real interest rate associated with it. The associated nominal interest rates depend on the assumed rate of inflation.

Balance sheet

ASSETS

Amount (£m)

75	Loans to companies, 5% real interest, 15.5% nominal at 10% inflation
25	Reserve assets, 4% real interest, 14.4% nominal at 10% inflation
$\overline{100}$	

LIABILITIES

90	Deposits, 4% real interest, 14.4% nominal at 10% inflation
10	Shareholders capital
$\overline{100}$	

With *no inflation*, the interest being received and paid by the bank is simply the real rate. We assume a tax rate of 40% on the bank's profits. The profit and loss statement is then:

Profit and loss account

	Amount (£m)
Interest received on loans to companies (75×0.05)	3.75
Interest received on reserve assets (25×0.04)	1.00
	$\overline{4.75}$
Interest paid on deposits (90×0.04)	3.60
Taxable profit	$\overline{1.15}$
Tax	0.46
After-tax profit	$\overline{0.69}$

On shareholders capital of £10 m, the bank is earning an after-tax profit of almost 7 per cent. If the bank intends to grow at 4 per cent annually in real terms while maintaining the existing proportions on its balance sheet, then £0.40 m of the after-tax profit needs to be kept in the business and the remainder can be paid out as a dividend to shareholders.

With *10 per cent inflation*, the corresponding figures will be as follows:

	Amount (£m)
Interest received on loans to companies (75×0.155)	11.625
Interest received on reserve assets (25×0.144)	3.600
	$\overline{15.225}$
Interest paid on deposits (90×0.144)	12.960
Taxable Profit	$\overline{2.265}$
Tax	0.906
After-tax profit	$\overline{1.359}$

On first appearance, it looks as though inflation has made the bank more profitable. After-tax profit has apparently risen from £0.69 m to £1.359 m; but this is entirely misleading. With an inflation rate of 10 per cent, the shareholders' capital must go from £10 m to £11 m simply in order to retain its real value. The only gain to shareholders is the remaining £0.359 m in end-of-year money which is only worth £0.326 m in beginning-of-the-year money. If the bank wants to increase its real capital base at 4 per cent per year it will be unable to pay any dividend to its shareholders. Either the bank will have to go to its shareholders from time to time to get injections of new capital (and the shareholders will hardly be enthusiastic) or the bank must accept that its growth must be stunted by the tax and inflation environment in which it operates.

One way of looking at the impact of inflation on banks is to say that, in this example, the effective tax rate has grown from 40 per cent with no inflation to 72 per cent with 10 per cent inflation. No business can flourish with effective tax rates at these very high levels. Notice that this effect of inflation is specific to a business such as banking which has a large part of its assets denominated in monetary units. A property company, with real assets (buildings) and monetary liabilities (debt) can have its tax rate lowered by inflation.

Of course, there are many countries with significant inflation where the banking sector flourishes. There are two ways in which this may occur. One is the situation in which the government owns the major banks. This is the case in France, Italy and Spain. The banking sector can be used as an instrument of economic policy and can work behind the scenes to support particular industries in accordance with political priorities. In the United Kingdom the Bank of England did, until 1971, operate direct credit controls designed to encourage banks to lend to particular sectors, for example to manufacturing industry rather than to property developers. The banking system tended to find ways around the controls and their effectiveness was limited.

Another approach is that banks should take equity stakes in companies. This gives them a 'real' asset which will tend to rise in value with inflation. German and Spanish banks, for example, have large shareholdings in industry. This certainly makes life easier for the banks, but it is not value-maximising for the bank's shareholders. We have already seen that they prefer to hold equity stakes directly rather than indirectly. This escape route is not open to British banks. The German and Spanish banks are less sensitive to shareholders' interests and seem under no strong pressure to give up their equity holdings.

There are, therefore, good reasons for the relatively weak condition of UK banks. The poor competitive position of the banks will be one factor leading to the size and success of the Stock Exchange in Britain. There are several others. In continental Europe, invasions, defeats and hyperinflation in the first half of the twentieth century have forced the rebuilding of the corporate structure from ground zero. British companies are typically older-established and have often come to the Stock Exchange as a result of inheritance taxes or the dispersion of shares to increasingly remote family descendants with no emotional or managerial links to the company. Family-controlled large companies are still common in continental Europe.

14.4.2 The UK pension system

Pension arrangements in the United Kingdom also have a major influence on the financial markets. In contrast to policy in continental Europe, in the United Kingdom the state only offers a small basic pension. Occupational pension schemes, typically set up by individual companies for their employees, make up the difference. These are funded in the sense that investments are purchased to cover future pension payment obligations. Most continental state schemes do not build up an investment fund. They are 'pay-as-you-go' schemes. The pensions of each generation are paid by the contributions of the next.

Because most UK schemes offer pensions based on salary at retirement they need to buy real (not monetary) assets to match this real liability. Shares fit this requirement well. Since contributions to pension schemes are tax deductible for both employee and employer, and the returns earned by the fund are tax-free, pension funds are a very attractive way to save. Many individuals opt to make additional voluntary contributions (AVCs) to their occupational pension scheme rather than save directly on their own account. These tax advantages have caused pension funds to expand over the past few decades to the point that they own almost a third of all the listed shares in the United Kingdom, as demonstrated in Table 14.1.

As with many other features of the UK financial markets, pension funds have grown without any very active government involvement, other than that financial provision for old age was generally to be encouraged and that tax benefits were therefore appropriate. An unwelcome spotlight was thrown on the UK pensions world by the death of Mr Robert Maxwell in 1991 and the revelation that hundreds of millions of pounds were missing from the pension funds of companies that he controlled. It was immediately clear that the legal and regulatory framework for the vast system of UK occupational pensions was inadequate. Indeed, it turned out that pension schemes fell legally under the law of trusts and that trust law had been originally designed to protect the property of knights in the middle ages when they went away on crusades. The Goode committee was set up to look at this matter. It reported in 1993 and legislation is expected in 1995.

One of the most difficult and controversial features of new pensions legislation is the proposal for statutory solvency requirements for pension funds. The value of the investments held by a pension fund at a particular date should be sufficient to cover the pension rights acquired by members at that date. In the event of a shortfall, the company would be required to make up the difference over a short time period.

This innocuous-seeming proposal has the potential to transform the structure of the financial markets in the United Kingdom. As we have seen, pension funds are at present very heavily invested in shares and shares are risky. In October 1987, the UK stock market fell by 30 per cent over a period of 2 days. Actuaries, the professional advisers on pension fund matters, have not been concerned about this because equities in the United Kingdom have had a good record of returns over the long-term, and the long term is the appropriate time-scale in which to view pension funds. A new solvency test could substantially change this picture. Pension funds could not invest heavily in shares, for fear that a sudden fall in the market could create a situation of technical insolvency and the sponsoring company would be forced to make large unforeseen contributions to the scheme. Since a sharp fall in the stock exchange is likely to be an indicator of difficult times for company finances, the calls for extra pension fund contributions could come just at the time when they would be most difficult to meet.

If pension funds could not take the risk of putting most of their money into shares, they would have to switch to alternative investments (perhaps index-linked bonds) which would be less risky, and a quite different financial system would have to develop. It will be extremely interesting to see the final form in which legislation emerges.

Pension funds and other institutional investors have not been interested in developing long-term relationships with companies and their managements. However, their more short-term approach, which has involved active trading of shares, means that they have been active in pressing for the modernisation of Stock Exchange trading practices. The Take Over Panel (1968), the abolition of minimum commissions on share-dealing and the other 'Big Bang' reforms (1986), the prohibition of insider dealing (1985), the increase in the amount of information given in company accounts (a continuous process during the 1970s and 1980s) have all resulted from pressure from institutional investors. These reforms have put the London market some distance ahead of continental Europe. Evidence of this competitive advantage of the trading mechanisms of the London market can be seen in the growth of Stock Exchange Automatic Quotations (SEAQ) International, a system for trading the shares of non-UK companies in London. Some companies in continental Europe, particularly from Scandinavia, have been active in courting UK institutional investors.

14.4.3 *Takeovers*

Takeovers have been far more common in Britain than in continental Europe. Many takeovers are friendly but, equally, many are not. Because companies lack controlling shareholders, many UK companies are potential takeover targets. There is a 'market for corporate control' in which shareholders can oust existing managers if another management team offers a better deal. The defending management and the challengers will put their arguments in circulars to shareholders and press advertisements. The whole process is very public and very expensive.

Unsuccessful managers are also removed in other financial systems. In Germany and Japan it would probably fall to the company's bankers, who would have a close long-term relationship with the company including representation on the board, to press for a management change. There would be much less publicity for this type of change. The interests of the bankers, of course, will not be quite the same as the interests of the shareholders.

14.5 An evaluation of the financial system in the United Kingdom

The discussion above has been a wide-ranging overview of the government policies and other forces that have shaped the financial markets in the United Kingdom. Since the system in the United Kingdom is so different from that in most of our partner countries in the European Union, it is not surprising that there is considerable debate on the merits of the British approach. There are good points to be made on both sides, and we shall end this chapter by looking briefly at the arguments of both the supporters and the opponents.

14.5.1 *The case for UK financial market policies*

Let us conclude by setting out briefly the arguments for and against the financial markets policies in the United Kingdom compared with those in Germany or other continental countries. The UK system has produced the largest market for risk capital in Europe. As a result, British companies have had a financial base on which to grow into world class competitors, a development which was also encouraged by the abolition of all exchange controls in 1979. The level of Foreign Direct Investment from the United Kingdom illustrates this strength clearly.

Risk capital is available in Britain partly because shareholders are offered a fair deal. They can get rid of incompetent or self-serving management. The UK corporate world is a meritocracy; promotion comes on the basis of talent and not because you were born into the right family or belong to the right political party.

The financial markets are generally clean and becoming cleaner. The government has shown itself willing to pass reforming legislation and to act against abuses through the courts. There have been a number of very high profile (and very expensive) cases in which leading company directors have been accused of abuse. The success rate of the Serious Fraud Office in obtaining convictions has not been impressive, but the prosecutions are likely to have a useful deterrent effect in the financial markets generally.

Shareholders are better at allocating their own funds than are politicians or bankers working on their behalf. Shareholders have been brutally realistic in observing those sectors of the economy which were in long-term decline or in which Britain did not have a competitive advantage. They have steered the UK economy away from metal-beating and textiles and towards service and leisure industries, branded consumer goods and health-care products (especially drugs). They have given the United Kingdom a strong position in the growth industries of the future.

The clearest evidence of the success of UK policy towards financial markets is the success of UK financial sector companies in selling their services overseas. London is the leading financial centre in Europe. It is a centre for international banking and share dealing and its expertise in privatisation and corporate restructuring are in demand throughout the world. A host of other high value professional services: legal, accounting, property valuation, insurance, etc., are flourishing on the basis of Britain's highly developed financial markets. The financial markets are the source of many well-paid jobs.

14.5.2 *The case against UK financial market policies*

So far as industrial and commercial development is concerned, the main task of the financial markets is to provide low cost finance. This the UK system fails to do. Bank finance is the first choice for most companies. The transaction is simple and cheap. The borrower provides whatever information the lender needs. However, mainly because of the poor inflation record in the United Kingdom bank finance, other than short-term funding, is scarce in Britain and there is only a small market for corporate bonds. Companies are forced into the stock market to raise equity capital.

Equity from the Stock Exchange is expensive, because it is risk capital and investors demand extra return for extra risk. In the United Kingdom the propensity of the economy to lurch from slump to boom and back again adds to risk and so adds to the expense. Equity is also expensive because its tax treatment is less favourable than debt and because of all the ancillary costs of providing a constant flow of information to shareholders. Senior managers, for example, must expect to field a steady stream of questions from investment analysts and must make presentations to institutional investors. Raising funds by issuing new shares is a highly complex and expensive exercise involving lawyers, accountants, merchant bankers, stockbrokers and underwriters. Finally, shares are an expensive form of finance because of the inefficiencies due to moral hazard and insider dealing. Most of these problems can be avoided in family companies whose shares are not traded on the Stock Exchange and where there is no split between ownership and management.

The stock market is ill-adapted to meet the needs of small companies. It is hard to keep track of what they are doing and there will not be a steady flow of trading in the shares. Consequently, UK companies, as a result of friendly or unfriendly amalgamations, have tended to grow large and diverse. The main activity at Head Office will be financial management; raising funds; preparing accounts and handling investor relations. The top managers will have a financial or accounting background. They may have little understanding of the technologies on which their manufacturing processes are based or the markets that they serve. They are, therefore, incapable of identifying new products or new manufacturing processes. In a changing world they are incapable of innovation. They preside over carefully audited decline.

The managers' reluctance to innovate is enhanced by the reward structure within which they operate. The greatest threat to their own careers is for their company to be taken over. Their primary objective is to avoid this. They must do what their shareholders want. They dare not use the forecasts of their own skilled and experienced staff to embark on a policy that goes against current conventional wisdom. Indeed, they will be reluctant to adopt any policy that reduces next year's profits even if the long-run effect would be highly beneficial. Their management will be directed towards producing a steady upward trend in earnings per share, and creative accounting will be one of the main management skills required. Management will have a short-term perspective, looking towards the next half-yearly profit number. Long-term development of the business will have a lesser priority.

Takeovers are greatly over-rated as a discipline for poor managers. They are public relations contests rather than genuine choices between different management policies. With most shareholders' real knowledge of the company based on nothing more than a few pages of accounts and some glossy photographs, it cannot be anything else. At least in Germany management changes are based on inside knowledge.

The takeover game is essentially run by and for the merchant banks. They act as advisers to aggressors and victims and, in exchange for large fees, orchestrate the whole show from just off-stage. A company which stays aloof from the process and refuses to pay tribute to the merchant banker is likely to be set up as a victim. The Guinness trial showed how large amounts of money could be offered to 'friends' and 'supporters' in a takeover battle in irregular and unauthorised ways which hovered on the margins of corruption. At the end of a lengthy trial the purpose and destination of some multi-million-pound payments to Swiss bank accounts was still unclear.

Shareholders in the United Kingdom have a short-term outlook and view their shares as trading chips. They should accept that, as proprietors, they must take some responsibility for the long-term development of their companies.

14.6 Conclusion

There are strongly held views on both sides of the argument. Critics of the UK financial markets sound more convincing when detailing their charges than when proposing remedies. If UK shareholders are too quick to sell their shares to a takeover raider, how are they to be prevented or dissuaded from doing so.

Would it help if shareholders were refused voting rights until they had held their shares for 6 months? Could more non-executive directors help bridge the information gap between companies and their shareholders? Or are both these ideas mere tinkering?

The arguments for and against the present structure of the UK financial markets may seem closely balanced; but surely the greatest handicap from which they have suffered has been inflation. It is inflation that has damaged the banking system and artificially stimulated stock market activity. It is also inflation that stokes the takeover market. The great wave in takeover activity towards the end of the 1980s was fuelled by an increase in the money supply which left banks with a surplus of money to lend. The merchant banks were quick to conjure up takeover deals which helped them to solve their problem.

If the fundamental problem of inflation can be solved, possibly through a single European currency, the United Kingdom might perhaps have the best of all worlds as far as its financial markets are concerned. An efficient, well-regulated stock exchange; fixed interest finance available to companies at reasonable rates and on reasonable terms; and an overall cost of capital for industrial and commercial companies that will help them to compete successfully on a global basis.

Questions for discussion

1. Will the system of corporate finance in Britain come to model itself on continental Europe, or will continental Europe move in the direction of the United Kingdom?
2. Would you agree that in the United Kingdom shareholders have more powers than they can properly use?
3. In view of the difficulty in controlling insider trading, should directors and managers be prohibited from buying, selling or owning shares in their companies?
4. Does Britain need a state-controlled Investment Bank?
5. If inflation damages financial markets, why have successive British governments not controlled inflation more effectively?
6. Should company managements have greater protection against takeover bids?
7. Does Britain's large expenditure on Foreign Direct Investment weaken the British economy?

References and further reading

Bank of England Quarterly Bulletin (various issues).
Clarke, W.M. (1991) *How the City of London Works: An introduction to its financial markets*, London: Waterlow.

Julius, D. (1990) *Global Companies and Public Policy: The growing challenge or foreign direct investment*, London: The Royal Institute of Public Affairs.

Mayer, C. and Alexander, I. (1990) 'Banks and securities markets: corporate financing in Germany and the United Kingdom' *Journal of the Japanese and International Economies* 4 (4) December pp. 450–75.

National Association of Pension Funds (1990) *Creative Tension*, London: National Association of Pension Funds.

Peasnell, K.W. and Ward, C.W.R. (1985) *British Financial Markets and Institutions*, Hemel Hempstead: Prentice Hall.

Seldon, A. (ed.) (1988) *Financial Regulation – or Over-regulation?*, London: Institute of Economic Affairs.

The Economist (various issues).

Thomas, W.A. (1986) *The Big Bang*, Oxford: Philip Allan.

PART 3

International economics

CHAPTER 15

The exchange rate: what price sterling?

HUGH FLEMING

15.1   Introduction

The exchange rate for a currency is simply the price of one currency in terms of another. It is, however, a price which probably attracts more interest and attention than any other single price. As our discussion develops we will see that, generally speaking, it is changes in the price which attract most interest. Television and newspapers provide us with daily information on movements of the exchange rate for sterling against the US dollar and the German Deutschmark in particular, and also movements in what is called 'sterling's trade-weighted index' – a concept we will deal with later in the chapter.

In considering the exchange rate for sterling we will divide our discussion into three parts. First we will deal with the determinants of the exchange rate for a currency. Secondly, we will consider why the exchange rate and changes in the exchange rate are important for the domestic economy. Finally, we will look at the sterling experience over the last decade, concluding with a brief glimpse at the implications of the Maastricht Treaty.

15.2   Determination of the exchange rate

As already noted, the exchange rate is simply the price of one currency in terms of another and, as with all prices (in the absence of direct controls), is determined by the forces of supply and demand. The supply of, and demand for the currency are the direct outcome of the economic decisions which make up a country's balance of payments account. These economic decisions, although international, are no different from any other economic decisions. They reflect consumers preferring foreign-produced goods to domestically produced goods, producers seeking lowest cost sources of inputs, wealth holders seeking highest rates of return, and so on. Exports and an inward flow of capital generate an inflow of currency and appear as credit items while imports and an outward flow of capital appear as debit items. Thus credit items in the current and capital accounts generate a demand for the currency while debit items generate a supply. If there is a balance of payments surplus then there is an excess demand for the currency at the existing price (exchange rate) and there is excess supply when there is a balance of payments deficit. It is true that the official statistics always show the balance of payments to be in balance, but this is purely because the balance of payments account is a conventional bookkeeping exercise. Balance (credits equal to debits) is ensured through accommodating transactions carried out by the Bank of England operating on behalf of the government and the inclusion of an (accounting) balancing item.

Economists' models of exchange rate determination have become increasingly sophisticated (and complex!) over the last two decades, but at a simple level we can readily identify the principal economic variables in the determination process.

We may postulate the following:

$$\text{Net demand for currency} = \text{balance of payments}; \tag{15.1}$$

$$\text{Balance of payments} = \text{current account} + \text{capital account}; \tag{15.2}$$

$$\text{Current account} = (X - M) + (i^*A^* - iA); \tag{15.3}$$

$$\text{Capital account} = (\Delta A^* - \Delta A); \tag{15.4}$$

where X = exports, including services, M = imports, including services, A^* = foreign assets held by UK residents, i^* = foreign interest rate, A = UK assets held by non-residents, i = UK interest rate, ΔA^* and ΔA = changes in UK holdings of foreign assets and non-resident holdings of UK assets. The term $(i^*A^* - iA)$ may be thought of as net investment income.

We may further postulate:

$$X = f\ (Y^*, (p/p^*)e);$$
$$M = f\ (Y, (p/p^*)e);$$
$$(\Delta A^* - \Delta A) = f\ (i, i^*); \tag{15.5}$$

where Y^* = foreign income, Y = UK income level, p = domestic price level, p^* = foreign price level, e = nominal exchange rate.

The set of equations 15.5 identify and relate together a small number of important economic variables. Exports are a function of foreign income and the ratio of domestic prices relative to foreign prices, adjusted by the exchange rate, i.e. exports depend upon foreign income and the real exchange rate. Similarly, imports are a function of domestic income and the real exchange rate while changing asset holdings (resident and non-resident) depend upon domestic and foreign rates of return, represented here as the domestic and foreign rates of interest. We have seven relevant variables; two sets of income levels, two sets of prices, two sets of interest rates and the nominal exchange rate. Note that any given nominal exchange rate will indirectly influence movements in the nominal exchange rate since it influences the demands for exports and imports, and consequently the demand for and supply of the currency.

We can consider the outcome in terms of a simple supply and demand analysis of the foreign exchange market. Figure 15.1 shows the demand for and supply of sterling. In the absence of government intervention the demand for sterling reflects the demand for UK exports and the foreign demand for UK assets while the supply of sterling reflects UK import demand and UK residents' demand for foreign assets. The market-determined exchange rate is £1 = $1.60 on a turnover of £300 bn.

This buying and selling of currency in respect of trade and capital flows takes place on the foreign exchange market. It is not currency as such which is being exchanged – this is basically confined to tourism and illegal activity – but bank deposits denominated in different currencies. The foreign exchange market is a huge worldwide market, although London remains the largest, single component of that market. The last major survey of foreign exchange market activity was carried out by 26 central banks in April 1992 (*Bank of England Quarterly Bulletin*, 1992). Valued in US dollars as a common measuring rod, the survey revealed an average turnover of some one thousand billion (a trillion) dollars *per day*.

Average daily turnover in London was some three hundred billion dollars, of which some 26 per cent involved transactions in sterling. A key feature of the foreign exchange market, and it is of considerable relevance to our later discussion, is that upwards of 90 per cent of all this activity is a reflection not of international trade flows but of international capital flows. We can understand the implications quite simply by considering a rise in US interest rates.

In Figure 15.2 the balance of payments is initially in balance at a sterling–dollar exchange rate of £1 = $1.60, i.e. this is the market clearing exchange rate. A rise in US interest rates means that funds held on deposit in New York now earn a (relatively) higher rate of return than was previously the case.

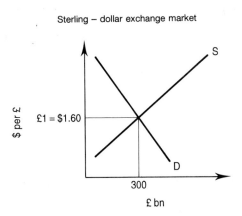

Sterling – dollar exchange market

Figure 15.1 $/£ exchange rate.

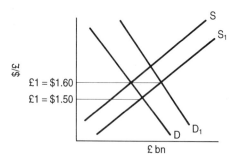

Figure 15.2   Determination of sterling exchange rate.

Other things being equal there is now an incentive to move funds from London to New York. The supply curve in Figure 15.2 shifts out to the right (S_1) as wealth holders supply sterling in exchange for dollars to place on deposit in New York. With the new supply curve S_1 the market-determined exchange rate falls to £1 = \$1.50. Suppose the UK government, for whatever reason, would like to see the exchange rate stable at £1 = \$1.60. This can be achieved if it can shift the demand curve to D_1.

   The UK government could itself deal in the foreign exchange market. It could enter the marketplace as a purchaser buying up its own currency, using its holdings of foreign currency reserves to finance the purchase. Of course, its ability to do this depends on its official reserve holdings which necessarily diminish in time with purchasing. Alternatively, it may stimulate increased demand for sterling by raising UK interest rates so that the incentive to move funds to New York is removed. This, as we shall see, becomes a crucial issue for the UK government, not in terms of the sterling–dollar exchange rate, but for the sterling–Deutschmark exchange rate.

15.2.1   *The exchange rate and the domestic economy*

As stated before, the exchange rate is a price, no different in principle from the price of any other good or service. Yet it commands great attention. In a speech in June 1994 (*Bank of England Quarterly Bulletin*, 1994) the Governor of the Bank of England stated: 'in terms of national policies in pursuit of stability, the exchange rate is far too important a price to be ignored'. What is it about the exchange rate that merits such special attention?

   The exchange rate is the mechanism through which the prices of domestic goods and services are converted into foreign currency prices and through which the prices of foreign goods and services are converted into domestic currency prices. Any given value for the exchange rate carries implications for domestic employment levels and domestic inflation levels. A fall in the exchange rate for sterling – a depreciation of the currency – simply means that sterling is worth less. It is not necessarily worth less in terms of domestic usage, but it is worth less relative to other currencies.

As a consequence foreigners get more pounds for their dollar or Deutschmark, etc., while UK residents have to give up more pounds to acquire dollars and Deutschmarks. The outcome of the depreciation is that UK products are now relatively cheaper compared to foreign products. Such a development should be beneficial for the level of UK output and employment. With UK products now relatively more competitive we might expect an increase in demand in the export sector and in the import-competing sector as foreigners are faced with relatively cheaper UK products and UK residents substitute domestic products for relatively more expensive foreign goods. Two points should be borne in mind. Any such outcome is unlikely to be immediately apparent. At any point in time there will be substantial contracts in the pipeline at the old set of relative prices. Changes in the pattern of demand will not be evident until reordering takes place. Secondly, and more important, the extent of any change will depend upon the price elasticities of the demand for exports and imports, the cross-elasticity of demand for UK products and foreign products and the elasticity of supply of UK products.

While we may hope for beneficial effects on output and employment, the same fall in the exchange rate may have less desirable implications for domestic inflation. If there are foreign inputs into the production process and demand for such imported inputs is price inelastic, then UK firms experience an increase in their costs of production through higher import prices. If the imported goods are final goods and demand is price inelastic there will be a direct impact on the consumer price index – a widely used measure of inflation. In general terms we may argue that a fall in the exchange rate could be good for employment but it could be bad for inflation. Of course, the argument is reversed if there is a rise in the exchange rate.

15.2.2   *Three concepts of the exchange rate*

At the beginning of the chapter we defined the exchange rate as the price of one currency in terms of another, and the discussion above referred to a fall or rise in the exchange rate. Yet a country which engages widely in international trade has exchange rates for its currency against the currencies of all of the countries with whom it has international economic transactions. If we are interested in assessing what is happening to a currency on a global basis, then framing the discussion in terms of 'the' exchange rate is overly simplistic. A consideration of movements in, for instance, the sterling–Deutschmark exchange rate need not tell us anything about the UK position *vis-à-vis* the United States. A wider view may be required, depending on the issue which we seek to address. Three views of the exchange rate are commonly adopted.

(a) The bilateral nominal exchange rate

It is the rate which has been implicit in our discussion so far. This is the rate which we observe being set on the foreign exchange market day by day – indeed, minute by minute – and which is reported by the media. Thus £1 = 2.24 Deutschmarks, £1 = $1.51, and so on. Examining one particular exchange rate may allow us to arrive at certain judgements in terms of bilateral comparisons, but no more than that. As the 1980s unfolded, considerable attention was paid to the nominal exchange rate, not with regard to any implications for exports or imports but as an indicator of monetary policy. We will deal with this view of the exchange rate in the final section.

(b) The effective exchange rate index

If we are interested in the global performance of a currency we need a wider measure than a single bilateral exchange rate. An analogy would be a situation where we formed a judgement about inflation by looking at the price of only one product.

In the foreign exchange market it is quite common to see the nominal exchange of a currency rising against one foreign currency while it falls against another foreign currency. To establish the overall picture exchange rate indexes are constructed to measure the average value of a currency relative to a group of other currencies. An exchange rate index is a weighted average of the currency's value against the other currencies in the group, where the weights reflect the importance of each currency to international trade, i.e. it is a trade-weighted index.

Thus, if 20 per cent of total UK trade was with Germany and 15 per cent was with France the construction of the index involves multiplying the sterling–Deutschmark exchange rate by 0.2, the sterling–French franc rate by 0.15 and summing the result (including all major trading partners, the weights of course sum to one) (*Bank of England Quarterly Bulletin*, 1988).

(c) The real exchange rate

If we want to know how the competitive position of the United Kingdom is changing over time then we need to look, not at the nominal exchange rate, but at the real exchange rate. The real exchange rate is the nominal exchange rate adjusted for price level changes. For example, if sterling falls in value by 5 per cent against the Deutschmark and UK inflation is 5 per cent higher than in Germany, then there is no change in the relative competitive position of the United Kingdom. The depreciation of the nominal exchange rate has simply offset the inflation differential and there is no change in the real exchange rate. It is when there is a fall in the real exchange rate that the United Kingdom's relative competitive position improves.

15.3 The course of sterling

Up to the mid-1980s attention was primarily focused on the sterling–US dollar exchange rate. The United States was (and still is) the world's major economic power and the 'new' international monetary order introduced after the Second World War established the US dollar as the linchpin of the world financial system. In 1979 the European Monetary System (EMS) was established, of which the principal feature was the Exchange Rate Mechanism (ERM), which we discuss below. As a member of the European Economic Community (now the European Union) the United Kingdom was automatically a member of the EMS but chose not to participate in the ERM. The decision reflected both economic and political factors. At some levels there was undoubtedly antipathy towards increasing European integration. Yet equally, from an economic standpoint, there was an influence on sterling which did not apply to other member countries' currencies. By the beginning of the decade the United Kingdom had emerged as a major oil producer, and changing oil prices significantly influenced the value of sterling. Sterling at the time was what came to be known as a 'petrocurrency'. Oil is priced in US dollars, hence the sterling–dollar exchange rate remained the main focus of attention.

Towards the end of the 1980s there was a change of emphasis. First, North Sea oil production had peaked and the importance of oil prices lessened. Secondly, and more important, the exchange rate was increasingly viewed as an indicator of domestic monetary conditions. The basic aim of policy was the control of inflation, and in particular to bring inflation into line with major low-inflation competitors. In practice, the German rate of inflation was the principal target. The essence of the exchange rate argument is that a depreciating exchange rate is indicative of monetary conditions which are, in relative terms, too easy. A depreciating exchange rate is taken to reflect expectations that future domestic inflation is going to be higher than competitors and that monetary policy should therefore be tightened. Implicit in the argument was that UK monetary policy be kept in line with German monetary policy. This view of the exchange rate as a monetary indicator was one reason for the emergence of a policy of 'shadowing' the Deutschmark, i.e. trying to keep the sterling-Deutschmark exchange rate relatively stable. A second reason was undoubtedly a preparatory move towards eventual membership of the ERM, although the two reasons are closely interlinked.

When we look at the sterling-Deutschmark exchange rate (Table 15.1) we find, beginning in 1981, a prolonged, albeit gradual, sterling depreciation. From mid-1987, Chancellor Lawson began the policy of stabilising the exchange rate, targeting a rate of around £1 = DM 3. What became known as the Lawson experiment was to last some two-and-a-half years (Figure 15.3).

The policy gave rise to considerable controversy and debate (much of it political); nevertheless, considerable stability was achieved from the outset of the policy until its abandonment in late 1989 following the resignation of the

Table 15.1 Quarterly Deutschmark/pound exchange rate

1980	1	3.99	1984	1	3.87	1988	1	3.01	1992	1	2.86
	2	4.13		2	3.78		2	3.14		2	2.91
	3	4.22		3	3.78		3	3.16		3	2.78
	4	4.55		4	3.71		4	3.17		4	2.44
1981	1	4.81	1985	1	3.63	1989	1	3.23	1993	1	2.41
	2	4.73		2	3.88		2	3.14		2	2.48
	3	4.47		3	3.92		3	3.07		3	2.52
	4	4.22		4	3.71		4	2.87		4	2.51
1982	1	4.33	1986	1	3.38	1990	1	2.80	1994	1	2.56
	2	4.23		2	3.38		2	2.81		2	2.49
	3	4.28		3	3.11		3	2.96		3	2.42
	4	4.13		4	2.87		4	2.92		4	
1983	1	3.68	1987	1	2.83	1991	1	2.91			
	2	3.86		2	2.96		2	2.93			
	3	3.99		3	2.97		3	2.93			
	4	3.93		4	2.99		4	2.88			

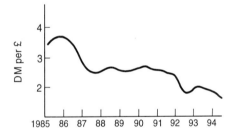

Figure 15.3 DM/£ exhange rate.

chancellor, who spoke in the Commons of a long and bitter debate over exchange rate policy. The abandonment of the policy witnessed a resumption of the downward movement of sterling. It can certainly be debated whether or not £1 = DM 3 was a wise choice of exchange rate target, but the episode gave credence to the view that the exchange rate could be successfully managed. Through 1990 increasing pressure from within Europe and growing influence of 'pro-Europeans' in government led to the decision to join the ERM in October 1990.

15.4   Sterling and the exchange rate mechanism

Joining the ERM involves setting a central rate for the currency against the European Currency Unit (ECU). The ECU is a 'composite currency', i.e. it is based upon a basket of currencies. The currencies of all member countries of the European Union go to make up the basket. Each is given a weight which reflects a country's share of Union Gross National Product and its share of intra-Union trade.

The ECU provides the numeraire for the ERM. With each participating country having an agreed central rate for its currency against the ECU, we can derive bilateral exchange rates. Thus, in October 1990 we had:

£ central rate   1 ECU = £0.696904

DM central rate   1 ECU = DM 2.05586

£/DM bilateral $£1 = DM \dfrac{2.05586}{0.696904} = DM\ 2.95$

Around the central rate was a permitted band of variation (6 per cent in the case of the United Kingdom). The band of variation places a ceiling and a floor within which the exchange rate may fluctuate, as illustrated in Figure 15.4.

The commitment to an (essentially) fixed exchange rate imposes a constraint on domestic macroeconomic policy, particularly monetary policy. The attraction of such a commitment had come to be seen as giving credibility to policy-makers with regard to controlling inflation. A fixed exchange rate cannot be sustained over time if a country's rate of inflation is seriously out of line with rates of inflation in other countries. The constraint on monetary policy is to be found in the reduced room for manoeuvre on interest rates. We examine the arguments in Figure 15.5.

Looking at the inflation argument first, we can characterise it in terms of a shift in both supply and demand curves. If the UK rate of inflation is markedly higher than its major trading partners then UK products become less competitive and we may expect to export less (the demand curve shifts to the left from D to D_1) and we may expect to import more (the supply curve moves to the right to S_1). The effect is to push the exchange rate to the floor (A), and the authorities are obliged to take action to prevent any further fall. They can enter the marketplace as purchasers of their own currency, using foreign

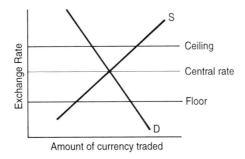

Figure 15.4   The exchange rate mechanism.

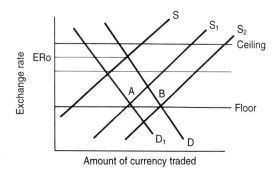

Figure 15.5 The exchange rate constraint.

currency reserves to finance the purchase. Such a course of action cannot, of course, be sustained, since reserves are finite and will be exhausted. This, as we shall see, can happen very quickly. Equally the authorities can boost the demand for the currency by raising interest rates, although this has implications for domestic economic activity.

The mechanism may also result in reduced room for manoeuvre with respect to domestic interest rates. As implied above, there is no problem in regard to raising interest rates, but this is not necessarily the case with regard to cutting interest rates, or indeed keeping them constant. Other things being equal a cut in UK interest rates or a rise in, for instance, German interest rates reduces the attractiveness of holding funds in London as against Frankfurt. The outcome is a flow of funds out of the United Kingdom. From our initial exchange rate (ER_o) there is a shift in the supply curve from S to S_2 and the exchange rate is again pushed to the floor (B).

While the needs of the domestic economy may be best served by reduced interest rates, such a reduction may lead to a capital outflow and put serious pressure on the exchange rate. Given the commitment to a fixed exchange rate, a reduction in interest rates may have to be foregone, or postponed until conditions in other member countries change. There is reduced autonomy in macroeconomic policy.

Sterling entered the ERM at an effective rate against the Deutschmark of £1 = DM 2.95, with the floor at approximately £1 = DM 2.78. Many observers took the view that the chosen exchange rate overvalued sterling, and was detrimental to the export prospects of UK industry, at a time when the economy was moving into deeper recession. Compounding the problem was rising interest rates in Germany, reflecting the enormous costs of the reunification programme. The UK government was faced with a classic dilemma associated with a fixed exchange rate system which we referred to above. It is quite clear that reductions in interest rates would have been desirable in terms of the domestic economy, yet it was equally clear that UK interest rates had to be kept in line – indeed, slightly above – German interest rates. Failure to do so would have generated a capital outflow putting pressure on the sterling exchange rate.

From the point of entry, sterling consistently traded below DM 2.95, and by late 1991/early 1992 it was trading below DM 2.90. It is true that UK interest rates did fall over this period but the cuts in interest rates were very small – generally a half per cent at a time – and the timing of interest rate cuts was as much dictated by what was happening in Germany as by conditions in the domestic economy.

With sterling in trouble by mid-1992, the UK government sought to convince the market of its commitment to the exchange rate by borrowing 10 bn ECUs to bolster reserves. The borrowing was an attempt to demonstrate the government's determination to defend the exchange rate and, for a brief period, sterling traded above the DM 2.90 figure. Any change in market sentiment provided only the briefest of respites, and sterling again came under pressure, culminating in the dramatic events of September 1992.

With sterling bumping along the floor, the market was aware of a scarcely concealed divergence of views between the UK government and the Bundesbank (the independent German Central Bank). The Bundesbank clearly took the view that there should be an exchange rate realignment, i.e. a sterling devaluation. The UK government took the view that the Bundesbank should cut interest rates and be prepared to buy sterling in the marketplace. The conflicting messages and associated uncertainty made sterling an ideal target for a speculative attack.

On 16 September, there was a massive wave of speculative sales of sterling. In an attempt to stem the tide, UK interest rates were raised by 2 per cent in the morning and a further 3 per cent increase was announced in the afternoon. This was an unprecedented course of action. The authorities also intervened heavily in the market in an attempt to maintain the price of the currency. It is estimated that anywhere between 16 and 20 bn dollars of reserves were used up in the purchase of sterling in the one day, almost one half of total reserves. As we mentioned earlier, reserves can disappear very quickly!

None of this action proved adequate. The 3 per cent increase came too late – although it is doubtful if it would have proved sufficient (Sweden, which shadowed the ERM, raised its overnight interest rate to 200 per cent!). In fact the 3 per cent increase, while announced, was not actually implemented. The government announced withdrawal from the ERM and the 2 per cent increase was reversed the following morning.

The episode was viewed by many as a humiliation for the government and was immediately dubbed 'Black Wednesday'. Prime Minister Major stated that sterling would not return to the ERM until its basic 'fault line' was remedied. This was a new concept and rectifying the so-called 'fault line' is generally taken to mean that Germany has to put the interests of other EU member countries before its own!

With sterling now floating on the market the exchange rate quickly fell, depreciating by some 15 per cent against the £1–DM 2.95 rate, or by some 9 per cent against the previous floor. Allowing sterling to float did, however, remove the constraint on interest rate policy. On 21 September, UK interest rates were cut a full percentage point to 9 per cent, the first time they had been below German rates for 11 years. With the lower exchange rate seen as beneficial to the export sector and the freedom to direct interest rate policy to the domestic economy many commentators quickly renamed the 16 September as 'Golden Wednesday'.

Sterling has continued to float and interest rate policy has indeed been directed to domestic economic developments. In a world of free capital movements the exchange rate for sterling cannot be unaffected by general turbulence in foreign exchange markets, but upheavals since September 1992 have been directed at other currencies, most notably the French franc in 1993. This resulted in a 'revised' ERM in which the permitted band of variation is plus or minus 15 per cent. On the basis of quarterly figures, Table 15.1 shows sterling trading from a low of £1 = DM 2.42 to £1 = DM 2.56. It is a range of variation which would sit quite comfortably in the 'new' ERM.

15.5   The future

The future is dominated by the continuing controversy over the Maastricht Treaty and the proposal for the introduction of a single currency in the European Union by 1999, or possibly even 1997. While the United Kingdom has negotiated an opt-out clause which would allow it not to participate, it is nevertheless instructive to note the conditions which must be satisfied if any member country is to participate. Four criteria must be satisfied:

1. A country's inflation rate must be no higher than 1.5 per cent above the three best performing countries.
2. A country's budget deficit must not be in excess of 3 per cent of GDP at market prices and total accumulated national debt must not exceed 60 per cent of GDP at market prices.
3. A country's currency must have observed the permitted fluctuation of the ERM for at least 2 years, i.e. no realignment has taken place.
4. A country's long-term interest rates must be no more than 2 per cent above the three best performing countries.

These are strong criteria. There is still considerable divergence in national inflation rates. Taking the consumer price index as a measure of inflation with 1990 as the base period we find that by the end of 1993 the indices for the three low-inflation countries, Denmark, France and Ireland, were in the range 106–108 compared to Spain (117), Portugal (129) and Greece (158). It is also the case that the fourth criterion, convergence of long-term interest rates, is dependent on the first criterion being realised.

Table 15.2 Maastricht budget conditions

	Budget deficit as % of GDP		Cumulative budget deficit as % of GDP	
	1990	1994	1990	1994
United Kingdom	−1.3	−7.4	34.7	52.3
Austria	−2.2	−3.8	56.4	58.6
Belgium	−5.7	−6.1	130.7	144.6
Denmark	−1.5	−5.1	59.5	69.7
Finland	5.3	−6.2	16.6	66.1
France	−1.5	−6.0	46.6	62.1
Germany	−2.1	−3.5	43.5	50.8
Greece	−18.1	−15.7	89.0	103.7
Ireland	−1.5	−3.2	98.7	89.6
Italy	−10.9	−8.7	100.5	116.5
Netherlands	−5.1	−4.3	76.5	81.9
Portugal	−5.3	−6.9	66.6	70.2
Spain	−3.9	−7.0	46.8	62.6
Sweden	4.2	−13.6	44.2	80.5

It is perhaps the second criterion which best illustrates the problems to be faced in progressing to the proposed union. Table 15.2 sets out the budget/GDP and national debt/GDP ratios for the Union member countries for 1990 and 1994. For 1994 no country satisfies the criterion, but more worryingly for proponents of monetary union, most countries have moved further away from the target rather than converging on it. Indeed, some countries are nowhere close to the targets, e.g. the Belgian, Greek or Italian national debt; or the Greek, Italian and Swedish budgets. Moving quickly to satisfy the targets will involve significant shifts in the fiscal stance of most member countries and very substantial adjustment costs for the domestic economies of these countries. Perhaps too much is made of the United Kingdom's opt-out clause.

15.6 Conclusion

The single currency debate will inevitably continue to dominate economic and political debate. At the present time even the 1999 timetable looks exceedingly optimistic. The economies of member countries will have to demonstrate much greater convergence than has hitherto been the case if anything other than a small handful of countries are to participate.

The sterling experience of ERM membership partially demonstrates the key issue which must be faced. The UK government found itself constrained in regard to interest rate policy. With a single currency there must be a single Central Bank. The United Kingdom itself is a currency union. For a given class of borrower or lender the rate of interest in Edinburgh cannot diverge from the rate of interest in London. Indeed, the United Kingdom and the Republic of Ireland formed a *de facto* currency union for over 50 years. With a single currency across the EU, the same interest rate proposition would apply to Paris *vis-à-vis* Rome *vis-à-vis* Madrid, etc.

Questions for discussion

1. To what extent do movements in the exchange rate reflect underlying economic considerations?
2. What are the potential costs and benefits of (a) an appreciating exchange rate, and (b) a depreciating exchange rate?
3. The Bank of England focuses on the effective exchange rate. Why should this be?
4. Why is the rate of interest important?
5. Membership of the ERM may impose constraints on domestic macro-economic policy. What do you consider to be the economic advantages and disadvantages of such constraints?
6. What problems do you envisage arising in meeting the Maastricht Treaty criteria?
7. Under what circumstances might the United Kingdom consider rejoining the ERM?

References and further reading

Bank of England Quarterly Bulletin November 1988 pp. 528–9.
Bank of England Quarterly Bulletin November 1992 pp. 408–15.
Bank of England Quarterly Bulletin August 1994 p. 257.
Curwen, P. (1992) *Understanding the UK Economy* 2nd edn Chapters 4, 5, London: Macmillan.
Johnson, C. (1991) *The Economy under Mrs. Thatcher*, London: Penguin.
Keegan, V. (1989) *Mr. Lawson's Gamble*, London: Hodder and Stoughton.
Sloman, J. (1991) *Economics* (especially Chapter 22), Hemel Hempstead: Harvester Wheatsheaf.
Walters, A. (1990) *Sterling in Danger*, London: Fontana.
Bank of England Quarterly Bulletins provide regular commentaries on developments related to sterling.

CHAPTER 16

The current account of the United Kingdom's balance of payments

THOMAS S. TORRANCE

16.1 Introduction

International transactions are an integral part of the economic life of the United Kingdom. As well as being home to one of the world's major capital markets, the United Kingdom is linked to the international economy by both visible trade (the export and import of physical goods and commodities) and by invisible trade. This latter category consists of the export and import of various kinds of services, and the receipt and payment abroad of financial obligations (largely of interest, profits and dividends, but also including a number of relatively smaller sums of unilateral transfer).

In 1993 the United Kingdom exported £121 bn of goods and earned £115 bn from trade in invisibles. On the import side, the country imported £135 bn worth of goods and paid out £112 bn for invisible items. In relation to the United Kingdom's gross domestic product (at factor cost) of £544.23 bn for the same year, it can be seen that these trade flows are sizeable and significant: the credits from visible and invisible exports amounted to over 43 per cent of GDP, while outgoing payments for visible and invisible imports came to more than 45 per cent of GDP. What these figures show is that at the present time a sum of about 45 per cent of the United Kingdom's GDP is involved each year in both outward and inward trade settlements. The UK economy is one of the most open in the world: whatever affects the United Kingdom's trade, is likely to have repercussions for important domestic economic factors such as the level of employment and general living standards.

16.2 The balance of payments statistics

Extensive details of the United Kingdom's register of transactions with the rest of the world economy are to be found in the balance of payments tables in many of the monthly and annual publications of the Central Statistical Office. The main specialist CSO publication in this area is the yearly *The Pink Book:*

United Kingdom Balance of Payments. Especially interesting are the long-run sets of figures going back to 1946, which are given and updated each year in the CSO's volume *Economic Trends Annual Supplement (ETAS).*

A balance of payments statement is an accounting record which provides a description for a given period of the state of an economy's relationship with the rest of the world. In the United Kingdom and elsewhere the convention is to divide the statement into two chief parts: the current account and the capital account. The former gives information for the time period in question on the relative outcomes of trade exports and imports, while the latter traces the flows of investment capital in and out of the economy. It is important to realise (as will shortly be explained) that these two sections of a balance of payments statement are necessarily connected: for a deficit (surplus) on current account, there has to be a corresponding surplus (deficit) on capital account. Therefore, the sum of any year's current and capital accounts should come to zero. In a simplified form, the UK balance of payments for 1993 is shown in Table 16.1.

In the current account, 'other transfers (net)' refers to net unilateral transfers of funds to and from the United Kingdom by both the government and the

Table 16.1   UK balance of payments 1993 (£m)

Current account		
Value of visible exports	+ 120 839	
Value of visible imports	− 134 519	
Visible trade balance	− 13 680	
Services (net)	+ 5 202	
Interest, profits, dividends (net)	+ 2 703	
Other transfers (net)	− 5 106	
Invisible trade balance	+ 2 799	
Current account balance		− 10 881
Capital account:		
Transactions in assets	− 162 797	
Transactions in liabilities	+ 174 939	
Net capital transactions	+ 12 142	
Capital account balance		+ 12 142
Balancing Item		− 1 261

Source: Central Statistical Office (1994c), Tables 16.1, 16.2, 16.3.

private sector. Examples of such transfers are government payments to and from the European Union and, involving the private sector, remittances to and from the United Kingdom between separated workers and their families. In gross terms, inward unilateral transfers in 1993 came to about £4.9 bn (60% government, 40% private sector); while outward transfers amounted to almost £10 bn (75% government, 25% private sector).

Turning now to the capital account as shown in Table 16.1, under the heading 'transactions in assets' is recorded the value of foreign assets that all UK residents (individuals, companies and the British government) acquired in 1993. The figure is given as a negative, because it represents a flow of money out of the country to overseas. It should be noted that under this heading is included any gain or loss of foreign currency from the Bank of England's official reserves (in 1993, these reserves in fact grew by £701 m). The immediately following heading of 'transactions in liabilities' records the value of UK assets obtained in 1993 by foreign individuals and institutions; the sum is given as positive because it describes a flow of money from abroad to the United Kingdom.

The 1993 balance of payments statement shows that the United Kingdom had a current account deficit of £10.89 bn. Given that the United Kingdom imported visibles and invisibles to a greater value than those exported, the difference has to be financed either by borrowing money from abroad or from the proceeds of the sale to foreigners of UK assets. This is the reason why any deficit on current account has to be reflected by a corresponding surplus on capital account. As previously mentioned, the current and capital accounts should be equal in value but opposite in sign and thus ought to sum to zero.

However, it is hardly ever the case that the collected statistical data shows the two parts of the balance of payments to be exactly equal in magnitude. In practice the existence of errors and omissions almost always prevents this from happening. To make allowance for statistical error, the balance of payments tables invariably include a feature called the 'balancing item' (which in 1993 came to £1.26 bn). In practice, it is current account plus capital account plus balancing item that sums to zero.

The balancing item is highly erratic with respect to both sign and size. Going back to 1970 it has normally been of positive sign, but has been negative six times (in 1970, 1972, 1975, 1982, 1987 and 1993). In absolute size over this period, the balancing item has varied between a negligible £4 m in 1975 to a massive £7.3 bn in 1990. Recently there has been debate on what area of the balance of payments is most likely to be the source of the errors and omissions that give rise for a need for a balancing item. After a study of this puzzle, the Bank of England (1990) concluded that capital account data, by nature difficult to identify and to record precisely, are less accurate than current account data. If this view is accepted, it implies that in 1993 the transactions in assets have been understated and/or the transactions in liabilities have been overstated.

However, the complete facts for this and earlier years are unlikely ever to be known for certain.

16.3 Historical outline of the UK current account from 1946

Trends in the UK current account are followed with great interest. The state of this part of the balance of payments is widely taken by politicians and economic commentators to be a highly important measure of the international health of the British economy. It is true that the balance of payments always balances: but in the case of a current account deficit, this is because borrowing from abroad (and the purchase of UK assets by foreigners) has made good the difference between what the country pays for its imports and what it earns from its exports. A persistent current account deficit is commonly taken as an indicator that the United Kingdom is not paying its way in the world; and, rightly or wrongly, the perception that the country is living beyond its means is frequently the cause of popular alarm and political pressure on the government to take remedial action.

The first step to understanding the British current account is to gain an informed perspective by viewing the facts of its development over a significant period of time. The long-run summary figures for the UK current account are given in Table 16.2. Until the 1980s it can be seen that the usual pattern was for the United Kingdom to run a visible trade deficit which was then wholly or largely offset by a surplus on invisibles. In the early 1980s, however, there were 3 years (1980, 1981 and 1982) in which both the trade in visibles and invisibles were in surplus. This short period of overall surplus was followed by the period up to the present in which the visible deficits are so large that they completely overwhelm the traditional surpluses earned on the trade in invisibles. At the end of 1993, the cumulative debt from successive annual current account deficits from 1986 exceeded, in terms of simple addition, the sum of £90 bn.

The current account details in Table 16.2 are the actual money figures, and take no account of the inflationary erosion of the domestic purchasing power of the pound. In December 1993, for instance, the RPI was just a fraction below eight times the RPI at the start of 1970. Distortions to the statistical data produced by inflation are easily removed by displaying the current account balance as a ratio of GDP, as in Figure 16.1. The most striking general feature of the graph can even be detected in the non-inflation-adjusted data of Table 16.2. This is that the current account until 1986 displays a distinct seesaw pattern, moving from deficit to surplus and then back into deficit in a roughly cyclical fashion.

Between 1952 and 1968 the amplitude of this oscillation was relatively modest: the largest surplus occurred in 1958 (1.73% of GDP) while the largest deficit was in 1964 (1.26%). The period immediately after World War II and prior to 1952, however, experienced more variable fluctuations.

Table 16.2   UK current account 1946–93 (£bn)

	Visible trade balance	Invisible trade balance	Current account balance
1946	− 0.10	− 0.13	− 0.23
1947	− 0.36	− 0.02	− 0.38
1948	− 0.15	+ 0.18	+ 0.03
1949	− 0.14	+ 0.14	0.00
1950	− 0.05	+ 0.36	+ 0.31
1951	− 0.69	+ 0.32	− 0.37
1952	− 0.28	+ 0.44	+ 0.16
1953	− 0.24	+ 0.39	+ 0.15
1954	− 0.20	+ 0.32	+ 0.12
1955	− 0.31	+ 0.16	− 0.15
1956	+ 0.05	+ 0.16	+ 0.21
1957	− 0.03	+ 0.26	+ 0.23
1958	+ 0.03	+ 0.32	+ 0.35
1959	− 0.12	+ 0.28	+ 0.16
1960	− 0.40	+ 0.16	− 0.24
1961	− 0.14	+ 0.18	+ 0.04
1962	− 0.10	+ 0.24	+ 0.14
1963	− 0.12	+ 0.23	+ 0.11
1964	− 0.54	+ 0.17	− 0.37
1965	− 0.26	+ 0.18	− 0.08
1966	− 0.11	+ 0.24	+ 0.13
1967	− 0.60	+ 0.32	− 0.28
1968	− 0.71	+ 0.45	− 0.26
1969	− 0.21	+ 0.69	+ 0.48
1970	− 0.01	+ 0.83	+ 0.82
1971	+ 0.21	+ 0.90	+ 1.12
1972	− 0.74	+ 0.94	+ 0.20
1973	− 2.57	+ 1.57	− 1.00
1974	− 5.23	+ 2.05	− 3.18
1975	− 3.26	+ 1.73	− 1.53
1976	− 3.96	+ 3.19	− 0.77
1977	− 2.32	+ 2.37	+ 0.05
1978	− 1.59	+ 2.71	+ 1.12
1979	− 3.34	+ 2.89	− 0.45
1980	+ 1.36	+ 1.49	+ 2.85
1981	+ 3.25	+ 3.50	+ 6.75
1982	+ 1.91	+ 2.74	+ 4.65
1983	− 1.54	+ 5.07	+ 3.53
1984	− 5.34	+ 6.82	+ 1.48
1985	− 3.35	+ 5.58	+ 2.23
1986	− 9.56	+ 8.69	− 0.87
1987	− 11.58	+ 6.60	− 4.98
1988	− 21.48	+ 4.86	− 16.62
1989	− 24.68	+ 2.17	− 22.51
1990	− 18.81	+ 0.54	− 18.27
1991	− 10.28	+ 2.63	− 7.65
1992	− 13.41	+ 2.87	− 10.54
1993	− 13.68	+ 2.80	− 10.88

Source: Central Statistical Office (1994a), Table 1.16; Central Statistical Office (1994c), Table 16.1; Central Statistical Office (1993), Tables 1.1, 1.3.

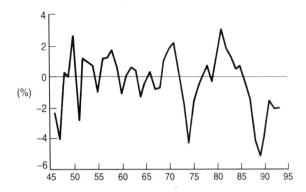

Figure 16.1   Current account as percentage of GDP, 1946–93.

1947 saw a deep deficit of 4.02 per cent which was then followed 3 years later
by a conspicuously good surplus of 2.66 per cent, only to be replaced in 1951 by
a wide 2.88 per cent deficit. After 1968 the comparatively stable run of gentle
swings between deficit and surplus ended, and the economy entered a period
of tumultuous variability in the behaviour of the current account. The deficit of
1974 broke the post-war record of 1947 and reached a remarkable 4.21 per cent
of GDP. In 1981, however, the position was reversed with the strongest post-
war surplus at 3.08 per cent of GDP. By 1986 the current account was back in
deficit, and in 1989 and 1990 it had slid to the extent of being a yawning 5.10
per cent and 3.82 per cent of GDP. In the period up to the present, the last year
of surplus was 1985 (at the modest level of 0.73%). Most recently, 1991, 1992
and 1993 experienced percentage deficits of 1.55 per cent, 2.05 per cent and
2.00 per cent, respectively.

16.4   The absorption approach to the current account

As well as recording and charting the current account, economists are
interested in explaining its behaviour. At the moment there are two broad
types of approach to understanding the current account, the first of which is
known as the 'absorption approach'.[1] This was originally developed in 1952 by
the International Monetary Fund economist Sidney Alexander.

The absorption approach to the current account operates in the context of the
circular flow of income of an economy. The starting point is that in any
economy aggregate expenditure (or aggregate demand) is given by the
following expression:

$$y^d = c + i + g + (x - m),$$ (15.1)

where y^d stands for aggregate expenditure (aggregate demand); c, for
consumption expenditure; i, investment expenditure (gross domestic fixed

capital formation plus net additions to inventory stocks); g, government expenditure on final resources; x, revenue obtained from the sale of exports; and m, expenditure on imports. In equation 15.1, the sum of the expenditures represented by $(c + i + g)$ is referred to as domestic absorption of goods and services.

In the circular flow of income, income is earned by using owned factors of production (which include human skill) to engage in the creation of goods and the provision of services. This income is equal to the value of produced output, and the various ways that it is disposed of is shown in the following:

$$y = c + s + t, \tag{15.2}$$

where y stands for national income (or output); s, for the value of private sector (personal and company) saving; and t, for the value of taxation paid to government.

Circular flow equilibrium is defined by the national accounting identity that aggregate expenditure has the same value as national income, namely:

$$y^d = y. \tag{15.3}$$

After substitution, the following expression is obtained from equations 15.1, 15.2 and 15.3

$$(c + i + g) + (x - m) = (c + s + t). \tag{15.4}$$

And from this, the following two conditional propositions can be validly derived:

$$\text{if } (c + i + g) > (c + s + t) \text{ then } (x < m); \tag{15.5}$$

and,

$$\text{if } (c + i + g) < (c + s + t) \text{ then } (x > m). \tag{15.6}$$

Equations 15.5 and 15.6 assert important connections between domestic absorption, national income or output, and the current account balance. First, according to equation 15.5, when absorption exceeds output, then exports are invariably lower than imports. (This should be obvious if equation 15.4 is considered: if $(c + i + g)$ is greater than $(c + s + t)$ then the term $(x - m)$ must take a negative value, i.e. x must have a lower absolute size than m.) Secondly, with the content of equation 15.6 (when absorption is less than output), then exports are necessarily greater than imports.

A number of further interesting inferences can be drawn from the basic equation 15.4. For instance, it can be deduced that if the aim is to raise the value of the $(x - m)$ component, this is only possible if domestic absorption is reduced and/or income is increased. Since the consumption element is common to both absorption and income, a decrease in the former involves essentially a fall in i or g (or both), while a rise in the latter entails a rise in s or t (or both).

These notable connections can be viewed more clearly if equation 15.4 is rewritten in a way that enables it to be compared to the UK statistical data published by the CSO. After rearrangement, equation 15.4 can be presented as follows:

$$(s - i) + (t - g) + (m - x) = 0. \tag{15.7}$$

In this form, the three terms $(s - i)$, $(t - g)$ and $(m - x)$ stand for the financial surplus (if positive) or deficit (if negative) of the main sectors of the economy. These are, respectively, the private, public and overseas sectors. The private sector consists of the personal and investor-owned company domains, the public sector consists of central and local government along with state-owned enterprises such as the Post Office, while the overseas sector is simply the CSO's name for the rest of the world. The $(m - x)$ term, it should be noted, is simply the United Kingdom's current account balance but with the sign reversed: thus, for example, if the United Kingdom has a current account deficit (i.e. $(x - m)$ is negative) then the overseas sector is recorded by the CSO as being in surplus (with $(m - x)$ taking a positive sign).

In non-inflation-adjusted terms, the data relating to the financial surplus or deficit of the three sectors of the UK economy from 1985 onwards are shown in Table 16.3. To take 1989 as an illustrative year: the large £22.51 bn current account deficit of the United Kingdom is shown in Table 16.3 as a surplus of the same size for the overseas sector. The sector counterparts of this surplus are the £27.74 bn deficit of the private sector plus the slightly off-setting £5.23 bn surplus of the public sector. (Because of residual error, the figures for the years 1991, 1992 and 1993 do not sum exactly to zero.)

As a proportion of GDP (at factor cost), the three UK sector balances from 1948 to 1993 are shown in Figure 16.2. In Figure 16.3 the public and private

Table 16.3 UK sector financial balance 1985–93 (£m)

	Private sector $(s - i)$	Public sector $(t - g)$	Overseas sector $(m - x)$
1985	+ 12 465	− 10 227	− 2 238
1986	+ 7183	− 8054	+ 871
1987	− 466	− 4517	+ 4983
1988	− 23 003	+ 6386	+ 16 617
1989	− 27 739	+ 5227	+ 22 512
1990	− 16 195	− 2073	+ 18 268
1991	+ 7050	− 15 147	+ 7652
1992	+ 26 410	− 36 996	+ 10 539
1993	+ 37 331	− 48 622	+ 10 881

Source: Central Statistical Office (1994a), Table 1.10; Central Statistical Office (1994b), Table 2.9.

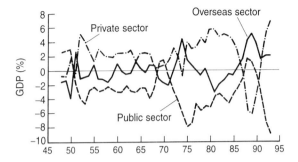

Figure 16.2   Financial surplus or deficit by sector, 1948–93.

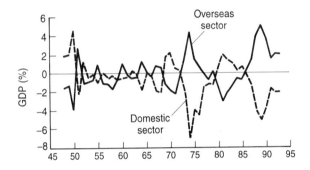

Figure 16.3   Overseas and domestic sectors, 1948–93.

sector balances of Figure 16.2 have been added together to show the balance of the overall domestic sector. In both figures, the graph for the overseas sector balance shows, with a change of sign, the current account balance plus any non-recurrent overseas capital grant to or from the UK government. (For a number of years, residual error prevents the sum of the overseas and other sector balances coming precisely to zero.) Historically it can be seen that the private sector has almost always been in financial surplus: the most conspicuous deviation from this general rule is the period 1987–1990, during which the consumption and investment expenditure of the private sector exploded in an unsustainable credit-financed boom. As well as the late 1980s and 1990, the years 1948, 1949, 1951 and 1974 were also episodes of overall, but less spectacular, private sector deficit. However, these years apart, the usual position was of private sector surplus combined with public sector deficit. In this situation, an overseas sector surplus (i.e. a current account deficit) was inevitably generated whenever the public sector deficit exceeded the private sector surplus. This seems to hint that since the 1940s it is the state of the public sector financial balance that has had a predominant role in the creation of a UK current account deficit. This suggestion receives support from the fact that over the stretch of 46 years from 1948 to 1993, the public sector was in surplus only seven times (1948, 1949, 1950, 1969, 1970, 1988 and 1989), and in all but two of these occasions there was also a current account surplus. The two exceptions here were 1988 and 1989, when gigantic private sector deficits swamped the substantial public sector surpluses.

16.5 The absorption approach: some implications

It was argued earlier that the reversal of a current account deficit is only possible alongside a fall in the ratio of domestic absorption to output (income). This ratio would fall if, the other variable remaining constant, either absorption fell or output increased. Over a short-run time horizon, it is unrealistic to expect technological developments to deliver output growth via productivity improvements. It therefore follows that if all available resources within an economy are fully employed, the only possible route to an improvement in the current account is a reduction in the absolute level of domestic absorption. That is to say, under full employment, a current account in deficit can only be improved if expenditure from $(c + i + g)$ is reduced.

When referring to the modern UK economy, however, it is realistic to assume the existence of some unused capacity (unemployed skill and capital). In this situation, a current account deficit could be diminished by an increase in output as well as by a fall in absorption. But, and this is the significant point, for an increase in output to have this consequence, it must not be accompanied by an absorption increase (or at least, it must not be accompanied by an absorption increase of the same or greater percentage).

In terms of equation 15.4, the current account balance will improve if output increases but absorption remains constant (or rises by a smaller percentage). Given that an increase in output (y) is always matched by an increase in aggregate expenditure (y^d), the ideal sequence of events, from the point of view of securing a current account improvement, is for the increase in expenditure to stem from an expansion of net exports $(x - m)$ rather than absorption $(c + i + g)$. In other words, an output increase will improve the current balance provided it is accompanied by a reduction in the relative share of aggregate expenditure that is devoted to domestic absorption and to an expansion in the proportion of expenditure that comes from outside the economy.

In the United Kingdom, however, the long-run (1946–93) statistical data indicate a different story: the data show that rapid rises in output growth have almost always been associated with corresponding increases in absorption, rather than with improvements in net exports. In Figure 16.4 the current account balance, as a percentage of GDP at factor cost, is shown with a graph of the annual change in real GDP. From Figure 16.4, it is evident that an increase in the rate of change of output growth has tended to worsen the

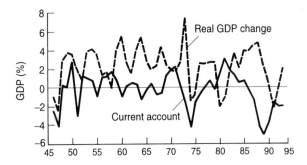

Figure 16.4   Current account (as % GDP) and real GDP change, 1946–93.

current account balance; this directly implies that over this time period the tendency in the UK economy has been for a rise in the growth rate to be linked with an increase, rather than a decrease, in the proportion of total expenditure going on domestic absorption. Since the mid-1940s, in other words, output growth in the United Kingdom has not been export-led.

16.6   The elasticities approach to the current account

The second important type of analysis of the current account is the 'Elasticities Approach'. This theory, in the shape that it has today, owes its formation to the economists Alfred Marshall (1842–1924) and Abba Lerner (1905–82). Marshall in 1879, and Lerner again and independently in 1944, developed the principal theorem of this approach, and it is with their two names that the theory is now identified.

The elasticities approach is so-called because its central hypothesis is that the quantities demanded of exports and imports are price sensitive or 'elastic'. What is known as the Marshall–Lerner theorem (which will not be proved as a theoretical proposition here) concerns the effects of a currency depreciation on a current account balance. The theorem is that when the sum of the foreign-price elasticity of demand for exports and the domestic-price elasticity of demand for imports comes to more than 1 (unity), a currency depreciation improves the current account balance.

Research surveys (Artus and Knight, 1984) show that for most developed economies today the medium- and long-run export and import elasticities do in fact sum to unity or above. Of course, what is of central interest is whether, when this stipulated circumstance holds, the current account balance behaves under the influence of exchange rate changes as the Marshall–Lerner theorem predicts.

On the elasticities approach, the respective equations for export (Qx) and import (Qm) volumes are postulated to be as follows:

$$Qx = k(y_f, P_x, E.P/P_f); \tag{15.8}$$

and,

$$Qm = k(y, P_m, E.P/P_f), \tag{15.9}$$

where k stands for the functional relation; y_f for the level of the foreign country's national income; y, for the level of domestic national income; P_x, for the foreign currency price of exported goods and services; P_m, for the domestic price of imported goods and services; E, for the foreign exchange rate of the domestic currency; P, for the domestic price level; and P_f, for the foreign country's price level.

In equations 15.8 and 15.9 the market (or 'nominal') exchange rate E represents the current number of foreign currency units per unit of domestic currency. In the setting of the United Kingdom, E describes a rate such as, for instance, DM 3.00 per £1. The expression $E.P/P_f$ is what economists call the 'real exchange rate', which is the nominal exchange rate adjusted to take account of declines (from a chosen base year) in the relative domestic purchasing powers of the two currencies as a result of inflation. To give an example: suppose that in a base year the nominal (and real) exchange rate for the pound against the Deutschmark is DM 3.00; and that five years later, after which the UK price level doubles but the German price level remains the same, the nominal rate is still DM 3.00. In these circumstances, although the nominal exchange rate is unchanged the real rate, compared to that prevailing in the base year, has appreciated sharply to DM 6.00.

It is changes in the real exchange rate and not changes in the nominal rate that measure movements over time in the international competitiveness of a country's exports. Thus if UK prices double but German prices remain the same, the real exchange rate of the pound against the Deutschmark will rise unless the nominal exchange rate falls by 50 per cent to compensate. The chief consequence of a rising real exchange rate is that goods and services exported from the United Kingdom become unattractively priced in Deutschmark terms in the German market. In general, for an economy's exports to remain internationally competitive, the nominal exchange rate E should change in such a way that over time the real exchange rate does not drift upwards.

Under the elasticities approach, then, a currency depreciation leads to increased demand abroad for exports and a reduced demand domestically for imports; and, if the Marshall–Lerner theorem is satisfied, the current account balance improves. But is the situation really as simple as this?

It is a statement of the obvious that the behaviour of exports and imports cannot be considered in isolation from the rest of the wider economy. If the elasticities approach is to have real-world application it has to be considered dynamically, that is, in the overall setting of a functioning economy in which individual markets affect and mutually interact with each other over time in complex ways.

In a context of full employment (coupled with a constant level of domestic absorption), a current account deficit cannot be removed by a real depreciation of the domestic currency. The reason is this. Outside the economy, a depreciation would generate a higher level of demand for exported goods and services, but since supply could not be increased the additional demand from abroad could not be satisfied and export earnings in domestic currency would therefore remain the same as previously. Within the economy, because output could not be lifted, any attempt to substitute domestic in place of the temporarily more expensive imported goods would cause the price level to rise to the point at which the price of imported goods no longer appeared relatively expensive. The overall result would be that the same expenditure as previously would be directed to imports (even though, being at a higher unit price, a smaller physical volume of goods and services would be purchased from abroad).

It is clear, therefore, that the elasticities approach has relevance only when an economy is operating at less than full capacity: if a currency depreciation does indeed increase export sales, the additional goods for export must actually have been supplied. The chief presupposition of the elasticities theory, however, is not this postulate of unused capacity, important though it is. Rather, it is the tacit assumption that a fall in the real exchange rate tends to lead to a decrease in the proportion of aggregate expenditure committed to domestic absorption (and vice versa, for a rise in the real exchange rate).

The initial effect of a change in relative prices caused by a currency depreciation is to raise demand for exports and to cut demand for imports. With unused capacity in the economy, a change in demand of this kind results in an increase in domestic output: exports rise and, on account of consumers seeking to purchase domestic goods in place of relatively more expensive imports, the production of import substitutes increases. On the elasticities approach, a currency depreciation does not merely have the effect of raising domestic output but it is also held to improve the current balance. The second conclusion here, however, is the contentious part of the elasticities theory.

Even if the Marshall–Lerner theorem is satisfied, an increase in output that follows a currency depreciation will improve a current account balance only if the income earned from the production of the additional output is itself not expended in absorption (or if absorption subsequently rises by a smaller proportion than the output/income increase). If this condition is met, absorption becomes a smaller proportion of the higher level of output than of the lower level that existed prior to the depreciation. It is this fall in the proportion of income going on absorption that is responsible for the improved current balance, rather than the currency depreciation itself.

The above condition may not of course be satisfied: it is perfectly possible that as output rises following a currency depreciation, the proportion of income expended on absorption rises. And in such a case, the result of the depreciation would be a worsening of the current balance. Such a development could well happen if, for instance, a fall in the exchange rate to a more internationally competitive level induced an expansion in investment expenditure that was sufficiently large to raise the ratio of absorption to output (income).

Thus, once the dynamic or further consequences for an economy of a fall in a currency's real rate are considered, the effect of such a change on the current account balance is essentially undetermined: it could be in either direction. To illustrate the claim that relatively high and low real exchange rates are not automatically associated with current account surpluses and deficits, respectively, it is instructive to examine the two most recent decades of the United Kingdom's experience.

The United Kingdom's current account balance since 1946 has already been given by Figure 16.1. The graph of this balance, as portrayed by Figure 16.1, for the years 1970 to 1993 should now be compared to the graphs of the real exchange rates of the pound against the Deutschmark and the US dollar over the same period as given by Figures 16.5 and 16.6. (The combined behaviour of these two real exchange rates provides a good indication of the international price-competitiveness of the UK economy.) Over this period the German

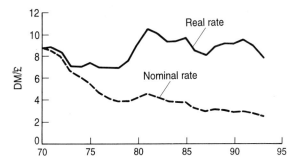

Figure 16.5   DM/£FX rate, 1970–93 (nominal and real, base year: 1970).

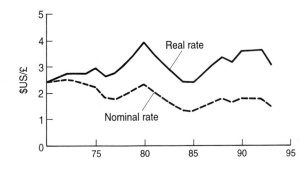

Figure 16.6 $US/£FX rate, 1970–93 (nominal and real, base year: 1970).

currency depreciated in real terms by about 9.5 per cent, while the American currency appreciated in real terms by approximately 28 per cent. Despite these underlying trends, the year-to-year changes in real rates do not appear to have the effects predicted by the elasticities approach. As can be seen by inspection of Figures 16.1, 16.5 and 16.6, the great plunges into current account deficit of 1974 and 1989 are not correlated with any sudden real appreciation of the pound; and, similarly, the peak UK current account surplus of 1981 is not associated with a dramatic real depreciation of the pound.

If an economy possesses unused productive capacity, a fall in the real exchange rate acts directly to raise the level of output and employment. Since this is obviously a desirable effect, the real exchange rate is rightly considered by policy-makers and their advisers to be a critical variable within an economy. However, although the real exchange rate is an influential factor affecting the overall level of economic activity, this is not the same thing as saying that the real exchange rate is closely related to any particular state of the current account balance. The implicit assumption that the growth in output stimulated by a currency depreciation will normally be followed by a fall in the proportion of income spent on absorption is an important weakness of the elasticities approach.

16.7   Conclusion: is a current account deficit damaging?

Those concerned with the formation of government policy frequently take it as axiomatic that a current account deficit is undesirable. A deficit is viewed as a signal that the economy is becoming internationally uncompetitive, unable to pay for the import of goods and services by a corresponding outward flow of exports. The analogy of a spendthrift individual is habitually invoked: the result of living beyond one's means over a lengthy period often ends in personal insolvency and the misery of the bankruptcy court. How accurate is this comparison and how seriously should it be taken?

With most advanced industrial countries, a current account deficit can be financed into the indefinite future by the willing inflow of foreign capital but which over time produces a build-up of foreign debt upon which a growing sum of interest has to be paid. Whether this is good or bad depends very much on the exact nature of the 'overabundant' imports. If domestic absorption exceeds output because of a high volume of imported capital goods such as industrial machinery, then it could well be true that these investment items were being used to produce eventually a strong growth in output, an output that would be greater than future absorption and which would itself generate the exports to service and pay off the foreign debt acquired. On the other hand, if the excess of absorption over output was on account of a vast government deficit that was leading to a consumption boom of imported goods, these imports could not be viewed in a similarly favourable light.

As a general rule it seems sensible to regard a current account deficit as undesirable only if the predictable long-run effect is to cause foreign indebtedness to accumulate at a faster rate than the economy's real rate of growth. If this undesirable eventuality should occur, the earlier analogy with the spendthrift individual, encumbering himself with a rising burden of debt that he never realistically expects to repay or service, appears appropriate, but not otherwise.

In the United Kingdom there exists a Queen's Award for Exports but not a Queen's Award for Imports! The suggestion that there should be an Award for Imports would strike most people as misguided, even preposterous. In a mild way this public reaction reflects an ingrained attitude that, almost as a reflex, tends to be prejudiced against imports as such; but just as a sharp kitchen knife is not an intrinsically dangerous object (although, in the hands of a small child, it can be that), so modern economic theory provides no grounds for an absolute bias against imports and importers.

To stress that imports can be crucial for economic growth and can in time serve to generate new flows of export revenues is not to say that a current account deficit should never be a matter of concern. A glance back at Table 16.3 shows that the United Kingdom's present-day current account deficit is caused not by a surge of investment by the private sector but by a public sector deficit of a size that the government itself accepts as too large and liable to be a dead-weight burden on future taxpayers. From this it is reasonable to conclude that today's current account deficit, enabling personal consumption to be maintained from imported goods, is not the sort to be warmly welcomed. As the inevitable counterpart of the government's own budget deficit, the United Kingdom's current account deficit is increasing the country's gross foreign debt without adding proportionately to the country's stock of productive business assets.

Over the next few years the primary task of economic management for the British government must be to try to devise a more suitable balance between its own spending and collected tax revenue and, if possible, to bring this about without a contraction in the level of aggregate expenditure so rapid as to destabilise the level of national income. Even on the pessimistic assumption of little or no real growth in output, the chosen policy objective could in principle be attained if exports increased in line with a gradual fall in government spending. In terms of the earlier equation 15.1, this scenario involves a change in the composition but not the level of y^d, with an increase in x compensating for a fall in g. If this could be achieved it would result in a decrease in the absorption/output ratio (thus removing the current account deficit), without causing an unpalatable decline in output (national income).

In the real world, however, governments are rarely able to realise accurately ideal outcomes laid down by theoretical blueprints. The conspicuous weakness of the suggested plan is that there is no guaranteed means available to the

British government for positively inducing a growth in exports to take the place of a decline in its own spending, thus maintaining the existing level of aggregate expenditure in the economy.

While it is to be hoped that the present budget and current account deficits can be smoothly eliminated there must, nevertheless, be a good probability that as absorption is reigned in, output too will also suffer some decline. The old familiar pattern, illustrated in Figure 16.4, of an improvement in the UK current account being associated with, at very best, a fall in the output growth rate, may well be about to stage a further appearance.

Questions for discussion

1. Is a country with a current account surplus necessarily a net exporter of capital?
2. How convincing is the view of the Bank of England that the balancing item in the yearly balance of payments figures is more likely to arise from errors in the compilation of the capital account statistics than those of the current account?
3. If the current account consistently shows a net inflow under 'interest, profits and dividends', does this imply that the United Kingdom is a net international creditor?
4. Can any conclusions about the structure of the UK economy be drawn from the fact that since 1948 (see Table 16.2) the invisible trade balance has always been in surplus?
5. Was the current account balance more volatile from 1970 onwards in comparison to the 1950s and 1960s? If this was so, what might be the causes?
6. Under the absorption approach, what would happen to the current account balance if domestic investment exceeded all private saving *and* government spending was greater than all tax revenue?
7. Is a current account deficit identical to an overseas sector surplus? Does Figure 16.2 suggest that since 1948 it is the public sector financial deficit that has largely been responsible for generating the overseas sector surplus?
8. If the United Kingdom experiences higher inflation than Germany while the nominal exchange rate of the pound against the Deutschmark remains unchanged, what happens to the pound's real exchange rate? Why is the real exchange rate of the pound important for the UK economy?
9. What conditions and assumptions have to hold before a real depreciation of the domestic currency will correct a current account deficit?
10. Is a current account deficit always a sign of underlying economic weakness of some kind? If not, should there be a Queen's Award for imports?

Note

1. Strictly, there is a further theory of the current account known as the 'Monetary Approach to the Balance of Payments' (MABP). This is basically an extension of the Absorption Approach, and for this reason is not discussed as a separate theory in this chapter. Under the MABP, an increase in domestic absorption is produced by a rate of increase in the domestic money stock that is faster than the rate of growth of the population's willingness to hold money. Thus, on the MABP, a current account deficit is caused by a too-rapid rate of monetary growth and is, accordingly, corrected by a monetary contraction. The origins of the MABP lie with a 1957 paper by the IMF economist Jacques J. Polak (1957).

References and further reading

Alexander, S.S. (1952) 'Effects of a devaluation on a trade balance' *IMF Staff Papers* (2) pp. 263–78.

Artus, J.R. and Knight, M.D. (1984) *Issues in the Assessment of the Exchange Rates of Industrial Countries* (Occasional Paper no.29), Washington, D.C.: International Monetary Fund.

Bank of England (1990) 'Problems associated with balance of payments statistics' in *Bank of England Quarterly Bulletin* 30(4) pp. 497–9.

Bank of England (1994) 'The external balance sheet of the United Kingdom: recent developments' in *Bank of England Quarterly Bulletin* 34(4) pp. 355–61.

Central Statistical Office (1993) *The Pink Book 1993: United Kingdom balance of payments*, London: HMSO.

Central Statistical Office (1994a) *Economic Trends Annual Supplement*, London: HMSO.

Central Statistical Office (1994b) *Economic Trends 489 July*, London: HMSO.

Central Statistical Office (1994c) *Monthly Digest of Statistics* 583 July, London: HMSO.

Curwen, P. (ed.)(1992) *Understanding the UK Economy* 2nd edn, Chapter 6, London: Macmillan.

Frenkel, J.A. and Johnson, H.G. (1976), *The Monetary Approach to the Balance of Payments*, London: Allen & Unwin.

Griffiths, A. and Wall, S. (1993) *Applied Economics* 5th edn, Chapter 25, London: Longman.

Heffernan, S. and Sinclair, P. (1990) *Modern International Economics* Chapter 8, Oxford: Blackwell.

International Monetary Fund (1994) *International Financial Statistics Yearbook*, Washington, DC: International Monetary Fund.

Polak, J.J. (1957). 'Monetary analysis of income formation and payments problems' *IMF Staff Papers* VI (1) pp 1–50.

Vane, H.R. and Thompson, J.L. (1993) *An Introduction to Macroeconomic Policy* 4th edn, Chapter 6, Hemel Hempstead: Harvester Wheatsheaf.

Winters, L.A. (1991) *International Economics* 4th edn, Chapters 17–21, London: HarperCollins.

CHAPTER 17

UK trade and trade policy

SHU-MEI GAO

17.1 Introduction

The United Kingdom was the first major, and for many years the dominant, trading nation in the world. In today's highly interdependent and open world, a substantial share of UK domestic output is exported and a large part of total expenditure is spent on imported items. International trade has become an increasingly important part in the economic life of the United Kingdom.

This chapter is concerned with the trends in United Kingdom trade and the UK's trade policy in practice. Section 17.1 examines various explanations to the cause and direction of international trade. Section 17.2 looks at changes in the structure of UK trade during the last 30 years or so and examines the factors which brought about these changes. Section 17.3 introduces instruments of trade policy such as tariffs and non-tariff barriers while the following section looks at the effects of the GATT and the European Union on the United Kingdom's trade policy. The last section gives a summary and conclusion.

17.2 Why do countries trade with each other?

17.2.1 Explanations based on differences between countries

The classical treatment of international trade is represented by the theory of comparative advantage. It was first stated by the English economist, David Ricardo (1772–1823) in 1817 in his book entitled *The Principles of Political Economy and Taxation*. The theory of comparative advantage regards the cause of trade as differences in the relative costs of production between countries. Ricardo showed that it was not necessary for a country to have an absolute cost advantage in the production of a good to engage in beneficial trade. Even if one country's absolute costs of producing all goods are higher than another, as long as its relative costs of producing different goods are different from the latter, trade between them can take place and benefit both of them. Therefore the law of comparative advantage regards the relative efficiency in the production of different goods as the determinant of trade. Countries gain by specialising in and exporting the goods they produce relatively efficiently and trading with each other.

Ricardo showed that differences in the relative costs of production are an important cause of international trade. However, he did not explain where the differences come from. Two Swedish economists, Eli Heckscher (1879–1952) and Bertil Ohlin[1] (1899–1979) demonstrated that differences in costs of production exist because countries have different relative factor endowments. If a country has a relatively abundant supply of one factor of production, then that factor will be relatively cheaper in that country. When a good is produced using this relatively abundant factor relatively intensively, this good would also be cheaper. Therefore a country is expected to have its comparative advantage in goods whose production uses its relatively abundant factor more intensively. Thus the Heckscher–Ohlin model concluded that countries will export goods whose production is relatively intensive in the factors which they possess in relatively abundant supply.

A common feature of comparative advantage and the Heckscher–Ohlin model is that they are both based on the assumptions of perfect competition and constant returns to scale, and that the output of each industry is homogeneous between countries and the factors of production are identical and perfectly mobile within a country. A car is a car; there should be no difference between a British car and a German car. A worker in the British textile industry is no different from a worker in the British food industry. International variations in production technology or factor endowments determine in which goods a country has a comparative advantage and where it has a comparative disadvantage; and the pattern of trade follows naturally. Countries export the goods in which they have a comparative advantage and import those in which they have a comparative disadvantage. Therefore the pattern of trade they predict is inter-industry trade, i.e. trade between different industries. There is no room for the simultaneous import and export of the same good within the same industry, i.e. intra-industry trade.

In reality, however, both inter-industry trade and intra-industry trade take place. That developing countries export materials and primary products to industrialised countries in exchange for manufactured goods is a good example of inter-industry trade. Intra-industry trade, however, is a dominant component of trade in manufactured goods among industrialised countries. With the establishment of the EEC, the phenomenon of intra-industry trade among member countries became a particularly distinguished feature in international trade. Contrary to the predictions of inter-industry trade (for example, suggesting that French grain would exchange for German machinery), much of the trade that happened was within the same industry (for example, German cars are traded for French cars). How is intra-industry trade to be explained?

17.2.2 *Explaining intra-industry trade*

The phenomenon of intra-industry trade, in part, is a statistical aggregation problem due to the difficulty of defining an industry. International trade data are recorded according to categories defined at different levels of disaggregation. The most common classification system in international trade is the Standard International Trade Classification (SITC), now in its third revision. SITC divides industries into 10 major sections,[2] with each section being divided into up to 10 divisions; in turn, each division is divided into up to 10 groups, and so on. SITC is numerical, with more digits indicating greater detail. Table 17.1 is an example of SITC classification. It is apparent from the example that an industry at the three-digit level would have a higher share of intra-industry trade than that defined at the four-digit level. Nevertheless, most studies in intra-industry trade regard the three-digit SITC group as an industry.

In contrast to the above theories of inter-industry trade, the explanations of intra-industry trade are centred on scale economies and product differentiation. First, product differentiation is related to the fact that people have diversified preferences for different commodities. The initial development of products within a country normally reflects the domestic pattern of preferences. Secondly, the tendency and presence of economies of scale in industrial production induce firms to narrow down the range of products produced and concentrate on the production of particular products for which domestic demand is the greatest. The combination of different preferences and economies of scale provides the basis for international trade within the same industry.

Let us take cars, for an example. Some people prefer a big family car, some a mini, some a sports car, and so on. If every type of car were met by domestic production, then the car producers would be unable to reap the benefits of economies of scale. It is very likely that the prices would be so high for some types of cars that people would be unwilling to buy them. Therefore,

Table 17.1 An example of Standard International Trade Classification

Section 7:	Machinery and transport equipment
Division 77:	Electrical machinery, apparatus & appliances
Group 775:	Household type, electrical and non-electrical equipment
Subgroup 775.1:	Household laundry equipment, whether or not electrical
Sub-subgroup 775.11:	Household laundry-type washing machine (including machine with wash & dry), each of a dry linen capacity net 10 kg

producers of cars tend to specialise in a limited range of cars where domestic demand is the greatest to benefit from economies of scale. With international trade, each manufacturer of cars faces a much larger market. If each of them specialises in a limited range of products and sell them to different countries, then they can reap the benefit of economies of scale while consumers worldwide enjoy a much wider choice of cars.

17.3   Trends and structure of UK trade

International trade refers to exchanges of goods and services across national boundaries. The shipment of physical goods and commodities is called visible trade because this kind of trade is observable. International trade also involves invisible trade. Invisible trade includes three parts: first the export and import of services such as shipping, banking and tourism; secondly the receipt and payment of interest, profits and dividends; and thirdly some unilateral transfers. They are called invisible trade because they are basically financial transactions and do not involve shipments of physical objects.

In value terms visible trade, i.e. imports and exports of goods, accounted for about 80 per cent of UK trade in goods and services in 1993. Therefore we concentrate on visible trade. In this section we look at the longer-term trends in UK trade. We shall examine the changes in the composition of the UK trade, first by commodity and then by region. We shall then focus on the trade performance of the United Kingdom in manufacturing goods compared with other major industrialised countries. We will find evidence that there is a general trend of decline in the international competitive performance of UK manufacturing trade, although the trend has been reversed to some extent since the second half of the 1980s.

17.3.1   Commodity composition of UK trade

The traditional pattern of UK trade involved UK manufactures being exchanged for food and basic materials with the bulk of trade being with the Commonwealth countries. This has changed dramatically, however, especially in the 1970s when several important events happened. Three factors in particular have affected UK trade. The first two factors are closely related: one is the oil price rise in 1973 and the further increase that took place in 1979, and the other is the exploitation of North Sea oil. The third factor is the United Kingdom's accession to the European Union.

Figures 17.1 and 17.2 show the commodity composition of UK exports and imports since 1960. In terms of exports, the importance of manufactures to UK trade has not changed during the last 30 years. Semi-manufactures and finished manufactures exports together constitute around 80 per cent of UK exports in merchandise goods during this period, except for the years of 1979–85, when the exports of fuel increased, with the importance of finished

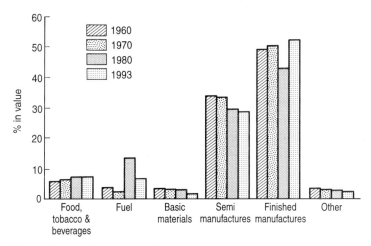

Figure 17.1 Commodity composition of UK exports.
Source: Annual Abstract of Statistics, various issues.

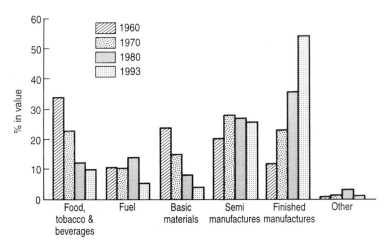

Figure 17.2 Commodity composition of UK imports.
Source: Annual Abstract of Statistics, various issues.

manufactures increased slightly matched by the equivalent decline of semi-finished manufactures. Finished manufactured goods accounted for around half of UK exports from 1960 to 1978 and during 1979–85 this share was reduced to about 40 per cent, again reflecting the relative importance of fuel exports during this period. However, from the second half of the 1980s we have seen a steady increase in finished manufactured exports.[3] By 1993 they accounted for about 53 per cent of UK exports. The rise in manufactured exports is a result of structural improvements in the United Kingdom's export performance. The importance of fuel in UK exports from 1979 to 1985 was the result of North Sea oil development. In general, the export composition of UK trade has been rather stable since 1960.

In contrast to exports, the commodity composition of UK imports has changed dramatically. Historically the United Kingdom has been an importer of food and basic materials. In 1960, food and beverages accounted for more than one-third of imports while basic materials accounted for 30 per cent. By 1993 food and basic materials together constituted only about 14 per cent of total imports. The fall in food imports can be attributed to two factors: first, an increasing proportion of food demand is met by domestic production and secondly, a falling share of personal expenditure is spent on food. The decline in imports of basic materials reflects the tendency for producer countries to undertake processing of primary products up to the semi-finished or even finished stage. The falls in food and basic materials imports are mirrored by an increase in the proportion of manufactured goods imports. The share of manufactured goods constituted around 54 per cent of UK imports in 1993, compared with only 13 per cent in 1960. This reflects the increased importance of intra-industry trade in UK manufactures which we will further examine in the following sections. For fuels, the share increased dramatically during 1974–5 after the oil price rise. It then returned to about the earlier levels from 1976 as a result of North Sea oil development. From 1986 the expenditure on fuel imports was reduced dramatically due to self-sufficiency in fuel and the fall in the oil price.

17.3.2   Regional composition of UK trade

Figures 17.3 and 17.4 show the regional composition of UK imports and exports since 1960. The most striking feature is that UK trade with the EU has increased substantially during the last 30 years or so. It should be noted that the importance of EU members had already increased since the 1960s before the United Kingdom's accession, although after 1973 this process accelerated somewhat. In value terms, both EU shares of UK imports and exports were around 26 per cent in 1966, whereas by 1993, these shares had nearly doubled. The increases in trade with the EU countries have occurred at the expense of other regions. First, the importance of Commonwealth Countries in UK trade has declined dramatically, especially Canada, New Zealand and Australia. Secondly, the dependence on trade with non-oil developing countries is reduced especially on the export side. Thirdly, the importance of other developed countries to UK trade has also been reduced; imports from North America, especially, were reduced. The share of oil exporting countries in UK imports peaked in 1974 due to the oil price rise; it then kept falling. This

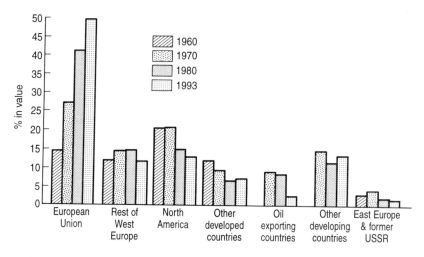

Figure 17.3 UK exports by destination.
Source: Annual Abstract of Statistics, various issues.

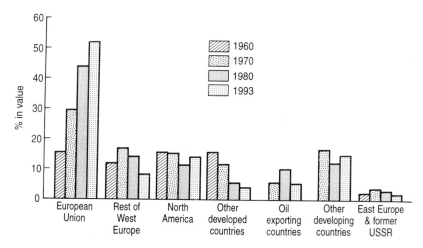

Figure 17.4 UK imports by source.
Source: Annual Abstract of Statistics, various issues.

reflected the declining importance of the oil exporting countries as a source of UK imports because of the development of North Sea Oil. The oil exporting countries, however, became important markets for UK exports during 1975–83 as a result of their increased demand due to the increased income brought by the oil price rises in this period. From the second half of the 1980s, the share of UK exports to the oil exporting countries returned to the pre-1973 level. The importance of Japan as a supplier to the UK market has increased steadily over time, but it still only supplies about 6 per cent of UK imports.

17.3.3 UK manufactures export performance

As observed above, manufacturing exports have been very important to the United Kingdom, and as far as the United Kingdom's own export composition is concerned manufacturing exports still constitute an important share. However, the United Kingdom has long experienced a declining proportion in manufacturing exports. Table 17.2 shows the volume indexes and unit value indexes of United Kingdom and other major developed countries' manufactured exports.

Table 17.2 shows that UK manufacturing exports growth in volume terms

Table 17.2 Volume and unit value indexes of manufactured exports

Volume indexes of manufacturing exports (1980 = 100)							
	1960	1965	1970	1975	1980	1985	1990
Developed countries	21	31	53	73	100	120	156
UK	43	50	68	85	100	106	142
USA	27	35	49	75	100	82	135
Japan	8	19	39	64	100	144	164
Germany	22	33	59	74	100	129	159
France	21	29	49	74	100	109	152
Canada	18	27	58	70	100	151	193
Italy	13	27	49	70	100	127	143

Unit value indexes of manufacturing exports (1980 = 100)							
	1960	1965	1970	1975	1980	1985	1990
Developed countries	29	31	34	63	100	86	136
UK	24	26	28	50	100	79	132
USA	33	34	41	65	100	123	145
Japan	36	32	37	66	100	95	136
Germany	27	29	31	64	100	75	137
France	28	30	32	64	100	81	130
Canada	43	41	47	70	100	105	121
Italy	33	32	35	63	100	81	160

Note: Value indexes are compiled in US dollars. Before 1985, developed economies include Belgium, Luxembourg, USA, Japan, Former West Germany, Canada, Netherlands, Sweden, Switzerland, United Kingdom, Italy and France. After 1985, apart from the above countries, all other EU and EFTA countries are included in the Developed Countries indexes.
Source: UN Statistical Yearbook, 1983/84, 1993.

fell short of the growth by the developed countries as a group in the 1960–85 period, and far short of the major industrialised countries listed in the Table. However, from the second half of the 1980s, UK manufacturing exports grew very rapidly in volume and outgrew most of the major industrialised countries. How are the changes explained?

The progressive decline of the United Kingdom's share in the total exports of manufactured goods of developed countries and the increased penetration[4] of the UK market have often been interpreted as evidence of a general lack of competitive edge in British industry to foreign industry. One measure of competitiveness is the relative prices of traded goods between the United Kingdom and her trading partners. Changes in the relative prices of traded goods can be caused by two factors: one is productivity and, therefore, unit labour costs, and the other is the movements in exchange rates. As mentioned in Section 17.1.1, relative prices are very important in the direction of trade. Other things being equal, a fall in relative prices between the United Kingdom and other countries could lead to an increase in the demand for British-made goods. Empirical studies on the effect of relative prices on export performance are not conclusive, however. Caves and Krause (1980) suggest that there were relative price changes in the 1970s either because of exchange rate changes or inflation. However, due to real wage resistance, the United Kingdom could not achieve a sustained improvement in competitiveness. A study by the Bank of England (1994) shows that UK relative costs and prices did not fall in the second half of the 1980s when the United Kingdom's manufacturing exports grew rapidly, although the delayed effect of the fall in relative costs and prices in the first half of the 1980s may have had an impact.

Relative prices or costs are important in determining the direction of trade; however, other factors also affect trade. One important factor is the different rates of growth in demand in the United Kingdom and elsewhere. The Bank of England (1994) shows that between 1970 and 1985, the decline in the UK share in her major export markets' manufacturing imports was in part the result of the slower-than-average growth in the markets. Between 1985 and 1990, the increase in UK export market share was partly a result of faster-than-average growth in those markets.

Therefore, empirical evidence suggests that changes in the relative prices of UK exports and the different relative growth rates of demand in the United Kingdom and abroad seem to explain the changes in UK manufacturing exports only in part. This is hardly surprising, because it is extremely difficult to isolate the causes of trade performance due to the fact that there are different interrelated factors involved and the weight attached to each is difficult to establish and may vary over time.

With regard to the better performance of UK manufacturing exports, the Bank of England (1994) suggests that this is due to the structural improvement which is represented by an increased level of demand for and supply of UK produced manufactured goods at given levels of the exchange rate, and of aggregate demand. One factor suggested by Muellbauer and Murphy (1990) is that UK exports in the 1980s benefited from a fall in the growth of world trade relative to output. Landesmann and Snell (1993) suggest that the United Kingdom may have benefited from bilateral trade barriers between the United States and Japan as there are observed worsening trade shares for these two countries.

Now we turn to the unit-value indexes of UK manufactures exports. Unlike the volume indexes, UK unit-value indexes of manufactures exports growth is more or less in line with the developed countries. The different movement between the volume and unit-value indexes suggests that changes in export volumes, rather than prices, accounted for most of the decline of UK manufactures in world total exports.

17.3.4   Import penetration and export sales of UK trade

In the above section we considered mainly the export performance of UK manufactured goods. In this section we further consider UK manufactures trade, but in terms of both imports and exports. Figures 17.5 and 17.6 show the ratio of imports to home demand and the ratio of exports to manufacturer's sales for a number of important manufacturing industries. The former ratio indicates the extent to which foreign imports compete with domestically

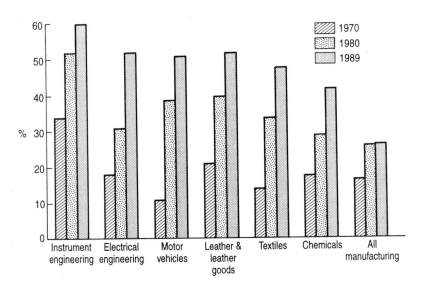

Figure 17.5   Import penetration ratio of manufacturing industries.
Source: Annual Abstract of Statistics, 1981 and 1994.

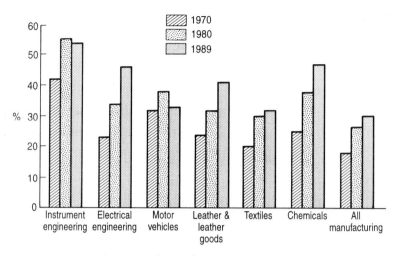

Figure 17.6 Export/sales ratio of manufacturing industries.
Source: Annual Abstract of Statistics, 1981 and 1994.

produced goods while the latter shows the relative importance of exports to total home production.

17.4 Trade policy

National governments adopt various policies towards international trade. These policies are designed with the objective of protecting domestic producers against foreign competition.

Tariffs are the oldest form of trade policy. They are taxes levied on foreign goods entering into the country. They may be levied as a certain percentage of the value of imports, for example, a 17 per cent tariff is imposed on clothing items entering EU countries. Tariffs may also be levied as a specific amount per unit of import, for example, £2 per barrel of oil imported. In either case, the tariff will increase the cost of imports.

Tariffs have traditionally been used as a source of government revenue. However, import duties are generally introduced not only to provide revenue but to protect particular domestic producers. The Corn Law in the early nineteenth century, for example, was used by the UK government to protect agriculture from import competition. The importance of tariffs has declined in modern times largely as a result of successive rounds of tariff reductions, especially in manufactured goods, achieved through GATT.

However, due to the rise of unemployment and slow growth in industrial countries during the 1970s and 1980s, and changes in comparative advantage and competitiveness, the use of non-tariff barriers (NTBs) in the form of quantitative restrictions, subsidies, and administrative measures have become prevalent. This is known as the 'new protectionism', in comparison to the use of tariffs referred to as the 'old protectionism'.

The most widespread use of NTBs is in the form of 'Voluntary Export Restraints' (VERs) or 'Orderly Marketing Arrangements' (OMAs). Both measures are quantitative restrictions on exports of a product, agreed between the exporting country and the importing country. They are normally negotiated for a specific period and administered by the exporting country. Exporting countries enter this kind of agreement because they face a threat that, otherwise, they may be subject to unilateral, and most likely, more stringent limitations.

The classical argument for trade protection is the infant industry argument. It is argued that a domestic firm may have a long-term comparative advantage in a product, but be discouraged from the starting point because of set-up costs and the initial losses before the learning-by-doing effects are realised. Hence a trade barrier may be desirable to protect the infant industry from foreign competition during the initial period, and then be removed when the domestic industry becomes competitive. The infant industry argument has been used in less developed countries, but it does not explain the existence of protection in long-established industries in the industrialised countries such as textiles and clothing. The infant industry argument also has flaws in itself. In particular, the fact that it is costly and time consuming to establish an industry is not an argument for government intervention, especially in advanced market economies. If there is no market failure, and if an industry is supposed to be able to earn high returns on factors of production, why do private investors not develop the industry without government intervention? Sometimes it is argued that private investors take into account only the current returns in an industry and fail to take into account the future prospects, but this is not consistent with market behaviour.

More recent arguments for trade protection are the strategic trade policy arguments. The arguments stem from a recognition that most industries do not operate under perfectly competitive market conditions as described by the theory of comparative advantage. If international markets are imperfect then firms in the industry will be able to make excess returns. These excess returns will create a divergence between private and social benefits, and protection could then be justified by the proposition that strategic trade policy can shift the terms of international trade to the domestic industry's advantage. Clearly, these strategic trade policy arguments rest on the idea that an individual country can gain through protection. This naturally leads us to ask whether protection would result in any worldwide benefit or merely involves a transfer of wealth from one country to another. In the latter case, then it would inevitably lead to retaliation. Therefore, we have to treat these arguments cautiously unless concrete empirical evidence suggests otherwise.

17.5 UK trade policy in practice

The United Kingdom's trade policy since the Second World War has been significantly influenced by the international environment. The GATT and the European Union are particularly important to the United Kingdom's trade policy.

The 1930s saw widespread protectionism when countries retaliated against each other by imposing tariffs and quotas during the Great Depression. International trade and prosperity were greatly reduced as a consequence. To avoid repetition of the inter-war experiences, the General Agreement on Tariffs and Trade (GATT) was established in 1947 and became effective on 1 January 1948. The objectives of GATT are to reduce and remove trade barriers in international trade. The reduction and removal of trade barriers under GATT take place through a succession of multinational trade negotiations, which are called rounds. There have so far been eight rounds of GATT negotiations and the most recent Uruguay Round was concluded in 1993.

The Uruguay Round has covered virtually every sector of world trade. For the first time, trade in services is brought into GATT multilateral disciplines. Subsidies in agriculture are set to be reduced. Trade protection in textiles and clothing under the Multi-fibre Agreement (MFA) will be phased out gradually over the next ten years. From 1995 GATT is replaced by the World Trade Organisation (WTO), based in Geneva, with all members of GATT as contracting parties.

Unlike the multilateral tariff reductions of the GATT, the European Union[5] has aimed at the reduction and removal of internal trade barriers among its member countries only. By 1977 all industrial tariffs between EU members at that time and the European Free Trade Association (EFTA) members were removed. The most significant step taken by the EU since then is the Single Market initiative, which became fully effective on 1 January 1993. With the Single Market, national boundaries between member countries no longer exist as far as trade is concerned. Therefore trade within the EU is, in principle at least, completely free.

The Common External Tariff (CET) forms an integral part of the European Union and it has provided the basis for the Union's Common Commercial Policy (CCP). Therefore, the European Union negotiates trade policy as a single entity in international and bilateral negotiations and decisions on trade policy are mostly taken at the European Union level rather than at the individual national level.

The EU has played an active part in all the GATT negotiations on the basis of common positions which have frequently been the result of long and painful intra-EU bargaining. The CET has been progressively reduced, reaching an average of about 5 per cent after the implementation of the Tokyo Round (1979) agreements. However, high tariffs have survived in some sensitive sectors such as textiles and clothing as well as consumer electronics. The recently concluded Uruguay Round of GATT negotiations has reached agreement on the progressive liberalisation of textiles and clothing trade, as indicated above.

Probably the most important trade policy of the EU, and one of most concern to the United Kingdom, is the Common Agricultural Policy (CAP). Agriculture has been outside the GATT framework from the very beginning, largely because of the insistence of the United States that it keeps its domestic policies on agriculture outside international agreement. The subsequent development of the EU's CAP has made the Americans regret bitterly their earlier approach. The CAP gives preferences to the Union through a system of variable import levies and export subsidies. The former ensure that imports cannot sell below domestically produced goods while the latter is intended to cover the difference between the EU and world prices. The costs of the CAP are borne by EU taxpayers. A nation such as the United Kingdom, which consumes food and pays taxes to the EU but has a below average per capita agricultural output, is clearly penalised by the CAP.

Because of its strongly discriminatory nature, the CAP has attracted a great deal of criticism from other countries, especially the United States. The strong resistance of the EU kept agricultural trade practices outside the GATT framework until the Uruguay Round. However, due to the high cost of the CAP and strengthening international pressure, the EU has finally agreed to cut its agricultural subsidies progressively.

Since the Second World War, the United Kingdom has faced a persistent problem with her balance of payments. The United Kingdom adopted quantitative restrictions on imports in the 1950s and the Labour governments in the 1960s imposed a temporary import surcharge, but changes in the international trade environment have greatly affected the United Kingdom's trade policy. As a member of GATT (and now the new WTO), the United Kingdom has had to comply with the successive GATT rounds of tariff reductions. As a member of the EU, her trade relations with developing countries and the rest of Europe are also changed. Under the Lomé Convention, all imports to the EU from many of the least developed countries are duty free. Less developed countries (LDCs) have also been granted more favourable treatment under the Generalised System of Preferences (GSP). The EU has conducted its trade with LDCs under the GSP since 1971, and the previous duty-free trade between Britain and the Commonwealth countries was mostly replaced by the GSP tariff regime. Hence for Britain's trading partners in the Commonwealth, the move to GSP rules usually entailed a less favourable tariff regime than had operated previously. EFTA, of which the United Kingdom was a member, has long had free trade with the EU. Finally, the EU also has a preferential trading agreement with Mediterranean countries.

The changes in Eastern Europe have also had an impact on the EU's trade policy. The EU has signed, with Hungary, Poland, the Czech Republic, the Slovak Republic, Romania and Bulgaria, the so-called Europe Agreements.

These agreements are intended to create a free trade area within a period of 10 years, with a shorter timetable of liberalisation on the EU side.

17.6 Summary and conclusion

International trade occurs because countries are different. Countries are different in their production efficiency, their factor endowments, or their preferences. By specialising in things they do relatively well and exchanging with each other, all countries benefit. International trade also takes place because countries can exploit economies of scale through trade.

International trade is an important part of the United Kingdom's economic life. The traditional trade pattern of exporting manufactures in exchange for food and basic materials, with the bulk of trade taking place between the United Kingdom and the Commonwealth countries, has changed dramatically, especially since the 1970s. The most striking change in the commodity composition of UK trade is the rapid increase of manufacturing imports and the declining share of UK manufacturing exports in world trade. The higher import penetration of manufactured goods reflects the relative importance of intra-industry trade in manufactures between the United Kingdom and other developed countries and the declining importance of food and basic materials in UK imports. The falling share of UK manufactures in world exports during 1960–85 was related to the declining competitiveness of UK industry, although it is very difficult to isolate the precise factors that caused this decline. The improved performance of UK manufactured exports from the late 1980s is regarded by some as the revival of UK competitiveness in international trade. In terms of regional composition, the European Union has become increasingly important to the United Kingdom as a trade partner with the importance of Commonwealth countries, other developing countries and North America correspondingly reduced.

Both tariff barriers and non-tariff barriers are employed by national governments to protect domestic industries from foreign competition. The use of NTBs has become very popular from the 1970s. The justification for the use of trade barriers includes the traditional infant industry argument and the more recent strategic trade policy arguments. These arguments are not without flaws and have to be treated with care.

The international trade environment has changed significantly compared with the first half of the century. GATT and the subsequent multilateral trade negotiations under GATT have greatly lowered tariff barriers, particularly in manufactures. The recent Uruguay Round has covered nearly every aspect of international trade. For the first time in more than 30 years, trade in textiles and clothing will be brought into GATT disciplines. Trade in agriculture will be liberalised progressively. The European Union has made significant progress in liberalising trade among its member countries. The EU has a common commercial policy and most trade policy decisions are taken at the Union level.

Being a member of GATT (now the WTO) and the EU, the United Kingdom has become very open in international trade.

Questions for discussion

1. According to the theory of comparative advantage, what are the causes of international trade and what do they imply about its likely direction?
2. The Heckscher–Ohlin model of international trade suggests that different factor endowments are a major cause of international trade. Can you find some examples of such trade in real life?
3. What are the major differences between the assumptions of theories explaining inter-industry trade and intra-industry trade?
4. How has the phenomenon of intra-industry trade been explained?
5. What are the major changes in the commodity composition of UK trade during the last 30 years? What are the causes of these changes?
6. The United Kingdom has long experienced a declining share in world manufacturing trade. What are the factors that brought about this decline?
7. There has been a steady improvement in the United Kingdom's manufacturing exports performance since the second half of the 1980s. What are the explanations for this change?
8. Assess the impact of the United Kingdom's European Union membership on the trade pattern and trade policy of the United Kingdom.
9. What are the major instruments of trade policy?
10. Examine the validity of infant industry and the strategic trade policy arguments for the use of trade policy.

Notes

1. Ohlin received the Nobel Prize in economics in 1977.
2. The 10 sections are as follows. Section 0 is food and live animals; section 1 is beverages and tobacco; section 2 crude materials; section 3 fuels; section 4 animal and vegetable oils; section 5 chemicals; section 6 manufactured goods; section 7 machinery and transport equipment; section 8 miscellaneous manufactured goods; section 9 miscellaneous.
3. See Section 17.3.3 for more detailed information about this change and for a fuller analysis of UK manufacturing exports performance.
4. See Section 17.3.4 for details on the import penetration of manufactured goods in the UK market.
5. For information on the European Union, see Chapter 18.

References and further reading

Bank of England (1994) 'UK trade – long term trends and recent development' *Bank of England Quarterly Bulletin* August pp. 223 – 30.

Caves, R.E. and Krause, L.B. (eds) (1980) *Britain's Economic Performance*, Washington: Brookings Institution.

Central Statistical Office (various years) *Annual Abstract of Statistics*, London: HMSO.

Forman-Peck, J. (1991) 'Trade and balance of payments' in Crafts, N.F.R. and Woodward, N. (eds) *The British Economy since 1945*, Oxford: Clarendon Press.

Greenaway, D. (1983) *Current Issues in International Trade*, London: Macmillan.

Hecksher, E. (1919) 'The effect of foreign trade on the distribution of income' *Ekonomisk Tidskerift* 21 pp. 497–512. (A new translation is provided by Flam and Flanders (1991) (eds) in *Hecksher – Ohlin Trade Theory*, Cambridge, Mass: MIT Press.

Hewer, A. (1980) 'Manufacturing industry in the seventies: an assessment of import penetration and export performance' *Economic Trends* 320 pp. 97–109.

Hine, R.C. (1985) *The Political Economy of European Trade*, Hemel Hempstead: Harvester Wheatsheaf.

Landesmann, M. and Snell, A (1993) 'Structural shift in the manufacturing export performance of OECD economies' *Journal of Applied Econometrics* 8 pp. 149–62.

Mansell, K. (1980) 'UK visible trade in the post-war years' *Economic Trends* 324 pp.136–50.

Muellbauer, J. and Murphy, A. (1990) 'Is the UK balance of payments sustainable?' *Economic Policy* 11 October pp. 348–82.

Ohlin, B. (1933) *Interregional and International Trade*, Cambridge, Mass: Harvard University Press.

Ricardo, D. (1963) *The Principles of Political Economy and Taxation*, Homewood, Il.: Irwin.

CHAPTER 18

The European Union's impact on UK economic policy

ANDREW SCOTT

18.1 Introduction

After two unsuccessful applications during the 1960s, Britain (along with Ireland and Denmark) finally became a member of the then European Community[1] on 1 January 1973. This was the first enlargement of the European Union (EU) which, until then, included only the six founder-member countries of France, West Germany, Italy, Belgium, the Netherlands and Luxembourg. In 1981 Greece became the 10th member of the EU, while in 1986 the accession of Spain and Portugal took Community membership to 12 member countries. The mid-1990s have witnessed a further enlargement, with the accession of three EFTA countries – Finland, Sweden and Austria – from 1 January 1995. Interestingly, Norway voted against joining the Union at that point. At the end of the decade, it is possible that some of the former centrally planned, East European states might already be negotiating their membership.

In this chapter we examine the structure and economic policies of the European Union. In Section 18.2 we set out the basic analytical framework used by economists to examine the economic effect of international integration. In Section 18.3 we examine the development of the Union's economic policy and the manner in which this has impacted on the British economy. In Section 18.4 we consider the future development of the Union and in Section 18.5 we offer some concluding thoughts.

18.2 International economic integration

18.2.1 Basic concepts

The European Union is first and foremost an economic arrangement. It is based on the creation of a *common market* (Treaty of Rome, Article 3). A common market is an area in which all goods, services, capital and labour that originate in one participating (or member) country shall enjoy unfettered access to all other participating (or member) countries. Economic integration occurs as a consequence of the removal of those barriers that currently segment both national product (goods and services) markets and national factor (labour and capital) markets. As we now see, a common market is one of four distinct stages, or levels, of international economic integration.

Free trade area

A free trade area describes a situation in which all physical barriers to trade (in both goods and services) between member countries are removed. Thus tariff barriers and import quotas are eliminated and consumers throughout the area are able to buy products from the lowest cost supplier inside the area. However, in the free trade area each country continues to have complete freedom to determine trade policy towards non- participating countries. This means that customs posts between members of the free trade area must be retained to ensure that products originating in non-participating countries are not 'deflected' to one country through a partner country which has a less restrictive external trade policy.

Economic theory tells us that the process of commodity arbitrage will ensure that an immediate impact of participation in a free trade area will be the removal of all national price differences for identical goods – that is, the 'law of one price' for traded goods and services will pertain within the area. However, because countries retain national control over trade policy with non-participating countries, the law of one price will not extend to imports originating outside the area.

Customs union

A customs union is a free trade area which also provides for a *common external tariff* with respect to trade with non-participating countries. Because the customs union is characterised by a single, common, external trade policy, imports to the customs union are subject to identical treatment regardless of the country through which these enter the union. Consequently, all internal economic frontiers in the customs union can be completely dismantled. In a customs union the law of one price will, in principle, also apply to imports originating outside the union.

Common market

A common market is a customs union with the additional provision that labour and capital (factors of production) are free to move within the area. The common market represents a higher stage in the process of economic integration as not only are national product markets integrated, as is the case with the customs union, but so too are national factor markets.

An important economic consequence of the shift from a customs union to a common market is that the law of one price that hitherto has applied only to trade products should now operate with equal force in factor markets. This suggests that in a common market there will be a tendency towards the equalisation of factor returns; that is, national differences in both wage rates and interest payments on capital invested will be removed as both labour and capital move within the common market to take advantage of the highest returns available.

Economic and monetary union

An economic and monetary union is a common market in which national monetary and fiscal policies are unified. Essentially the members of an economic and monetary union surrender autonomy over virtually all the instruments of national economic (monetary and fiscal) policy. National economies effectively vanish to be replaced by one super-economy in which countries become constituent states or regions. An economic and monetary union combines all of the characteristics of a common market, but goes further. Monetary union means that national currencies disappear to be replaced by a single, common, currency. Consequently, national central banks are replaced by a union-wide central bank which alone determines the monetary policy for the union as a whole.

18.2.2 Integration and economic efficiency

(a) The static effects

The economic effects of integration are analysed using a framework developed by Professor Jacob Viner during the 1950s and universally referred to as 'customs union theory'. Before Viner's contribution, the dominant view was that integration must raise economic welfare among the participating countries, as it involved the dismantling of trade barriers and was thus a step in the direction of universal free trade. In short, integration would *always* benefit the participating countries as they would be able to exploit the classical gains from trade. Viner suggested that this view was incorrect. This somewhat paradoxical conclusion emerges from the distinction Viner drew between 'trade creation' and 'trade diversion'.

Trade creation refers to additional (or new) trade that is created between partners in the customs union following the removal of trade barriers. Thereafter, consumers throughout the union have access to the lowest cost supplier and inefficient producers – those who previously survived only by virtue of protection from external competition – are forced out of business. The result is an improvement in the efficiency of resource allocation throughout the union and a corresponding increase in consumer welfare. The extent to which trade creating gains are available to a potential member of a customs union will be a key factor in determining the merits of membership.

Trade diversion, which is welfare reducing for the union as a whole, occurs when membership of a customs union results in consumers switching from a low-cost supplier outside the union to a higher-cost source of supply inside the union. Trade diversion occurs because all tariffs on imports from the partner countries are removed, whereas the tariff continues to apply to imports originating outside the union. The import tax has two effects. First, it protects national suppliers from more efficient external suppliers and secondly, it redistributes income from consumers to beneficiaries of subsequent higher public spending or lower taxes (see Sloman, 1991, Chapter 21).

In practice, membership of a customs union is likely to involve elements of trade creation and trade diversion. As we will see this was certainly true when Britain joined the EU. The extent to which welfare-enhancing trade creation or welfare-reducing trade diversion dominates will depend very much on the specific characteristics of the countries forming the union. However, we can make some general observations on the basis of Viner's two welfare effects.

Trade creation will be greater the more intense is the degree of competition in the industrial structures of the countries forming the customs union. This conclusion follows from the fact that a greater share of high-cost production will be displaced when the removal of trade barriers is between economies which have competitive rather than complementary production structures.

The extent to which trade diversion occurs will depend upon the height of the tariff imposed for the union as a whole. The higher the external tariff protecting the union as a whole then the greater is the likelihood that trade diversion will occur. This conclusion can be most easily understood if one remembers that a customs union which has a zero external tariff is in fact satisfying the condition of universal free trade.

The larger the size of the union – in terms of number of countries participating – then the less likely is trade diversion. Again, in the extreme case in which every country is a member of the union we would effectively have a situation of universal free trade. On the other hand, trade diversion is more likely where only a few countries are involved, as this restricts the opportunity for a relocation of production and consumption.

In practice economists have found the magnitudes of these static effects to be extremely small. In the most studied case, that of the EU, trade creation has been estimated at less than 1 per cent of Union GDP while the magnitude of measured trade diversion has been significantly below this. Although the European Union has been found to be net trade creating, and therefore has raised welfare to consumers, the extent of the gain has been very small. Furthermore, it is widely acknowledged that the static effects of international integration will almost certainly be exceeded by the dynamic effects. These dynamic effects are *not* captured in Viner's comparative static framework.

(b) The dynamic effects

A common criticism of Viner's contribution to the theory of international economic integration is that although he did clarify conditions under which integration would reduce economic efficiency, his analysis focuses exclusively on the static or *impact* effects of the customs union. By so doing, a number of sources of potential economic gain, which together would be likely to exceed trade diverting losses, were ignored. These are the *dynamic* effects of integration. In theory, dynamic effects refer to the consequences of international integration that directly influence the rate of economic growth of the members of the union over time. It is commonly assumed that these dynamic effects are positive in that together they will raise the rate of growth for the union as a whole above the rate which would otherwise be expected. There are two principal sources of dynamic gain from international integration.

The first is *scale economies* in production. Economies of scale refer to the reduction in the unit costs of production that occurs with an increase in the scale of production. After the union has been formed, producers in individual member states will be able to export freely to partner country markets. As a result output will increase and unit costs will fall. The central point is that scale economies provide an added source of consumer gains from international integration. The rate of economic growth is improved as economies of scale release resources to be used in the production of other goods and services. Further, economies of scale may generate additional gains through *external trade creation* which occurs when the cost savings in production allow producers to increase their share of non-union member markets. This increases further the union-wide rate of economic growth.

The second dynamic gain commonly associated with a customs union derives from the intensification of competition that results as barriers to trade are removed. With the removal of barriers, domestic firms now find that their hitherto protected domestic market is being contested by foreign rivals. This forces management to improve its performance in controlling production and administrative costs.

Together, economies of scale and competitive effects constitute the main sources of dynamic gains from economic integration. This does not, however, exhaust all the possible dynamic gains. For example, it is possible that membership of a customs union will cause an acceleration in the pace of technological development if the growth in firm size associated with servicing a larger market increases the earnings available for corporate research and development. Further, servicing a larger market means that the risks associated with research and development can be spread over a higher number of consumers. A conclusion from the analysis of dynamic effects arising from international integration is that even where membership of a customs union results in a measure of trade diversion adversely affecting economic welfare in one country, this might be more than compensated for by the dynamic gains from integration.

18.3   The economics of the European Union

18.3.1   *The foundations of the common market*

The European Union is first and foremost an economic arrangement based on the principles of a common market. Consequently the Treaty of Rome establishing the European Economic Community (as it was called at that time) provides for the elimination of all barriers to the free internal movement of goods, services, capital and labour and the adoption of a common external policy concerning trade between member and non-member countries. It also seeks to ensure that this liberalisation of intra-Community trade would result in greater competition within the Union, leading to gains in consumer welfare, by setting out the basic principles of a common competition policy to apply in all member countries.

It was realised from the outset that establishing a common market would be a lengthy process. Not only would this involve the abolition of a large number of formal impediments to implementing the 'four freedoms' (i.e. the free movement of goods, services, capital and labour), there was also a wide range of technical obstacles in the form of national laws and regulations that would have to be harmonised before a common market could become a reality. This too would take time. However, in order that the foundation of the common market could speedily be put in place, the Treaty of Rome set out a 12-year timetable during which the minimum steps of eliminating all formal barriers (i.e. tariffs and quotas) to intra-Community trade would take place. In practice, this was achieved by July 1968, some 18 months ahead of schedule. The same timetable was successfully applied to the introduction of a common external tariff. Of course, the common external tariff did not mean that all elements in the external economic policy of member countries were harmonised and determined at the Union level. Non-tariff barriers to trade remained firmly under the control of individual member countries and these were used, in part at least, to compensate for the loss of national sovereignty over formal trade policies.

In addition to establishing the free trade basis of the common market, the Treaty of Rome called for the introduction of a common agricultural policy (CAP) and a common transport policy. Although a common transport policy never materialised, the CAP was in place by the mid-1960s. Thereafter, all aspects relating to agricultural policy in Union countries were determined exclusively at the Union level. The two key objectives of the CAP were to provide a fair income to farmers and to ensure that consumers had reliable access to foodstuffs at reasonable prices. The former would be secured through the principle of intervention buying or selling by Union agencies with a view to ensuring that market prices never differ significantly from a predetermined 'target' price. This target price is fixed by agreement between the agricultural ministers from the member countries, and should reflect the interests of consumers as well as those of producers. In practice, however, the interests of consumers have been secondary to the political need to fix the target price at that level that ensures a reasonable income is received by the least efficient farmer. The result has been that efficient producers have tended to increase production as much as possible in order to take advantage of the relatively high (compared to world market) Union prices, thereby creating the massive agricultural surpluses that have become such a feature of Union farming.

Finally, under the Treaty of Rome a European Social Fund (ESF) and a European Investment Bank (EIB) were established. Both agencies were intended to facilitate the transition to a common market. The ESF would assist by providing finance for retraining and resettling unemployed labour while the EIB was to contribute to the 'balanced and steady development of the common market' by providing investment funds for the purpose of aiding the development of backward regions, modernising undertakings or financing schemes of interest to more than one member country.

Initially the Community's economic and social policies were financed from a common budget to which member countries directly contributed revenues. However, from 1980 the Community's budget has been financed by so-called *own resources*. Under this arrangement revenues accruing from the operation of the common external tariff, the agricultural levy, a share of VAT collected in each member state and (from 1988) a contribution based on national GNP are designated as Union revenues to be assigned to the common budget.

By the end of the 1960s, therefore, the Union had successfully laid the foundation of a common market. The intra-Community movement of goods had been freed from all tariff restraints, a common external tariff had been introduced, the CAP was in place, a common indirect taxation system (VAT) had been agreed upon, and limited progress had been made in removing the barriers to the free internal movement of both labour and capital. Despite this, however, significant obstacles to the creation of a 'common market' remained.

The free movement of goods remained an unfulfilled objective due to the plethora of non-tariff barriers (NTBs) to trade that extended over a vast range of consumer and capital goods and which continued to segment national markets and, consequently, undermine competition. Therefore, consumers throughout the Union were failing to enjoy the full benefits of integration as domestic producers remained relatively immune from competition in these (still protected) markets. Many of these NTBs were technical in nature, and took the form of minimum product standards justified on the basis of health and safety. Although Article 100 of the Rome Treaty did empower the Commission to issue proposals for harmonising standards where necessary for the functioning of the common market, these proposals had to have the unanimuous support of the Council of Ministers. Elsewhere, other NTBs continued to distort trade: preferential public procurement, state subsidies to domestic industry and administrative barriers constituted deliberate attempts by national authorities to undermine competition in the Union.

Little progress had been made in achieving free trade in services. On the one hand, for those services purchased by government there was clear national favouritism. This continued throughout the 1970s despite the publication of Commission directives in 1974 and 1976 outlawing this practice. For financial services (banking, insurance, etc.), on the other hand, there were two problems. First, there was an analogous 'health and safety' problem to that preventing comprehensive product market integration, i.e. consumers might find it difficult to take legal action against a services supplier located in a different country. Secondly, for trade in *financial* services to be genuinely free, there would have to be no restrictions on the free movement of capital between member states. The objective of free movement of capital (Articles 67–73) was far from being achieved because member states were simply unwilling to relinquish capital (exchange) controls as an instrument of their macro economic policy.

Finally, although the free movement of labour had become a reality in 1968, when the principle of national priority was abandoned, this did not require member states to recognise professional standards and qualifications awarded elsewhere in the Union. Consequently, the free movement of labour was effectively restricted to a very small subset of the labour supply.

18.3.2   British membership of the EU

Britain's membership of the Union coincided with attempts to accelerate the process of economic integration. In 1969 the Heads of Government of the six founder members had set themselves the target of achieving full economic and monetary union by 1980. In addition, moves would be made to build upon the successes of the 1960s by deepening the degree of integration in both product and factor markets by further measures of both negative and positive integration.

In practice, however, the 1970s turned out to be a disappointing decade for the Union. Rather than building on the successes of the 1960s, the 1970s saw a 'turning-inwards' of national economic policies throughout the Union such that by the end of the decade the process of economic integration had been thrown into reverse. The global recession that was triggered by the oil price rise in 1973 intensified the pressure on governments to protect national producers from foreign competition. In the Union this resulted in an increase in the incidence of non-tariff barriers to trade and not the progressive dismantling of these measures of hidden protectionism that had been planned. At the same time the exchange rate stability that had been a feature of the 1950s and 1960s gave way to a period of considerable volatility with the demise of the Bretton Woods regime in the early 1970s. Finally, rather than removing barriers to the free movement of capital, member countries tended to raise these barriers to even greater heights during the 1970s in an attempt to insulate domestic monetary policy from external forces.

Britain's relations with the Union deteriorated alarmingly during the second half of the 1970s. Despite the result of the consultative referendum conducted in 1975, at which two-thirds of those voting approved of membership of the EU on the renegotiated terms secured by the Labour government, opinion polls soon began to record public disapproval of British membership. There were three main reasons for this change in public opinion.

First, the operation of the CAP manifestly ran counter to the interests of British consumers. In order to protect Union farmers from imports, foodstuffs originating outside the Union were subject to a levy that raised their selling price to slightly above the minimum price which Union farmers were guaranteed. Because world prices were almost always below EU intervention prices, consumers of non-Community foodstuffs bore the full force of this protection. And because the lion's share of the United Kingdom's substantial food imports did come from countries outside the Union, British consumers found themselves disadvantaged by the CAP as food prices increased significantly post-membership.

A second problem related to the net contribution that the British government was making by the end of the 1970s. The CAP was by far the single biggest element of Union expenditure – accounting for up to 75 per cent of total expenditure from the common Union budget. As a net importer of foodstuffs Britain did not benefit from CAP spending. Instead, as food imported from non-EC countries attracted a levy under the rules of the CAP, Britain made a comparatively high gross contribution to the common budget. Even although Britain was a net beneficiary from other aspects of Union policy, most notably the European Regional Development Fund (ERDF), the final result was that Britain was making a net contribution to the Union by 1979 of approximately £1 bn per year. Not only was this widely held to be unfair given the United Kingdom's relatively low share of Union GDP, it was also seen to be linked to an agricultural policy that was capable only of generating enormous surpluses of unwanted foodstuffs.

Finally, Union membership was regarded by many as being partly responsible for the erosion of Britain's manufacturing industry and the associated rise in unemployment. There were two elements to this view. The first concerned the impact of exposing a weakened industry in Britain to the full force of continental competition – especially from Germany. While the proponents of British membership of the Union had steadfastly maintained that greater competition was necessary to shock Britain's industry out of its complacency, critics insisted that this would result in the further decline of manufacturing and, by extension, Britain's already weak balance of payments position. Certainly the evidence by the late 1970s seemed to support the anti-common market lobby. A second adverse consequence of EU membership identified mainly by left-wing critics was that the free-market basis on which the European Union was founded would impose severe constraints on the conduct of national industrial policy in Britain, particularly trade controls and industrial interventionism.

Even with the benefit of hindsight it is difficult to assess whether, on balance, membership of the European Union contributed significantly to the economic problems that Britain experienced during the 1970s. Certainly there is no doubt that the CAP operated to the detriment both of economic efficiency and the British consumer. Not only were consumers required to pay higher prices for foodstuffs after EU membership, but the protectionist element of the CAP encouraged an increase in output from Union farmers when lower cost supplies were available outside the Union. In short, the CAP resulted in trade diversion and, consequently, effected a lowering of economic efficiency and consumer welfare throughout the EU. Moreover, the CAP was directly responsible for the emergence of an unacceptable outcome with regard to Britain's net contribution to the Union budget. On the other hand, however, it is very difficult to attribute the problems of British manufacturing industry during the 1970s to membership of the EU. There is ample evidence that by the time Britain joined the Union its manufacturing industry was already displaying symptoms of long-term decline; and although the exposure to greater competition from other EU partners might well have added to these problems, almost certainly membership of itself did not create any fundamentally new problems.

18.3.3   *Economic integration during the 1980s*

By the end of the 1970s the progress in European economic integration had come virtually to a standstill. Moreover, a political crisis raged over Britain's insistence that both the Union budget and the CAP be fundamentally reformed. This political crisis reached its zenith in the early 1980s when the combative and nationalistic negotiating stance adopted by the new British premier, Margaret Thatcher, replaced the low-key approach preferred by the previous Labour administration. Mrs Thatcher's demands for an immediate reduction in Britain's net contribution to the EU budget were speedily rewarded with temporary rebates over the period 1980–3. In 1984 a 'permanent' solution was found in the form of the British abatement whereby Britain was entitled to claim a rebate from the budget of up to two-thirds of the difference between its share of VAT contributions to the common budget and payments received from that budget.

Britain's aloof stance from the Union increased during this period. In 1979 the European Monetary System (EMS) was introduced as a mechanism designed to create a 'zone of monetary stability' within the European Union.

Since the demise of the Bretton Woods fixed exchange rate arrangements in 1973, exchange rates between EU member states had become increasingly volatile. This reflected, in part, a tendency for individual governments to direct monetary policy at achieving internal objectives without full regard to the external consequences of that policy. At the same time, severing the link between currencies relaxed the pressure on high inflation economies to bring their inflation rate into line with better performing trading partners. As a result, by the end of the 1970s a flexible exchange rate regime was regarded as carrying with it an unacceptable inflationary bias. In turn, the combination of increased exchange rate volatility and high rates of inflation was inhibiting intra-Community trade, thereby jeopardising the gains from economic integration.

The EMS represented a return to a fixed exchange rate arrangement for the EU for the explicit purpose of stabilising the Community's monetary arrangements. Despite the fact that the EMS had its origins in a speech delivered by the then President of the European Union, (Lord) Roy Jenkins, it was not regarded by its French and German architects as a vehicle for launching European monetary union. As we discuss below, however, by the end of the 1980s the EMS had become a vehicle for monetary union. The anti-inflation discipline of the EMS was provided by the exchange rate mechanism (ERM) which defined a maximum permissable deviation for each currency of $\pm$ 2.25 per cemt ($\pm$ 6% for the lira) from a central rate against the ECU – this being a weighted basket of all other currencies in the arrangement. When a currency reached either limit in this range, a combination of domestic policy changes and diversified intervention would be used to stabilise the currency.

Although the United Kingdom did become a member of the EMS, at the very outset the government opted not to participate in the ERM. The main reason for this was that domestic economic policy at that time was based on control of the money supply. Had Britain become a member of the ERM then monetary policy, including interest rate policy, would have to be determined with respect maintaining the declared exchange rate rather than solely domestic considerations such as the level of unemployment or the rate of economic growth. The United Kingdom remained outside of the ERM for the whole of the 1980s, eventually joining the arrangement in October, 1990. However, Britain's membership of the ERM was comparatively short-lived, with sterling exiting the system amid crisis conditions in September 1992. By that time it was clear that there was a fundamental inconsistency between the monetary policy stance necessary to counter domestic recessionary forces and that required to maintain the prevailing exchange rate arrangement with other EU partner countries. Ultimately it was domestic considerations that prevailed.

The UK position with respect to the ERM attracted criticism from many quarters during the 1980s. However, the initial decision to remain outside the arrangement, and the decision to join, have to be seen in the context of the key economic issue that dominated the European Union over the 1980s.

time was right for launching such an ambitious project. The fixed exchange rate arrangement – the Exchange Rate Mechanism (ERM) – which lay at the heart of the European Monetary System (EMS) appeared to have become stable, implying that a progressive convergence in national monetary policies within the participating countries was in any case occurring. If monetary policies were anyway informally converging around a common monetary policy, there would be little controversy in taking the next step to transferring control for essentially similar monetary policies to a common authority. As we discuss in greater detail below, it soon became clear that the stability displayed by the ERM in the growth years of the late 1980s could not be sustained with the onset of recession and the extraordinary conditions surrounding German re-unification.

The Conservative government in the United Kingdom remained extremely sceptical on the issue of monetary union. Domestic political pressure along with significant doubts surrounding the economic consequences of monetary union persuaded Prime Minister John Major that it was not in Britain's interests to make a firm commitment to monetary union. Consequently the TEU includes an opt-out clause whereby the United Kingdom reserves the right not to participate in the single currency arrangement. Subsequently, the Danish Government also secured an opt-out from the monetary union provisions of the TEU. The British position also prevailed on the matter of EU social policy. It had been an aim of some member states that the TEU should include a fourth pillar dealing with social rights and conditions of workers. However, in the face of stiff UK opposition this fourth pillar was relegated to the status of protocol to the TEU with the result that any decisions adopted by EU member states within the social policy area would not have legal force and, consequently, not be binding on individual member states.

In the period that has elapsed since the signing of the TEU there has been a perceptible shift in the balance of opinion concerning progress to monetary union. The TEU had an extremely difficult passage through a number of EU Parliaments. In Denmark the electorate initially rejected the TEU through a referendum, only consenting in a second referendum after the Danish government had secured an opt-out for Denmark from the commitment to move to monetary union. In France the TEU secured the narrowest of majorities in a referendum, while in the United Kingdom the TEU met fierce opposition as it passed through the Parliamentary process with many demanding that the United Kingdom, too, should decide the matter by a public referendum. Only in Ireland did the public express overwhelming support for the Treaty, explained in part no doubt by the fact that Ireland enjoys significant financial benefits by virtue of the operation of the Union's structural funds (see below). Even in those countries where support for the TEU was firmer, it nevertheless became clear that public opinion was increasingly coming to question the direction which European integration was taking. At the very least the debate surrounding the TEU demonstrated that the period of 'passive acquiesence' on the part of Europe's citizens had come to an end.

18.4   Present developments in the European Union

The increasingly troubled economic agenda now faced by the EU is attributable to the decisions taken in the two intergovernmental conferences that produced the Single European Act and the Treaty on European Union. In this section we focus on two internal policy matters; structural policies and monetary union. In both cases the EU has undertaken far-reaching decisions. In the former we have witnessed a significant increase in funds applied towards increasing the economic and social cohesion of the EU. Increasingly, the value of EU structural policies is coming under scrutiny. In the latter case the TEU commits the EU to introducing monetary union by the end of this decade. Monetary union undoubtedly represents the most dramatic shift in European economic arrangements attempted this century. In this section we consider the economic issues that this proposal raises.

18.4.1   Structural policies

In the preceding section we noted that the SEA amended the Rome Treaty by calling for greater efforts to be made to achieve closer economic and social cohesion across the EU. This led to a series of reform proposals designed both to increase the resources available to the Commission to deploy through instruments of regional economic assistance, and to ensure that these instruments operated with greater efficiency than previously.

Economic integration in Europe has always raised fears among the less prosperous regions that they would not share fully in the economic benefits accruing to the area as a whole. While regional disparities in per capita income and levels of employment are commonplace in modern economies, and have traditionally been addressed by instruments of regional economic assistance, successive enlargements of the EU (with the exception of the 1995 enlargement referred to in the introduction) have brought in countries which are at a lower level of economic development than the original six members. The accession of Ireland (1973), Greece (1981) and Spain and Portugal (1986) in particular increased considerably the extent of the economic divide between the richest and poorest regions. Moreover, in addition to the problems of economic backwardness characterising the poorer regions, the EU has regions within the more prosperous member states that were suffering from problems created by the long-term decline of traditional economic activities – shipbuilding, textile production, coal mining and heavy engineering. These regions are characterised by a high incidence of long-term unemployment and significant material deprivation.

The case for a common, EU regional policy which sees a transfer of resources from the prosperous to the less prosperous regions – usually involving an international transfer of assistance – rests on two related propositions.

The first is that the benefits arising from economic integration – that is, the elimination of all barriers to trade – tend to be unevenly distributed with some countries tending to gain more than others. Consider, for instance, the case of the single market programme. Much of the total gain from completing the single market arises due to cost savings associated with the rationalisation of economic activity with inefficient (protected) firms losing out to their more efficient competitors as barriers to market access are removed. Where the benefits from market completion are unevenly distributed geographically, regions that lose economic activity may need to be compensated for their loss by regions that gain. Otherwise there is little incentive for them to continue with the integration process. If, however, the now more prosperous regions are prepared to transfer part of these gains to assist the poorer regions, and to the extent that this assistance is aimed at improving the economic potential of these regions, then it will be in their long-term interests – as well as in the interests of the poorer regions – to participate in the integration process.

The second reason for implementing EU-wide regional policy is more explicitly political and follows from the difficulties that would arise should inter-regional disparities in material conditions between Europe's regions continuously widen. In that event, political support for continuing the process of integration might lessen in the less favoured countries with the result that some member states would come to question the wisdom of membership of the EU. In the final instance support for economic integration will be shaped, in part, by the ability of all member state governments to demonstrate that EU membership is doing no net harm to their economy, or that any damage that is being done is more than compensated for by common action.

Although the Union has had a regional development policy in place since 1975, it was not until the reforms implemented as a direct result of the SEA that this policy began to make a real contribution to resolving the regional problem in the Union. These reforms were implemented in January 1989 and, arguably, led to the establishment – for the first time – of a genuinely common regional policy. Until the 1989 reforms, EU spending on regional assistance had suffered from inadequate resources being spread too thinly over too wide an area.

The 1989 reforms to the operation of the structural funds were based on four principles:

1. Concentration of assistance upon the regions in greatest need.
2. Partnership between local, national and EU agencies in developing and delivering regional economic assistance programmes.
3. Programming of assistance to ensure continuity in the process of regional economic development

4. Additionality whereby EU financial assistance must be matched by equivalent funds being made available from domestic sources in the member states involved.

The decision to concentrate regional assistance resulted in three 'objective regions'. Objective 1 regions are defined as regions in which per capita income is below 75 per cent of the Union average (i.e. the underdeveloped regions) and to which 80 per cent of the entire regional development budget should be applied. Objective 2 regions, which are regions suffering from industrial decline, and Objective 3 regions, are defined as rural and peripheral areas within the EU. In addition, the reforms prioritised two further instruments of economic assistance (under Objectives 3 and 4) relating to support for measures to promote employment prospects for young people and for the long-term unemployed. In both cases eligibility for assistance was determined by need and support would be provided to any area within the EU. Although the changes to the operation of the structural policies could, in themselves, be expected to improve conditions in the qualifying regions, it was also agreed that the resources available to structural operations should be doubled in real terms over the 5-year planning period 1989–93.

To achieve this aim, however, changes in the arrangements for financing the common budget were needed. Prior to 1988, the EU budget was financed from three sources – monies raised by the operation of the EU's common external tariff and from the variable levy applied to imports of agricultural produce, and a share (up to 1.4%) of VAT receipts collected by member states calculated on a common basis. The 1988 budget reforms saw the introduction of a 'fourth' financial resource. Thereafter, should the revenue accruing from the first three sources be insufficient to meet the EU's spending plans (which would be the case given the decision to double the funds available to structural operations) then member states will make up the deficit by a direct contribution according to their relative wealth as measured by GDP. In order that there would be a ceiling on overall EU spending, it was agreed that spending under common policies should not exceed a fixed percentage of the total GNP of the European Union. This budget ceiling was set at 1.20 per cent for 1989 rising to a maximum of 1.27 per cent by 1992. Further, it was agreed that the rate of increase of spending on the Common Agricultural Policy (the major item of common expenditure) should be held down in order that more resources would be available for the structural operations.

The UK government led by Prime Minister Margaret Thatcher strongly resisted the reform package (commonly known as the Delors I package). While endorsing proposals to hold down spending under the CAP, Mrs Thatcher was opposed to increasing the resources available to the structural funds. Her opposition was based on two considerations. First, that higher EU spending would increase even further the United Kingdom's net payments to the common budget (i.e. the difference between contributions made to the budget and payments received as a result of the operation of common EU policies). As a relatively prosperous member state, the United Kingdom would enjoy limited benefits from the reforms. Secondly, it was felt that the proposed reforms would increase the powers of the European Commission thereby hastening the development of a federal Europe. Instead, it was argued, the way forward for the poorer countries was to undertake domestic economic reforms.

It is generally accepted that the 1988 reforms to the structural funds have played a positive role in improving the economic prospects in the Union's weakest regions – those eligible under the Objective 1 provisions. Objective 1 assistance is concentrated primarily in the Union's four poorest countries – Spain, Portugal, Greece and Ireland, the so-called 'cohesion countries' – although large parts of Southern Italy and parts of the United Kingdom also are eligible for assistance. In these countries the application of structural fund assistance has had a discernible impact on employment and output. These are relatively weak economies with the result that EU assistance represents a significant injection to the circular flow of income. Elsewhere, the effect of the structural funds has been more difficult to measure. Objective 2 areas tend to be located in mature industrial economies where the relative effect of EU financial assistance is very difficult to assess. It is likely that the application of EU funds – in conjunction with domestic regional assistance – has had a beneficial impact on these regions through the resultant improvement in the provision of economic infrastructure and (re)training of labour. In turn we would expect this to result in an increase in net investment and employment growth. However, any such effects are difficult to detect in large economies susceptible to normal cyclical variations.

By the end of the decade EU spending under the structural funds will represent some 36 per cent of total EU expenditure, representing a significant growth relative to other EU policies during the period since the late 1980s. While the United Kingdom does benefit from the structural funds under all the Objective criteria, it remains true that the bulk of assistance is directed to the four cohesion countries. The debate that occurred in 1992 regarding the Union's financial framework until the end of the decade pointed to some dissatisfaction among the richer, Northern EU member states over the matter of increasing the intra-Union transfer of funds to the Union's Southern members. This suggests that the operation of the structural funds will continue to attract the close attention of the richer member states and that further development of cohesion policies will be carefully monitored.

18.4.2 *Monetary union*

The TEU (Council of the European Communities, 1992) commits the member states of the European Union to implementing policies as are necessary to achieve a staged transition to full monetary union by 1999 at the latest (see TEU, Title VI, Articles 102a-109m and Protocols 3,4,5,10,11). The TEU provisions cover both the economic and monetary policy conditions that have to be met by member states in the run-up to monetary unon and the accompanying institutional changes that are required to manage the monetary union upon its inception. The TEU envisages monetary union being achieved in the course of a three-stage transition period in which each stage is associated with specific policy changes and institutional developments that together create the necessary conditions for a monetary union to operate. This dual-track approach to establishing monetary union involving contemporaneous institutional and policy changes is known as a 'parallel' strategy.

Stage 1 of the transition to monetary union was deemed to have begun in 1990 and was to last until 31 December 1993. During Stage 1, very much a preparatory stage, the currencies of all member states should be within the narrow band of the ERM and all intra-EU restrictions on capital movements should be dismantled. Stage 2 would begin on 1 January 1994 and would involve the creation of the European Monetary Institute (EMI) which will be the forerunner of the European Central Bank (ECB) that will, ultimately, be responsible for implementing the common monetary policy. During Stage 2 EU member states would progressively align monetary policies as necessary to achieve convergence between nominal variables (see below). Moreover, all member state central banks would become wholly independent from national governments during the second stage. Stage 3 will begin, at the earliest, on 1 January, 1997 but only if a majority of member states satisfy the convergence criteria by that date. If this is not the case, monetary union will not begin until 1 January 1999, at which time all those member states that do meet the convergence criteria will adopt a single currency, with the other member states acceding to monetary union as and when the necessary economic criteria have been met.

The central feature of a monetary union is the circulation of a common, single currency: i.e. one that is legal tender in all participating countries and which replaces national currencies. It is a necessary feature of a monetary union that responsibility for matters pertaining to monetary policy (supply of money, interest rate policy, international monetary arrangements) are trans-ferred from the central banks of individual countries to a single Central Bank covering the entire monetary union.

As noted above, the TEU sets out a number of 'convergence criteria' that have to be met by EU member states before they can be deemed eligible to participate in monetary union. These criteria are intended to ensure that all countries have achieved nominal economic convergence prior to adopting the single currency. Otherwise there would be a risk of the arrangement as a whole being destabilised as a consequence of conditions in particular member states. The convergence criteria – all of which must be met by each country – are:

(i)   The achievement of a high degree of price stability such that the average rate of inflation over the preceding year does not exceed by more than 1.5 percentage points that recorded by the three best performing member states in terms of price stability.
(ii) The observance of the normal fluctuation margins provided for by the ERM of the EMS, for at least 2 years, without devaluing against the currency of any other member state.
(iii) That long-term nominal interest rates should not, over the preceding year, have exceeded by more than 2 percentage points that of, at most, the three best performing member states in terms of price stability.
(iv) The budgetary position of countries applying for inclusion in the final stage of monetary union must demonstrate that an excessive deficit situation does not exist. An excessive deficit exists when either of two reference values are breached: (a) where the ratio of planned or actual government deficit to gross domestic product exceeds 3 per cent and (b) where the ratio of government debt to gross domestic prices exceeds 60 per cent.

It is widely acknowledged that the adoption of a single currency between EU member states will produce tangible economic benefits. The European Commission proposed four general sources of gain from the introduction of a single currency.

Efficiency and growth

The introduction of a single currency for the Union will eliminate the transactions costs of exchanging Union currencies. Moreover, movement to a single EU currency will remove exchange rate volatility and uncertainty – both of which undermine   intra-EU trade – and this could be expected to encourage businesses to invest in greater productive capacity targeted at the export market. In turn, this will lead to greater growth for the economy as a whole.

Price stability

The Commission suggests that the introduction of a single currency will force inflation in the EU to converge to the lowest rate. This will benefit the EU as price stability is itself advantageous for efficient resource allocation.

Public finance

Because national budget deficits can no longer be financed by an expansion in the domestic money supply, and in the light of the excessive deficit provisions referred to above, governments will be forced to discipline their borrowing and this will lead to lower interest rates and, by extension, greater investment.

External gains

The EU single currency (ECU) would be a major player in the global economy. The Commission insist that this will further benefit the Union by leading to lower costs in international trade, ensuring that there are more ECU denominated financial issues managed by European banks, implying smaller needs for holding (costly) reserves of foreign currencies, and also producing some financial gains via seigniorage.

Undoubtedly, some part of the proposed benefits of monetary union will accrue to the EU as a whole. However, the critics argue, against such benefits – many of which are contested – must be weighed certain costs that will arise from monetary union. Critics of monetary union claim that while transaction cost savings will accrue as a result of monetary union, these costs are extremely small. Moreover there is, it is claimed, little evidence that actual or expected exchange rate fluctuations interfere significantly with intra-EU trade flows. However, the main objection to monetary union is that this will remove from national governments the exchange rate as an instrument of economic policy. The concern is particularly acute where some parts of a monetary union are subject to external 'shocks' (such as a loss in demand for a product) to which the rest of the monetary union are not subject. In such instances the government of the 'shocked' area will be unable to respond by an exchange rate adjustment and, moreover, might also find that the room for responding to the shock by fiscal policy is restricted by virtue of the excessive deficit criteria referred to earlier. Of course, precisely the same problem arises in current monetary unions. It is possible to imagine an external shock which would adversely affect one part of the United Kingdom but leave the rest unaffected. Imagine, for instance, that there is a reduction in demand for Scottish whisky and that the result is a rise in unemployment and a fall in output in the North of Scotland. It is unlikely in this case that the UK government would opt to devalue the pound to assist Scottish whisky exports as such a policy might well have negative consequences for the UK economy as a whole. However, in such cases we could anticipate two adjustment mechanisms operating that do not require a change in the exchange rate. First, unemployed labour in the North of Scotland might move southwards to find employment thereby alleviating, in part, the problem. Secondly, we would expect that compensating fiscal flows would automatically be triggered through the operation of national unemployment and social welfare provisions. This too would partially offset the problem in the North of Scotland. The problem for the EU, argue the opponents to monetary union, is that the arrangements set out in the TEU do not provide for the development of a common fiscal policy. Further, the experience with labour mobility on a European scale does not suggest that labour will migrate to the extent required if one is to regard this as an adjustment mechanism.

Whether the benefits of a monetary union outweigh the costs is extremely difficult to determine before the event. Essentially the problem is one of comparing microeconomic benefits with potential macroeconomic costs; similar to the problem of comparing apples to oranges. None the less the European Union is committed to moving fairly speedily in the direction of monetary union. The committment to monetary union does not appear to have been significantly weakened by the recent currency turbulence. Indeed, many advocates of monetary union insist that the events of September 1992, when the British and Italian currencies were forced out of the ERM, and August 1993, when the ± currency bands of 6 per cent and 2.25 per cent were replaced by a single band of ± 15 per cent, establish only more forcefully the importance of a rapid move to monetary union.

Others, however, take precisely the opposite lesson from these events. Critics argue that in both instances the underlying problem was a basic policy incompatibility between the economies of the EU and that this was detected by the markets which then acted in anticipation of a justified exchange rate realignment. In other words, the fiscal–monetary policy mix in some parts of the EU as required by prevailing economic conditions differed from the policy mix required in other parts. While it is correct that such exchange rate volatility would have been avoided had these countries already been participating in a monetary union, the problem would simply have manifested itself in other ways – by regionally diverging levels of output and employment within the single currency area.

The UK opt-out from the monetary union provisions of the TEU mean that no decision surrounding the conduct of domestic economic policy need follow the dictates of that Treaty. Moreover, the United Kingdom is not obliged to participate in the monetary union even should all of the convergence criteria be satisfied. However, this does not mean that the United Kingdom will remain unaffected by monetary union. Should there be gains from membership of a monetary union then the United Kingdom will not enjoy these as long as it stands on the outside. By the same token, all costs from monetary union will be avoided. In the final instance it is impossible to be 'for' or 'against' the principle of European monetary union as such on strictly economic grounds. After all, all national economies in the 15 EU member states are monetary unions: why should these be acceptable, in economic terms, when the idea of a European monetary union should not be? In practice it is necessary to consider the actual provisions that will support the monetary union before deciding on the likely consequences. As implied above, much of the concern surrounding the TEU provisions for monetary union is that these provide insufficient guarantees that a country will be better off inside the union than outside it. Consequently, while the principle of monetary union within the EU might be valid, the actual version of monetary union being proposed is not necessarily the best one.

18.5   Conclusions

In this chapter we have investigated the evolution of the economic policies of the European Union. It is clear that the EU has, progressively, come to occupy a more important position with respect to the economic function of the British government, as it has with respect to economic policy in all 15 member countries. Moreover, there is little doubt that this process will accelerate in the next decade. The completion of the single market more or less on schedule represented a significant achievement in terms of market access and resource allocation throughout the EU. Undoubtedly, it poses challenges and opportunities for British firms and their response to these challenges will help shape the economic future of the United Kingdom. Beyond this the commitment to establishing monetary union in the EU does seem likely to be fulfilled, although not before 1 January 1999. Even then, almost certainly, only a handful of EU member states will satisfy the convergence criteria and move towards monetary unification. If, as seems likely, the United Kingdom will not be in this first group, this does not mean that the United Kingdom will remain unaffected by the change. To the extent that monetary union conveys advantages upon participating countries – and this might be particularly true in the financial products sectors – then the United Kingdom stands to lose relative ground to competitor countries.

As the EU approaches the end of the decade it is not only internal matters that dominate the agenda. From 1 January 1995 the EU increased in size to 15 member states with the accession of Sweden, Finland and Austria. This accession was relatively trouble-free for the EU as a whole. The new members are all relatively prosperous economies that together impose no new net burden to EU budgetary arrangements. However if, as seems probable, the EU will be contemplating the membership of central European countries by the end of the decade then matters will be considerably more complex. Not only does a European Union of upwards of 20 member states require an entirely different institutional structure than prevailing at the present time, but it will involve a dramatic increase in the financial burden placed upon the common EU budget. As matters stand at present the four probable members from central Europe – the Czech and Slovak Republics, Poland and Hungary – would be eligible for significant payments under both the Union's common agricultural policy and the structural fund programmes. This raises sensitive questions concerning cross-border transfers of funds from the richer member states to their poorer partner member states. Countries such as the United Kingdom, as the EU's more prosperous member states, might question the direct costs associated with an enlarged Union. In addition to the direct burden of enlargement, the EU as a whole is likely to experience the adjustment problems arising as countries whose comparative advantage lies in the production of agricultural products, textiles, chemicals and steel products accede to the EU. Finally, it is worth stressing that both the deepening and the widening of the Union are bound to change the part played by the Union on the global economic stage.

Questions for discussion

1. What is the difference between a free trade area and a common market?
2. Define the conditions necessary for an economic union to be realised. What are the implications of such a union for the conduct of economic policy in the participating countries?
3. What do you understand by the terms *trade creation* and *trade diversion*? What insights does this give in respect of a country's membership of a customs union?
4. What do you understand by the expression *completing the internal market*? How is this likely to improve consumer welfare in the European Union?
5. Why is regional policy an important aspect of the European Community's economic policies?
6. What are the costs and benefits of a monetary union?

Note

1. Now referred to as the European Union, following the coming into effect of the Maastrich Treaty.

References and further reading

Bulmer, S., George, S. and Scott, A. (1992) *The United Kingdom and EU Membership Evaluated*, London: Frances Pinter.

Cecchini, P. (1988) *The European Challenge 1992: The benefits of a single market*, Aldershot: Gower Press.

Council of the European Communities (1992) *Treaty on European Union*, Brussels: Office for Official Publications of the European Communities.

El-Agraa, A. (1994) *The Economics of the European Union* 4th edn, Hemel Hempstead: Philip Allan.

European Commission (1985) *White Paper* 'Completing the Internal Market', Brussels: European Commission.

Foreign Office (1967) *Treaty setting up The European Economic Community, Rome, 25th March 1957*, London: HMSO.

Hitiris, T. (1991) *European Union Economics*, Hemel Hempstead: Harvester Wheatsheaf.

Pinder, J. (1991) *European Union: The building of a union*, Oxford: Oxford University Press.

Sloman, J. (1991) *Economics*, Hemel Hempstead: Harvester Wheatsheaf.

Swann, D. (1992) *The Economics of the Common Market*, London: Penguin Books.

Tsoukalis, L. (1994) *The New European Economy* 2nd edn, Oxford: Oxford University Press.

Index